VOLUME 602

NOVEMBER 2005

THE ANNALS

of The American Academy of Political
and Social Science

ROBERT W. PEARSON, *Executive Editor*
LAWRENCE W. SHERMAN, *Editor*

Developmental Criminology and Its Discontents: Trajectories of Crime from Childhood to Old Age

Special Editors of this Volume
ROBERT J. SAMPSON
Harvard University
JOHN H. LAUB
University of Maryland

SAGE Publications Ⓢ Thousand Oaks · London · New Delhi

The American Academy of Political and Social Science

3814 Walnut Street, Fels Institute of Government, University of Pennsylvania,
Philadelphia, PA 19104-6197; (215) 746-6500; (215) 898-1202 (fax); www.aapss.org

Origin and Purpose. The Academy was organized December 14, 1889, to promote the progress of political and social science, especially through publications and meetings. The Academy does not take sides in controverted questions, but seeks to gather and present reliable information to assist the public in forming an intelligent and accurate judgment.

Meetings. The Academy occasionally holds a meeting in the spring extending over two days.

Publications. THE ANNALS of The American Academy of Political and Social Science is the bimonthly publication of the Academy. Each issue contains articles on some prominent social or political problem, written at the invitation of the editors. Also, monographs are published from time to time, numbers of which are distributed to pertinent professional organizations. These volumes constitute important reference works on the topics with which they deal, and they are extensively cited by authorities throughout the United States and abroad. The papers presented at the meetings of the Academy are included in THE ANNALS.

Membership. Each member of the Academy receives THE ANNALS and may attend the meetings of the Academy. Membership is open only to individuals. Annual dues: $84.00 for the regular paperbound edition (clothbound, $121.00). Members may also purchase single issues of THE ANNALS for $17.00 each (clothbound, $26.00). Student memberships are available for $53.00.

Subscriptions. THE ANNALS of The American Academy of Political and Social Science (ISSN 0002-7162) (J295) is published six times annually—in January, March, May, July, September, and November— by Sage Publications, 2455 Teller Road, Thousand Oaks, CA 91320. Telephone: (800) 818-SAGE (7243) and (805) 499-9774; FAX/Order line: (805) 499-0871; E-mail: journals@sagepub.com. Copyright © 2005 by The American Academy of Political and Social Science. Institutions may subscribe to THE ANNALS at the annual rate: $577.00 (clothbound, $652.00).

Periodicals postage paid at Thousand Oaks, California, and at additional mailing offices.

Single issues of THE ANNALS may be obtained by individuals who are not members of the Academy for $34.00 each (clothbound, $37.00). Single issues of THE ANNALS have proven to be excellent supplementary texts for classroom use. Direct inquiries regarding adoptions to THE ANNALS c/o Sage Publications (address below).

All correspondence concerning membership in the Academy, dues renewals, inquiries about membership status, and/or purchase of single issues of THE ANNALS should be sent to THE ANNALS c/o Sage Publications, 2455 Teller Road, Thousand Oaks, CA 91320. Telephone: (800) 818-SAGE (7243) and (805) 499-9774; FAX/Order line: (805) 499-0871. E-mail: journals@sagepub.com. *Please note that orders under $30 must be prepaid.* Sage affiliates in London and India will assist institutional subscribers abroad with regard to orders, claims, and inquiries for both subscriptions and single issues.

Printed on recycled, acid-free paper

THE ANNALS

© 2005 by The American Academy of Political and Social Science

Editorial Office: 3814 Walnut Street, Fels Institute for Government, University of Pennsylvania, Philadelphia, PA 19104-6197.

For information about membership° (individuals only) and subscriptions (institutions), address:

Sage Publications
2455 Teller Road
Thousand Oaks, CA 91320

For Sage Publications: Joseph Riser and Esmeralda Hernandez

From India and South Asia,
write to:
SAGE PUBLICATIONS INDIA Pvt Ltd
B-42 Panchsheel Enclave, P.O. Box 4109
New Delhi 110 017
INDIA

From Europe, the Middle East,
and Africa, write to:
SAGE PUBLICATIONS LTD
1 Oliver's Yard, 55 City Road
London EC1Y 1SP
UNITED KINGDOM

°Please note that members of the Academy receive THE ANNALS with their membership.
International Standard Serial Number ISSN 0002-7162
International Standard Book Number 1-4129-3679-9 (Vol. 602, 2005 paper)
International Standard Book Number ISBN 1-4129-3678-0 (Vol. 602, 2005 cloth)
Manufactured in the United States of America. First printing, November 2005.

The articles appearing in *The Annals* are abstracted or indexed in Academic Abstracts, Academic Search, America: History and Life, Asia Pacific Database, Book Review Index, CAB Abstracts Database, Central Asia: Abstracts & Index, Communication Abstracts, Corporate ResourceNET, Criminal Justice Abstracts, Current Citations Express, Current Contents: Social & Behavioral Sciences, Documentation in Public Administration, e-JEL, EconLit, Expanded Academic Index, Guide to Social Science & Religion in Periodical Literature, Health Business FullTEXT, HealthSTAR FullTEXT, Historical Abstracts, International Bibliography of the Social Sciences, International Political Science Abstracts, ISI Basic Social Sciences Index, Journal of Economic Literature on CD, LEXIS-NEXIS, MasterFILE FullTEXT, Middle East: Abstracts & Index, North Africa: Abstracts & Index, PAIS International, Periodical Abstracts, Political Science Abstracts, Psychological Abstracts, PsycINFO, Sage Public Administration Abstracts, Social Science Source, Social Sciences Citation Index, Social Sciences Index Full Text, Social Services Abstracts, Social Work Abstracts, Sociological Abstracts, Southeast Asia: Abstracts & Index, Standard Periodical Directory (SPD), TOPICsearch, Wilson OmniFile V, and Wilson Social Sciences Index/Abstracts, and are available on microfilm from ProQuest, Ann Arbor, Michigan.

Information about membership rates, institutional subscriptions, and back issue prices may be found on the facing page.

Advertising. Current rates and specifications may be obtained by writing to *The Annals* Advertising and Promotion Manager at the Thousand Oaks office (address above).

Claims. Claims for undelivered copies must be made no later than six months following month of publication. The publisher will supply missing copies when losses have been sustained in transit and when the reserve stock will permit.

Change of Address. Six weeks' advance notice must be given when notifying of change of address to ensure proper identification. Please specify name of journal. POSTMASTER: Send address changes to: *The Annals* of The American Academy of Political and Social Science, c/o Sage Publications, 2455 Teller Road, Thousand Oaks, CA 91320.

THE ANNALS

OF THE AMERICAN ACADEMY OF POLITICAL AND SOCIAL SCIENCE

Volume 602

November 2005

IN THIS ISSUE:

Developmental Criminology and Its Discontents: Trajectories of Crime from Childhood to Old Age

Special Editors: ROBERT J. SAMPSON
JOHN H. LAUB

Section Three:
Multiple Patterns of Offending

Section Four:
Final Thoughts

Section Five:
Quick Read Synopsis

ON THE COVER: *The Two Paths,* reproduced for this cover from a late nineteenth-century original lithograph provided by volume contributor Richard E. Tremblay.

Preface

By
ROBERT J. SAMPSON
and
JOHN H. LAUB

Unbeknownst to us at the time, the idea for this special issue was born two years ago. In November 2003, we participated in a Presidential Plenary session at the annual meeting of the American Society of Criminology (ASC) in Denver, Colorado. As then–ASC President, John Laub organized and chaired the session, titled "Age, Crime, and Human Development: The Future of Life-Course Criminology." Since the early 1980s, age, crime, and human development have animated the field of criminology, so he thought it would be a good idea to revisit these topics, especially with an eye to the future of life-course criminology. Laub invited four scholars whom he felt represented a diverse set of protagonists in ongoing debates about age, crime, and human development. Robert Sampson, Harvard University, agreed to serve as the principal speaker for this session. He presented material from *Shared Beginnings, Divergent Lives: Delinquent Boys to Age 70* (Laub and

Robert J. Sampson is chairman of the Department of Sociology and Henry Ford II Professor of the Social Sciences at Harvard University. His recent work focuses on the limits of the prediction paradigm in criminology, durable forms of urban inequality, networks of community social organization, and theories of civil society.

John H. Laub is a professor of criminology and criminal justice in the Department of Criminology and Criminal Justice at the University of Maryland at College Park. His areas of research include crime and deviance over the life course, juvenile delinquency and juvenile justice, and the history of criminology. He has published widely, including most recently Shared Beginnings, Divergent Lives: Delinquent Boys to Age 70, *coauthored with Robert Sampson (Harvard University Press, 2003). This book is the 2004 recipient of the Michael J. Hindelang Book Award from the American Society of Criminology and the 2005 recipient of the Outstanding Book Award from the Academy of Criminal Justice Sciences.*

NOTE: We thank Stacey Bosick, Harvard University, who served as managing editor for this volume, for her hard work and good humor throughout the process. We also thank Robert Pearson and Julie Odland of the *Annals* for their patience and support.

DOI: 10.1177/0002716205280574

Sampson 2003) and a recent article from the ASC's flagship journal *Criminology*: "Life-Course Desisters? Trajectories of Crime among Delinquent Boys Followed to Age 70" (Sampson and Laub 2003). The three invited commentators were Alfred Blumstein of Carnegie Mellon University, Joan McCord of Temple University, and Richard Tremblay of the University of Montreal.

Quite frankly, we were surprised by the response to this session. First off, we played to a packed house, a rarity for an ASC session! Second, and more important, there was a buzz in the air about the ideas presented, discussed, and debated. Topics covered included patterns of crime by age—from infancy to late adulthood; criminal career topics such as onset, continuation, termination, and career length; the viability of developmental and taxonomic theories of crime; the suitability of the Glueck archives to test such theories; and the prospects for marrying longitudinal and experimental studies. We think it is safe to say that the session was a success because of the intellectual excitement it generated not only during the session but also in the hallways and bars afterwards.

Shortly after the ASC meeting, Julie Horney, dean of the School of Criminal Justice at the University of Albany, approached us about organizing a symposium to be held at Albany that would build on the ideas and discussion initiated at the ASC session. Independently and at the same time, Robert Pearson, executive director of the American Academy of Political and Social Science, contacted us about putting together a special issue of the *Annals* building on the ASC session. Something was clearly in the air, and we enthusiastically agreed to do both, not thinking of course about all the hard work to come.

Yet with much help we were able to persevere. Funding from the School of Criminal Justice at the University of Albany and the National Consortium on Violence Research (with many thanks to Al Blumstein) allowed the planning and execution of the inaugural Albany Symposium on Crime and Justice: "Developmental Criminology and Its Discontents: Offender Typologies and Trajectories of Crime," which took place on the campus of the University of Albany on April 28 and 29, 2005. Our idea was not to simply replicate the ASC plenary session but branch out with the opportunity for significant critical discussion. We ultimately decided and organized to have three major papers presented at the symposium. The first paper was by Robert Sampson and John Laub: "A Life-Course View of the Development of Crime"; the second paper was by Daniel Nagin and Richard Tremblay: "What Has Been Learned from Group-Based Trajectory Modeling? Examples from Physical Aggression and Other Problem Behaviors"; and the third paper was by Terence Thornberry: "Explaining Multiple Patterns of Offending across the Life Course."

To promote discussion and debate, we invited two commentators on each paper who would deliver formal remarks for approximately thirty minutes each. We were very pleased at the lineup of major figures who agreed to take on this assignment. They included Michael Gottfredson and Lee Robins (Sampson and Laub), Barbara Maughan and Stephen Raudenbush (Nagin and Tremblay), and Janet Lauritsen and Wayne Osgood (Thornberry). We sought commentators who were thoughtful yet critical—as Sampson said in an earlier e-mail to Laub, "Having fans comment on our papers is about the most boring thing I can imagine." So we aimed for scholarly independence of thought and overall we believe we hit the bull's eye. (Our only disappointment is that Terrie Moffitt was unable to accept an invitation as a critic on Sampson and Laub.) We also asked Al Blumstein, long associated with the criminal-career paradigm and a panelist on the original ASC session, to provide an overview of the symposium and offer some recommendations for future research and theoretical development.

Like the ASC session in 2003, the response to the Albany Symposium far exceeded our expectations. Almost two hundred participants came from all over the country, and for two days ideas, agreements, and disagreements were presented, discussed, and, at times, fiercely debated. We are pleased that the full set of revised papers and commentaries from the Albany symposium are presented here in this special issue of the *Annals*, retitled to reflect the final broad swath of topics addressed: "Developmental Criminology and Its Discontents: Trajectories of Crime from Childhood to Old Age." In addition, we offered each paper presenter the opportunity to respond to the two commentators, and these responses are included here along with Al Blumstein's overview paper of the central issues raised at the symposium.

Finally, to round things out, we commissioned a review essay from Hans-Jurgen Kerner of Germany on three recent books by the symposium's main authors that addresses topics central to the developmental criminology and thus this special volume: John H. Laub and Robert J. Sampson's (2003) *Shared Beginnings, Divergent Lives*; Daniel S. Nagin's (2005) *Group-Based Modeling of Development*; and Terence P. Thornberry, Marvin D. Krohn, Alan J. Lizotte, Carolyn A. Smith, and Kimberly Tobin's (2003), *Gangs and Delinquency in Developmental Perspective*. We aimed to select a reviewer who was not in one of the intellectual "camps" at issue, who was not a collaborator in any way with the book authors and thus independent, had an international perspective, and possessed impeccable intellectual integrity. On all accounts, Hans fit the bill, and we are pleased to include his insightful review.

Throughout the history of criminology, intellectual debates have created excitement and controversy, but even more important, these debates have shaped the theoretical and research agenda for years to come. Some of the topics that come to mind are the debates about official and self-report data on the correlates of offending during the 1960s and 1970s, the problems and prospects for theoretical integration during the 1970s and 1980s, and most recently, the debate regarding the criminal career paradigm, age and crime, and causes of crime during the 1980s and 1990s. Several issues of similar weight are discussed in the articles that follow, including debates about the patterns of continuity and change in offending, the role of taxonomic theories in criminology, the prospects for accurately predicting crime, theories of crime over the life course, and the origins and consequences of crime and violence and other problem behaviors. We see these issues as paramount in criminology and hope that the production of this volume will be viewed as a historical moment for the field in future assessments of key developments in criminology.

Dedication to Joan McCord

Joan McCord, a respected colleague and friend, passed away on February 24, 2004, at the age of seventy-three. Joan approached her work and lived her life in the same fashion, with a fervent zeal and excitement. Most important, she was not afraid to speak her mind on any and all issues; she would have felt wonderfully at home at the Albany Symposium. Indeed, when we initially told Joan about the symposium idea, her infectious grin said it all. As most readers will know, she was also an indefatigable champion of longitudinal research and of using scientific data in the formulation of theory and policy. The fields of criminology and criminal justice are much stronger because of her unflagging efforts and her extraordinary hard work. We dedicate this volume—covering many topics near and dear to her heart—to Joan's memory.

References

Laub, John H., and Robert J. Sampson. 2003. *Shared beginnings, divergent lives: delinquent boys to age 70.* Cambridge, MA: Harvard University Press.

Nagin, Daniel S. 2005. *Group-based modeling of development.* Cambridge, MA: Harvard University Press.

Sampson, Robert J., and John H. Laub. 2003. Life-course desisters? Trajectories of crime among delinquent boys followed to age 70. *Criminology* 41-301-39.

Thornberry, Terence P., Marvin D. Krohn, Alan J. Lizotte, Carolyn A. Smith, and Kimberly Tobin. 2003. *Gangs and delinquency in developmental perspective.* Cambridge: Cambridge University Press.

SECTION ONE

A Life-Course View

A Life-Course View of the Development of Crime

ROBERT J. SAMPSON
and
JOHN H. LAUB

In this article, the authors present a life-course perspective on crime and a critique of the developmental criminology paradigm. Their fundamental argument is that persistent offending and desistance—or trajectories of crime—can be meaningfully understood within the same theoretical framework, namely, a revised age-graded theory of informal social control. The authors examine three major issues. First, they analyze data that undermine the idea that developmentally distinct groups of offenders can be explained by unique causal processes. Second, they revisit the concept of turning points from a time-varying view of key life events. Third, they stress the overlooked importance of human agency in the development of crime. The authors' life-course theory envisions development as the constant interaction between individuals and their environment, coupled with random developmental noise and a purposeful human agency that they distinguish from rational choice. Contrary to influential developmental theories in criminology, the authors thus conceptualize crime as an emergent process reducible neither to the individual nor the environment.

Keywords: crime; development; trajectories; life course; typologies; prediction; desistance

In this article, we argue for a life-course perspective on trajectories of crime, focusing on the question of whether (and why) adolescent

Robert J. Sampson is chairman of the Department of Sociology and Henry Ford II Professor of the Social Sciences at Harvard University. His recent work focuses on the limits of the prediction paradigm in criminology, durable forms of urban inequality, networks of community social organization, and theories of civil society.

John H. Laub is a professor of criminology and criminal justice in the Department of Criminology and Criminal Justice at the University of Maryland at College Park. His areas of research include crime and deviance over the life course, juvenile delinquency and juvenile justice, and the history of criminology. He has published widely, including, most recently, Shared Beginnings, Divergent Lives: Delinquent Boys to Age 70, *coauthored with Robert Sampson (Harvard University Press, 2003). This book is the 2004 recipient of the Michael J. Hindelang Book Award from the American Society of Criminology and the 2005 recipient of the Outstanding Book Award from the Academy of Criminal Justice Sciences.*

DOI: 10.1177/0002716205280075

delinquents persist or desist from crime as they age across the adult life course. The growing tendency in developmental perspectives on crime, often called "developmental criminology," is to subdivide the offender population and assume different causal influences at different stages of the "criminal career." For example, it is now commonplace to assert that certain childhood factors uniquely explain persistent adult offenders, whereas another set of causal factors explain desistance in adolescence. A variation on this theme is that a small group of offenders continue to commit crimes at a persistently high rate as they grow older. In direct contrast, another view posits an "invariant" effect of age—that regardless of stable between-individual differences, all offenders will commit fewer crimes as they age.

Although at first it may seem counterintuitive, our fundamental argument is that persistent offending and desistance—and hence trajectories of crime—can be meaningfully understood within the same theoretical framework. We do not argue that offender typologies are without merit, and in fact some of our analysis will estimate group-based trajectories of crime. Rather, our strategy is to start with the assumption of generality and see how far it takes us in understanding patterns of criminal offending across the full age range of the life course. We explore this logic in five sections, beginning with a summary of results from our prior research. This work serves as our point of departure for new analyses and theoretical reflection on key issues in life-course criminology. We specifically review, albeit in brief, the main results from *Crime in the Making: Pathways and Turning Points through Life* (Sampson and Laub 1993) and the more recent *Shared Beginnings, Divergent Lives: Delinquent Boys to Age 70* (Laub and Sampson 2003) that bear most directly on this article. We then take on three major issues.

1. A life-course view of the idea of developmentally distinct groups that have unique causes. Here we revisit our position on typologies of crime, focusing on the dual taxonomy theory of Moffitt (1993) with the goal to identify points of agreement and disagreement. We present new analyses on the predictability of age at desistance and the life-course trajectory of crimes that are minor in nature. According to Moffitt (1993, 1994, forthcoming), to assess the validity of a life-course persistent versus adolescent-limited typology of offenders one must consider a sufficiently broad range of criminal and antisocial behaviors. We agree. We also concur that offender trajectory groups are of continuing analytic value and that there *are* men who offend at a high rate in adulthood. The main points of disagreement appear to be that (1) we find life-course desistance is the norm for all men and all crimes, including minor forms of deviance; and (2) we question the *prospective* or predictive power of offender groups and whether they are causally distinct with respect to later trajectories.

NOTE: This article was presented at the Albany Symposium on Crime and Justice, "Developmental Criminology and Its Discontents: Offender Typologies and Trajectories of Crime," State University of New York at Albany, April 28-29, 2005. We thank Elaine Eggleston Doherty and Stacey J. Bosick for their assistance.

2. *A revised life-course view of turning points.* Unlike unusual events (e.g., Great Depression, war), many events are frequently recurring—people move in and out of various states over the life course in a repeated events fashion. We ask, How is this fact reconciled with the notion of long-term "development" or "growth"? We observe that developmental theory works well with many phenomena—the question here is what about crime and its time-varying predictors? We use marriage as a prime example and highlight results of work in progress that attempts to estimate the causal effects of marriage on crime. We find that conditioning on long-term histories of both outcome and treatment, the *same* man exhibits lower rates of crime in the state of marriage compared to not being in the state of marriage. We discuss how this finding fits a developmental theory of crime and the general idea of turning points.

3. *A life-course view that takes human agency seriously.* Developmental criminology, in practice if not in theory, tends to emphasize the notion that people get "locked" into certain trajectories. One of the lessons of prospective longitudinal research is that there is considerable heterogeneity in adult outcomes that cannot be predicted in advance. In this section, we highlight a life-course view that emphasizes human agency and choice over the life span, underscoring how people construct their lives within the context of ongoing constraints. From this view, trajectories are interpreted not from a lens of unfolding inevitability but rather continuous social reproduction. We want to ask the hard question of how men with a criminal past go about prospectively *creating* their own trajectories.

The final section of the article considers the implications of these findings and theoretical reflections for the conception of development generally and life-course criminology in particular.

Crime in the Making and the Origins of Life-Course Criminology

Unraveling Juvenile Delinquency, along with subsequent follow-ups conducted by Sheldon and Eleanor Glueck of the Harvard Law School, is one of the most influential research projects in the history of criminological research (Glueck and Glueck 1950, 1968). The Gluecks' data were derived from a three-wave prospective study of juvenile and adult criminal behavior that began in 1940. The research design involved a sample of five hundred male delinquents aged ten to seventeen and five hundred male nondelinquents aged ten to seventeen matched case by case on age, race/ethnicity, IQ, and low-income residence in Boston. Extensive data were collected on the one thousand boys at three points in time—ages fourteen, twenty-five, and thirty-two. Over the period 1987 to 1993, we reconstructed, augmented, and analyzed these longitudinal data that, owing to the Gluecks' hard work over many years, are immensely rich and will likely never be repeated given modern institutional review board restrictions (e.g., wide-ranging interviews with teachers, neighbors, and employers; detailed psychiatric and physical assessments; extensive searches of multiple agency records).

In *Crime in the Making*, we developed a theoretical framework to explain childhood antisocial behavior, adolescent delinquency, and crime in early adulthood. The general organizing principle was that crime is more likely to occur when an individual's bond to society is attenuated. Our analysis of the causes of delinquency shared much in common with the focus in classical control theory (Hirschi 1969) on adolescence, but the reality of later life-course milestones required us to develop a modified theoretical perspective. After all, the transition to young adulthood brings with it new social control institutions and potential turning points that go well beyond adolescence. We thus developed an *age-graded* theory emphasizing informal social controls that are manifested in shifting and possibly transformative ways as individuals age (see Sampson and Laub 1993). For example, we focused on parenting styles (supervision, warmth, consistent discipline) and emotional attachment to parents in childhood; school attachment and peers in adolescence; and marital stability, military service, and employment in adulthood. Although these are manifestly distinct domains that are age graded, we argued that there are higher-order commonalities with respect to the concept of social connectivity through time.

Stability and change in criminal behavior over the life course

The delinquents and nondelinquents in the Gluecks' study displayed considerable between-individual stability in crime and many problematic behaviors well into adulthood. This stability held independent of age, IQ, ethnicity, and neighborhood SES. Indeed, delinquency and other forms of antisocial conduct in childhood were strongly related to troublesome adult behavior across a variety of experiences (e.g., crime, military offenses, economic dependence, and marital discord). But why? One of the mechanisms of continuity that we emphasized was "cumulative disadvantage," whereby serious delinquency and its nearly inevitable correlates (such as incarceration) undermined later bonds of social control (such as employability), which in turn enhanced the chances of continued offending (see also Sampson and Laub 1997).

At the same time, we found that job stability and marital attachment in adulthood were significantly related to *changes* in adult crime—the stronger the adult ties to work and family, the less crime and deviance among both delinquents and nondelinquent controls. We even found that strong marital attachment inhibits crime and deviance regardless of that spouse's own deviant behavior and that job instability fosters crime regardless of heavy drinking. Despite differences in early childhood experiences, adult social bonds to work and family thus had similar consequences for the life-course trajectories of the five hundred delinquents and five hundred nondelinquent controls. These results were consistent for a wide variety of crime outcome measures, control variables (e.g., childhood antisocial behavior and individual-difference constructs), and analytical techniques ranging from methods that accounted for persistent unobserved heterogeneity in criminal propensity to analyses of qualitative data.

Taken as a whole, these findings suggested to us that social ties embedded in adult transitions (e.g., marital attachment, job stability) explain variations in crime unaccounted for by childhood propensities. This empirical regularity supports a dual concern with continuity and change in the life course. A fundamental thesis of our age-graded theory of informal social control was that whereas individual traits and childhood experiences are important for understanding behavioral stability, experiences in adolescence and adulthood can redirect criminal trajectories in either a more positive or more negative manner. In this sense, we argue that all stages of the life course matter and that "turning points" are crucial for understanding processes of adult change. Drawing on the life-course paradigm (Elder 1985), we conceptualized a turning point as an alteration or deflection in a long-term pathway or trajectory that was initiated at an earlier point in time (see also Rutter 1996).

Shared Beginnings, Divergent Lives: An Overview

Crime in the Making raised many unanswered questions, and in its concluding chapter we highlighted directions for future research and theoretical development that appeared fruitful. Two of these directions seemed especially relevant for developmental/life-course theories of crime, namely, the merging of quantitative and qualitative data and further understanding of age and crime (Sampson and Laub 1993, 251-53). For example, what about crime in middle age? Older age? Is there really such a thing as a lifelong career criminal—or what have been dubbed "life-course persisters" (LCPs)? If so, can this group be prospectively identified? Another set of questions turned on the use of qualitative narratives to delve deeper into a person-based exploration of the life course. Can narratives help us unpack mechanisms that connect salient life events across the life course, especially personal choice and situational context? In our view, life-history narratives combined with quantitative approaches can be used to develop a richer and more comprehensive picture of why some men persist in offending and others stop. We made moves toward a narrative-based inquiry in *Crime in the Making* but were forced to rely on the Gluecks' written records rather than our own original interviews.

These motivations led us to follow up the Glueck men to the present. Our study involved three sources of new data collection—criminal record checks (local and national), death record checks (local and national), and personal interviews with a sample of fifty-two of the original Glueck delinquents. The sample of men to interview was strategically selected to ensure variability in trajectories of adult crime. More specifically, using criminal history records we classified eligible men into strata that reflected persistence in crime, desistance, and "zigzag" offending patterns, including late desistance and late onset of violence (see Laub and Sampson 2003, chap. 4, for more details). The combined data represent a roughly fifty-year window from which to update the Glueck men's lives at the close of the twentieth century and connect them to life experiences all the way back to early childhood. We believe these data represent the longest longitudinal study to date in criminology of the same men. The following sections briefly summarize the key findings.

Age and crime

Our analyses showed that, on one hand, the aggregate age-crime curve is not the same as individual age-crime trajectories, lending apparent support to one of the major claims of the criminal career model. There is enormous variability in peak ages of offending, for example, and age at desistance varied markedly across the Glueck men (Laub and Sampson 2003, chap. 5). On the other hand, we found that crime declines with age even for active offenders and that trajectories of desistance cannot be prospectively identified based on typological accounts rooted in childhood and individual differences. That is, offenses eventually decline for all groups of offenders identified according to extant theory and a multitude of childhood and adolescent risk factors. Whether low IQ, aggressive temperament, or early onset of antisocial behavior, desistance processes are at work even for the highest-risk and predicted life-course persistent offenders. While prognoses from childhood factors such as these are modestly accurate in predicting stable differences in later offending, they did not yield distinct groupings that were valid prospectively for troubled kids. Not only was prediction poor at the individual level, our data raised questions about the sorts of categorically distinct groupings that dominate theoretical and policy discussions (e.g., "life-course persistent offender," "superpredator"). These groupings tended to wither when placed under the microscope of long-term observation (Laub and Sampson 2003, chap. 5; Sampson and Laub 2003).

We thus concluded that a middle-ground position was necessary in the criminal careers debate—yes, there is enormous variability in individual age-crime curves such that it renders the aggregate curve descriptive of few people, and yes, age has a direct effect on offending such that life-course desistance is the more accurate label. We believe this compromise position, which we subject to further testing in this article, has general implications for assessing key assumptions of developmental criminology and rethinking its conceptual meaning.

Mechanisms of desistance

A second goal of our book was to exploit life-history narratives to better understand patterns of stability and change in offending over the life course. In our narrative interviews, we asked the men to describe turning points in their life. We also had the men fill out life-history calendars so that we could more accurately determine the sequencing of major life events. Several turning points were implicated in the process of desistance from crime, including marriage/spouses, military service, reform school, work, and residential change. The mechanisms underlying the desistance process are consistent with the general idea of social control. Namely, what appears to be important about institutional or structural turning points is that they all involve, to varying degrees, (1) new situations that "knife off" the past from the present, (2) new situations that provide both supervision and monitoring as well as new opportunities of social support and growth, (3) new situations that change and structure routine activities, and (4) new situations that provide the opportunity for identity transformation (for details, see Laub and Sampson 2003, chaps. 6-8). The lesson we drew is that involvement in institutions such as marriage, work, and the military reorders short-term situational inducements to crime and, over time, redirects long-term commitments to conformity. In making the case for the importance of the adult life course, we have referred to involvement in these institutions as turning points because they can change trajectories over time (Laub and Sampson 1993; Sampson and Laub 1993).

[W]e find life-course desistance is the norm for all men and all crimes, including minor forms of deviance; and . . . we question the prospective *or predictive power of offender groups and whether they are causally distinct with respect to later trajectories.*

A potential objection, however, is that turning points are a result of selection bias or, put differently, the unobserved characteristics of the person (e.g., Gottfredson and Hirschi 1990). To shed further light on life events, we exploited the longitudinal nature of the long-term data to examine within-individual change, where the unit of variation is across time. As such, stable characteristics of the person are held constant and we can exploit changes in social location, such as marriage, in terms of deviations from a person's expected trajectory. Holding age constant and allowing individual heterogeneity in age effects, we found that *when* in a state of marriage, the propensity to crime was lower for the same person than when not in marriage. Similar results were found for military service and steady employment. Quantitative models of within-individual change thus give statistical evidence of the probabilistic enhancement of desistance associated with life-course events like marriage, military service, and employment (Laub and Sampson 2003, chap. 9).

With this brief summary as a backdrop, we can now turn to the heart of the current article's concern with group-based typologies, turning points, and human agency.

Group-Based Typologies

> A small group of persons is shown engaging in antisocial behavior of one sort or another at every stage of life. I have labeled these persons *life-course-persistent* to reflect the *continuous course* of their antisocial behavior. (Moffitt 1993, 676, italics added)

> Thus, in defiance of "regression to the mean," extremely antisocial persons remain extreme on measures taken at later ages and in different situations. (Moffitt 1994, 10)

The "group" question is one of the most salient in modern developmental criminology. Here we revisit issues relating to Moffitt's (1993) dual taxonomy theory and group-based theories more generally (see Patterson and Yoerger 1993; Loeber and Hay 1997). One of the major strengths of our data is that they allow us to examine within-individual variability in crime over nearly the entire life course. Moreover, the original design in *Unraveling Juvenile Delinquency* targeted serious, persistent delinquents in adolescence, providing an important opportunity to assess patterns of continuity and change in crime for a population of high interest and concern to both criminal career theory and policy efforts that target high-risk children.

The question we address here is whether our tests to date set up a "straw man" argument. In response to our research, Moffitt (forthcoming) claimed as much, arguing first and foremost that nowhere does her theory predict a "flat rate" of criminal offending for LCPs. By persistent, in other words, she simply means "high rate" over time in the between-individual mode of comparison (i.e., stability). We acknowledge that we did (and still do) read in the original theory an insistence that adult crime should be relatively flat for the distinct group of LCPs, for that is how persistence is typically defined (e.g., "continuous," "degrading only slowly"). Moreover, if the differences of note are really on a continuum with respect to levels of offending, then the idea of a distinct group is weakened. In defense of our interpretation, we would note that many others apparently read the theory in a similar way. Consider the following independent assessment (other similar interpretations are found in Cullen and Agnew 2003, 450; Thornberry 1997, 2; Benson 2001, 86):

> The second group of offenders in Moffitt's taxonomy, "life-course-persistent," is hypothesized to engage in antisocial activities and criminal acts throughout the life span. . . . Unlike their adolescence-limited counterparts, life-course-persistent offenders continue their criminal involvement throughout most of their lives (*i.e., they are unlikely to desist*). (Piquero, Farrington, and Blumstein 2003, 398, italics added)

Even more striking, consider Nagin's (2005, 183) recent book where he graphs a flat expectation trajectory derived from Moffitt's theory and states, "The life-course persistent trajectory is flat and high, whereas the adolescent-limited trajectory rises and falls with age" (p. 182).

Moffit's (forthcoming) clarification clears the air considerably, for if the theory is that "high rate yet declining with age" equals life-course persistent, then we have little or no disagreement, and in fact our data (and that of many others) clearly supports the assertion that there are high-rate offenders. We remain a bit puzzled, however, because this concept would then seem to revert back to the classic "chronic offenders" from the Wolfgang, Figlio, and Sellin (1972) birth cohort study. In other words, in the clarified or revised position, it is not clear to us what is new or different in the "life-course-persistent" concept versus "chronic" other than the label.

A second line of critique is that we did not examine a population-based study and as a result cannot fully test the dual taxonomy theory. We fully agree in one important sense—we cannot assess the validity of the adolescence-limited hypothesis. Much of the testing of Moffitt's (1993) theory requires a population-based sample, and the limitations of our data conflict with the ideal testing conditions she prefers. So we are in agreement here as well. The apparent exception is that we remain convinced that our data are quite relevant to examining long-term trajectories of crime and thus the existence of life-course persistent offender groups. As we have argued elsewhere (Laub and Sampson 2003, 113), it would be hard to write an analytic script that would be more conducive to finding troubled adult men than the one laid out in the behavioral story of the delinquent group in the Gluecks' *Unraveling Juvenile Delinquency* (Glueck and Glueck 1950). These five hundred men generated some ten thousand criminal and deviant offenses to age seventy.

[W]e highlight a life-course view that emphasizes human agency and choice over the life span, underscoring how people construct their lives within the context of ongoing constraints. From this view, trajectories are interpreted not from a lens of unfolding inevitability but rather continuous social reproduction.

Thus, it seems not at all a straw-man argument to say that if we cannot find convincing evidence that a life-course persistent group can be prospectively identified in these data based on theoretical risk factors at the individual level in childhood and adolescence, then that aspect of the theory is in trouble. Our finding confirms what some have called the Robins paradox, namely, antisocial behavior in children is one of the best predictors of antisocial behavior in adults, yet most antisocial children do not grow up to be antisocial adults (Robins 1978). In retrospect, high-rate adult offenders will almost always be drawn from the pool of high-risk children, but looking forward from high-risk children, we cannot distinguish well who will persist or desist as adults.

A third line of critique of our work was advanced by Blumstein (2003), who suggested that if one calculated rates of offending ("lambda") among "active offenders" as well as offenders distinguished by crime types and various combinations thereof, evidence of LCPs might be found. We are open to the possibility that if one decomposes the data into smaller and smaller subgroups, a subset of men may be found that *in retrospect* appear to look somewhat flat in their offending for some period of the adult life course. But to our mind, these exceptions may merely prove the rule. Here we are admittedly old-fashioned in our approach to data—if one has to search hard and long for patterns that one cannot otherwise see, we are skeptical about the replicability and generality of the results, especially in light of sample selection strategies based on the dependent variable. We further wonder about the overall import of the findings for theory and public policy (for an earlier exchange along similar lines, see Gottfredson and Hirschi 1986; Blumstein, Cohen, and Farrington 1988). For us, the key question remains: Is there a predictable group of offenders who commit crime at a high rate and maintain that high rate of offending over the full life course with some degree of persistence?

Revisiting the predictability of persistence

We now turn to critiques of our work that we address with further data analyses. Moffitt (forthcoming) contends that we did not consider offenses by LCPs that are minor in nature from a legal perspective but that nonetheless capture important dimensions of deviant or antisocial activities in adulthood. Crime, in the sense of serious predatory offending, for example, might be declining over time but "bad behavior" will not. We assess this important argument by measuring within-individual variations in relatively minor offenses that tap various types of deviant behavior. Specifically, we calculated person-year counts of "other" offenses recorded in arrest histories—disorderly conduct, vagrancy, gambling, speeding, conspiracy, lewdness, impersonation of a police officer, resisting arrest, desertion, nonsupport, and hunting near a dwelling.

Although these offenses are by definition violations in a legal sense, they reflect the type of antisocial tendencies that Moffitt has emphasized, especially family conflict (see Moffitt 1993, 680; Moffitt, forthcoming). It is further true that the information we analyze is by definition based on official record keeping, but we would emphasize that our comparisons are *within* individuals. It is hard to imagine why a fifty-five-year-old man, for example, compared to the same man at fifty, would be any more or less likely to be arrested for nonsupport of children or gambling. Within-individual trajectories do not compare different groups or cohorts of men with different characteristics often thought to influence processing (e.g., race and social class). And it turns out that the Glueck men as adults engaged in all sorts of deviant activities that the Boston police appeared only too happy to record—indeed, there were more than three thousand arrests for these minor offenses! We do not have data on things like being fired from jobs, but then again, that kind of behavior is not illegal or of a rule-breaking kind and thus remains outside the bounds of a theory of crime and deviance.

To assess the predictability of trajectories of offending relating to miscellaneous minor offenses, we employ the validated child-risk predictor used in Sampson and Laub (2003) based on a summary of thirteen measures listed in Table 1. These measures are derived from multiple sources (parents, teachers, official records, and the boys themselves) that tap classic *individual-difference* risk factors and the observed propensity to offend of the boys in their early years and adolescence. Measures of individual differences include some of the most venerable and sturdy predictors of crime, especially cognitive abilities (Moffitt 1994, 16), temperament (Moffitt 1993, 695), personality traits (Caspi et al. 1994; Hawkins et al. 2000), and childhood behaviors (Moffitt 1994, 15). In addition, guided by the substantial body of research on criminal careers, we focused on early and frequent involvement in crime and delinquency (Blumstein et al. 1986, 72, 94).

[C]rime is more likely to occur when an individual's bond to society is attenuated.

Verbal intelligence (see Moffitt 1993) was assessed using the Wechsler-Bellevue IQ test and coded into eight categories ranging from one (120 and above) to eight (59 and below). The mean verbal IQ for the delinquent sample was 88.6. We also examine the full-scale IQ score that includes both math and verbal skills, unrecoded. From detailed psychiatric assessments of the boy, we use four dichotomous variables of personality traits: extroverted ("uninhibited in regard to motor responses to stimuli"), adventurous ("desirous of change, excitement, or risk"), egocentric ("self-centered"), and aggressive ("inclined to impose one's will on others"). To capture the early onset of childhood behavior, we used self-reported age of onset of misbehavior, a dichotomous indicator based on teacher and parent reports of the subject engaging in violent and habitual temper tantrums while growing up, and a report from the mother as to whether the subject was overly restless and irritable growing up (we labeled this "difficult child").

The level of delinquent conduct in adolescence was measured in several ways. We used an indicator of the average annual frequency of arrests in adolescence while not incarcerated and a composite scale (ranging from 1 to 26) based on unof-

TABLE 1

CHILD AND ADOLESCENT RISK FACTORS MEASURED BEFORE ADULTHOOD (YOUNGER THAN SEVENTEEN)

Cognitive
  Measured intelligence (IQ, Full-Scale Wechsler-Bellevue)
  Verbal IQ (Wechsler-Bellevue)
Psychiatric assessments
  Extroversion
  Adventurousness
  Egocentricity
  Aggressiveness
Early onset/conduct disorder
  Age of onset of misbehavior (self-reported)
  Age at first arrest (police)
  Age at first incarceration (correctional)
  Violent temper tantrums (teacher and parent reports)
  Difficult child behavior (mother reports)
Antisocial behavior
  Frequency of arrest per days free (up to age seventeen)
  "Unofficial" delinquency (self-, parent, and teacher reports)

ficial self-, parent, and teacher reports of delinquent behavior (e.g., stealing, vandalism) and other misconduct (e.g., truancy, running away) not necessarily known to the police. Following the logic of the criminal career approach, we also included measures of the age at first arrest and age at first incarceration for each boy. Overall, the delinquency measures capture both the level and the developmental pattern of official and unofficial behavior up to an average of about fourteen years of age for each boy.

To assess summary patterns, we followed the logic of risk factor theory by giving emphasis to the *combination of individual-level risks within the person*. We combined standardized indicators of all thirteen variables in a single child-risk indicator, with constituent items scored such that a high value indicated either the presence of antisocial behavior or an individual-level risk (e.g., low verbal IQ, engaging in tantrums, early age of onset of antisocial behavior, and so on). We then looked at the distribution across all boys and created a group at highest risk for what Moffitt would call *life-course persistent* offenders—namely, those boys in the upper 20 percent of the distribution. The bottom 80 percent group is defined as low risk. What is important to point out is that the groups were defined prospectively with respect to adult offending, as all the measurement was completed prior to age seventeen. Other than delinquency, which we separate out in a later analysis, the vast majority of measures refer to individual differences of the boys in childhood. The prospective ability of these measures to predict later involvement in crime was demonstrated in earlier work (Sampson and Laub 1993, 92). Thus, while retrospective reporting is a concern we fully acknowledge, the multimethod and multireporter approach, combined with the diversity of measures and their demonstrated validity in predicting stability of offending, speaks to the utility of considering the link between childhood risk and trajectories of crime throughout life.

When we examine the predictive power of childhood risk groups, the dominant pattern is parallel offender trajectories by age and no evidence of distinct developmental pathways. We demonstrate this pattern in several different ways, beginning in Figure 1 with the predicted probability of offending for the most general outcome—total crime (sum of violent, property, alcohol/drug, and other offenses). This replicates the main picture painted in Laub and Sampson (2003, chap. 5). Next we turn to the "raw data" trajectories for the predatory crimes (violent and property offenses) emphasized in traditional criminological theory (see Figure 2). We present the raw data because some critics have wondered whether our smoothing of the data through age-expected trajectories might have masked subgroups of offenders. Even without smoothing, however, one sees a sharp rise and then decline in predatory offense counts for both risk groups, with the main difference in the level of offending. In Figure 3, even the relatively messy trajectories for alcohol- and drug-related offenses reveal remarkably similar patterns for each child-risk group. As predicted by Moffitt (1993, 1994), there are definitely men who offend well into middle age, yet as is also evident in our data, the same pattern holds for both childhood risk groups, and a sharp decline in offending (desistance) is the eventual pattern for all men.

In Figure 4, we turn to the key findings predicting the miscellaneous offenses described earlier from age seven to seventy by childhood risk. Once again the same pattern is displayed as found for other offense types—both child-risk groups show parallel patterns of offending with sharp declines in crime by age. Figure 5 replicates these results using smoothed age-crime trajectories, with strikingly similar patterns. In short, there is no prospective evidence of a flat-line offending trajectory when we examine raw or smoothed age-crime patterns for various crime types, including minor forms of illegal activity and deviance. In analyses not shown, these findings hold up when incarceration and active offender designations are taken into account and when we disaggregate childhood risk into constituent measures (see also Sampson and Laub 2003).

Childhood risk in family adversity

As another test, we conducted analyses that interacted individual-risk characteristics, both the overall scale and constituent measures, with criminogenic family environments during the turbulent years of child and adolescent development. A long history of research, including on the Gluecks' data, has shown that family structural conditions (e.g., poverty, large family size, and residential mobility) and family social processes (e.g., poor supervision, erratic/threatening discipline, and weak parental attachment) are strong predictors of adolescent delinquency (see Sampson and Laub 1993, chap. 4). Moffitt (1993) argued that when a child's vulnerability is compounded with such negative family conditions, life-course-persistent offending is most likely.

FIGURE 1
PREDICTED TOTAL OFFENSE TRAJECTORIES: AGE
SMOOTHED, SEVEN TO SEVENTY, BY CHILDHOOD RISK

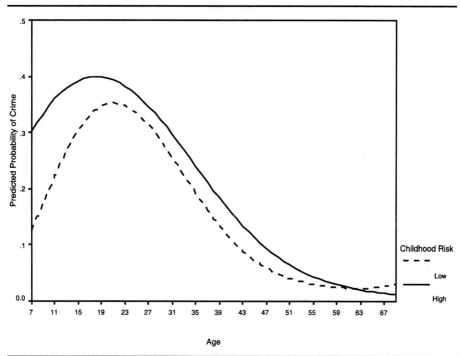

Drawing on Sampson and Laub (1993), we conducted a principal components analysis that reduced the dimensionality of a set of theoretically and empirically salient items measuring family adversity. Two key dimensions emerged, the first defined by high residential mobility, parental emotional instability, low maternal supervision, and hostility between father and son. Poverty, large families, and erratic/harsh methods of discipline defined the second dimension. We then selected those boys who were in the upper half of the distribution of each orthogonal factor (hence approximately 25 percent of the boys) *and* who were in the upper 20 percent of the distribution of the individual-level childhood-risk score. In other words, we examined the interaction of the multiple indicators, with the end result that approximately 4 percent of the delinquent group members are defined as truly high risk. These boys experienced not only the extremes of criminogenic family environments; they were vulnerable from the start based on multiple childhood risks.

In Figure 6, we present the raw plots of trajectories of "other" offending for the boys at the highest child and family risk compared with the rest of the delinquent group. Perhaps not surprisingly, the rate of offending for the high-risk group is

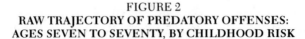

FIGURE 2
RAW TRAJECTORY OF PREDATORY OFFENSES:
AGES SEVEN TO SEVENTY, BY CHILDHOOD RISK

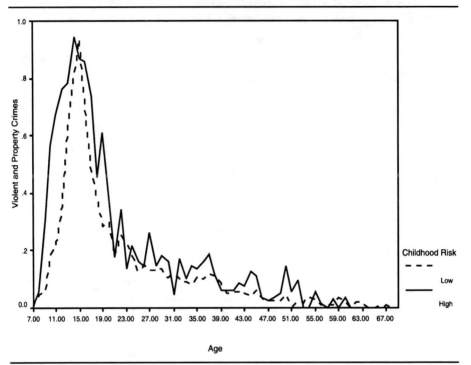

higher in the early years up to the point of the traditional peak age of offending—
about age fifteen. Thereafter, the rate of offending drops off, and these boys desist
just like all other boys in the study. Amazingly, in fact, the rates of offending are
higher in later life for the group predicted to be at *lower risk* based on early child
and family circumstances. But the big picture is clear—the age-crime curves look
the same as in the earlier figures, where we see increasing and then declining
involvement in crime for all risk groups. Our basic conclusion thus continues to
hold, namely, that desistance and aging out of crime appear to reflect a general
(almost fractal) process for all groups of offenders.

Latent class models of desistance

So far, we have restricted our analysis to prospectively defined groups of offenders based on childhood and adolescent risk factors. A quite different approach is to
take the full life course as a given and ask whether there are distinct and latent
offender groups based on ex post trajectories of offending. And if so, can the resulting trajectory groups be linked to preexisting or childhood differences? Despite its

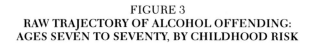

FIGURE 3
RAW TRAJECTORY OF ALCOHOL OFFENDING:
AGES SEVEN TO SEVENTY, BY CHILDHOOD RISK

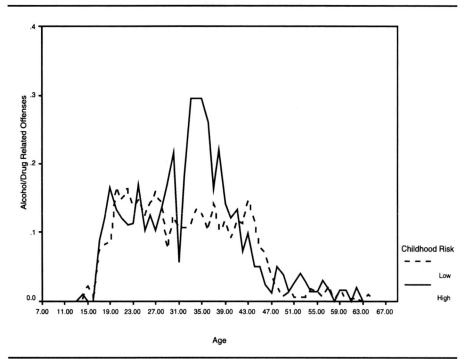

prospective nature, in the analysis above we might have masked underlying trajectory groups, such as life-course persisters.

Nagin's (2005) semiparametric group-based modeling approach offers an innovative way to satisfy our objective. In general, the mixed Poisson model assumes that the population is comprised of discrete Poisson distributions with respect to the rate of offending. Each trajectory assumes a polynomial relationship that links age and crime. Based on our earlier analysis, we use a cubic function of age for the seven to seventy models and estimate the equation,

$$\log(\lambda_{it}^j) = \beta_0^j + \beta_1^j (AGE)_{it} + \beta_2^j (AGE^2)_{it} + \beta_3^j (AGE^3)_{it},$$

where λ_{it}^j is the predicted rate of offending for person i in group j for time period t, AGE_{it} is the age of person i for time period t, AGE_{it}^2 is the squared age of person i for time period t, and AGE_{it}^3 is the cubed age of person i for time period t; and the coefficients β_0^j, β_1^j, β_2^j, and β_3^j structure the shape of the trajectory for each group j. Although every individual in each group is constrained to the same slope and intercept of that trajectory, these parameters, which determine the level and shape of the trajectory, are free to vary by group.

FIGURE 4
RAW TRAJECTORY OF "OTHER" OFFENSES:
AGES SEVEN TO SEVENTY, BY CHILDHOOD RISK

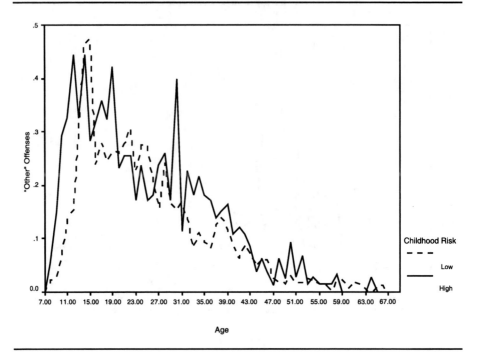

Figure 7 shows the results from semiparametric mixed Poisson models for "other" crimes. Again, heterogeneity in trajectories is present and the data firmly reject a simple typology of two offender groups. There are instead five groups of offending patterns by age for "other" offenses, similar to patterns for total offending as well as crime specific trajectories (see Laub and Sampson 2003, 104-6). Most important to our discussion here is that the differences across groups seem to be age at desistance and rate of offending, but with all groups eventually declining with age. Furthermore, we see in Table 2 that the different subgroups in the data for "other" offenses are not *systematically* predicted by key constituent indicators of our child-risk measure (for similar results for total crime, see Laub and Sampson 2003, 108-9).

For good measure, we also consider in Table 2 two measures of considerable interest in intergenerational studies of the transmission of crime risk—the criminality/deviance of parents and parental mental health status. Parental risk is not a consistent predictor. Interestingly, the group that peaks the latest in terms of other offenses (group 2, in their late thirties) has the *lowest* score on parental criminality and second lowest score on mental disturbance. Overall, the patterns in Table 2 are

FIGURE 5
PREDICTED "OTHER" OFFENSE TRAJECTORIES: AGE
SMOOTHED, SEVEN TO SEVENTY, BY CHILDHOOD RISK

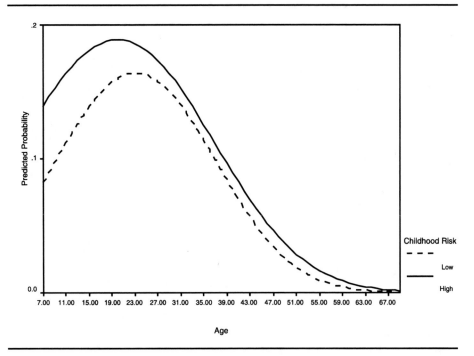

contradictory and do not add up to a consistent story about the past as prologue (cf. Glueck and Glueck 1968).

Age at desistance

Finally, we address in more detail the notion that it may not be the rate of individual offending that is at issue but the length of criminal career (Moffitt, forthcoming). More precisely, the question we pose is, Do those prospectively predicted to be high-rate offenders, or LCPs, offend to a later point in their lives than the low-risk group? Because we have not specifically addressed this argument before, we present in Table 3 the age at last offense for all crime types by the childhood risk factor. The bottom line is that we do not see consistent evidence of differential age at termination based on prospective childhood risk. Note that none of the mean ages at termination across five different crime types differ significantly by group. These results maintain when we examine the age at last offense taking into account both childhood risk and family risk factors together (see Table 4). Thus, there is no evidence in the Glueck data that prospectively defined life-course-persistent

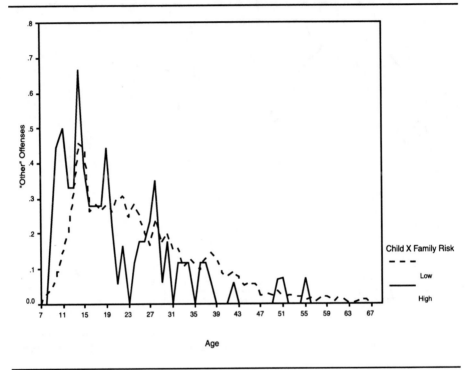

FIGURE 6
RAW TRAJECTORY OF "OTHER" OFFENDING:
AGES SEVEN TO SEVENTY, BY CHILD/FAMILY RISK

offenders display "unusually extended offending careers" (Moffitt, forthcoming) over the life course once conditioned on a troubled adolescence.

Summary

We believe our analyses on minor or miscellaneous offenses and age at termination, in conjunction with reanalyses of raw data trajectories from our previous work, again raise questions about what might be termed the causal theory of groups and the idea that offender groupings are prospectively valid. While our analyses focused on Moffitt's taxonomy, the most detailed and articulate statement of a group-based theory to date, our results have implications for other group-based theories of crime trajectories (e.g., Patterson and Yoerger 1993; Loeber and Hay 1997). We would add that empirical research has by now firmly rejected the notion that there are only two groups of latent-class offenders. Setting aside the present study, Piquero (2005) has recently and independently provided an exten-

FIGURE 7
TRAJECTORIES OF OFFENDING FOR
"OTHER" OFFENSES: AGES SEVEN TO SEVENTY

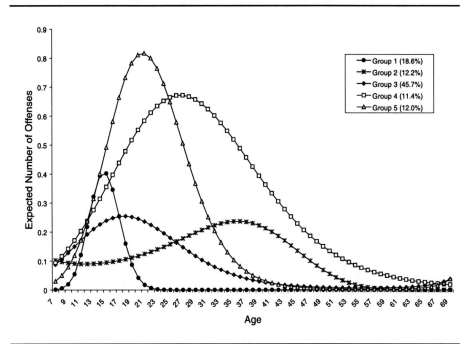

sive review of more than fifty studies of trajectories of crime, *none* of which yielded a two-group solution. The extant evidence thus seems clear that while there are high-rate offenders who evince relative stability in their criminal and deviant offending patterns compared to others, they still decline with age. Second, there is little evidence that there are categorical groupings of men with distinct offender trajectories that can be accurately or meaningfully predicted in the prospective sense among high-risk adolescent delinquents.

If these are the facts, we hazard to guess that their overall interpretation is still like a glass half-full or half-empty scenario—a veritable Rorschach test. Although we were critical of Gottfredson and Hirschi (1990) in our earlier work (Sampson and Laub 1993), and still do maintain an age-graded theory, like them we are now inclined to see in the data from Figures 1 through 7 the overwhelming power of age in predicting desistance from crime. If age is the driving factor, it follows, as they originally argued, that typologies of offender trajectory groups are (inherently?) limiting when it comes to meaningful inferences about the developmental causes of crime.

TABLE 2

COMPARISON OF SELECTED CHILDHOOD AND ADOLESCENT RISK FACTORS
BY "OTHER" CRIMES TRAJECTORY GROUP (N OF CASES APPEAR IN PARENTHESES)

	Group 1 (97)	Group 2 (52)	Group 3 (229)	Group 4 (51)	Group 5 (51)
Individual differences					
Full scale IQ	92.4 (97)	90.9 (52)	91.2 (229)	91.8 (51)	91.5 (51)
Verbal IQ	3.70 (97)	3.35 (52)	3.52 (229)	3.35 (51)	3.31 (51)
Percentage extroverted	54 (97)	62 (52)	57 (229)	67 (51)	51 (51)
Percentage adventurous	47 (97)	58 (52)	56 (229)	65 (51)	53 (51)
Percentage egocentric	16 (97)	10 (52)	14 (229)	8 (51)	12 (51)
Percentage aggressive	18 (97)	15 (52)	17 (229)	10 (51)	12 (51)
Parent/child disposition					
Parental crime/alcoholism	1.92 (97)	1.88 (52)	2.02 (229)	2.14 (51)	2.02 (51)
Parental instability	.84 (92)	.83 (48)	.87 (222)	1.10 (48)	.78 (51)
Percentage tantrums	35.0 (97)	26.9 (52)	41.0 (229)	45.1 (51)	51.0 (51)
Percentage difficult child	61.0 (95)	62.7 (51)	56.9 (225)	60.8 (51)	57.1 (49)
Percentage early onset	7.1 (84)	8.3 (48)	17.3 (197)	13.3 (45)	9.3 (43)
Adolescent delinquency					
Arrest frequency (ages seven to seventeen)	.376 (97)	.362 (52)	.443 (229)	.479 (51)	.447 (51)
Unofficial delinquency (younger than seventeen)	13.5 (97)	14.0 (52)	14.3 (229)	15.3 (51)	14.7 (51)

TABLE 3
AGE AT LAST OFFENSE BY CHILDHOOD RISK FACTOR

	Risk	N	Mean	Standard Deviation
Total crime	No	364	37.44	13.48
	Yes	92	38.65	13.64
Property	No	350	26.21	12.73
	Yes	89	26.92	11.58
Violence	No	196	31.10	13.39
	Yes	59	32.25	13.20
Alcohol/drug	No	209	36.10	12.04
	Yes	56	39.29	10.97
Other	No	356	32.72	13.23
	Yes	91	33.83	13.68

NOTE: No *t-test* comparisons are significant.

TABLE 4
AGE AT LAST OFFENSE BY CHILD/FAMILY RISK FACTOR

	Risk	N	Mean	Standard Deviation
Total crime	No	434	37.96	13.43
	Yes	18	33.39	14.59
Property	No	419	26.48	12.59
	Yes	17	23.76	11.17
Violence	No	241	31.42	13.28
	Yes	7	32.57	19.07
Alcohol/drug	No	252	36.94	11.87
	Yes	10	33.60	12.47
Other	No	425	33.07	13.26
	Yes	18	28.56	13.78

NOTE: No *t-test* comparisons are significant.

A Revised View of the Casual Importance of Turning Points

The second major issue to which we now turn is the role of "turning points" in development and growth. To date, our work has tended to conceptualize turning points in terms of singular, sometimes rare events (e.g., serving in military during wartime). Recently, we have begun to modify this view in light of the fact that many important life events are repeating in nature. For illustrative purposes, we examine here the institution of marriage.

Why is marriage important in the process of desistance from crime? There appear to be at least five mechanisms of desistance, none of which are to our knowledge limited to the particular historical period or demographic subgroups repre-sented in the Gluecks' data. Consistent with the general turning point processes discussed above, theoretically marriage has the potential to lead to one or more of the following in the lives of criminal men: (1) a "knifing off" of the past from the present; (2) opportunities for investment in new relationships that offer social sup-port, growth, and new social networks; (3) forms of direct and indirect supervision and monitoring of behavior; (4) structured routines that center more on family life and less on unstructured time with peers; and (5) situations that provide an oppor-tunity for identity transformation and that allow for the emergence of a new self or script, what Hill (1971) described as the "movement from a hell-raiser to a family man."

It follows from this theoretical conceptualization that the mechanisms associ-ated with marriage are not a constant once set in motion and thus vary through time. The spousal monitoring of drinking patterns, for example, is predicted to vary over time depending on the state of whether one is in or out of a marital relation-ship. Consider further the demographic reality that people enter and exit (and often reenter) marriage over time. Sampson, Laub, and Wimer (2005) followed through on this observation by conceptualizing the potential causal effect of being in the state of marriage (which hypothetically could be randomly or exogenously induced) with the state of nonmarriage *for the same person*. In dynamic terms, marriage is thus not seen as a single turning point but as part of a potential causal dynamic over the life course. We further hypothesize that the effect of marriage on desistance from crime is independent of the developmental history of the person—in this sense, the marriage effect is "nondevelopmental."

Causal effects and the life course

The biggest threat to the validity of any analysis claiming causal effects of a social state like marriage is to account for the nonrandom selection of individuals into the state itself. Marriage is not a random event, and homophily in partner characteris-tics is well established, even though it is simultaneously true that fortuitous events influence mating patterns. To the extent that marriage is influenced by individual self-selection, the marriage-crime relationship is potentially spurious. Indeed, selection is the main critique put forth by those suspicious of social forces (e.g., Gottfredson and Hirschi 1990). Since marriage cannot be randomized in practice, the canonical solution to date has been to "control" for a host of potentially con-founding factors, most notably lagged states of crime itself and other factors that may cause both crime and later marriage, such as prior crime and deviance, per-sonality, unemployment, and so on. Instrumental variables are also possible, but in practice they have not proven effective. Moreover, controlling past values of the treatment or outcome results in biased estimates because such a method controls for the very pathways that are hypothesized to lead to crime.

In recent work, we have addressed this conundrum through a multipronged approach that combines a longitudinal fixed-effects analysis of changes in marriage and crime over the life course with recently pioneered methods for identifying causal effects using observational data—what are typically called "counterfactual methods" of causal inference (Sampson, Laub, and Wimer 2005). Drawing from the language of randomized experiments, counterfactual methods conceptualize causal effects as the effect of a definable "treatment" (e.g., marriage) on some outcome (e.g., likelihood of committing a crime). In this case, one would divide the sample population into a treatment group (those who marry) and a control group (those who do not marry). When examining the causal effect of the treatment, counterfactual methods assume that each individual has two "potential outcomes," at least theoretically. The first is the outcome that the individual demonstrates under the treatment condition, which we will call Y_i^t. The second is the outcome that the individual demonstrates under the control condition, which we will call Y_i^c. For each individual, however, only one of these outcomes can be actually observed at the same time. We can thus recast questions of causality as a "missing data problem" of the unobserved counterfactual (Winship and Morgan 1999), one that is solved in experimentation through randomization. Assuming equivalence of controls and treatments, in other words, permits the estimation of the causal effect, $\overline{Y}_t - \overline{Y}_c$.

Observational data are another matter. When dealing with a treatment at one point in time, one statistical solution is propensity score matching (see Rosenbaum and Rubin [1983] for a formal discussion; see Morgan [2001] and Harding [2003] for empirical examples). With this technique, one can model the propensity that each individual receives the treatment and then create two groups by matching those who did or did not receive the treatment on this propensity score. This strategy has been shown to yield consistent and unbiased estimates of causal effects, as long as all potential confounding factors are included in the model used to create the propensity score. The surprising outcome is that matching on the propensity score fully balances the treatment and control groups on *all* of the covariates used in modeling the propensity of receiving the treatment, allowing the identification of the causal effect by $\overline{Y}_t - \overline{Y}_c$.

In a recent article, we applied this model, but because of space constraints we note here just the basic results (for details, see Sampson, Laub, and Wimer 2005). Our essential strategy was to exploit the rich individual baseline data and time-varying covariates over the full life course to model the propensity to marriage. Rather than control for the proverbial "kitchen sink" in estimating crime, the inverse proportional treatment weighting (IPTW) method forces conceptual clarity in the sense of distinguishing between pretreatment confounders and post-treatment outcomes. From IQ to the cumulative history of both the outcome and treatment itself, we accounted for twenty baseline covariates and approximately a dozen time-varying confounders measured from widely varying sources—many of which predict the course of marriage as theoretically expected. For example, all the childhood and family adversity risk factors noted earlier were considered as baseline (pre–first marriage) covariates, and employment, military service, offspring, and crime itself were modeled as time-varying covariates (cumulative history up to the year before a marriage observation).

To give an example, married men who had a high probability of being married at any given age based on their marital, criminal, employment, military, and offspring history were effectively "downweighted" in the IPTW analysis for that year. Such person-periods reflect a higher degree of "selection" into the observed treatment status given values on confounding covariate histories that make them especially likely to be married (or unmarried). As a result, we do not want them to contribute as much information to the estimation of the causal effect of marriage on crime. On the other hand, married men with low probabilities of being married (but who actually marry) at a given age based on the same histories provide more information, and they are therefore "upweighted" when estimating the final causal effect.

In sum, in our revised framework we see marriage not as a singular turning point but as a potential causal force in desistance that operates as a dynamic, time-varying process through time.

Applying this counterfactual modeling strategy that weights observations by the inverse probability of men being in the state of marriage as predicted by observed covariates and prior treatment history, we found that being married is associated with a 35 percent average reduction in the probability of crime for our sample of fifty-two men assessed from ages seventeen to seventy. This finding was maintained for our full sample of nearly five hundred men examined from ages seventeen to thirty-two (Sampson, Laub, and Wimer 2005). Thus, we view this basic finding as robust and consistent with the notion that marriage causally inhibits crime over the life course. Given the extensive list of baseline and cumulative history covariates, omitted confounders would have to be implausibly large to overturn the basic results we obtained under a number of different model specifications and assumptions.

In sum, in our revised framework we see marriage not as a singular turning point but as a potential causal force in desistance that operates as a dynamic, time-varying process through time. Changes in crime *or* marriage can happen in any year, and the explicit point of the counterfactual model is to estimate these associations with the cumulative history of both outcome and covariates explicitly controlled. Given the nature of the results, we raise the question whether the metaphor of development is the proper one when it comes to understanding time-varying turning points over the adult life course. We return to this issue in the conclusion.

Reflections on the Importance of Agency and Choice

A vital feature that emerged from our life-history narratives was the role of human agency—the purposeful execution of choice and individual will (Matza 1964)—in the process of desisting from crime. As a result, the men we studied were active participants in the process of going straight. We discovered that personal conceptions about the past and future were often transformed as men maneuvered through the transition from adolescence to adulthood. Cohler (1982) has noted that a subjective reconstruction of self is especially likely at times of transition (see also Emirbayer and Mische 1998; Maruna 2001). Many men engaged in "transformative action" in the desistance process. Although informed by the past, agency points toward the future (and hence a future self). Projective actions in the transition from adolescence to adulthood that we uncovered were the advancement of a new sense of self and identity as a desister from crime or, perhaps more aptly, as a family man, hard worker, and good provider.

It also appears that human agency is vitally important for understanding persistent offending over the life course. Some men simply insist on a criminal lifestyle, not out of impulsivity or lack of knowledge of future consequences, but rather because of the rewards of crime itself (Katz 1988) or a willful resistance to perceived domination (Butterfield 1995; Sherman 1993). Persistent offenders knowingly engage in these activities at the expense of a future self. As revealed in many of our life-history narratives, crime was viewed as attractive, exciting, and seductive despite the future pains usually called forth as a result. Calculated and articulated resistance to authority was a recurrent theme in lives of persistent offenders. The men's defiance seemed to have been fueled by a perceived sense of injustice resulting from a pattern of corrosive contacts with officials of the criminal justice system, coupled with a general sense of working-class alienation from elite society. Many persistent offenders see "the system" (criminal justice and work alike) as unfair and corrupt (see also Willis 1977).

In crucial ways, then, persistent crime is more than a weakening of social bonds, and desistance is more than the presence of a social bond, as one might be led to conclude (mistakenly) from *Crime in the Making*. At a meta-theoretical level, our long-term follow-up data direct us to insist that a focus purely on institutional, or structural, turning points and opportunities is incomplete, for such opportunities are mediated by perceptions and human decision making. The process of desistance is complex, and many men made a commitment to go straight without even realizing it. Before they knew it, they had invested so much in a marriage or a job that they did not want to risk losing their investment. Drawing on the work of Becker (1960), this is what we call "desistance by default" (Laub and Sampson 2003, 278-

79). Even if below the surface of active consciousness, actions to desist are in a fundamental sense willed by the offender, bringing a richer meaning to the notion of commitment. Further support for this idea is that the men who desisted from crime, but even those who persisted, accepted responsibility for their actions and freely admitted getting into trouble. They did not, for the most part, offer excuses. Tough times due to the Great Depression, uncaring parents, poor schools, discrimination based on ethnicity and class, and the like were not invoked to explain their criminal pasts. One man captured this opinion the best when he was asked to assess his life and said, "Not because of my mother and father. Because of me. I'm the one that made it shitty."

---

*[P]ersistent crime is more than a
weakening of social bonds, and desistance
is more than the presence of a social bond.*

In ongoing work (Laub and Sampson 2005), we make what we believe is a crucial distinction between human agency and rational choice, one that runs opposite to the recent claim by Paternoster and Bushway (2004, 1) that "if you believe in agency you need to adopt a rational choice perspective." From a rational choice perspective, agency is a matter of preferences (e.g., attitudes toward time and attitudes toward others) and how preferences can be used to change or modify inputs or exogenous events like employment and marriage (Paternoster and Bushway 2004). In our view, the rational choice approach views agency as a static entity representing the stable part of the person as well as within-individual variation over time that is largely driven by age. What is lacking in rational choice is the recognition that we "construct our preferences. We choose preferences and actions jointly, in part, to discover—or construct—new preferences that are currently unknown" (March 1978, 596). At this time, we know little about how preferences are formed (see Vaughan 1998). It is thus not surprising that Hechter and Kanazawa (1997, 195) concluded that "the mechanisms for individual action in rational choice theory are descriptively problematic." Perhaps more important, we argue that human agency cannot be divorced from the situation or context, once again making choice situated or relational rather than a property of the person or even the environment; agency is constitutive of both.

In short, human beings make choices to participate in crime or not, and life-course criminology has been remiss to have left agency—which is essentially human social action—largely out of the theoretical picture. We seek to reposition human agency as a central element in understanding crime and deviance over the life course (Laub and Sampson 2003, chaps. 6-8; see also Wikström 2004). To be sure, *Shared Beginnings* is an incomplete response, for we did not develop an explicit theory of human agency replete with testable causal hypotheses. Our theoretical claim here is simply that the data make clear that agency is a crucial ingredient in causation and thus will be a first-order challenge for future work in life-course criminology (see Laub and Sampson [2005] for further theoretical development).

Implications for Developmental (Life-Course?) Criminology

Development . . . is literally an unfolding or unrolling of something that is already present and in some way preformed.
                                                              —Richard Lewontin (2000)

We close by considering the implications of our analyses of group-based theories of crime, turning points, and human agency for a broader understanding of human development over the life course—issues that are at the very heart of developmental criminology. Relying on what Wordsworth argued was a central insight from Shakespeare—that the child is father to the man—criminologists have addressed in intense fashion how developmental processes are linked to the onset, continuation, and cessation of criminal and antisocial behavior. Much has been learned, and it is fair to say that developmental criminology is now ascendant.

In our view, however, the meaning of development in developmental criminology remains fuzzy and has not been subjected to theoretical interrogation. The biologist Richard Lewontin (2000, 5) has argued that "the term *development* is a metaphor that carries with it a prior commitment to the nature of the process." Using the analogy of a photographic image, Lewontin argues that the way the term *development* is used implies a process that makes the latent image apparent. From our perspective, this seems to be what much of developmental criminological theory is all about, that is, offering a perspective wherein the environment offers a "set of enabling conditions" that allow individual traits to express themselves over time. Although reciprocal interactions with the environment are often mentioned, the typical working assumption seems to be that offenders are following a preprogrammed line of development in a crucial respect—an unwinding, an unfolding, or an unrolling of what is fundamentally "already there." The underlying view of development as a predetermined unfolding is ultimately linked to a typological understanding of the world—different internal programs will have different outcomes for individuals of a different type.

Debates about development in the social sciences are not new (see, for example, the exchange between Dannefer [1984] and Baltes and Nesselroade [1984]), and we are not saying that development reduces to biological processes only. Still, while most developmentalists allude to social interactions as real, in the end most embrace a focus that emphasizes the primacy of early childhood attributes that are presumed to be stable over the life course in a between-individual sense. How else can we understand the fixation on the prediction of later crime from childhood characteristics? It is indisputable that throughout the history of criminology, one of the dominant themes is past as prologue. This continues and finds full expression in the area of addiction research, where we seem to have come full circle from the crude biology of Cesare Lombroso to the current fascination with DNA sequencing and brain imaging as the promise of the future.

In our life-course theory of crime, we seek to return development to where it probably should have been all along, conceived as the constant interaction between individuals and their environment, coupled with purposeful human agency and "random developmental noise."

In our life-course theory of crime, we seek to return development to where it probably should have been all along, conceived as the constant interaction between individuals and their environment, coupled with purposeful human agency and "random developmental noise" (Lewontin 2000, 35-36). According to Elder (1998), human agency is one of the key principles of the life-course perspective. The principle states that "individuals construct their own life course through the choices and actions they take within the opportunities and constraints of history and social circumstances" (p. 4). The recognition of developmental noise implies that "the organism is determined neither by its genes nor by its environment *nor even by interaction between them*, but bears a significant mark of random processes" (Lewontin 2000, 38, italics added). The challenge is that human agency and random processes are ever-present realities, making prediction once again problematic. It further follows that long-term patterns of offending among high-risk populations cannot be divined by individual differences (for example, low verbal IQ, temperament), childhood behavior (for example, early onset of misbehavior), or even adolescent characteristics (for example, chronic juvenile offending).

A key difference between the present life-course perspective and most developmental criminology can be clarified by asking what would happen in an imagined world of perfect measurement. Even if *all* risk factors (including social controls!) were measured without error, our framework posits the continuous influence of human agency and randomizing events, leading again to heterogeneity in outcomes, emergent processes, and a lack of causal prediction. The logic of prediction that drives the search for early risk factors takes nearly the opposite view. Indeed, one gets the sense from "early interveners" that it is just a matter of time before risk factors are measured well enough (from the human genome?) that the false positive problem will finally become ancient history. From the perspective of our theory, this is simply wishful thinking, and we instead predict continued heterogeneity in criminal offending over the life course no matter what the childhood classification scheme of the future. Some "destined" offenders will always start late or refrain from crime altogether, whereas some "innocents" will always start early and continue for long periods of time. And a sizable portion of the offending population will always display a zigzag pattern of offending over long time periods.

Whither groups and offender typologies?

As noted, another strand of developmental theory has focused on offender typologies and the idea of causally distinct and durable groupings through time. We believe that tendencies to reify offender groups as categorically distinct rather than as approximations or heuristic devices runs a considerable risk of reinforcing a "metaphorical imagery." This risk of typologies is related to the larger issue of development as a packaged unfolding as discussed above. After many years of searching, however, there is little reliable or replicable evidence of a *foretold* LCP or career criminal on populations of interest, the organizing focus of the "prediction" paradigm in criminal justice generally and selective incapacitation in particular.

The problem was identified by Travis Hirschi more than thirty years ago—"The problem with the typological approach is that it begs the question of causal homogeneity by focusing exclusively on the question of behavioral homogeneity" (1969, 53). As we witnessed in our long-term follow-up data, it seems likely that offender groupings follow a fairly continuous distribution across predictor or etiological variables. A key finding from our analyses, for example, is that the underlying processes of desistance follow a remarkably similar path for *all* offenders, albeit at different rates and ages, and that age-graded factors (e.g., marriage in adulthood) predict the probability of crime conditioning on the cumulative (developmental) history of the person. It is therefore at least arguable that persistent offending and desistance from crime can be explained by a general age-graded theory of informal social control that emphasizes social ties, routine activities, and human agency (Laub and Sampson 2003).

By raising critical questions about typological approaches, we are not arguing that groups or grouping techniques have no place in criminology. As discussed earlier, groups serve many useful purposes, and methods such as trajectory-group analysis (Nagin 2005) are some of the most innovative to come along in recent criminology. Moreover, the main innovator of the method, Daniel Nagin, has himself warned against the reification of groups and the dangers it presents (2005). The latent class method is not the problem any more than regression techniques are the problem when incorrectly interpreted in causal rather than associational terms.

We see, then, a growing consensus on the potential dangers and benefits of trajectory groups, a development we believe is healthy for the field. Our position is that the line of contention, if one remains, turns on the theoretical interpretation of an offender trajectory. Moving away from the metaphor of development, we see offender trajectories of the sort analyzed in Nagin (2005) and in Laub and Sampson (2003) as being *continually socially produced over time*. This conceptualization is a far cry from what we see as the dominant (and unreflective) interpretation in criminology that rests on a notion analogous to traveling by train—one gets on a trajectory and ends up at a later point directed by the plan set down at the beginning (barring an accident, of course, thereby limiting social influences to the error term; see also Dannefer 1984). We believe this distinction is not merely a matter of semantics and goes to the very heart of modern views of causality and prediction in the social sciences. Our conceptualization of crime as an emergent process can be accommodated by trajectory analysis but not necessarily by developmental theory as currently practiced in criminology.

Concluding thoughts

We view this article and our larger project as offering a dual critique of social science theory and current policy about crime over the life course. Developmentalists seem to believe that childhood and adolescent risk characteristics are what *really* matter—witness the undeniable rise and dominance of the "early risk-factor" paradigm. Our work simply pleads for balance in the other direction, but this move in no way denies the reality of the stability of individual differences. Again, the prescient work by Lee Robins (1978) and the ensuing idea of the Robins paradox discussed earlier serve as an excellent point of common reference.

Not to be overlooked and equally important, our work is inherently critical of "structuralist" approaches in sociological criminology wherein it is argued that location in the social structure, namely, poverty and social class, are what really matter. We hardly believe that all bad actors would simply desist from crime if they were given jobs. Pure deprivation or materialist theories are not just antediluvian but wrong by offenders' own accounts. Our recent work even questions the idea that some inferred from *Crime in the Making*—that institutional turning points are purely exogenous events that act on individuals. The men we studied in *Shared Beginnings, Divergent Lives* were not blank slates any more than they were rational actors in an unconstrained market of life chances. They were active participants in constructing their lives—including turning points. We were thus compelled to take seriously purposeful human action under conditions of constraint. At the same time, we did see evidence that certain institutions, such as marriage, predicted crime even when each man served as his own control.

How can these seemingly opposite views be reconciled? Although not readily apparent at first glance, we believe the concept of *emergence* unifies the three themes of this article. By studying the group question, we learned that long-term outcomes cannot be easily predicted. By emphasizing time-varying events, we learned that stability and change do not neatly fit a simple linear "growth" model of development. By listening and taking seriously what the Glueck men told us about their lives, in their own words, we learned that human agency is an important element in constructing trajectories over the life course. Each theme shares in common the idea of criminal behavior as a socially emergent and contextually shaped property.

From our perspective, the implied next step is to reconcile the idea of choice or agency with a structural notion of turning points. We refer to this idea as "situated choice" (Laub and Sampson 2003, 281-82; 2005). As Abbott (1997, 102) has written, "A major turning point has the potential to open a system the way a key has the potential to open a lock . . . action is necessary to complete the turning." In this instance, individual action needs to align with the social structure to produce behavioral change and to maintain change (or stability) over the life course. Choice alone without structures of support, or the offering of support alone absent a decision to desist, however inchoate, seems destined to fail. Thus, neither agency nor structural location can by itself explain the life course of crime (cf. Wikström 2004). Studying them simultaneously permits discovery of the emergent ways that turning points across the adult life course align with purposive actions and, yes, stable individual differences.

References

Abbott, Andrew. 1997. On the concept of turning point. *Comparative Social Research* 16:85-105.

Baltes, Paul, and John Nesselroade. 1984. Paradigm lost and paradigm regained: Critique of Dannefer's portrayal of life-span developmental psychology. *American Sociological Review* 49:841-47.

Becker, Howard S. 1960. Notes on the concept of commitment. *American Journal of Sociology* 66:32-40.

Benson, Michael L. 2001. *Crime and the life course: An introduction.* Los Angeles: Roxbury.

Blumstein, Alfred. 2003. Age, crime, and human development: The future of life-course criminology. Presidential Plenary Session, discussant paper presented at the annual meeting of the American Society of Criminology, Denver, CO.

Blumstein, Alfred, Jacqueline Cohen, and David P. Farrington. 1988. Criminal career research: Its value for criminology. *Criminology* 26:1-35.

Blumstein, Alfred, Jacqueline Cohen, Jeffrey Roth, and Christy Visher, eds. 1986. *Criminal careers and career criminals.* Washington, DC: National Academy Press.

Butterfield, Fox. 1995. *All God's children: The Bosket family and the American tradition of violence.* New York: Knopf.

Caspi, Avshalom, Terrie E. Moffitt, Phil A. Silva, Magda Stouthamer-Loeber, Robert F. Krueger, and Pamela S. Schmutte. 1994. Are some people crime-prone? Replications of the personality-crime relationship across countries, genders, races, and methods. *Criminology* 32:163-95.

Cohler, Bertram J. 1982. Personal narrative and life course. In *Life span development and behavior,* vol. 4, ed. Paul B. Baltes and Orville G. Brim Jr., 205-41. New York: Academic Press.

Cullen, Francis, and Robert Agnew. 2003. *Criminological theory: Past to present essential readings*. 2nd ed. Los Angeles: Roxbury.

Dannefer, Dale. 1984. Adult development and social theory: A paradigmatic reappraisal. *American Sociological Review* 49:100-116.

Elder, Glen H., Jr. 1985. Perspectives on the life course. In *Life course dynamics*, ed. Glen H. Elder Jr., 23-49. Ithaca, NY: Cornell University Press.

———. 1998. The life course as developmental theory. *Child Development* 69:1-12.

Emirbayer, Mustafa, and Ann Mische. 1998. What is agency? *American Journal of Sociology* 103:962-1023.

Glueck, Sheldon, and Eleanor Glueck. 1950. *Unraveling juvenile delinquency*. New York: The Commonwealth Fund.

———. 1968. *Delinquents and nondelinquents in perspective*. Cambridge, MA: Harvard University Press.

Gottfredson, Michael R., and Travis Hirschi. 1986. The true value of lambda would appear to be zero: An essay on career criminals, criminal careers, selective incapacitation, cohort studies, and related topics. *Criminology* 24:213-34.

———. 1990. *A general theory of crime*. Stanford, CA: Stanford University Press.

Harding, David J. 2003. Counterfactual models of neighborhood effects: The effect of neighborhood poverty on dropping out and teenage pregnancy. *American Journal of Sociology* 109:676-719.

Hawkins, J. David, Todd I. Herrenkohl, David P. Farrington, Devon Brewer, Richard F. Catalano, Tracy W. Harachi, and Lynn Cothern. 2000. *Predictors of youth violence*. Washington, DC: U.S. Department of Justice.

Hechter, Michael, and Satoshi Kanazawa. 1997. Sociological rational choice theory. *Annual Review of Sociology* 23:191-214.

Hill, Thomas W. 1971. From hell-raiser to family man. In *Conformity and conflict: Readings in cultural anthropology*, ed. James P. Spradley and David W. McCurdy, 186-200. Boston: Little, Brown.

Hirschi, Travis. 1969. *Causes of delinquency*. Berkeley: University of California Press.

Katz, Jack. 1988. *Seductions of crime*. New York: Basic Books.

Laub, John H., and Robert J. Sampson. 1993. Turning points in the life course: Why change matters to the study of crime. *Criminology* 31:301-25.

———. 2003. *Shared beginnings, divergent lives: Delinquent boys to age 70*. Cambridge, MA: Harvard University Press.

———. 2005. Human agency in the criminal careers of 500 Boston men, circa 1925-1995. Paper presented at the workshop on Agency and Human Development under Conditions of Social Change, Jena, Germany, June 4-6.

Lewontin, Richard. 2000. *The triple helix: Gene, organism, and environment*. Cambridge, MA: Harvard University Press.

Loeber, Rolf, and Dale Hay. 1997. Key issues in the development of aggression and violence from childhood to early adulthood. *Annual Review of Psychology* 48:371-410.

March, James G. 1978. Bounded rationality, ambiguity, and the engineering of choice. *Bell Journal of Economics* 9:587-608.

Maruna, Shadd. 2001. *Making good: How ex-convicts reform and rebuild their lives*. Washington, DC: American Psychological Association Books.

Matza, David. 1964. *Delinquency and drift*. New York: Wiley.

Moffitt, Terrie E. 1993. Adolescence-limited and life-course-persistent antisocial behavior: A developmental taxonomy. *Psychological Review* 100:674-701.

———. 1994. Natural histories of delinquency. In *Cross-national longitudinal research on human development and criminal behavior*, ed. Elmar G. M. Weitekamp and Hans-Jurgen Kerner, 3-61. Dordrecht, the Netherlands: Kluwer Academic.

———. Forthcoming. Life-course persistent versus adolescence-limited antisocial behavior. In *Developmental psychopathology*, 2nd ed., ed. D. Cicchetti and D. Cohen. New York: Wiley.

Morgan, Stephen L. 2001. Counterfactuals, causal effect heterogeneity, and the Catholic school effect on learning. *Sociology of Education* 74:341-74.

Nagin, Daniel S. 2005. *Group-based modeling of development*. Cambridge, MA: Harvard University Press.

Paternoster, Ray, and Shawn Bushway. 2004. Rational choice, personal agency, and us. Paper presented at the annual meeting of the American Society of Criminology, Nashville, TN.

Patterson, Gerald R., and Karen Yoerger. 1993. Developmental models for delinquent behavior. In *Mental disorder and crime*, ed. Sheilagh Hodgins, 140-72. Newbury Park, CA: Sage.

Piquero, Alex. 2005. What have we learned about the natural history of criminal offending through longitudinal studies? Paper presented at the National Institute of Justice, Washington, DC.

Piquero, Alex R., David P. Farrington, and Alfred Blumstein. 2003. The criminal career paradigm: Background and recent developments. In *Crime and justice: A review of research*, vol. 30, ed. Michael Tonry. Chicago: University of Chicago Press.

Robins, Lee N. 1978. Sturdy childhood predictors of adult antisocial behavior: Replications from longitudinal studies. *Psychological Medicine* 8:611-22.

Rosenbaum, Paul, and Donald Rubin. 1983. The central role of the propensity score in observational studies for causal effects. *Biometrika* 70:41-55.

Rutter, Michael. 1996. Transitions and turning points in developmental psychopathology: As applied to the age span between childhood and mid-adulthood. *International Journal of Behavioral Development* 19:603-26.

Sampson, Robert J., and John H. Laub. 1993. *Crime in the making: Pathways and turning points through life.* Cambridge, MA: Harvard University Press.

———. 1997. A life-course theory of cumulative disadvantage and the stability of delinquency. In *Developmental theories of crime and delinquency*, ed. Terence P. Thornberry, 133-61. New Brunswick, NJ: Transaction Publishers.

———. 2003. Life-course desisters? Trajectories of crime among delinquent boys followed to age 70. *Criminology* 41:301-39.

Sampson, Robert J., John H. Laub, and Christopher Wimer. 2005. Assessing causal effects of marriage on crime: Within-individual change over the life course. Manuscript, Cambridge, MA: Harvard University.

Sherman, Lawrence W. 1993. Defiance, deterrence, and irrelevance: A theory of the criminal sanction. *Journal of Research in Crime and Delinquency* 30:445-73.

Thornberry, Terence P., ed. 1997. *Developmental theories of crime and delinquency.* New Brunswick, NJ: Transaction Publishers.

Vaughan, Diane. 1998. Rational choice, situated action, and the social control of organizations. *Law and Society Review* 32:23-61.

Wikström, Per-Olof. 2004. Crime as alternative: Towards a cross-level situational action theory of crime causation. In *Beyond empiricism: Institutions and intentions in the study of crime*, ed. Joan McCord. New Brunswick, NJ: Transaction Publishers.

Willis, Paul E. 1977. *Learning to labour: How working class kids get working class jobs.* Farnborough, UK: Saxon House.

Winship, Christopher, and Stephen L. Morgan. 1999. The estimation of causal effects from observational data. *Annual Review of Sociology* 25:659-707.

Wolfgang, Marvin, Robert Figlio, and Thorsten Sellin. 1972. *Delinquency in a birth cohort.* Chicago: University of Chicago Press.

Offender Classifications and Treatment Effects in Developmental Criminology: A Propensity/ Event Consideration

By
MICHAEL R.
GOTTFREDSON

Developmental criminology has raised the prospect that empirical classifications of offenders based on variations in the age of offending will assist in the prediction of and explanation for crime and delinquency. Additionally, developmental criminology suggests that events late in the life course may alter offending propensities in significant ways. Recent empirical works provide compelling evidence about these claims and provide support for general theories of the causes of crime and delinquency. Some of this recent research is analyzed from the perspective of a propensity/event theory.

Keywords: developmental studies of crime; offender classifications; crime theory; self-control

E fforts to classify the offender population have a long tradition in empirical criminology (Gottfredson and Tonry 1987). Classification is, after all, an element of most sciences and rests on the expectation that grouping like cases together and separate from unlike cases will add either predictive or explanatory value. Interest in typologies is frequently associated with efforts to discover differential treatment amenability, under the assumption that not all offenders are alike—they differ in the motives for their offenses; in the meaning that offenses have for them; and, perhaps, in their susceptibility to intervention, to therapy, or to offending reductions from incapacitation.

There are important methodological issues involved in empirical classification, including the selection and measurement of elements around which to classify, the rules used to assess

Michael R. Gottfredson is a professor of criminology, law, and society and of sociology and executive vice chancellor at the University of California, Irvine. He received his A.B. from the University of California, Davis, and Ph.D. from the State University of New York at Albany. He is the coauthor or editor of Control Theories of Crime and Delinquency *(2003),* The Generality of Deviance *(1994),* A General Theory of Crime *(1990),* Decisionmaking in Criminal Justice *(1988), and* Victims of Personal Crime *(1978), as well as numerous articles in criminology.*

DOI: 10.1177/0002716205279937

similarity and difference, and the reliability of empirically derived classes. As with most methodological questions in the behavioral sciences, these issues cannot be adequately resolved independent of theories about the causes of the behavior in question, because every empirical classification technique presumes the appropriateness of the elements pertinent to the identification of similarities and differences. In contrast to the typological approach to causal understanding are the general theories, theories that seek to explain crime and delinquency by understanding the individual and group differences that generally differentiate rates of crime and delinquency. Recent strong claims made for offender types (Moffitt 1993) and developments in empirical classification methodologies (Nagin and Land 1993) have stimulated reconsideration of the virtues of typologies in criminology as opposed to general theories.

What distinguishes current typological research from the long tradition is the promise from developmental criminology that by adding age (or time) as a dimension of similarity and difference, offender typologies might yield enhanced prediction or more complete explanation for offending. This has produced a growing body of sophisticated and important work (Nagin and Land 1993; Nagin and Tremblay 2005; Ezell and Cohen 2005) enabled both by a large increase in data sets that involve repeated measures on the same subjects over time and by adoption of sophisticated statistical methods employed in the assessment of similarity and difference.

Classification has also long been held to be important by criminologists on the "crime" side of the problem, because some scholars regard the study of crime itself as too heterogeneous a subject for useful science. These scholars instead prefer to study subclasses of offending, such as white-collar crime or violence. Some do both—creating offender typologies for special forms of crime or delinquency (e.g., Nagin and Tremblay 1999).

For several reasons, not all scholars are equally sanguine about the prospects for criminology of the typological approach. Reasons for skepticism may include

- evidence of substantial versatility in offending,
- evidence for general propensities for crime and deviance,
- a preference for parsimony,
- uncertainty about the effectiveness of differential treatment,
- concern about the policy use resulting from the putative identification of certain types of offenders (e.g., chronic, high-rate offenders), and
- substantial advances in general explanatory models for crime and delinquency.

Although it is undeniably true that in some ways all offenders are alike, just as in some ways all offenders are unique, the typologist's problem is to identify those ways in which some offenders are alike and different from others in nontrivial ways, in ways that enable better prediction than achieved by generalists or more satisfying explanation than provided by global theories. The developmental typologist's problem is to do so in a way that makes time (or age) essential.

In this context (among many others), the recent work of Robert Sampson and John Laub is critically important (Sampson and Laub 1993, 2005; Laub and

Sampson 2003). Not only are their hard-earned data the most important in the field, but the framework of their studies and the sophistication of their analysis make their research compelling. For present purposes, two sets of findings in their recent work should be considered in an interrelated way: (1) their analyses of the likelihood of enhanced predictions of offending over the life course, using development of typologies focused on the timing of offending at different ages; and (2) their analyses suggesting that some events during the adult life course have major effects on the probability of future offending, events that, for analytical purposes, may be termed "treatment" effects. As Sampson and Laub (2005) suggested, these findings have major implications for longstanding discussions about the meaning of age effects, the notion of "careers" in criminology, and the validity of general theories (cf. Hirschi and Gottfredson 1983, 1995; Gottfredson and Hirschi 1986, 1990). It may prove useful to discuss these issues for criminology by focusing for the moment on a distinction between crime and criminality, or between what Travis Hirschi and I referred to as the distinction between events and propensities (Hirschi and Gottfredson 1986).

Offenses and Offenders

Criminal and delinquent acts are events. They take place in time and in space and require certain, minimally necessary elements (Hindelang, Gottfredson, and Garofalo 1978; Cohen and Felson 1979; Gottfredson and Hirschi 1990). Among these are a suitably motivated actor who is unrestrained from acting, a target of the motivation, and their intersection in time and in space. At the same time, individuals differ in their tendency to engage in delinquency and crime, and it is known that such differences are remarkably robust over time and place. In recent years, criminology has made very substantial progress in the analysis of crime, thought of in this way (e.g., Felson 2002; Osgood et al. 1996). Theories of offending tend to focus attention on either motivation (attempting to specify why certain targets are attractive to certain people) or restraint (attempting to specify why certain people do not act, given target attractiveness). Individual or group differences in either motivation or restraint may be referred to as the propensity to offend. Our own theory emphasizes the restraint model and attempts to describe how individuals come to differ in their susceptibility to (mostly) informal controls on behavior (Gottfredson and Hirschi 1990).

Once created, these differences influence both the tendency to commit crimes and delinquencies and the environments and life circumstances that make delinquency or crime (events) more or less likely. Propensities and events are not independent of one another; propensities that affect one life circumstance (e.g., school completion) quite clearly affect others (employment prospects, marriage, place of residence), and certain life circumstances affect opportunities for criminal involvement. Laub and Sampson (2003) have referred to the results of the complex selection process as "cumulative disadvantage." This complexity is one reason we initially referred to our perspective as a "propensity-event" theory of crime

(Gottfredson and Hirschi 1989), a perspective that has since generated considerable research and much empirical support (Gottfredson, forthcoming). Although it too is a developmental theory, it places special emphasis on socialization experiences in the early years in life and on the lifelong influences that childhood experiences seem to have.

The difficult methodological and conceptual tasks for propensity-event theories is to partition the correlates of delinquency and crime into the propensity category and into the event category, under the circumstance that, once developed, propensity can strongly influence life circumstances, perhaps even particularly those social and environmental circumstances conducive to crime. So, for example, "gang members are more likely to engage in certain criminal acts, presumably at least partly because the group provides them with an advantage relative to some victims" (event) but also because some individuals are more likely to join gangs to begin with (propensity) (Gottfredson and Hirschi 1989, 63). Similarly,

> The use of alcohol is governed in part by those characteristics indexing . . . [propensity] and this is probably the principal reason for the association between alcohol consumption and crime. . . . At the same time, alcohol may also increase the probability of some types of crime independent of the criminality of the offender because it relates to emotionality, sense of immunity, or lack of motor control. School failure makes for probable unsupervised time during the day when houses are unoccupied and thus more suitable targets for burglary. School failure thus indexes . . . [propensity] and also increases the likelihood of crime over and above that to be expected from the . . . [propensity] of the offender. (Gottfredson and Hirschi 1989, 63)

Once made, the distinction between events and dispositions can be used to clarify some of the issues in the developmental research and to sharpen the predictions made by general as opposed to specialized theories or typologies of crime and delinquency. However easy to make in theory, the distinction is very difficult to practice in research.

From Concepts to Indicators

The oft-cited admonition that "it seems implausible to argue that all variables are related to crime in the same way at all ages" (Farrington 1986, 229) is, of course, one justification for developmental typologies. Given the recent results of Laub and Sampson (2003), such a circumstance now hardly seems implausible at all; rather, a general causal system is more consistent with their data than is the notion of differential causal structures for different offender types. These are indeed critical findings, since without causal significance (and without predictive validity, also shown by Laub and Sampson) the import of statistically generated typologies is problematic.

It is also important to recognize, however, that consistency of relationships for *variables* at all ages is most certainly not what causal theories require; rather, theories expect that their concepts, properly measured, will predict differences in offending over the life course. The distinction between variables and indicators, although elementary, is crucial. An example that helps illustrate the matter is the meaning of marriage effects sometimes reported in developmental studies.

Sampson and Laub (1993, 2003) showed, along with a considerable body of research, that there is substantial stability over the life course in the differences between people in offending and that there is a very general decline in offending with age for everyone. Indeed, given the very high quality of both their data and their analysis, their conclusion that crime declines with age even among their most active offenders is fundamentally important and inconsistent with the trend toward age-based typologies.

[T]he typologist's problem is to identify those ways in which some offenders are alike and different from others in nontrivial ways.

Sampson and Laub (1993, 2003) also found that changes in life circumstance, such as marriage and jobs, are associated with changes in criminal behavior (cf., for example, Cernkovich and Giordano 2001). In propensity-event theories, such changes in offending can come about either because the propensity for involvement in crime and related behaviors changes or because the opportunities to engage in crime change. The meaning of the variable "marriage" is thus of considerable importance. Laub and Sampson (2003) described in detail the several hypotheses consistent with the marriage effect. For the moment, we will focus on just two of them that are especially interesting to propensity-event theories (although this does not do justice to the complexity of their argument). Differences in self-control established in childhood may persist strongly despite changes in social circumstance later in life as suggested by Gottfredson and Hirschi (1990), and/or the effect of social controls may be somewhat variable throughout adulthood as suggested by Sampson and Laub (1993). Changes in life circumstances like marriage may result from changes in disposition (attitudinal change or increased personal bonds), and they certainly also affect opportunities for crime (restrictions on going out at night looking for fun). Married persons, as opposed to unmarried persons at similar ages, have different lifestyles associated with opportunities for crime (Hindelang, Gottfredson, and Garofalo 1978). So, setting aside for the moment selection problems,[1] is the effect of marriage propensity or event? Both of these interpretations for the effect are plausible and are even perhaps a matter of degree. A similar analysis could be made of the effects reported in developmental research for, as examples, area of residence, peer group membership, or employment.

Separating propensities (whatever the theoretical source) from events is a notoriously difficult problem for nonexperimental research to solve. But taking control theory as an example, it seems fair to argue that the control theory concepts of "attachment to others" and "self-control" (self-imposed limitations on the pursuit of self-interest) must have considerable temporal durability to be thought of as strong dispositions that shape much behavior. After all, in control theories these concepts are the source of the stable individual differences among people that help explain the main finding of over-time stability of between-subject differences in the first place. So, it seems reasonable to ask the question, consistent with the study of treatment effects generally, Does the marriage effect last after the treatment (marriage) is taken away? Is it a disposition change (e.g., bonding) or an opportunity restriction?

At least some evidence seems to come down on the event side of the matter. For example, in their study of short-term changes in life circumstances (such as marriage) for recently convicted offenders, Horney, Osgood, and Marshall (1995) found that these effects are rather fleeting—during the state of marriage, crime is temporarily reduced, but it returns once the marriage state is over. It is a difficult conceptual matter to argue that attachment or bonding (strong forces in control theory) or self-control can be so fleeting—as a matter of fact, that seems to be the opposite of bonding and more consistent with, say, opportunity restrictions or incapacitation. Similar results are reported by Sampson and Laub (2005): "Holding age constant and allowing individual heterogeneity in age effects we found that *when* in a state of marriage, the propensity to crime was lower for the same person than when not in marriage. Similar results were found for military service and steady employment." An analogy to some findings for parole supervision may be apt. During the period of supervision, some offending seems to be reduced, due perhaps to lifestyle restrictions placed as a condition of release from prison (be in at night, be subject to random searches, be restricted from associating with delinquent peers) (Gottfredson, Mitchell-Herzfeld, and Flanagan 1982).

For control theories, the meaning of the marriage variable is age dependent, and thus its effects are presumed to differ at different points in the life course. Due in part to the effect of self-control, marriage at age fifteen has different meaning from marriage at age twenty-eight, or even at fifty-seven. At very young ages, marriage may index low self-control (see Martino, Collins, and Ellickson 2004), during the early to late thirties higher levels, and so on. (Jobs also have a similar age-dependent meaning in control theory.) And repeated marriage may signify low rather than high self-control. In any event, not all marriage effects are inconsistent with general, propensity/event theories. In fact, these general theories might help to reconcile what seem to be inconsistent findings with respect to effect of marriage in the literature—sometimes appearing, sometimes not (e.g., contrast Stouthamer-Loeber et al. [2004] with Laub and Sampson [2003]).

The event-propensity distinction is also useful for conceptualizing and measuring the dependent variable in delinquency research. The event quality of acts clouds a clear meaning for or interpretation of measures of crime and delinquency. Consider, for example, the creative study of aggression by Nagin and Tremblay (1999), which is notable for the very early ages during which measures of aggression are taken and for the study of "trajectories" from ages six to fifteen. In this study, one measure of aggression, based on teacher's behavioral ratings (childhood physical aggression score) generally declines from the earliest to the later measurements (p. 1184). The second measure, adolescent physical aggression scores, indexed by the self-reports of the subjects, is either flat or peaks between the ages of fourteen and seventeen. How should one interpret the relation between these two different measures of aggression and age? The answer may be provided by focusing on the event quality of delinquencies and how this affects the two different methods of measurement for the two age groups used in the study. The first measure is based (presumably) on behavior in the classroom and thus subject to teacher assessment; the second is based on the children's reports, regardless of the place of occurrence.

It is entirely possible that virtually all children, as they age from six to thirteen, reduce their delinquency in highly structured, adult-supervised settings such as the classroom. In classrooms, "childlike" behavior is both increasingly less tolerated and less possible as children age, even as they generally increase their delinquency elsewhere. The variables "kicking, hitting, and biting" may mean one thing to teachers for children at age six and quite another at age thirteen. Children who bite others in the first grade may be unruly, but those who do so in the seventh grade are presumably removed from school. This distribution of "aggression" behaves over age exactly like what control theory would predict for a socialization effect—during the treatment (teacher socialization), over time, the very young children virtually all learn to control their misconduct when observed and sanctioned for it—some more than others, but increasingly so up to eight or nine years old. Meanwhile, the self-report data by age from the Nagin and Trembly (1999) study behave like standard crime data, although the range of ages is too restricted to infer much about the general trend, especially with very low-rate samples.

These are, of course, only hypotheses, but they illustrate the potential of parsing propensities from events, some of which inhere in the measures of crime themselves.[2] And if these ideas are modestly correct, they indicate that one general theory (control theory) could readily account for what seem to some developmental researchers to be different onsets and markedly different trajectories over a portion of the life course.

Age Effects

With apologies to Kurt Lewin, it might be said that nothing is as practical as a good fact. And as Laub and Sampson (2003) showed, the age effect continues to be a good fact. It looks like the general decline in offending with age is ubiquitous—or so nearly so that there is much to be risked by ignoring it. Research strongly implies that the warning that the aggregate age-crime curve may mislead because it combines prevalence with incidence (Farrington 1986) seems to be a false alarm.

Classification methods or concepts that only result in partitioning an underlying continuum (e.g., Moffitt 1993), such as the age distribution of crime seems to be, at best only attenuate propensity correlations and at worst result in empirical groupings with little etiological significance. The general age effect, it seems, even survives empirical classification schemes built on recidivists (Ezell and Cohen 2005). This replicates the well-known fact, reliably reported, that even in samples of incarcerated offenders followed up for long periods of time, offending declines significantly with age (Gottfredson and Gottfredson 1994).

[W]ithout causal significance . . . the import of statistically generated typologies is problematic.

The consequence of examining the full range of age effects over the life course was dramatically illustrated by Sampson and Laub (2003, 565-69), who reported, "Hence . . . the classic age crime pattern . . . is replicated even within a population that was selected for their serious, persistent delinquent activity. . . . Aging out of crime is the norm—even the most serious delinquents desist." They referred to the pattern for serious offenders in their data as fractal of the overall distribution.

The implication of this fact for offender typologies is enormous. For example, taken together, all these data provide a strong refutation to Moffitt's (1993) typology, predicting as it does that age is unrelated to offending for highly active offenders. It now seems that we can safely dispense with the notion of the "life-course persisters" in our theories of criminality.

Fundamentally, the Laub and Sampson (2003) study cautions us about the consequences of restrictions of the range of the age variable in developmental studies that try to assess the age effect. For example, in Bushway, Thornberry, and Krohn (2003, 144) age effects look to the authors to be quite variable, a finding discrepant from the repeated finding of the general age effect. But the range of ages studied is quite limited. And with the exception of the group called "late starters," and those who do not offend at all, most of the groups seem to have their peak age within a three-year period of one another and to decline subsequently. Their "late-starter" group makes up 10 percent of their sample. Recent work suggests that we might expect a general decline over age once the range is less restricted. There is also room for caution in empirical classifications based on data that find so-called "late onset" cases in their data. Elander et al. (2000) found upon careful inspection evidence of at least minor juvenile delinquency in every case of their "late-onset" cases classified on the basis of convictions. And their "late-onset" cases had more instances of major mental illness before, rather than after, the "onset."

In the recidivism study of discharges from California Youth Authority prisons, reported by Ezell and Cohen (2005), despite efforts designed to maximize the classification of cases discrepant from the aggregate crime curve, they could find no group for which offending did not decline with age, even with a restricted range of ages on their follow-up; and for most of their empirically created groups identified via their latent class method, the peak age of arrest (the crime measure used in the study) varied from about 14 to 16.5. It remains for future research to attempt badly needed reliability or replication analyses for the empirical typologies produced by both sets of researchers, given the tendency of the empirical methods employed to capitalize on chance variations in the samples.

The practical implications of the age effect

At least in part, serious efforts to identify offender typologies by age were stimulated by an interest in the policy implications of criminal careers. It thus seems fair now to ask, after a couple of decades of high-quality longitudinal research, whether the policy implications of the age invariant thesis or the criminal career thesis seem most consistent with the facts as we now know them. The predictions derived from a ubiquitous decline in offending with age are readily stated (Gottfredson and Hirschi 1990):

- Incapacitation will be inefficacious in reducing the crime rate.
- Absent control group comparisons, all treatments permitting selection by the offender postadolescence will appear to be effective (as long as the follow-up is long enough).
- Programs that seek to change the propensity for crime at a young age have the best chance of substantial individual crime reductions by changing the life course of offending.

Each of these expectations derived from the age effect appear to have strong empirical support (Gottfredson, forthcoming). Such policy findings, in turn, help validate the fact itself.

Human Agency Choice in Propensity Theory

Sampson and Laub (2005) made a case for the reintroduction of the person as an actor in crime theory. General propensity-event theories, such as self-control theory, are also comfortable with the idea of human agency (Hirschi and Gottfredson 1990). Low self-control does not require crime any more than high self-control prohibits it. The general tendency to engage in or refrain from acts of short-term self-interest can be overcome by minimal barriers, by opportunities, and by decisions. Excellent work on offender decision making and experimental research on the effects of sanctions and incentives indicate the important role of decision making in offending. Thus, the focus on choice or human agency as a vital component to explanations of criminal behavior is an important contribution of the Sampson and Laub work, one that seems to be highly consistent with the control perspective that they adopt. But in this regard, we continue to caution that self-reports of dispositions need external validation, and we continue to suggest behavioral measures for indicators of disposition, not filtered through the responses of the subjects themselves, to tap this concept reliably.

Years ago in an important contribution, David Matza (1964) worried about the problem of overdetermined actors in theories of crime and delinquency. Laub and Sampson (2003), in their impressive study, issue the same warning. At the same time, they hold out the reasonable prospect that a general theory can account for differences in propensity that have a high degree of stability, a theory that allows for change in offending at different times in life, a theory that recognizes the general decline in crime with age, and a theory that dispenses with offender classifications that have little added predictive or explanatory value. Criminology will be greatly advantaged by attending to these implications of their research.

Notes

1. Selection bias is the first refuge of a propensity theorist when confronted with treatment effects in nonrandomized quasi-experimental studies. Although statistical methods have advanced measurably in recent years, the essential problem of "holding constant" propensity and thus potential selection bias in nonexperimental developmental studies remains (see Hirschi and Gottfredson 1995).

2. We have made an analogous argument about studies of the age effect for such subclassifications as white-collar crime—the setting in which such crimes can take place are themselves both propensity affected and age dependent (Hirschi and Gottfredson 1987).

References

Bushway, Shawn D., Terrence P. Thornberry, and Marvin D. Krohn. 2003. Desistance as a developmental process: A comparison of static and dynamic approaches. *Journal of Quantitative Criminology* 19:129-53.

Cernkovich, Stephen A., and Peggy C. Giordano. 2001. Stability and change in antisocial behavior: The transition from adolescence to early adulthood. *Criminology* 39 (2): 371-410.

Cohen, Lawrence, and Marcus Felson. 1979. Social change and crime rate trends: A routine activity approach. *American Sociological Review* 44:588-608.

Elander, James, Michael Rutter, Emily Simonoff, and Andrew Pickles. 2000. Explanations for apparent late onset criminality in a high-risk sample of children followed up in adult life. *British Journal of Criminology* 40:497-509.

Ezell, Michael E., and Lawrence E. Cohen. 2005. *Desisting from crime.* Oxford: Oxford University Press.

Farrington, David P. 1986. Age and crime. In *Crime and justice: A review of research*, vol. 7, ed. Michael Tonry and Norval Morris. Chicago: University of Chicago Press.

Felson, Marcus. 2002. *Crime in everyday life.* Thousand Oaks, CA: Pine Forge Press.

Gottfredson, Don M., and Michael Tonry. 1987. Prediction and classification: Criminal justice decision-making. In *Crime and justice: An annual review of research*, vol. 9, ed. Michael Tonry and Norval Morris. Chicago: University of Chicago Press.

Gottfredson, Michael. Forthcoming. The empirical status of theory in criminology. In *Advances in criminological theory*, vol. 15, ed. K. Blevins, F. Cullen, and J. Wright. New Brunswick, NJ: Transaction.

Gottfredson, Michael, and Travis Hirschi. 1986. The true value of lambda would appear to be zero: An essay on career criminals, criminal careers, selective incapacitation, cohort studies, and related topics. *Criminology* 24:212-34.

———. 1989. A propensity-event theory of crime. In *Advances in criminological theory*, vol. 1, ed. Freda Adler and William S. Laufer. New Brunswick, NJ: Transaction.

———. 1990. *A general theory of crime*. Stanford, CA: Stanford University Press.

Gottfredson, Michael, Susan Mitchell-Herzfeld, and Timothy J. Flanagan. 1982. Another look at the effectiveness of parole supervision. *Journal of Research in Crime and Delinquency* 19:277-98.

Gottfredson, Stephen D., and Don M. Gottfredson. 1994. Behavioral prediction and the problem of incapacitation. *Criminology* 32 (3): 441-74.

Hindelang, Michael, Michael Gottfredson, and James Garofalo. 1978. *Victims of personal crime*. Cambridge, UK: Ballinger.

Hirschi, Travis, and Michael Gottfredson. 1983. Age and the explanation of crime. *American Journal of Sociology* 89:552-84.

———. 1986. The distinction between crime and criminality. In *Critique and explanation: Essays in honor of Gwynne Nettler*, ed. Timothy F. Hartnagel and Robert A. Silverman. New Brunswick, NJ: Transaction.

———. 1987. Causes of white collar crime. *Criminology* 25:949-74.

———. 1990. Substantive positivism and the idea of crime. *Rationality and Society* 2 (4): 412-28.

———. 1995. Control theory and the life-course perspective. *Studies of Crime and Crime Prevention* 4 (2): 131-42.

Horney, Janet D., D. Wayne Osgood, and Inke H. Marshall. 1995. Criminal careers in the short-term: Intraindividual variability in crime and its relation to local life circumstances. *American Sociological Review* 60:655-73.

Laub, John H., and Robert J. Sampson. 2003. *Shared beginnings, divergent lives*. Cambridge, MA: Harvard University Press.

Martino, Steven C., Rebecca L. Collins, and Phyllis L. Ellickson. 2004. Substance use and early marriage. *Journal of Marriage and Family* 66:244-57.

Matza, David. 1964. *Delinquency and drift*. New York: Wiley.

Moffitt, Terrie E. 1993. Adolescence-limited and life-course-persistent antisocial behavior: A developmental taxonomy. *Psychological Review* 4:674-701.

Nagin, Daniel S., and Kenneth C. Land. 1993. Age, criminal careers, and population heterogeneity: Specification and estimation of a nonparametric, mixed poisson model. *Criminology*. 31:327-62.

Nagin, Daniel S., and Richard E. Tremblay. 1999. Trajectories of boys' physical aggression, opposition, and hyperactivity on the path to physically violent and nonviolent juvenile delinquency. *Child Development* 70:1181-96.

———. 2005. What has been learned from group-based trajectory modeling? Examples from physical aggression and other problem behaviors. Paper presented at the Albany Symposium on Crime and Justice, State University of New York at Albany, April 28-29.

Osgood, D. Wayne, Janet K. Wilson, Patrick M. O'Malley, Jerald G. Bachman, and Lloyd D. Johnston. 1996. Routine activities and individual deviant behavior. *American Sociological Review* 61:635-55.

Sampson, Robert J., and John H. Laub. 1993. *Crime in the making: Pathways and turning points through life*. Cambridge, MA: Harvard University Press.

———. 2005. A life-course view of the development of crime. Paper presented at the Albany Symposium on Crime and Justice, State University of New York at Albany, April 28-29.

Stouthamer-Loeber, Magda, Evelyn Wei, Rolf Loeber, and Ann S. Masten. 2004. Desistance from persistent serious delinquency in the transition to adulthood. *Development and Psychopathology* 16:897-918.

Explaining When Arrests End for Serious Juvenile Offenders: Comments on the Sampson and Laub Study

LEE N. ROBINS

This article comments on the article by Sampson and Laub in this issue. It congratulates them on locating and interviewing at approximately age seventy a large proportion of the survivors of the Glueck and Glueck (1968) study. It also points out problems, some resulting from the impact of privacy regulations. Other problems arose from the age of the subjects at follow-up, resulting in half being already deceased; from asking men to explain their desistance from crime, when they may not understand it themselves; and from the methods of testing childhood predictors of desistance. The study results apply only to serious juvenile delinquents and cannot be assumed to generalize to crime in general, including that which begins later and includes white-collar criminals. Preliminary studies to serve as the basis for such a broad approach are suggested.

Keywords: desistance; incarceration; trajectories; marriage

I am pleased to have been chosen as a discussant of the Sampson and Laub article (2005 [this volume]) reporting the first follow-up of a group of juvenile delinquents to age seventy. It is of particular interest to me because I too followed a sample made up principally of delinquents identified initially at about the same age (Robins 1966). The Sampson and Laub sample started with the five hundred youngsters originally identified by the Gluecks in Massachusetts reformatories and followed until age thirty-two (Glueck and Glueck 1968). My sample had attended one of the first child guidance clinics in

Lee N. Robins, Ph.D. is an emeritus University Professor of Social Science and a member of the Department of Psychiatry at Washington University in St. Louis. In the 1950s and 1960s, she conducted a study similar to that of Sampson and Laub, following into their forties a sample of children attending one of the first child guidance clinics in America, most of whom had been referred by the St. Louis Juvenile Court. Since then, she has conducted epidemiologic studies of black schoolboys followed into their thirties, Vietnam veterans exposed to heroin, older black and white men to understand their different suicide rates, and general adult populations to assess their psychiatric disorders.

DOI: 10.1177/0002716205280362

the country, a clinic set up to serve the St. Louis Juvenile Court. In addition to the delinquents referred by the court, it also accepted referrals from social agencies and directly from parents. I followed that sample and a matched control group into their forties, a record length of follow-up in those days. Sampson and Laub used the data collected by the Gluecks to describe the earlier life of their subjects; similarly, I used the clinic's records to describe my subjects' childhoods. For both Sampson and Laub and my group, having records for these subjects dating approximately from our own dates of birth solved the problem inherent in follow-up studies of human beings—that the researchers age with the same speed as the research subjects, making it impossible for one group of researchers to personally observe the whole life span of their subjects. Like Sampson and Laub, I found that most delinquents had adult arrest records but also that most had stopped being arrested years before follow-up. Indeed, in many ways the findings are strikingly consistent between our studies.

Like Sampson and Laub, my study interviewed subjects at follow-up to learn about desistance and our subjects' explanations for it, including what Sampson and Laub call "turning points." For those who reported desistance, our questions were, "You mentioned behaving in certain ways when you were young [and we reminded them of what they had told us]. About what age did you start to change? How did you happen to stop doing these things? Do you have any ideas about why you began to settle down then? Do you think your stopping was connected with any particular experience you had? With any particular person's influence?"

Achievements

Sampson and Laub's study is an impressive achievement in a number of ways. They located or found deceased a very large proportion of their sample. They found current addresses for 181 of those presumed to be still alive, a remarkable 79 percent of these elderly men.

They searched Massachusetts police and FBI records to determine the nature of the crimes each man had committed and the age at which his last crime occurred. They identified events in the Glueck follow-up data and in their own interviews that appear to have accelerated desistance. Their finding that *rewarding* life experiences, such as marriage and a steady job, can bring about earlier desistance from crime than would occur inevitably through aging, with its associated illnesses and decline in physical stamina, gives hope that interventions that improve the likelihood of marriage and working will improve the lives of former criminals as well as protect the property and lives of their potential victims. While most of their evidence for the impact of marriage and jobs comes from the original interviews and record searches by the Gluecks when the men were aged thirty-two, the interviews they themselves conducted with fifty-two survivors at age seventy substantiate those earlier findings.

Additional Materials That Would Have Been Useful

These achievements were attained despite considerable difficulties in carrying out this study. Its authors are keenly aware of some of the obstacles they have confronted in trying to get clear-cut answers to questions about differing trajectories over time and what accounts for those differences. I will review some of the difficulties they have faced and present some ideas that might reduce these problems for future follow-up studies.

Arrests and incarceration. The Gluecks had collected arrest information for their sample three times. As well as arrests, they collected information about incarceration—when it happened and for how long. Sampson and Laub also carried out three successive projects with this sample: first, to put the original Glueck data into excellent order and reanalyze it using modern statistical methods; second, to update the arrest and death records (Sampson and Laub 1993); and third, to again update arrest records and death records and also to interview surviving subjects at about age seventy (Laub and Sampson 2003). They obtained arrest records from Massachusetts and from the FBI. Arrest records from other states were sought only to assist in locating their subjects, not routinely. They did not get records of incarcerations. Thus, they had richer data for most of their sample up to age thirty-two, at the time of the Gluecks' final data collection, than thereafter.

The major finding arising out of this data collection was that arrest records continued to decline with age, reaching a near-zero rate by age fifty, when the men averaged less than one arrest per ten years. The decline in arrest records was dramatic even though arrests secondary to an initial offense were included. Secondary arrests—for example, a parole violation—extend the length of the arrest history. A parole violation occurs after release from prison, perhaps years after the commission of the crime that resulted in the incarceration. One could argue that such arrests should not be counted because only some of the sample is at risk of having them. Similarly, a secondary arrest can occur long after an escape from prison for an escapee who has lived a crime-free life under a different name for many years before he is finally identified and returned to prison. Counting this as an arrest gives the man a late-life arrest, even though his last crime was the escape many years earlier. Again, only a few men are at risk of such arrests because most have not escaped from prison.

The absence of prison records after age thirty-two meant that Sampson and Laub did not know precisely when the men were at risk of arrest. This lack of information could have exaggerated the estimate of desistance by giving men credit for a crime-free life during their last incarceration. Recognizing this problem, the authors used only the Glueck data to calculate rates of crime for men they did not interview.

Crimes not appearing in arrest records. Not all crimes committed appear in police arrest records. As Sampson and Laub note, men will not appear in police records while they are in prison. But incarcerated men can commit offenses in prison against guards, against other prisoners, and against prison rules. If men have long incarcerations, there may be evidence for continuity of crime in their prison records long after the police record evidence has ended. During service in the military, crime may result in time in the brig or dishonorable discharge, but these crimes too are missing from police records. Luckily for the dating of desistance, prison and military service usually occur early in adulthood, so the omission of crimes in those settings should have little relevance to the authors' conclusion about the rarity of crime in the older years.

Age at desistance may be underestimated if a criminal's later crimes do not appear on his arrest record for other reasons as well. This happens if the latest crime was committed out of state and was not reported to the FBI, if it was never cleared, if it was attributed to the wrong person, if the victim chose not to press charges, or if the event was not considered to have been a crime—for example, the subject had stolen what was thought to be a "lost" wallet. Men may become more skillful in concealing their crimes with experience. If so, the last crime identified by interview would tend to be later than the last crime in the arrest record. If the interview date of the last crime is usually later than the police record's, the difference between interview and record dates could be used to calculate a correction factor when estimating the age at last crime for men not interviewed.

Deaths. The authors collected death records to exclude years after death in calculating desistance. Death records were collected from the state of Massachusetts and from the National Death Index. Half of the original sample was found to have died by the second effort to collect records in 1993. The authors suspect that a number of deaths were missed by the National Death Index. Some may have been missed because the men were known by other names, a not-unusual solution for men with a substantial police record, or because their bodies were never identified. Some may have been missed because the National Death Index was not established until 1979, while the Glueck's final check was at least eleven years earlier. It would have been helpful to report how many of the deaths found by the search of Massachusetts records were missing from the National Death Index to get an estimate for the number that would have been found if every state's vital statistics records had been searched both for the years prior to the establishment of the National Death Index and since that date.

While the search of death records may not have been exhaustive, it showed the expected elevated early death rate for men with criminal records compared with that of the general population.

Other limitations on the period of risk. There are limitations on the period of exposure to risk other than those due to death and incarceration. Illness may markedly reduce the period of exposure to risk of arrest. Obviously, men do not commit street crimes while they are confined to hospitals or to other treatment settings or to bed at home.

Age brings its own deterrents, even to the healthy. In our study, the most frequent explanation offered for desistance was "I just wasn't up to that kind of hassle any more." Successful crime takes skill, and as they age, criminals become aware that the rapid reaction time and agility needed to be a successful thief has deserted them, and the dangerousness that was pleasurably exciting in their youths only creates anxiety once they realize they are no longer in top physical form. Physical decline is surely one explanation for why there is so clear a relationship between desistance and age. But the speed of physical decline with aging is not uniform, and we have no way to assess how much decline an individual has experienced by a specific age. This unmeasured variation across individuals probably determines in part the variable length of an active criminal life.

Why did [Sampson and Laub] set so small a goal? Was it a result of their decision to do all the interviews themselves?

The interviews. To obtain interviews dealing with topics not available in records of crime and death, Sampson and Laub attempted to locate the 230 members of the initial sample of reformatory children presumed to still be alive.

Of the 181 located, 52 (29 percent) were personally interviewed by one of the authors, considerably more than the 40 (22 percent) they originally intended to interview. Why did they set so small a goal? Was it a result of their decision to do all the interviews themselves? They used an unstructured interview, presumably because they wanted freedom to follow every possible clue in the men's comments to reach an understanding of what caused desistance from crime. They may not have trusted others to improvise questions as well as they did, or they may have lacked funds to hire interviewers.

The Gluecks had interviewed as many of these men as they could find at age thirty-two. We had done the same, adding interviews with a close relative for those who died at age twenty-five or older. (We excluded men who died before age twenty-five because they had too few years as adults to allow a meaningful assessment of their adult outcomes.) Our clinic sample of 524 was about the same size as the Gluecks' 500 reformatory boys. Our original plan was to use trained interviewers to locate subjects, do initial interviews, and make an appointment for one of our two psychiatrists to do a psychiatric evaluation. We changed that plan, however, when we discovered how many subjects no longer lived in St. Louis. Our psychiatrists, like Sampson and Laub, had obligations that made extensive travel impossible, and we did not then have the confidence in telephone interviewing that we now share with Sampson and Laub. Instead, we trained medical students and psychiatric residents to give a semistructured psychiatric interview as well as the initial interview and sent them to interview subjects living out of town. The psychiatrists and I did some of the out-of-town interviews as well, exploiting every trip to a professional meeting held in a city to which subjects had moved. In all, interviews were completed with 82 percent of the sample.

Sampson and Laub wrote or phoned a request for an interview to 141 men, 36 of whom refused. Subtracting these and the 52 with whom they completed interviews leaves 53 invited but never heard from. Because some of these men may never have received the invitation, and others willing to be interviewed may have procrastinated about responding, it would seem reasonable to have gone to their homes and knocked on their doors to invite them in person. But the university's institutional review board (IRB), in its role of protecting potential respondents from invasion of privacy, refused to let the authors do so. Why a knock on the door is a greater intrusion than a telephone call is not obvious to me. It is surely less discriminatory since all the men considered for interview had a known address, but some of the impoverished among them did not have a telephone.

The authors' goal for these interviews was to learn why some men had early desistance while others' crimes persisted. The authors report that the selection of interview respondents was not random but based on number and type of crimes and age at desistance. They show the 52 interviewed men's trajectories divided into five types: 15 nonviolent offenders who had desisted, 4 violent offenders who had desisted, 14 persistent offenders, 5 zig-zag careers, and 14 sporadic offenders (men with no clear pattern of offenses). Each of these is a very small group from which to generalize about predictors of distinct offense careers. It is also notably asymmetrical, with extremely small groups of violent offenders who desisted and of those with zig-zag careers. How much larger would the groups have likely been if all 181 located subjects had been invited to be interviewed? If the rate of refusal and failure to respond to letters and telephone calls had been the same for the 40 subjects never invited as for those invited, an additional 15 respondents would have been interviewed, of whom perhaps 4 could be expected to be nonviolent desisters, 1 a violent offender who had desisted, 4 persistent offenders, 1 a zig-zag offender, and 5 sporadic offenders. The total would have been 67 interviewed, still a small number, because of the high death rate and the failure to be allowed to visit them at home if they had not responded to a letter or phone call.

A look at the data on age at last offense suggests that it might have been wise to do this follow-up at age fifty, rather than age seventy, because by then the number still committing crimes was already very small but deaths had occurred for only about 18 percent of the sample (see Laub and Sampson 2003, Figure 5.8). If 82 percent of the sample were alive then, and of those alive, 79 percent were again located, this would have provided a target group of 308 for interviewing. If all 308 were approached, and the rate of agreement to be interviewed was the same, there could have been 114 interviews, a little more than double the number accomplished at age seventy. Of course, that would have been a large workload, undoubtedly requiring the authors to train colleagues to conduct interviews in the same way that the authors did. This opportunity is long gone, but it can remind us of the need to develop criteria for making a decision about when the best time would be to carry out follow-ups in ongoing longitudinal studies.

Record Sources Not Tapped

Even without interviews, the Gluecks' study and ours could have given a reasonably good picture of these men's adult lives from the great variety of records we collected. Like Sampson and Laub, I obtained death certificates and arrest records. In addition, I got coroners' records, social agency records, prison records, military records, Veterans Administration records, psychiatric hospital records, credit ratings, and Social Security Administration earnings records. Access to medical records might have been very difficult had my coinvestigator not been a physician. For other kinds of records, these were indeed the "good old days" for research before access was limited by privacy concerns and vigilant IRBs. Indeed, the only refusal we got from agencies whose records we requested came from the FBI. And even that we circumvented pretty well. Friendly police chiefs copied many FBI rap sheets for us from their own files. (I am impressed that Sampson and Laub were able to get help from the FBI. They must have great powers of persuasion.) The Social Security Administration (SSA) would not give us identified earnings records but was willing to let us assign individual subjects to groups, for which we would receive grouped earnings records for the past ten years. We grouped them by diagnosis and gender, protecting our subjects' privacy by not telling the SSA what our groups meant. They sent us back grouped individual earnings records without personal identification. Happily, we found it possible to discover the identities of all but eleven cases because SSA earnings records at that time included the city in which the employer was located, and we had traced residences over the follow-up interval.

If Sampson and Laub had had access to these record sources, they probably could have scored for later ages many of the social setting items available up to age thirty-two from the Glueck record searches, even without increasing the proportion with whom they conducted personal interviews. Alas, current restrictions make it virtually impossible for follow-up studies to get records without the respondent's written permission. That rule makes records much less useful. Obviously, you cannot get permission from subjects who remain unlocated or who have died. Among subjects located alive, those who would give permission may not be an unbiased subsample of the whole. I have argued (Robins 1979) for relaxing the rules against record sharing for scientific research purposes, while keeping the restrictions intact when the purpose is administrative. Research subjects can be adequately protected in two ways—by not disclosing to the record-holding group, who do have an administrative interest in them, what characteristics make them of research interest, as well as by requiring their anonymity in all publications.

The lack of access to prison records was a particularly serious problem in estimating date of desistance. If his last arrest resulted in a jail sentence, the man was not at risk of arrest during the year or years of incarceration following that arrest. For men with multiple arrests, the chance that the last arrest would result in incarceration increased with age because incarceration becomes more common the larger the number of past arrests, a number that can grow but not diminish over time. The authors do not say whether they considered deaths or other periods not at risk in Figures 1 to 6, although they had death information for all, and incarcerations and military service for all before age thirty-two from the Glueck data, and for the full lifetime in the fifty-two men they interviewed.

Can We Have Confidence in the Men's Explanations for Their Desistance?

The detailed descriptions of the fifty-two interviews with the men in their seventies as recounted in the book *Shared Beginnings, Divergent Lives* (Laub and Sampson 2003) are fascinating and persuasive. One lesson they teach is that the same event can have a very different impact on different people. Take the reformatory experience, which the subjects all shared. For some, it was seen as a lifesaver, teaching them respect for authority and self-control and the value of a structured day. For others, it was seen as degrading and cruel, making them hate authority figures and making their prognosis even worse than it would otherwise have been.

As Sampson and Laub recognize, one needs caution in accepting the men's attribution of their changed behavior to the "turning points" in their lives because they are being asked to explain a life change that they themselves often do not understand very well. They may hesitate to admit their doubts because they want to be cooperative and helpful to the researcher. Many of the respondents in my study, like those in Sampson and Laub's, credited marriage and family responsibilities for their desistance. Indeed, I remember one of our respondents who said that he had been saved by the love of a good woman, his wife. The only problem with this explanation was that the desistance occurred only after his marriage to his third good wife! Sampson and Laub creatively tested the likelihood that the marriages reported in their interviews truly explain the desistance observed. The tests are ingenious and very persuasive. Their tests show an effect not explained by selection for marriage.

Another explanation we got that has some resonance with stories told by Sampson and Laub is the delight in ownership allowed by earnings from employment. One respondent told us that he had never owned anything before, but after he married and got a job and bought some furniture, he could not bear the thought of its being repossessed, and so he became a steady worker. Research concerned with overcoming poverty (Sheradden 1991) has shown similarly that accumulating assets has great utility for people on welfare, improving their personal well-being and civic behavior and their offspring's well-being. This recognition of the value of owning assets will, we hope, result in changes in the rules in states where owning anything of value is grounds for being thrown off the welfare rolls.

How could we increase our confidence in the causal role of life events such as marriage and owning assets as explanations for early desistance? The standard for good research in medical interventions is the "double-blind" experiment, in which neither the doctor nor the patient knows whether the patient has received an active pill or a placebo. It is hard to imagine achieving such scientific purity in proving causes of desistance from crime. Yet we can design interviews that keep respondents blind to our hypotheses about the life experiences that influence desistance. One method that should be an improvement would be to have each subject seen by two interviewers. One would ask for dates of life events hypothesized to be "turning points"; the other would ask about the dates of criminal activities. There would be no attempt to have the subject link answers to the two interviews. A computer program could be designed to count how often a life event preceded or followed a decrease in criminal behavior and the length of the interval between them. These data could be used in judging whether the timing is consistent with a causal interpretation.

Early Predictors Compared with More Proximal Predictors

One of the principal findings of the Sampson and Laub study is the lack of impact of childhood risk factors on the trajectory. The authors find that while childhood factors predict the level of offending, as previous studies have found (Robins and Ratcliff 1980; Robins 1993, Table 9.9; Lacourse et al. 2002; Magdol et al. 1998; Roisman, Aguilar, and Egeland 2004, for example, and many others), they do not predict the trajectory. In their article in this issue, Sampson and Laub say, "When we examine the predictive power of childhood risk groups, the dominant pattern is parallel offender trajectories by age and no evidence of distinctive developmental pathways" (2005, 24). Their Table 4 shows no significant relationship between childhood risk and any type of crime or total crime. Nonetheless, one notes that for every crime type, those positive on childhood risk had a later mean age of termination. Figure 1 also suggests some relationship with trajectories because those with positive childhood risk have earlier onsets and more crimes up to age sixty-two.

These trends suggest that the lack of statistical significance may not be sufficient reason to discard the possibility of an effect of childhood risk on trajectories. In *Shared Beginnings, Divergent Lives*, Laub and Sampson (2003) described the thirteen childhood items they used as possible predictors. Each had been selected because it had been found in previous literature "to tap either classic individual-difference risk factors or the observed propensity to offend in the early years of the study" (p. 92). They then defined each item as positive when its score was high enough to identify only 20 percent of the sample (p. 93). A single childhood risk factor score was created by summing the number of items meeting this criterion for being positive. They took pride in the fact that this score was constructed independently of the adult arrest trajectory. It is true that had they selected individual items on the basis of their ability to predict age at desistance in this sample, they might have been taking advantage of purely chance associations.

Still, it is possible that the ability to predict trajectories from child and adolescent variables has been missed by diluting a truly predictive set of childhood factors with irrelevant items. This could be avoided by selecting only those juvenile variables that significantly forecast the adult trajectory. If no childhood variables significantly predict the trajectory, that would constitute persuasive evidence that the child and adolescent factors that predict adult crime do not predict its trajectory. On the other hand, if the results are positive for several items out of thirteen, this is a result better than chance since none or only one would be expected to be positive by chance alone out of thirteen. It would be legitimate to combine these positive items into a single predictor of trajectories. It is very likely that enough positive childhood predictors could be found using this approach because variables that predict number of arrests will by chance alone predict that the last arrest will be later for those predicted to have a large number of arrests than for those predicted to have few, simply because having more arrests will result in arrests over a broader time period. Only in the unlikely situation that the predictors of more adult arrests also predict a compression of the time span during which arrests occur would this effect on age at remission fail to appear.

Effect of Homogeneity on Causal Arguments

There is another possible explanation for this study's failure to find a role for childhood risk in predicting trajectories in addition to having diluted childhood predictors with nonpredictors. It lies in a very general principle: predictors of future variation cannot be found in homogeneous samples.

This study's sample is all white, and all have been in juvenile reformatories. These two selection criteria result in a sample at the extreme upper end of the range of childhood antisocial behavior. To see how extreme it is, consider the position of incarceration in possible official responses to juvenile crime. Many children who commit minor illegal acts have no police contacts. When a child's illegal behavior does come to police attention, the police frequently warn the child without creating any official record. When the crime is serious or police contacts have been frequent, the child is given a citation and has to appear in juvenile court. There the judge may dismiss the child with a warning, a fine, or a night in a detention center if he has not appeared in court frequently and if the crime is not serious. Sometimes, the judge will offer to excuse a child from incarceration if he agrees to enter drug treatment or join the military. Finally, there is a small percentage, usually made up of those who have already accumulated an extensive police record, who are sent to reformatories. This percentage is particularly small for *whites*. It is well known that blacks are overrepresented in the prison population. This could mean simply that a higher proportion of them commit the serious crimes that merit imprisonment.

However, in our epidemiologic catchment area (ECA) study (Robins and Regier 1991, 274), we found that whites in prisons had a history of much more antisocial behavior than blacks, indicating that blacks are more readily imprisoned than whites for equivalent crimes. To be sure, these were adults, but we found evidence that blacks' disadvantage is already visible in adolescence. Black youngsters had higher risks of being expelled from school given the same behavior problems as whites (Robins and Regier 1991, 270). Thus, this study's sample, white and incarcerated as adolescents, were probably all at quite high risk of adult criminality, even before their adolescent sentence to the reformatory. Even the "low" childhood risk group in reformatories would almost certainly have been found to be at "high" risk in a general population study.

[P]redictors of future variation cannot be found in homogeneous samples.

Many studies have had similar problems of homogeneity. For an example showing that the problem can apply if the childhood situation is homogeneously good rather than homogeneously bad, consider Vaillant's (1983) study of the course of alcohol problems followed in two samples: Harvard sophomores and the nondelinquent control sample from the Glueck study. The two samples were from different social classes, but neither had had serious early behavior problems. Not surprisingly, then, he found no childhood predictors of whether those with alcohol problems would become abstinent or whether their alcoholism would progress (p. 169). Homogenity is a problem at both ends of the continuum of childhood variables.

My own study followed white child guidance clinic cases, most referred by the Juvenile Court, and matched controls from the same neighborhoods. I found powerful childhood behavioral and family predictors of crime, substance abuse, and antisocial personality. But I worried about the lack of diversity in race. There was also the possibility that the children selected for referral to the clinic had been detected by the court as having psychiatric problems that might have made them particularly prone to adult difficulties. If they uniformly had such problems, they would not be as diverse as delinquents appearing in Juvenile Court. In addition, having appeared in Juvenile Court meant that they were less diverse than the total population of youngsters who committed crimes. My solution was to repeat the study in black schoolboys born and reared in St. Louis, some twenty years later, who were not selected for arrest or possible psychiatric problems. Happily, the findings from the child guidance clinic sample were replicated in that study (Robins, Murphy, and Woodruff 1971; Robins and Ratcliff 1980). These findings were again found to be independent of the age cohort studied as well as independent of place of rearing when they were replicated in two studies from broad geographic areas, a general population of Vietnam veterans born around 1950 (Robins 1978) and a general population study of American adults of all ages living in or near five different cities (Robins and Regier 1991, 266-68).

Homogeneity is a problem not only with respect to childhood behavior but also with respect to childhood environments. Studies of children adopted at an early age have found that the natural parents' antisocial behavior is a better predictor that the child will have an antisocial outcome than are characteristics of the adoptive home (Cadoret et al. 1995). While such studies have been cited as showing that juvenile antisocial behavior is mainly of genetic origin, an alternative interpretation is that this is an example of the impossibility of finding predictors in homogeneous groups. In adoptee studies, the reasons for the child's being available for adoption are various, as are the characteristics of the natural parents. Some of the parents are normal teenagers; some are ambitious people who fear that parenthood would endanger their pursuit of careers; some are people who refuse any responsibility for the products of their sexual activity; some of the fathers are rapists. The environment in the adoptive home is typically much less diverse. Prospective adoptive parents are carefully screened by social agencies. They are required to have an adequate, well-kept home, sufficient income to care for the child, no substance abuse, and no suspicion of illegal activities or other antisocial behavior. Thus, the heredity of adopted infants is diverse, while their families of rearing are relatively homogeneous. This probably leads to findings that exaggerate the importance of genetic factors in antisocial behavior and minimize the importance of the way the adopted children are reared.

The ideal longitudinal study looking for etiological factors determining an outcome chooses a sample diverse both in variables that are plausible predictors and in outcomes. One way to achieve this is to use the methods of modern epidemiological studies. Instead of choosing a very high risk sample and comparing it to a very low risk sample, as the Gluecks did, epidemiological studies sample the total population. They can oversample groups of special interest to have enough cases of them to study their particular outcomes. When prevalence rates for the whole sample are reported, the oversampled segments are down-weighted to the number that would have been found in a simple random sample. In my study of Vietnam veterans, we oversampled men whose urine was positive for heroin at the time of embarking for home so that we would have enough heroin users to study their outcomes when back in the United States (Robins, Davis, and Goodwin 1974). In the ECA study, we oversampled minority subjects and institutional residents (Eaton and Kessler 1985). This oversampling gave us enough prisoners to reach the conclusion about the readier imprisonment of blacks than whites that I mentioned earlier.

Sampson and Laub frequently mention their differences with Moffitt's (1993) conclusions (Laub and Sampson 2003). Perhaps the source of these differences lies in her epidemiological sample—a complete birth cohort. Like Sampson and

Laub, Moffitt joined her study when it was already under way, after the sample had already been chosen. The design gave her the whole range of childhood risk levels found in the population, maximizing the likelihood of finding them effective in predicting trajectories. However, because the sample included every birth in Dunedin, New Zealand, over a three-year period, she was not able to do any oversampling. Even given a sample of three thousand, she probably has too few children who were sent to a reformatory to compare their outcomes with those of the Glueck sample. In addition, her birth cohort has not yet reached an age by which most of those she calls life-course delinquents will have desisted. So I do not think comparing results of the Sampson and Laub study with hers is appropriate.

Conclusion

Indeed, comparison of the Sampson and Laub study with any other study of antisocial children is hampered by the fact that none other has dealt with so severely antisocial children and none other has so long a follow-up period. Among those at least somewhat comparable are the study of Pittsburgh boys from poor neighborhoods (Stouthamer-Loeber et al. 2004); Farrington's study of London boys from poor neighborhoods (Farrington and Hawkins 1991); the firstborns of young, poor mothers (Roisman, Aguilar, and Egeland 2004); boys removed from their homes because of parental inadequacy (Rutter, Quinton, and Hill 1990); children referred to a child guidance clinic by the Juvenile Court (Robins 1966); and black schoolboys attending segregated schools in St. Louis (Robins and Ratcliffe 1980). Despite the differences in severity and uniformity of juvenile antisocial behavior and in duration, these studies all agree with Sampson and Laub on certain important results: childhood and adolescent antisocial behavior are powerfully associated with limited education, and they predict criminality in young adult life, high unemployment rates, and unstable marriages. They also agree that some of the children with serious antisocial behavior in adolescence do not become highly antisocial adults and that those who do not have better employment records.

There are several ways of looking at these agreed-on outcomes. One might simply say (1) bad outcomes are all intercorrelated because they share predictors; and (2) prediction is never perfect because there are contributory variables we have not measured, and those we have measured are measured with error. Sampson and Laub have chosen the more ambitious task of trying to decide, when stable marriages occur despite the early antisocial behavior that would predict their absence, whether the stable marriages cause a shorter trajectory of criminal behavior. As we have discussed, this is a difficult task, given the data available to them. The question still remains open because the date of termination of criminality remains uncertain, given no information after age thirty-two about incarceration and unrecorded crimes, and because of the missing information for men not interviewed at follow-up about whether desistance or marriage came first.

The paper by Sampson and Laub has made an important contribution. It answered some questions resoundingly, and it made its authors think creatively about many issues still to be solved. It seems to provide a good argument for changing the focus of research on the longitudinal view of street crime from explanations of desistance to explanations for persistence. We now know that all street criminals desist, unless they die at an early age while still criminally active. But we do not know what keeps a minority of them active beyond their thirties.

[Sampson and Laub's article] seems to provide a good argument for changing the focus of research on the longitudinal view of street crime from explanations of desistance to explanations for persistence.

This study looks for turning points that explain earlier-than-expected desistance. The events in the life course that it identifies are certainly worthy of further study as experiences that might be fostered by social programs. We can imagine these findings serving as arguments for designing instruction for young criminals in how to judge the likelihood that a prospective mate will encourage home-centered activities and supervise the carrying out of responsibilities, in the behaviors needed to maintain their own prospective role as husbands, in the skills and reliability needed to get and keep jobs, and in making and adhering to budgets that allow accumulation of sufficient funds to purchase and keep durable assets.

These programs might result in a higher proportion of criminals experiencing the turning points reported by the men who had early desistance. If attendance is followed by improved stability of marriage and occupation and greater accumulation of assets, which in turn lower the age at desistance, that would be crucial evidence that these turning points do affect rates of common criminal behavior.

Of course, the criminals to whom these turning points would be relevant do not represent the whole range of criminals. Not all adult crime is committed by former juvenile delinquents, whose crimes are chiefly theft, assault, and public intoxication, and whose monetary gain from their crimes is typically slim. Missing from the current study are the CEOs of large corporations who commit theft on a really grand scale. Those criminals have to reach positions of power before they have the opportunity to steal large sums. This makes it unlikely that they came from the kinds of neighborhoods and families that this study's subjects did or had much in the way of youthful delinquency. They also seem to have more stable marriages, long-term jobs, and the ability to amass substantial assets. This small but important group appears to have quite a different trajectory from the men studied by Sampson and Laub. They begin their criminal careers later and continue their criminal activities at ages by which this study's subjects have long since quit. This difference may be explained not only by the delay in getting into positions of power but also by the fact that their crimes do not require much physical endurance or agility.

It would be a challenge at present to design a study whose sample could be predicted to include enough of these rare but very important white-collar criminals to learn how their risk factors compare with those of the well-studied street criminal. Because we know virtually nothing about their childhood predictors, the only viable study at present would appear to be a very large, and almost certainly unfundable, epidemiological sample.

To solve this problem, a worthwhile next step would be a study that begins with adult criminals rather than juveniles. A sample of adults, including substantial numbers of those convicted of the rarer crimes, could be interviewed about their early lives. Such a study would lay the groundwork for a prospective study that would select subjects in childhood with a more diverse set of criminogenic backgrounds and predictive early behavior patterns than the Gluecks' sample had. Following children selected on the basis of all the important predictors obtained retrospectively from adult criminals ranging across the full panorama of crimes should help us to better understand the predictors of crime and better understand its trajectories. As noted above, we would need to oversample children having the predictors of the rarer crimes, down-weighting these oversampled cases when we want to generalize about the best predictors of crime in general.

References

Cadoret, Remi J., William R Yates, Edward P. Troughton, George Woodworth, and Mark A. Stewart. 1995. Genetic-environmental interaction in the genesis of aggressivity and conduct disorders. *Archives of General Psychiatry* 52:916-24.

Eaton, William W., and Lawrence G. Kessler, eds. 1985. *Epidemiologic field methods in psychiatry: The NIMH epidemiologic catchment area project*. Orlando, FL: Academic Press.

Farrington, David P., and J. David Hawkins. 1991. Predicting participation, early onset, and later persistence in officially recorded offending. *Criminal Behavior and Mental Health* 1:1-33.

Glueck, Sheldon, and Eleanor Glueck. 1968. *Delinquents and nondelinquents in perspective*. Cambridge, MA: Harvard University Press.

Lacourse, Eric, Sylvana Côté, Daniel S. Nagin, F. Vitaro, M. Brendgen, and Richard E. Tremblay. 2002. A longitudinal-experimental approach to testing theories of antisocial behavior development. *Development and Psychopathology* 14:909-24.

Laub, John H., and Robert J. Sampson. 2003. *Shared beginnings, divergent lives: Delinquent boys to age 70*. Cambridge, MA: Harvard University Press.

Magdol, Lynn, Terrie E. Moffitt, Avshalom Caspi, and Philip A. Silva. 1998. Developmental antecedents of partner abuse: A prospective longitudinal study. *Journal of Abnormal Psychology* 107:375-89.

Moffitt, Terrie E. 1993. Adolescence-limited and life-course-persistent antisocial behavior: A developmental taxonomy. *Psychological Review* 100:674-701.

Robins, Lee N. 1966. *Deviant children grown up*. Baltimore: Williams & Wilkins.

———. 1978. Sturdy childhood predictions of adult outcomes. Replications from longitudinal studies. *Psychological Medicine* 8:611-22.

———. 1979. Privacy regulations and longitudinal studies. In *Regulation of scientific inquiry: Societal concerns with research*, AAAS Selected Symposium 37, ed. K. M. Wulff, 183-98. Boulder, CO: Westview.

———. 1993. Childhood conduct problems, adult psychopathology and crime. In *Mental disorder and crime*, ed. Sheilagh Hodgins, 173-93. Newbury Park, CA: Sage.

Robins, Lee N., Darlene H. Davis, and Donald W. Goodwin. 1974. Drug use by U.S. army enlisted men in Vietnam: A follow-up on their return home. *American Journal of Epidemiology* 99:235-49.

Robins, Lee, George E. Murphy, and Robert A. Woodruff. 1971. The adult psychiatric status of black schoolboys. *Archives of General Psychiatry* 24:338-45.

Robins, Lee N., and Kathryn S. Ratcliff. 1980. The long-term outcome of truancy. In *Out of school*, ed. Ian Berg and Lionel Hersov. Chichester, UK: John Wiley.

Robins, Lee N., and Darrel A. Regier. 1991. *Psychiatric disorders in America, The epidemiologic catchment area study*. New York: Free Press.

Roisman, Glen I., Benjamin Aguilar, and Byron Egeland. 2004. Antisocial behavior in the transition to adulthood: The independent and interactive roles of developmental history and emerging developmental tasks. *Development and Psychopathology* 16:857-71.

Rutter, Michael, David Quinton, and Jonathan Hill. 1990. Adult outcome of institution reared children: Males and females compared. In *Straight and devious pathways from childhood to adulthood*, ed. Lee Robins and Michael Rutter, 135-57. Cambridge: Cambridge University Press.

Sampson, Robert J., and John H. Laub. 1993. *Crime in the making: Pathways and turning points through life*. Cambridge, MA: Harvard University Press.

———. 2005. A life-course view of the development of crime. *Annals of the American Academy of Political and Social Sciences* 602:12-45.

Sherraden, Michael. 1991. *Assets and the poor: A new American welfare policy*. New York: M. E. Sharpe.

Stouthamer-Loeber, Magda, Evelyn Wei, Rolf Loeber, and Ann S. Masten. 2004. Desistance from persistent serious delinquency in the transition to adulthood. *Development and Psychopathology* 16:897-918.

Vaillant, George E. 1983. *The natural history of alcoholism*. Cambridge, MA: Harvard University Press.

RESPONSE

The authors respond to the commentaries of Michael Gottfredson and Lee Robins on their article "A Life-Course View of the Development of Crime." They delve further into the effect of marriage on crime, potential problems with sampling and research design, and how their data speak directly to related hypotheses and theories.

When Prediction Fails: From Crime-Prone Boys to Heterogeneity in Adulthood

By
ROBERT J. SAMPSON
and
JOHN H. LAUB

We are grateful to Michael Gottfredson and Lee Robins for taking our work so seriously and providing incisive commentary. As they are two of the leading and most influential scholars of age and deviant behavior anywhere, we are genuinely honored. The purpose of this response is to reflect on the overall themes of their comments, providing new data where appropriate. It is not our intention, nor do we think it productive, to focus on each and every point. We agree with many of their insights, so we take the opportunity to respond in a way that we hope is constructive and leads either to resolution of the relevant debate or strategies for future research.

Gottfredson and the Theme of Propensity

It will come as no surprise for readers of the symposium papers that we see a lot to like in Gottfredson's comments, so our response will be brief. In our view, one of the key points raised in the comment concerns the distinction between events and propensities to offend (for background, see Hirschi and Gottfredson 1986; Gottfredson and Hirschi 1989, 1990). Gottfredson and Hirschi (1989, 59) proposed that "crimes are short-term, circumscribed events that presuppose a peculiar set of necessary conditions (e.g., activity, opportunity, adversaries, victims, goods). Criminality, in contrast, refers to stable differences across individuals in the propensity to commit criminal or theo-

DOI: 10.1177/0002716205280575

73

retically equivalent acts." With regard to changes in offending over the life course due to life events such as marriage, Gottfredson (2005 [this volume], 50) states the problem as follows: "In propensity-event theories, such changes in offending can come about either because the propensity for involvement in crime and related behaviors changes or because the opportunities to engage in crime change."

We believe Gottfredson is probing us to articulate the effect and meaning of marriage in the context of propensity. We agree that the question of the specific mechanism (e.g., monitoring, social ties and support, norms) underlying the effect of marriage on crime is a high priority for future research, assuming the causal effect of marriage on crime can be established. We have been attempting to make headway on this issue, but even if a causal effect of marriage were established, that still leaves the mechanism unresolved. Drawing on Sampson and Laub (1993) and Laub and Sampson (2003), we believe marriage has an effect on *both* propensity and events or opportunities to offend. Specifically, in our earlier work, we conceived of marriage as a single turning point, largely affecting propensity. In our current work, we conceive of marriage in more dynamic terms reflecting the reality that people enter *and* exit (and often reenter) marriage through time, leading us to conceptualize the potential causal effect on crime of being in the state of marriage. This latter perspective stems from our focus on within-individual changes over time, both over the short term and long term. Additional evidence for the viewpoint that marriage affects both propensity and opportunities to offend can be found in our life-history narrative data (see Laub and Sampson 2003, chap. 6).

Robins and the Theme of Causal Homogeneity

We find much to like in Robins's (2005 [this volume]) commentary as well. But rather than dwelling on points of agreement, we shall focus on what we view as her most incisive critique—namely, that we underestimated the effect of causal "homogeneity" in the Gluecks' original sample (Glueck and Glueck 1950). Quite simply, given the Gluecks' design—boys who were incarcerated and selected based on their serious and persistent offending during childhood and adolescence—Robins contends that the sample is homogeneous on crucial childhood and adolescent variables of causal interest. For her, this is not an adequate data set to test Moffitt or other developmental theories of offending.

We acknowledge certain limitations of our research design and data that Robins outlines in her critique (e.g., small follow-up sample size, restricted scope of official records, possible retrospective bias in interviews). As we have argued before (see Laub and Sampson 2003; Sampson and Laub 2003), we also concur that our data cannot be used to definitively assess the validity of the adolescent-limited hypothesis of Moffitt (1993) or many of her specific predictions. Much of the testing of Moffitt's theory requires a population-based sample.

Moffitt's (1993) theory contains other and we believe equally important predictions, however, and our data speak directly to much of the developmental criminological paradigm. In particular, where our data are strong, and perhaps unsurpassed, is in providing the opportunity to examine long-term trajectories of crime and the existence of life-course persistent offender groups. It would be hard to invent a sample more conducive to finding troubled adult men than the delinquent group in the Gluecks' *Unraveling Juvenile Delinquency* (1950). These five hundred men generated some ten thousand criminal and deviant acts to age seventy (to our knowledge, the longest longitudinal study of criminal careers to date), and yet we have failed to find convincing evidence that a life-course persistent group can be prospectively or even retrospectively identified based on theoretical risk factors at the individual level in childhood and adolescence.

[W]here our data are strong, and perhaps unsurpassed, is in providing the opportunity to examine long-term trajectories of crime and the existence of life-course persistent offender groups.

It is difficult to reconcile these findings with the theoretical idea of a life-course persistent group (Moffitt 1993) and the idea of prediction writ large. We are not saying that adult crime cannot be predicted in general or that there are no adult offenders who persist longer than others. That point seems rather obvious and thus uninteresting. Rather, our argument is twofold in nature. One, all offenders eventually desist from crime—in this sense, the age effect is "invariant." Second, conditioned on delinquency or crime (the sorting reality of the juvenile and criminal justice system), we cannot predict long-term trajectories of offending. Robins claims this lack of prediction is because of causal homogeneity—the boys were delinquent and thus similar on causal variables. From this perspective, the boys were selected to become adult offenders, and any test of childhood prediction is therefore unfair.

Let us assume for a moment that the Glueck boys were perfectly homogeneous on all factors in childhood, including delinquency itself. Ironically, this scenario would only support our framework and the underlying theory of our article. Indeed, if heterogeneous adult outcomes exist when childhood factors are held constant, then by definition the childhood (developmental?) paradigm cannot provide the answer. We must look to factors in the adult life course, precisely the goal of much of our theoretical and empirical effort. So in a fundamental sense, we do not feel the sting in Robins's criticism for the specific analytic question we asked.

Another and even better reason to defend our position comes from simple facts in our data. While the boys were certainly restricted in variation more than a "normal population," considerable individual variation in the plethora of risk factors predicts later outcomes. The results in Table 1 directly assess Robins's concern. The table shows a series of logistic regression models predicting adult crime (coded 0 or 1) for each year from age seventeen to seventy using the summary measure of child risk as well as all thirteen constituent items found in the child risk scale. Contrary to Robins's expectations, most of the measures are in fact predictive of involvement in adult crime, attesting to the overall validity of the strategy we adopted in our article. In Table 1, we see that significant predictors of adult crime include measures of cognitive ability, assessments of personality tendencies (especially extroversion), violent tantrums and age at first incarceration, and antisocial behavior including the frequency of arrest per days free as a juvenile and "unofficial" delinquency as measured by self-, parent, *and* teacher reports of misbehavior. Moreover, many of these relationships are quite strong.

Overall, then, our measures meet Robins's criterion of "a truly predictive set of childhood factors." Consistent with our main article, it just happens that these factors predict a fractal set of age-crime curves (varying in level) rather than qualitatively distinct trajectory groups.

Representative Character of the Follow-Up Study

We would like to make a final point concerning the representativeness of our targeted long-term follow-up sample for life-history interviews. Several critics, including Robins, have questioned the nature of our selection criteria and the notion that our fifty-two men are similar to the rest of the five hundred delinquents in potentially causal variables. We briefly describe here our systematic strategy in sampling and show that in fact we ended up selecting a very representative subgroup of the delinquent sample.

Using criminal history records, our goal was to yield maximum variability in trajectories of adult crime. Our strategy was to classify eligible men into strata that reflected persistence in crime, desistance, and "zigzag" offending patterns, including late onset and late desistance of violence (Laub and Sampson 2003, 66-67). Our initial target goal was to complete about 40 in-person interviews, but with the thirty-five-year gap, we anticipated less than a 50 percent completion rate. Given limited resources, 40 of the located men were thus reserved as possible replicates for future study if funds permitted—but no attempt was ever made on our part to contact them. Of the pool of 141 men, we selected and interviewed 52. We encountered 27 refusals (including nonresponse to messages left on answering machines); 9 men were willing but seriously ill and declined for that reason; 53 men had an unlisted phone number and never contacted us in response to multiple mailings. Therefore, of those men we were able to talk with about the study ($N = 88$), 52 (59 percent) were interviewed and 36 (41 percent) refused or were unable for health reasons to be interviewed. Eliminating refusals due to illness, our rate of interview

TABLE 1

LOGISTIC REGRESSIONS PREDICTING ADULT CRIME EACH YEAR
FROM AGES SEVENTEEN TO SEVENTY BY SUMMARY RISK-FACTOR SCALE
AND CONSTITUENT ITEMS MEASURED IN CHILDHOOD/ADOLESCENCE
(YOUNGER THAN SEVENTEEN)

Childhood/Adolescent Predictor, Delinquents Younger than Seventeen	N of Person-Periods	B	SE	Wald	Significance Level
Child risk (summary)	19,697	.244	.046	27.502	.000
Verbal IQ	21,251	−.041	.011	13.685	.000
Full-scale IQ	21,251	−.003	.001	5.400	.020
Extroversion	21,251	.201	.038	27.391	.000
Adventurousness	21,251	.137	.038	12.932	.000
Egocentricity	21,251	−.123	.058	4.528	.033
Aggressiveness	21,251	−.157	.054	8.360	.004
Age of onset of misbehavior	18,591	.039	.059	0.428	.513
Age at first arrest	20,668	.006	.009	0.490	.484
Age at first incarceration	20,078	.027	.011	6.336	.012
Violent temper tantrums	21,251	.171	.038	20.033	.000
Difficult child behavior	20,870	.113	.039	8.552	.003
Frequency of arrest	20,668	.630	.072	77.466	.000
Unofficial delinquency	21,251	.041	.005	80.823	.000

participation was 66 percent. Both participation figures were beyond what we expected and compare favorably with other long-term follow-up studies with high risk samples (e.g., McCord and Ensminger 1997).

The bottom line of this effort with respect to a comparison of key factors can be seen in Table 2. When we separate the final follow-up sample from the rest of the delinquent group, the differences on a long list of factors is almost shockingly non-existent, especially given that our follow-up reached a relatively small proportion of the original group of men some thirty-five years after the Gluecks had last contacted them. Table 2 considers all our major child risk factors, measures of delinquency during adolescence, and a number of adult outcomes as well. Out of twenty-three specific comparisons and formal tests, there is only one significant difference, almost exactly what one would expect by chance at the .05 level. The data are thus clear and allow us to conclude that neither our sampling stratification scheme nor interview-based attrition (including death) served to create a sample of interviewed men that is distinct from the pool from which they were drawn.

Conclusion

The topics of stability and change in offenders and offenses, the age effect, offender classification, the prediction of crime, and general versus crime-specific theory has animated much of developmental/life-course criminology over the past

TABLE 2

**MEAN COMPARISONS AND SIGNIFICANCE OF DIFFERENCES:
GLUECK AND GLUECK (1950) DELINQUENT SAMPLE AND LAUB
AND SAMPSON (2003) FOLLOW-UP**

	Interviewed	N	Mean	SD	P of Difference
Full-scale IQ	No	428	91.27	13.15	.188
	Yes	52	93.79	11.96	
Verbal IQ	No	428	3.49	1.74	.720
	Yes	52	3.58	1.63	
Extroversion	No	428	0.55	0.50	.003
	Yes	52	0.75	0.44	
Adventurous	No	428	0.54	0.50	.314
	Yes	52	0.62	0.49	
Egocentric	No	428	0.13	0.34	.939
	Yes	52	0.13	0.35	
Aggressive	No	428	0.15	0.36	.421
	Yes	52	0.19	0.40	
Early onset	No	369	0.12	0.33	.275
	Yes	48	0.19	0.39	
Age of first arrest	No	428	11.97	2.08	.122
	Yes	52	11.50	2.12	
Age of first incarceration	No	414	13.41	1.82	.905
	Yes	52	13.44	1.61	
Tantrums	No	428	0.40	0.49	.836
	Yes	52	0.38	0.49	
Difficult child	No	419	0.59	0.49	.901
	Yes	52	0.60	0.50	
Arrest rate (seven to seventeen)	No	426	0.42	0.24	.430
	Yes	52	0.45	0.27	
Unofficial delinquency	No	428	14.22	4.18	.842
	Yes	52	14.35	4.07	
Parental instability	No	411	0.87	0.76	.797
	Yes	50	0.90	0.71	
Parental deviance	No	428	1.99	1.26	.796
	Yes	52	2.04	1.27	
Job stability (age twenty-five)	No	283	−0.42	2.45	.123
	Yes	43	−1.14	2.87	
Job stability (age thirty-two)	No	313	−1.12	2.46	.232
	Yes	45	−1.55	2.20	
Marital attachment (age twenty-five)	No	207	0.50	0.50	.742
	Yes	28	0.54	0.51	
Marital attachment (age thirty-two)	No	269	−0.39	2.02	.625
	Yes	42	−0.56	2.00	
Military duty	No	428	0.55	0.50	.263
	Yes	52	0.63	0.49	
Arrest rate (seventeen to twenty-five)	No	392	1.57	2.67	.362
	Yes	52	1.94	3.54	
Arrest rate (twenty-five to thirty-two)	No	369	0.94	2.02	.241
	Yes	51	1.68	4.41	
Child risk	No	404	0.19	0.39	.146
	Yes	52	0.29	0.46	

decade or so. We believe our article and subsequent commentary and discussion by Gottfredson and Robins offer important signposts for future developments in criminology. Eschewing childhood determinism, we offer our life-course conception of crime as a temporally emergent, socially interactive, and hence relational process as one of the core ideas to organize future theory and research on crime.

References

Glueck, Sheldon, and Eleanor Glueck. 1950. *Unraveling juvenile delinquency*. New York: The Commonwealth Fund.

Gottfredson, Michael R. 2005. Offender classifications and treatment effects in developmental criminology: A propensity/event consideration. *Annals of the American Academy of Political and Social Science* 602: 46-56.

Gottfredson, Michael R., and Travis Hirschi. 1989. A propensity-event theory of crime. In *Advances in criminological theory*, vol. 1, ed. Freda Adler and William Laufer, 57-67. New Brunswick, NJ: Transaction Books.

———. 1990. *A general theory of crime*. Stanford, CA: Stanford University Press.

Hirschi, Travis, and Michael R. Gottfredson. 1986. The distinction between crime and criminality. In *Critique and explanation*, ed. Timothy Hartnagel and Robert Silverman, 55-69. New Brunswick, NJ: Transaction Books.

Laub, John H., and Robert J. Sampson. 2003. *Shared beginnings, divergent lives: Delinquent boys to age 70*. Cambridge, MA: Harvard University Press.

McCord, Joan, and Margaret E. Ensminger. 1997. Multiple risks and comorbidity in an African-American population. *Criminal Behaviour and Mental Health* 7:339-52.

Moffitt, Terrie E. 1993. Adolescence-limited and life-course-persistent antisocial behavior: A developmental taxonomy. *Psychological Review* 100:674-701.

Robins, Lee N. 2005. Explaining when arrests end for serious juvenile offenders: Comments on the Sampson and Laub study. *Annals of the American Academy of Political and Social Science* 602:57-72.

Sampson, Robert J., and John H. Laub. 1993. *Crime in the making: Pathways and turning points through life*. Cambridge, MA: Harvard University Press.

———. 2003. Life-course desisters? Trajectories of crime among delinquent boys followed to age 70. *Criminology* 41:555-92.

SECTION TWO

Group-Based
Trajectory Modeling

What Has Been Learned from Group-Based Trajectory Modeling? Examples from Physical Aggression and Other Problem Behaviors

The focus of this article is group-based trajectory modeling. Its purpose is threefold. The first is to clarify the proper statistical interpretation of a trajectory group. The second is to summarize some key findings on the developmental course of aggression and other problem behaviors that have emerged from the application of group-based trajectory models and that in the authors' judgment are important to the fields of developmental criminology and developmental psychopathology. The third is to lay out some guidelines on the types of problems for which use of group-based trajectory modeling may be particularly productive.

Keywords: group-based trajectory modeling; physical aggression; trajectory group

By
DANIEL S. NAGIN
and
RICHARD E. TREMBLAY

Psychologists use the term *developmental trajectory* to describe the course of a behavior or outcome over age or time. Until about a decade ago, the two main branches of methodology for analyzing developmental trajectories were hierarchical modeling (Bryk and Raudenbush 1987, 1992; Goldstein 1995) and latent curve analysis (McArdle and Epstein 1987; Meredith and Tisak 1990; Muthén 1989; Willett and Sayer 1994). A 1993 article by Nagin and Land laid out a third alternative—group-

Daniel S. Nagin is Teresa and H. John Heinz III Professor of Public Policy and Statistics at the Heinz School, Carnegie Mellon University. He is an elected fellow of the American Society of Criminology and of the American Society for the Advancement of Science and is a 1985 recipient of the Northeastern Association of Tax Administrators Award for Excellence in Tax Administration. He is author of Group-Based Modeling of Development *(Harvard University Press, 2005).*

Richard E. Tremblay is Canada Research Chair in child development, professor of pediatrics/psychiatry/psychology, and director of the Research Unit on Children's Psychosocial Maladjustment at the University of Montreal. He is also the Joannes Groen Professor at Utrecht University in the Netherlands, director of the Centre of Excellence for Early Child Development, a fellow of the Royal Society of Canada, a fellow of the Academy of Experimental Criminology, and the Molson fellow of the Canadian Institute for Advanced Research.

DOI: 10.1177/0002716205280565

ANNALS, *AAPSS*, 602, November 2005

based trajectory modeling. The group-based trajectory model is a specialized application of finite mixture modeling. Using mixtures of suitably defined probability distributions, the method is designed to identify distinctive clusters of developmental trajectories within the population.

The introduction of "canned" software for estimating group-based models has resulted in a growing body of research based on this method. At this time, there are two excellent software alternatives for estimating group-based trajectories models. One is a SAS-based procedure called Proc Traj. It is described in Jones, Nagin, and Roeder (2001) and Jones and Nagin (2005) and in documentation available at www.ncovr.org. Proc Traj is designed to be inserted into the SAS software package. Once inserted, SAS treats it like any other standard SAS procedure. The other alternative is a widely used structural equation modeling software package called M-Plus, developed by Bengt Muthén, Linda Muthén, and colleagues (Muthén and Muthén 1998–2004). Piquero (2004) reported that more than fifty published articles use group-based trajectory modeling.

The purpose of this article is threefold. The first is to clarify the proper statistical interpretation of a trajectory group. The second is to summarize some key findings on the developmental course of aggression and other problem behaviors that have emerged from the application of group-based trajectory models, which in our judgment are important to the fields of developmental criminology and developmental psychopathology. The third is to lay out some guidelines on the types of problems for which use of group-based trajectory modeling may be particularly productive.

Group-Based Trajectory Modeling

As previously stated, hierarchical modeling and latent curve analysis are two important alternative approaches to the group-based methodology for modeling developmental processes. Like the group-based approach, these two alternatives are designed to provide a statistical tool for measuring and explaining differences across population members in their developmental course. Because all three approaches share the common goal of modeling individual-level heterogeneity in developmental trajectories, each must make technical assumptions about the distribution of trajectories in the population. It is these assumptions that distinguish the three approaches.

While the assumptions underlying hierarchical modeling and latent curve analysis differ in important respects, they also have important commonalities (MacCallum et al. 1997; Willett and Sayer 1994; Raudenbush 2001). For our purposes, one commonality is crucial: both model the population distribution of trajectories based on *continuous* distribution functions. Unconditional models estimate two key features of the population distribution of trajectory parameters—their mean and covariance structure. The former defines average growth within the population, and the latter calibrates the variance of growth throughout the population. Conditional models are designed to explain this variability by relating trajectory parameters to one or more explanatory variables. Modeling individual-level differences requires that assumptions be made about the distribution of trajectory parameters in the population. Both hierarchical modeling and latent curve analysis generally assume that the parameters are distributed throughout the population according to the multivariate normal distribution.

Group-based trajectory modeling takes a qualitatively different approach to modeling individual differences. Rather than assuming that the population distribution of trajectories varies continuously across individuals and in a fashion that can ultimately be explained by a particular multivariate distribution of population parameters (usually normal), it assumes that there may be clusters or groupings of distinctive developmental trajectories that themselves may reflect distinctive etiologies. In some applications, the groups may be literal entities. For example, the efficacy of some drugs depends on the users' genetic makeup. In many other application domains, however, the groups should not be thought of as literally distinct entities. They serve rather as a statistical approximation to a more complex underlying reality.

One use of finite mixture models is to approximate a continuous distribution function (Everitt and Hand 1981; Heckman and Singer 1984; Titterington, Smith, and Makov 1985). For example, Everitt and Hand (1981) described the use of a mixture of univariate normal distributions to approximate any unspecified univariate distribution function. McLachlan and Peel (2000, 8) described such use of finite mixture modeling as a "niche between parametric and nonparametric approaches to statistical estimation. . . . [M]ixture model-based approaches are parametric in that parametric forms are specified for the component density functions, but that they can also be regarded as nonparametric by allowing the number of components [groups] to grow." Similarly, Pickles and Angold (2003, 541) noted that "both theoretical and empirical work in statistics has shown that the nonparametric estimator of the underlying distribution, essentially the best fitting distribution, is just such a set of discrete classes of this kind, *even when the underlying distribution is continuous*." For this reason, the group-based trajectory method is often described as a semiparametric method (e.g., Nagin 1999, 2005; Nagin and Tremblay 1999, 2001a).

The idea of using a finite number of groups to approximate a continuous distribution is easily illustrated with an example. Suppose that panel A in Figure 1 depicts the population distribution of some behavior z. In panel B, this same distribution is replicated and overlaid with a histogram that approximates its shape. Panel B illustrates that any continuous distribution with finite end points can be approximated by a discrete distribution (i.e., a histogram) or alternatively by a finite number of "points of support" (i.e., the dark shaded "pillars"). A higher number of support points yields a discrete distribution that more closely approximates the true continuous distribution. However, simulation evidence reported in Brame, Nagin, and Wasserman (forthcoming) and Nagin (2005) suggests that relatively few points of support are required to approximate reasonably even complex continuous distributions of trajectories.

FIGURE 1
USING GROUPS TO APPROXIMATE AN UNKNOWN DISTRIBUTION

Panel A

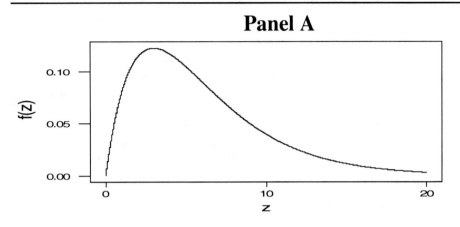

Panel B

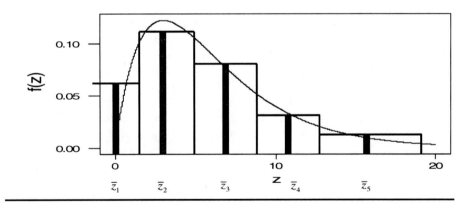

Why use groups to approximate a continuous population distribution? Heckman and Singer (1984) built upon the approximating capability of finite mixture models to construct a nonparametric maximum likelihood estimator for the distribution of unobservables in duration models. The motivation for this seminal innovation was their observation that social science theory rarely provides theoretical guidance on the distribution of unobserved individual differences, yet statistical models of duration data were often sensitive to the assumed form of the distribution of such differences. Their proposed estimator finessed the problem of having to specify a distribution of unobserved individual differences by approximating the distribution with a finite mixture model. This same motivation underlies the use of groups in group-based trajectory modeling—theory rarely provides guidance on the specific form of the population distribution of developmental trajectories. As McLachlan and Peel (2000, xix) observed, "Because of their flexibility, [finite] mixture models are being increasingly exploited as a convenient, semiparametric way in which to model unknown distributional shapes."

This brings us back to the key distinction between standard growth curve modeling and the group-based modeling method. Both approaches model individual trajectories with a polynomial relationship that links age to behavior. The approaches differ in their modeling strategy for incorporating population heterogeneity in the growth curve parameters (i.e., β_0, β_1, β_2, and β_3). In conventional growth curve modeling, the parameters describing individual-level trajectories are assumed to be distributed according to a specific function, usually the multivariate normal distribution. In the semiparametric group-based trajectory model, the distribution is approximated by a finite number of trajectory groups, aka points of support.

While users of conventional growth curve modeling have demonstrated great ingenuity in adapting the basic model to accommodate longitudinal data that is clearly not normally distributed (e.g., binary data or highly skewed data), these adaptations of the basic model do not resolve the more fundamental problem described by Raudenbush (2001): the standard growth curve modeling structure is not well adapted for modeling complex mixtures of developmental trajectories within a population in which population members are not following a common developmental process of growth or decline. He offered depression as an example. He observed, "It makes no sense to assume that everyone is increasing (or decreasing) in depression . . . many persons will never be high in depression, others will always be high, while others will become increasingly depressed" (p. 509). Instead, he recommended a multinomial statistical framework such as that provided by the group-based trajectory model. We return to this point in a later section, where we lay out guidelines on application domains in which group-based trajectory modeling may be particularly useful.

Useful Findings from Applications of Group-Based Trajectory Modeling

We next summarize some findings and conclusions that derive from group-based trajectory modeling that in our judgment showcase the strengths of the method. We organize these findings under three headings: (1) late onset physical aggression is the exception not the rule, (2) clarifying developmental taxonomies, and (3) clarifying the predictors and consequence of developmental trajectories. All of these involve important themes in developmental criminology and psychopathology.

At the outset, we emphasize that we are not suggesting that these results were not obtainable using some alternative method but only that the group-based approach greatly facilitated their discovery and communication. In the next section, we discuss guidelines for the types of analyses for which group-based modeling is particularly well suited.

Throughout this review, we will refer to trajectory groups as if they are literal entities. It should be understood that this is literary convenience for clear communication. As discussed in the prior section, trajectory groups, like all statistical models, are not literal depictions of reality. Rather, they are only meant as a convenient approximation. Our use of the term *trajectory group* is similar to the use of taxonomic distinctions in biology. Hugh Strickland, a leading zoologist and geologist who was trying to change traditions in zoological nomenclature, observed,

> Of course you will understand that by type-species I only mean a conventional distinction, referring only to words, not to things; and like human titles, only used as a matter of convenience. Nature knows no more type-species or "typical groups" than she does of Dukes and Marquesses. (cited in Burkhardt and Smith 1988, 216)

We reiterate this point because the pervasive use of group-based thinking in explaining the world around us and in structuring our economic and social institutions is testimony to the foundational role of groups in human cognition. Cognitive psychologists use the term *schemas* as a label for describing the cognitive role of groups. Anderson (1980, 128) defined schemas as "large complex units of knowledge that organize much of what we know about general categories of objects, classes of events, and *types of people* [italics added]." Anderson went on to observe, "Schematic thought is a powerful way to process complex sets of information. However, schematic thought is subject to biases and distortion" (p. 129). In the context of the present discussion, one such cognitive distortion is the reification of groups as nonexistent realities.

The risk of reification is particularly great when the groups are identified using a statistical method. The group's reality is reinforced by the patina of scientific objectivity that accompanies statistical analysis and by the very language that is used to describe the statistical findings, for example, "group 1, which comprises x percent of the population, is best labeled . . . "

The tendency to reify groups has important risks. One is in the conduct of public policy. If a group is small and its behavior is socially undesirable, such as committing crimes, the reification of the group as a distinct entity—rather than as an extreme on a continuum—may provoke draconian responses to the behavior, by creating the impression of a bright line of separation between "them" and "us." Human history is replete with tragic instances in which a fictional group-based separation is the first step in the dehumanization of the "them." Two other risks are not inherently insidious but still important. One is that reification creates the impression of the immutability of the groups. The reification of groups may also trigger a quixotic quest for assessment instruments designed to assign individuals to their true trajectory group. See Nagin and Tremblay (2005) for a discussion of these two risks.

Late onset physical aggression is the exception, not the rule

Two important scientific committees published reports in the 1990s on the causes and prevention of violence. The U.S. National Research Council panel concluded that "modern psychological perspectives emphasize that aggressive and violent behaviors are *learned* responses to frustration, that they can also be learned as instruments for achieving goals, and that the learning occurs by observing models of such behaviors. Such models may be observed in the family, among peers, elsewhere in the neighborhood, through the mass media, or in violent pornography, for example" (Reiss and Roth 1994, 7). Four years later, the report of the Human Capital Initiative Coordinating Committee on Reducing Violence (1996, 12) concluded, "In short, watching violent movies and television shows year after

---

[T]heories of desistance need to focus on multiple domains of behavior and the linkages between them.

---

year and listening to brutal lyrics set to throbbing music can change one's attitudes about antisocial, aggressive behavior. In children, it can lead to more aggressive behavior and also can evoke unwarranted fears and defensive actions. Whatever the violent content, movies and television exert powerful influences through visual imagery and dramatic characterizations; video games may have similar effects."

Over the past decade, the authors have collaborated on a series of studies that challenge the widely held view, articulated in these two blue-ribbon panel reports, that physical aggression is a learned behavior. Instead, we have argued that physical aggression is an innate behavioral tendency that does not need to be learned. Rather, it is a behavior that we must learn to control. Only a few studies have traced the developmental origins of physical aggression; the available evidence suggests that, on average, it peaks at a very young age—perhaps as young as two years old. Cairns, Cairns, and colleagues (Cairns and Cairns 1994; Cairns et al. 1989) found that physical aggression, on average, decreased rather steadily from ages ten to eighteen. Tremblay et al. (1999) reported a steady decline in physical aggression in a sample of Montreal males from ages six to fifteen. Similar results are found in a Pittsburgh, Pennsylvania–based longitudinal study (Loeber and Hay 1997). Studies of physical aggression prior to age six are even rarer, but the little evidence that is available suggests that humans begin physically aggressing others as soon as they have the physical capacity to do so (Tremblay et al. 1999, 2004).

Still, average tendencies may conceal the late emergence of physical aggression among subpopulations. It is on this point that group-based trajectory modeling has played a crucial methodological role in building the case against the view that the late emergence of physical aggression is the norm rather than the exception. Space does not permit a full summary of this evidence (but see Tremblay and Nagin [2005] for a full elaboration). Instead, we summarize evidence from several key studies that highlight the important methodological role group-based trajectory modeling has played in this inquiry into the developmental origins of physical aggression.

The first published study using group-based trajectory modeling that challenged the idea of late onset physical aggression was Nagin and Tremblay (1999). This study was based on a prospective longitudinal study of about one thousand white, French-speaking males from low-socioeconomic-status neighborhoods in Montreal. Among many other variables, the data include teacher ratings of physical aggression at age six and again at ages ten to fifteen. Teachers were asked to rate the frequency with which each boy kicks, bites, and/or hits other children; fights with other children; and bullies or intimidates other children. Figure 2 reports the preferred four-group trajectory model identified in that analysis. A group called "lows" is composed of individuals who display little or no physically aggressive behavior. This group is estimated to comprise about 15 percent of the sample population. A second group, comprising about 50 percent of the population, is best labeled "moderate declining." At age six, boys in this group displayed a modest level of physical aggression, but by age ten they had largely desisted. A third group, comprising about 30 percent of the population, is labeled "high declining." This group starts off scoring high on physical aggression at age six but scores far lower by age fifteen. Notwithstanding this marked decline, at age fifteen they continue to display a modest level of physical aggression. Finally, there is a small group of "chronics," making up less than 5 percent of the population, who display high levels of physical aggression throughout the observation period.

These trajectories are notable both for what is present and what is not present. As for what is present, all are stable or declining from age six on. Thus, over the period from age six to fifteen, there is no evidence of rising physical aggression even among a small subpopulation in these data. As for what is not present, we see no evidence of late-onset-like trajectories of physical aggression, namely, a trajectory that rises from a zero or negligible level at some point between six and fifteen. Because the trajectories are at their highest at age six, this suggests that to understand the developmental origins of physical aggression in these boys, we need to look back in time prior to age six rather than forward in time into their adolescence.

Our failure to find late-onset-type trajectories of physical aggression is not unique to these Montreal males. A follow-up analysis of five additional prospective longitudinal studies—one more from Canada, two from New Zealand, and two from the United States—again found no evidence of the onset of physical aggression after age six (Broidy et al. 2003).

It is also important to emphasize that the absence of late onset trajectories in these analyses of six different data sets from around the world is not an artifact of

FIGURE 2
TRAJECTORIES OF PHYSICAL AGGRESSION

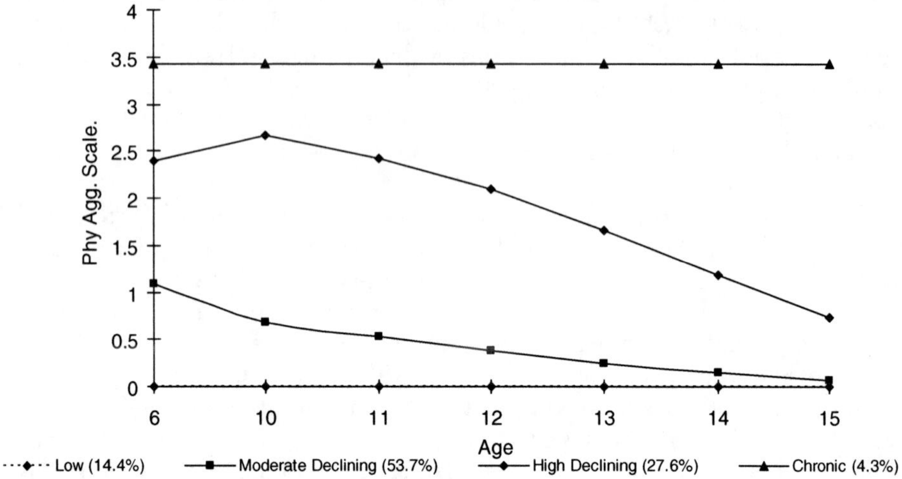

SOURCE: Nagin and Tremblay (1999).

the methodology itself. Figure 3 shows trajectories of indirect aggression reported in Côté, Vaillancourt, Barker, et al. (2004) from ages four to eight. The trajectories are the product of an analysis of a representative sample of about twelve hundred Canadian children. Indirect aggression was measured with five items (Lagerspetz, Bjorkqvist, and Peltonen 1988): "becomes friends with another as revenge," "says bad things behind the other's back," "when mad at someone, gets others to dislike him/her," "says to others: 'let's not be with him/her,' " and "tells the other one's secrets to a third person." Observe that for a sizable minority of children, about 30 percent of the sampled population, indirect aggression is rising over these ages. This is not terribly surprising because, unlike physical aggression, indirect aggression requires verbal facility and social awareness, two personal capacities that must be learned. By comparison, the three trajectories of physical aggression from ages two to eight that were also identified in this analysis were all declining.

Another important piece of evidence on the developmental course of physical aggression is reported in another analysis by Côté and colleagues (Côté, Vaillancourt, LeBlanc, et al., 2004). This analysis also used the same data set used in Côté, Vaillancourt, Barker, et al. (2004) but examined the developmental course of physical aggression from ages two to eleven in ten cohorts of approximately 1,000 children (N = 10,658). Group-based trajectory modeling again identified three trajectory groups, which are reported in Figure 4. One-third of children (31.1 percent) followed a *low desisting* trajectory, reflected in infrequent use of aggression in toddlerhood and virtually no aggression by preadolescence. The majority of children (52.2 percent) followed a *moderate desisting* trajectory, reflected in occasional use of aggression in toddlerhood and infrequent use by

FIGURE 3
TRAJECTORIES OF INDIRECT AGGRESSION

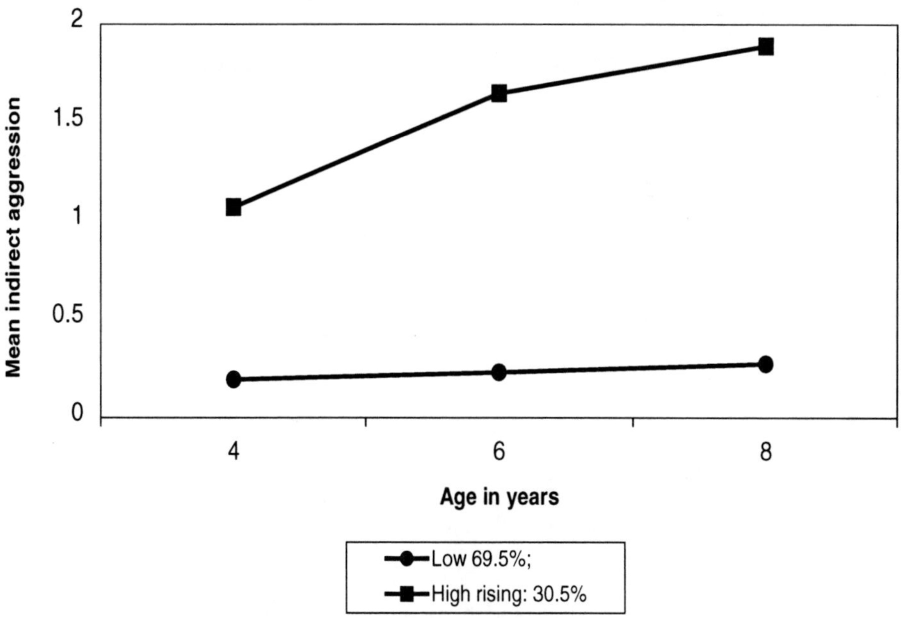

SOURCE: Côté, Vaillancourt, Barker, et al. (2004).

preadolescence. One-sixth of children (16.6 percent) followed a *high stable* trajectory of physical aggression. Here again we see no evidence of late-onset-type physical aggression trajectories even in a sample that includes measurement on children who were tracked from as early as two years of age.

Even if late onset of childhood physical aggression is highly unusual, this does not rule out the possibility that a sizable fraction of adolescents who were not physically aggressive as young children become violent during adolescence. Adolescence is a critical period in personal development. Parental control and influence generally diminishes and children take important steps toward independence. Unstructured time with peers increases, opportunities to organize life's activities without adult supervision grow, and experience with the successes and failures that determine life chances become more prominent (Osgood et al. 1996; Thornberry et al. 2003; Warr 2002). In various ways, each of these changes in life circumstances has been implicated in the onset of delinquency.

Brame, Nagin, and Tremblay (2001) and Nagin and Tremblay (2002) built from the findings of Nagin and Tremblay (1999) and Broidy et al. (2003) by exploring the linkage between trajectories of physical aggression in childhood and trajectories of violent delinquency in adolescence. Like Nagin and Tremblay (1999), both of these studies are also based on the Montreal longitudinal study. The key question that was addressed in each was whether there is any substantial evidence of late

FIGURE 4

TRAJECTORIES OF PHYSICAL AGGRESSION FROM AGES THREE TO ELEVEN

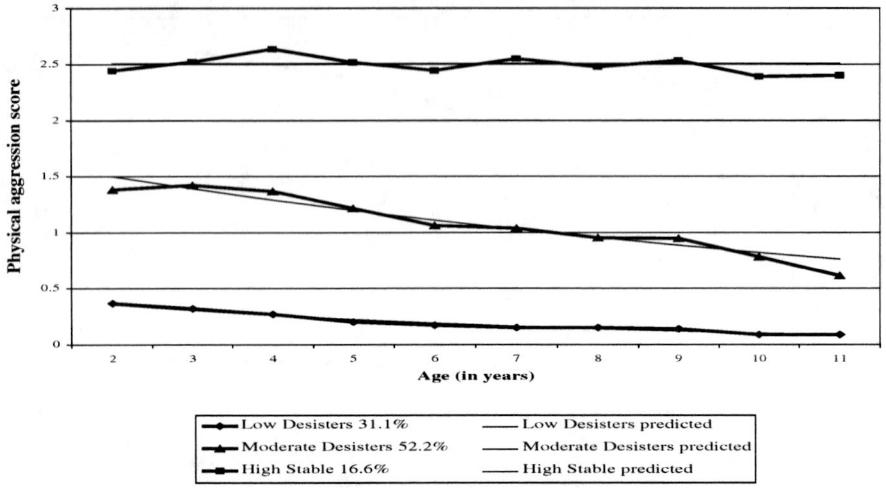

SOURCE: Côté, Vaillancourt, Barker, et al. (2004).

onset of physical aggression in adolescents among individuals with no history of childhood physical aggression, and if there is, whether that physical violence is chronic and sustained rather than episodic.

Both analyses are based on dual trajectories models, which are designed to explore the linkage between two distinct but conceptually related measurement series (Nagin and Tremblay 2001a; Nagin 2005). In both analyses, the two measurement series were physical aggression from six to thirteen based on the teacher ratings described above and self-reported violent delinquency from thirteen to seventeen. The self-reported violent delinquency scale sums the boy's report of the frequency with which he engaged in fistfighting, gang fighting, carrying/using a deadly weapon, threatening or attacking someone, and throwing an object at someone.

Brame, Nagin, and Tremblay (2001) used what Nagin (2005) called a constrained dual trajectory model. In the constrained model, each trajectory for childhood physical aggression is uniquely combined with a trajectory of adolescent violent delinquency. Figure 5 shows two of the seven combined trajectories that were reported in that analysis. Both groups display a consistently high level of physical aggression from age six to thirteen. Despite the similarity of their childhood aggression trajectories, the two groups display markedly different trajectories of violent delinquency in adolescence. At age thirteen, the self-reported violent delinquency of one group is higher than that of any other group. Their violence rises steadily to a peak at age fifteen and thereafter declines. This group was called the high childhood aggression/high adolescent violence group and was estimated to account for about 3 percent of the population. In contrast, the second group is made up of individuals who report a negligible level of violence in their adoles-

FIGURE 5
TWO TRAJECTORIES OF CHILDHOOD PHYSICAL
AGGRESSION AND ADOLESCENT VIOLENT DELINQUENCY
BASED ON THE CONSTRAINED DUAL TRAJECTORY MODEL

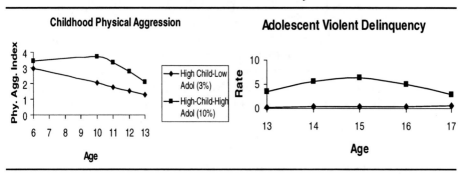

SOURCE: Brame, Nagin, and Tremblay (2001).

cence, despite their high aggression in childhood. This group, which was called the high childhood aggression/low adolescent violence group, was estimated to comprise 10 percent of the population.

The remaining five combined dual trajectories groups were distinguished by their levels of childhood physical aggression. A cluster of three groups were characterized by low and steadily declining physical aggression in childhood. The largest group, which was estimated to account for 33 percent of the population, self-reported virtually no violent delinquency in adolescence. A second group had a trajectory of adolescent violent delinquency that started off low at age thirteen but thereafter increased to a moderate level by ages sixteen to seventeen. We called this category the low childhood aggression/increasing adolescent aggression class. By contrast, the third latent class started off with a moderate level of self-reported aggression at age thirteen, but in the ensuing years their violence decreased gradually to a near-zero level. The latter two groups were of nearly equal size, about 11 percent to 13 percent of the population, respectively.

The final two groups were characterized by medium but declining levels of childhood physical aggression. The larger of the two groups, estimated to comprise 21 percent of the population, reported virtually no violent delinquency during adolescence. The other class, estimated to account for about 10 percent of the population, reported a relatively high but declining level of physical aggression during adolescence.

Thus, Brame, Nagin, and Tremblay (2001) found only one group that might be characterized as a late onset violence group. The group called the low childhood aggression/increasing adolescent aggression group was estimated to make up only 10 percent of the sampled population. The remaining 90 percent followed dual trajectories of either steady or declining physical aggression from ages six to seventeen.

The Nagin and Tremblay (2002) analysis was based on what Nagin (2005) called the general dual trajectory model. Three key outputs of the general dual model are (1) the shape of the trajectory of each group for both measurement series, (2) the probability of membership in each such trajectory group, and (3) the joint probability of membership in trajectory groups across behaviors. This final output is key. It provides the capacity for specifying the linkage between teacher-rated childhood physical aggression from ages six to thirteen with self-reported violent delinquency in adolescence from ages thirteen to seventeen. Thus, the general model relaxes the constraint of the model used in Brame, Nagin, and Tremblay (2001) of a unique identification between the trajectories of childhood physical aggression and of adolescent violence. The Nagin and Tremblay (2002) analysis examined whether this constraint might have been concealing more substantial evidence of late onset violence.

The trajectories of physical aggression from ages six to thirteen and violent delinquency from ages thirteen to seventeen are reported in Figures 6 and 7, respectively. The shapes and sizes of the childhood trajectories in Figure 6 are virtually identical to those reported in Nagin and Tremblay (1999) for the age period six to fifteen. The one exception concerns the size of the chronic group, which is nearly three times larger than in the earlier analysis, 11 percent versus 4 percent. We attribute the increased size of the chronic group to the two-year truncation in the observation period in this analysis.

The five trajectories in Figure 7 for the adolescent period, which had not been previously reported, deserve greater elaboration. The two largest trajectory groups, labeled the low 1 and 2 groups, combined to account for 65.8 percent of the population. These individuals average one or less on the seven-item inventory of self-reported violent delinquency described earlier. This amounts to responding with "1 or 2 times" in the past year to one item and "never" to the remaining six items. This finding suggests that a low level of physical aggression (e.g., an occasional fistfight) is normal among adolescent males.

Another perspective on this point is provided by consideration of the cumulative distribution of the sum of the individual-level self-reports of violent delinquency from ages thirteen to seventeen. To score 0 on this sum, the individual must report "never" to all seven items for all five years. Only about 10 percent of the sample so reported. The median score of about 5 corresponds, on average, to a response of "1 or 2 times per year" on only one item in the scale in each yearly assessment. Clearly, occasional physical aggression in adolescence is commonplace.

The one-third of the boys who engaged in more than occasional physical aggression are split among three groups: a high chronic group (6.6 percent) following the classic hump-shaped trajectory of delinquency, a declining group (13.3 percent) that starts at a rate that is nearly as high as the chronics at age thirteen but declines thereafter, and a rising group (15.3 percent) who are low at age thirteen but rise thereafter to a level that is about half that of the chronics. Note that because the declining group is twice the size of the chronic group, among the boys who start high at age thirteen, two in three are "desisters." This is consistent with our conten-

FIGURE 6
PHYSICAL AGGRESSION TRAJECTORIES FROM AGES SIX TO
THIRTEEN BASED ON THE GENERALIZED DUAL TRAJECTORY MODEL

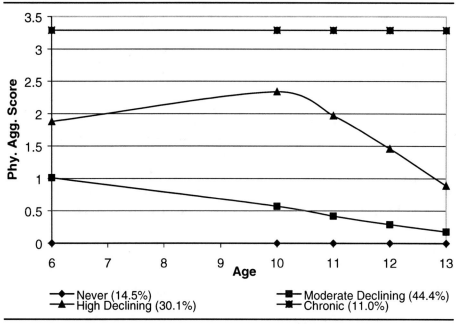

SOURCE: Nagin and Tremblay (2002).

tion that overall physical aggression tends to decline with age. Still, there is a very interesting group of "rising" boys. While they are a small minority of the population (16.5 percent), their size is nontrivial. Indeed, they comprise nearly 50 percent of the 35.3 percent in the three trajectory groups that engage in more than very occasional physical aggression.

How do the adolescent physical aggression trajectory groups link up with the childhood physical aggression trajectories? Table 1 reports the conditional probability of "transitioning" from each of the age six to thirteen physical aggression trajectory groups to the various age thirteen to seventeen violent delinquency trajectory groups. For example, the estimated probability of an individual in the moderate declining childhood group transitioning to either the low 1 or 2 adolescent trajectory group is .73. By contrast, the probability of his transitioning to the chronic group is less than .02.

The transition probabilities conform to long-standing results on the continuity of problem behaviors. Across the childhood physical aggression groups, the low childhood group is most likely to transit to the low 1 or 2 adolescent trajectories (.90), whereas the chronic group is least likely (.30) to transit to this group. In between are the moderate and high declining childhood physical aggression groups with probabilities of .73 and .53, respectively. Conversely, the low childhood group is least likely to join any of the three high adolescent trajectory groups

FIGURE 7
TRAJECTORIES OF VIOLENT DELINQUENCY FROM AGES THIRTEEN
TO SEVENTEEN BASED ON THE GENERALIZED DUAL TRAJECTORY MODEL

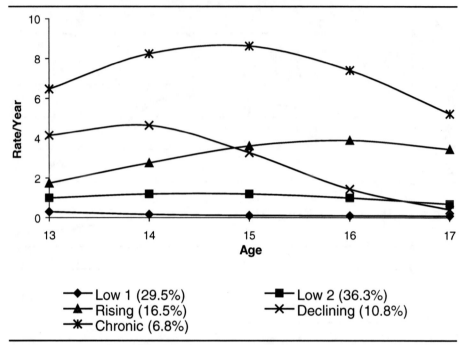

SOURCE: Nagin and Tremblay (2002).

TABLE 1

PROBABILITY OF ADOLESCENT VIOLENT
DELINQUENCY TRAJECTORY GROUP MEMBERSHIP CONDITIONAL
ON CHILDHOOD PHYSICAL AGGRESSION TRAJECTORY GROUP

	Adolescent Group			
Childhood Group	Low 1 & 2	Rising	Declining	Chronic
Low	.90	.09	.01	.00
Moderate declining	.73	.13	.12	.02
High declining	.53	.17	.19	.11
Chronic	.30	.27	.21	.22

($.10 = .09 + .01 + .00$) and the childhood chronics are most likely to transit to these trajectories ($.70 = .27 + .21 + .22$).

The transition probabilities are also consistent with prior research that finds generally declining physical aggression with age. For all groups, including the childhood chronics, the modal transition is to the low 1 or 2 adolescent trajectory groups. Furthermore, with the exception of the childhood chronic group, this probability exceeds .5. Conversely, the probability of boys in the two lowest childhood groups transiting to the chronic adolescent group is negligible. Still, a sizable minority of individuals in the two lowest childhood trajectory groups transit into one of the three higher adolescent trajectory groups—10 percent and 23 percent, respectively, for the low and moderate declining childhood groups.

The results of this application of group-based trajectory modeling suggest a more nuanced version of the "no late onset of physical aggression" hypothesis—physical aggression is mostly declining from childhood through adolescence. However, the finding that a small minority of boys appear to have a late onset physical aggression should not obscure the central finding that has emerged from these applications of group-based trajectory modeling. The dominant trend among all trajectory groups is either declining or stable physical aggression. Thus, to understand the developmental origins of physical aggression, it is imperative that studies begin at birth or (ideally) prenatally.

Longitudinal studies of physical aggression with large samples that were initiated before the 1990s focused on schoolchildren and adolescents. A few studies initiated in the past decade attempted to chart the developmental origins of physical aggression in the preschool years. Results indicate that physical aggression appears during the first year after birth (Tremblay 2004a, 2004b). All applications of group-based trajectory modeling show that the frequency of aggression increases rapidly during the second year after birth, reaches a peak between twenty-four and forty-two months after birth, and then decreases steadily (Côté, Vaillancourt, LeBlanc, et al. 2004; National Institute of Child Health and Development [NICHD] 2004; Tremblay et al. 2004). These data map on very well to the data from studies on school-age children described above. Thus, the story that is appearing from the patchwork of longitudinal studies from birth to adulthood is that the peak in frequency of physical aggression for humans is during early childhood, not during kindergarten, adolescence, or early adulthood. This suggests that rather than learning to physically aggress, children are learning not to physically aggress. From this perspective, it would be extremely surprising if there exists a significant group of individuals who never used physical aggression during the preschool years and initiated this behavior during adolescence. Based on the available data, we hypothesize that children with relatively low levels of physical aggression during the elementary school years who show an increase in physical aggression during adolescence were on a high trajectory during the preschool years. Only trajectory analyses with longitudinal data from infancy to late adolescence will enable us to test the "late onset" hypothesis.

Clarifying developmental taxonomies

There is a long tradition in developmental psychology of group-based theorizing about both normal and pathological development. Examples include theories of personality development (Caspi 1998), drug use (Kandel 1975), learning (Holyoak and Spellman 1993), language and conceptual development (Markman 1989), depression (Kasen et al. 2001), eating disorders (Tyrka, Graber, and Brooks-Gunn 2000), alcoholism (Cloninger 1987), anxiety (Cloninger 1986), and the development of prosocial behaviors such as conscience (Kochanska 1997) and of antisocial behaviors such as delinquency (Loeber 1991; Moffitt 1993; Patterson, DeBaryshe, and Ramsey 1989).

Human history is replete with tragic instances in which a fictional group-based separation is the first step in the dehumanization of the "them."

When testing these taxonomic theories, developmental researchers have commonly resorted to using assignment rules based on subjective categorization criteria to construct categories of developmental trajectories. For example, in their research on the developmental origins of violence, Haapasalo and Tremblay (1994) proposed a taxonomy composed of five groups—stable high fighters, desisting high fighters, late onset high fighters, variable high fighters, and nonfighters. These groups were created from the annual teacher ratings of a child's physical aggression in the previously described Montreal-based longitudinal study. Haapasalo and Tremblay labeled boys who scored high on this scale in any given year as "high fighters" for that year. They then defined rules for assigning individuals into their five-group taxonomy. These rules were based on the frequency and trend of each boy's classification as a high fighter. For example, "desisting high fighters" were boys who were high fighters in kindergarten but who were classified as high fighters in no more than one of the ensuing assessment periods.

Moffitt's (1993) well-known taxonomy is more parsimonious. She posited only two distinct developmental trajectories of problem behavior. One group follows what she calls a life course persistent (LCP) trajectory of antisocial behavior, and the other group is posited to follow an adolescent limited (AL) trajectory. In empirical tests of her theory, such as Moffitt et al. (1996), she has used classification rules conceptually similar to those used by Haapasalo and Tremblay (1994). LCPs are defined as individuals who score one or more standard deviations above the mean in three of four assessments of a conduct disorder index between the ages five and eleven and who also score at least one standard deviation above the mean in self-reported delinquency at least once at either age fifteen or eighteen. The ALs are defined as individuals who do not meet the LCP criteria for childhood conduct problems but who do achieve the LCP threshold for adolescent delinquency.[1]

While such assignment rules are generally reasonable, limitations and pitfalls are attendant on their use. One is that the existence of distinct developmental trajectories must be assumed a priori. Thus, the analysis cannot test for their presence, a fundamental shortcoming. A second and related pitfall is the risk of simultaneously "overfitting and underfitting" the data by creating trajectory groups that reflect only random variation and failing to identify unusual but still real developmental patterns. Third, ex ante specified rules provide no basis for calibrating the precision of individual classifications to the various groups that comprise the taxonomy. Thus, the uncertainty about an individual's group membership cannot be quantified in the form of probabilities.

To illustrate these limitations, consider the Haapasalo and Tremblay (1994) study. While Haapasalo and Tremblay proposed five taxonomic groups, the application of group-based trajectory analysis described in Nagin and Tremblay (1999) found that the four-group model shown in Figure 2 best fitted the data. The Nagin and Tremblay analysis provided formal statistical support for the presence of three of the groups hypothesized in the Haapasalo and Tremblay taxonomy: the stable high fighters (who correspond to the chronic trajectory group), the desisting high fighters (who correspond to the high declining trajectory group), and the nonfighters (who correspond to the low trajectory group). However, there was no evidence of a trajectory corresponding to Haapasalo and Tremblay's late onset high fighter group or of a variable high fighter group. These are examples of classifications that likely resulted from overfitting the data, where random variation is confounded with real structural differences.

Two other examples of the utility of the formal group-based trajectory method compared to ad hoc classification procedures are studies by Nagin, Farrington, and Moffitt (1995) and Lacourse et al. (2003). The former study was intended to test several predictions of Moffitt's (1993) two-group taxonomic theory, including testing for the very presence of the trajectories predicted by her taxonomy. Based on an analysis of a classic data set assembled by Farrington and West (1990), which included data on convictions from age ten to thirty-two in a sample of more than four hundred males from a poor neighborhood in London, three offending trajectories were found. These trajectories are shown in Figure 8. One trajectory, which peaks sharply in late adolescence, closely matches the adolescent limited group predicted by Moffitt's theory. The high-hump-shaped trajectory, labeled high chronic, is similar in some respects to Moffitt's second group, the LCP group. This group is already actively engaged in delinquency at age ten. However, their frequency of antisocial behavior, at least as measured by conviction, is very age-dependent—a pattern that is not anticipated by Moffitt's theory. It rises until about age eighteen and then begins a steady decline. By age thirty, it has dropped below its starting point at age ten and is about equal to the rate of a third group called low chronic offenders. This third group was not included in Moffitt's taxonomy. Thus, the application of the group-based method provides basic confirmation of the presence of the AL and LCP trajectories that Moffitt predicted in her taxonomy but also suggests that the LCP trajectory may be more age-dependent than antici-

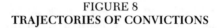

FIGURE 8
TRAJECTORIES OF CONVICTIONS

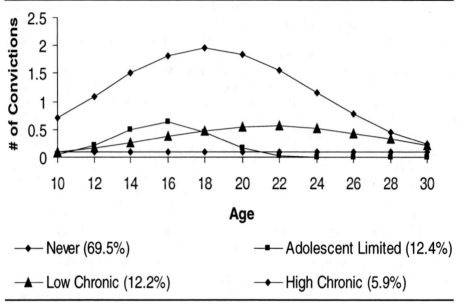

SOURCE: Nagin (2005).

pated by the theory. Moreover, it identified the low chronic trajectory, which was not predicted by the taxonomy.

In Lacourse et al. (2003), group-based trajectory modeling was used to analyze the developmental course of gang membership. This analysis was based on the same Montreal-based sample that forms the basis for the trajectories depicted in Figures 2 and 4 through 6. The trajectories of gang membership identified in this analysis were based an annual self-reports from age eleven to seventeen of delinquent group involvement in the past year. The resulting trajectories of probability of gang membership at each age are shown in Figure 9. One trajectory, called the never group, is estimated to make up 74.4 percent of the population. This group's probability of gang membership was very small over all ages. The second group, called the childhood onset group, began at age eleven with a high probability of gang membership that modestly rises till age fourteen and declines thereafter. The third group, called the adolescent onset group, had a near-zero probability of gang membership at age eleven, but thereafter the probability rose to a rate that actually exceeded that of the childhood onset group. The latter two groups are each estimated to constitute 12.8 percent of the sampled population.

The trajectories identified in the Lacourse et al. (2003) analysis illustrate two valuable properties of the group-based modeling approach compared to the use of classification rules. One is the capacity to identify qualitatively distinct developmental progressions that are not readily identifiable using ad hoc, ex ante classifica-

FIGURE 9
TRAJECTORIES OF GANG MEMBERSHIP

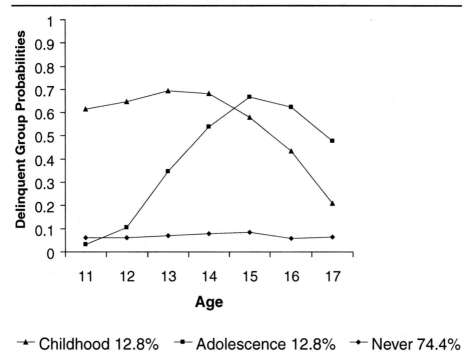

—▲— Childhood 12.8%   —■— Adolescence 12.8%   —♦— Never 74.4%

SOURCE: Lacourse et al. (2003).

tion rules. In principle, the childhood onset and adolescent onset groups shown in Figure 9 are identifiable ex ante, but given the specific developmental course of each, it would be very difficult to identify them without a formal statistical methodology. A second, closely related advantage also stems from the use of a formal statistical structure. It is because of this structure that the methodology has the capacity for distinguishing chance variation across individuals from real differences and for calibrating whether individual change is real or only random variation in behavior. Because the childhood and adolescent onset trajectories are the product of a formal statistical model, there is a firmer basis for their reality than if they had been constructed based on subjective classification rules.

Another important example of the clarifying role of the group-based trajectory model involves the taxonomic distinction in the criminal career model between being an active offender and a desistor. Bushway, Thornberry, and Krohn (2003) explored the distinction between what they call a "static" versus a "dynamic" definition of desistence in a sample of about nine hundred individuals from Rochester, New York, for whom they have self-reported data on general delinquency from ages thirteen to twenty-three. The static definition of desistance was specified in a form that conformed with much research in the tradition of the criminal career paradigm as articulated in the seminal work of Blumstein et al. (1986). Specifically, by the static definition, an individual was defined as a desistor if he or she self-reported committing at least one delinquent act prior to age eighteen but none thereafter. The dynamic definition was based on a comparison of trajectories of offending.

Application of the group-based trajectory modeling to the Rochester data yields the seven-group model shown in Figure 10. Two of these seven trajectories, called the very-low- and low-level offenders, involve individuals with very limited numbers of self-reported delinquent offenses during adolescence and young adulthood. They are basically nonoffenders. Collectively, these individuals were estimated to comprise 55 percent of the sample. They also accounted for 79 percent of so-called desistors by the static definition. Thus, if one were to compare desistors by the static definition with no offenders, the resulting analyses would amount to little more than a comparison of very infrequent offenders in adolescence with their counterparts who remained completely inactive in adolescence. By contrast, if the trajectory groups are used to define desistors, desistance is defined by a group that goes through a period of substantial offending followed by a decline to a diminished rate. By this definition, the bell-shaped desistors and possibly the intermittent offenders should be defined as desistors. Collectively, these two groups are estimated to comprise about 17 percent of the sampled population, a much smaller group than that defined by the static definition. Furthermore, there is little overlap in the population of desistors by these two definitions of desistance. In our judgment, the trajectory group-based definition of a desistor identifies a substantively far more interesting and distinctive group of individuals than the static definition.

Clarifying the predictors and consequences of developmental trajectories

Trajectory groups can be thought of as latent strata in longitudinal data (Haviland and Nagin forthcoming) that distinguish clusters of individuals following distinctive developmental paths. Theories of development provide much guidance on the predictors and likely consequences of favorable and unfavorable developmental trajectories. However, theory provides very little guidance on the functional form that relates risk and protective factors to alternative developmental trajectories and in turn relates the effects of the trajectories themselves to still other developmental consequences.

Figure 11 illustrates the importance of this functional form issue in the context of identifying the dose-response relationship between a single predictor, x, and a single outcome variable, y. Suppose y is a "bad" outcome (e.g., crime) and that we have a strong theoretical basis for stipulating that x aggravates the likelihood of a higher y. Mathematically, this prediction can be faithfully represented by any functional relationship in which y never declines with an increase in x. One possibility is that the relationship between y and x is well approximated by the linear equation A. However, there are other possibilities that are not well approximated by such a linear relationship. For example, the dose response relationship depicted by B is highly nonlinear—y only increases steeply after the dose of x exceeds $x°$. Curve C

FIGURE 10
TRAJECTORY OF SELF-REPORTED DELINQUENCY

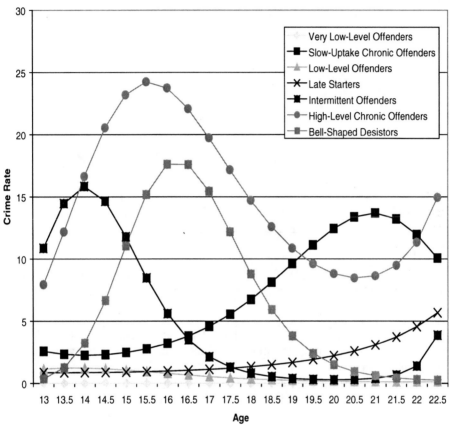

SOURCE: Bushway, Thornberry, and Krohn (2003).

depicts an even more extreme version of this threshold effect in which the positive association between x and y follows a step function in which y jumps to a new level y° once x exceeds x°. Each of these alternative response functions is consistent with the theoretical prediction that more x tends to aggravate y.

Figure 11 depicts the statistical complexities that may attend capturing the relationship between a single predictor variable and a single outcome variable. The statistical complexities that attend capturing the relationship between multiple predictors and developmental trajectories are even more daunting. One straightforward approach to begin exploring these complexities without assuming functional forms is by stratifying the outcome variable and then examining the relationship between the strata and other variables. One way of stratifying longitudinal data on development is by grouping individuals into the trajectory groups identi-

FIGURE 11
THREE HYPOTHETICAL DOSE RESPONSE RELATIONSHIPS

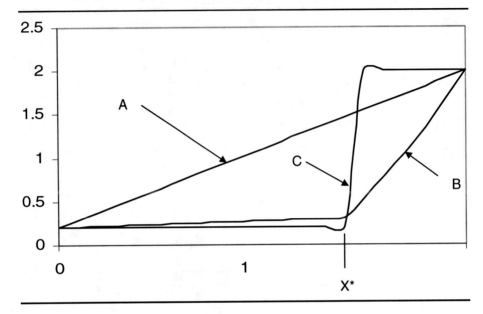

fied by group-based trajectory modeling. It is in this sense that the trajectory groups can be thought of as latent strata of individuals following distinctive developmental paths.

The remainder of the section summarizes results from three studies that we believe illustrate the utility of this form of data stratification.

Life-course trajectories of different types of offenders (Nagin, Farrington, and Moffitt 1995)

This article by Nagin, Farrington, and Moffitt (1995) explored the predictors and consequences of the trajectories depicted in Figure 8. Perhaps the most important finding of this study was that the seeming reformation of the individuals following the AL trajectory may have been more apparent than real. At ages fourteen and eighteen, the offending and other misconduct by the ALs and the high level chronics (HLCs) was generally statistically indistinguishable. Both groups self-reported similar levels of behaviors such as burglary, stealing, fighting, and drug use that in turn were significantly higher than the self-reported rates of individuals following the nonconviction (NC) trajectory.[2] Thus, during adolescence the behavioral trajectories based on conviction closely corresponded with behavioral patterns based on self-report of the study participants themselves.

By age thirty-two, however, this close correspondence between convictions record and self-reported behavior had evaporated. At this age, the HLCs and the low level chronics (LLCs) were still active offenders as measured by their nonnegligible conviction rate, whereas the ALs had seemingly been inactive offenders for a decade or more. However, the self-reports of offending suggested a far more complex reality. The self-reports on burglary were consistent with the conviction data. The HLCs and LLCs reported comparable levels of burglary, whereas the rates for the ALs and NCs were negligible. The ALs were also significantly more likely to be married and have a job than the LLCs and HCLs. However, the ALs' self-reported levels of theft, fighting outside the home, and illicit drug and alcohol use were indistinguishable from that of the HCLs and LLCs.

Thus, this investigation into the predictors and consequences of offending trajectories as measured by conviction raised a number of important issues of measurement and theory. As for measurement, the lack of correspondence of results between self- and official reports at age thirty-two is reminiscent of a much earlier controversy about the measurement of offender participation: incompatibility between results of official versus self-report studies of juvenile delinquency was a pivotal methodological issue for criminologists in the 1970s. Hindelang, Hirschi, and Weiss (1979) argued that the discrepancy was illusory because juvenile self-reports probably tap a more trivial domain of offending than do official data. It is not clear that the discrepancy identified in the Nagin, Farrington, and Moffitt (1995) study can be dispensed with as easily. The self-reports of the subjects in the London sample at age thirty-two tapped nontrivial offenses: drunk driving, fighting outside the home, drug use, burglary, and theft. To be sure, some convictions for certain of these offenses, such as drunk driving and brawling, are not included in the conviction counts. Thus, the discrepancy between self-report versus official-record findings may in part be a measurement artifact. This observation cannot fully resolve the discrepancy, however, because the convictions for theft and burglary were included in the conviction data. Thus, this study raised a new methodological issue—a discrepancy between official records and the self-reports of *adults* who reported *nontrivial* crimes. Resolution of this issue remains important to this day because almost all published findings about criminal careers rely on official data.

As for theory, this investigation raised important questions about the definition and explanation of desistance. The ALs had clearly desisted in some but not all domains of antisocial behavior. Their domain-specific reformation from crime raises important conceptual questions of what is meant by desistance. Nagin, Farrington, and Moffitt (1995) went on to point out the domains of reformation were seemingly not random. The men appeared to be avoiding forms of antisocial behavior that would most jeopardize their stakes in conformity. One theoretical implication of this speculation is that theories of desistance need to focus on multiple domains of behavior and the linkages between them.

Parental and early childhood predictors of persistent physical
aggression in boys from kindergarten to high school
(Nagin and Tremblay 2001b)

This article by Nagin and Tremblay (2001b) reported another example in which stratification into trajectory groups provided valuable insight into subtle but important differences that may distinguish behavioral trajectories. The analysis involved an investigation into the factors that discriminated among the four trajectories of physical aggression reported in Figure 2. A host of risk factors were identified that distinguished the two low physical aggression trajectories from the two high physical aggression trajectories. Concerning these risk factors, two findings stand out. First, the most powerful predictors of membership in a high aggression trajectory group were high levels of hyperactivity and opposition assessed in kindergarten. Individually, these risk factors increased the odds of membership in a high physical aggression trajectory by more than a factor of three. In combination, the increase is more than ninefold. Individually, these risks are comparable in magnitude to the impact of high serum cholesterol levels on risk of coronary heart disease (Truett, Jerome, and William 1967). In combination, they far exceed it.

The group-based trajectory model is well
suited for identifying and testing whether
the response to a turning point event or
treatment is contingent upon the individual's
developmental trajectory.

A second prominent finding concerned the predictive power of parental characteristics—only characteristics of the mother have predictive power. Whereas teen onset of parenthood and low educational attainment for mothers were significant predictors of their male child's high aggression, these characteristics of the father had no predictive power.

The prominent predictive power of mother characteristics again revealed itself in the analysis of factors that distinguished the two high physical aggression groups—the high declining trajectory and the chronic trajectory. Here we were concerned with identifying characteristics that distinguished the modestly large fraction of boys who start off displaying high levels of physical aggression but subsequently desist (28 percent) from the small but prominent group of chronics (4

percent) who continue their physical aggression unabated. Only two such characteristics were identified—the mother's low educational attainment and teenage
onset of childbearing. The odds of male offspring of poorly educated teenage
mothers not desisting from a high level of physical aggression at age six are 9.3
times greater than those of their counterparts without such mothers.

While this was the first analysis to document that these two mother characteristics distinguish persistence from desistance of chronic physical aggression, a large
body of evidence links teen onset of childbearing to a litany of unfavorable behaviors and outcomes for the offspring. These include conduct disorder and other
problem behaviors in childhood (Wakschlag et al. 2000), delinquency and school
drop out in adolescence (Furstenberg, Brooks-Gunn, and Morgan 1987; Morash
and Rucker 1989), and criminality as an adult (Grogger 1997; Pogarsky, Lizotte,
and Thornberry 2003).

This study does not explain why teen onset of motherhood and low maternal
education are risk factors for chronic physical aggression in her offspring. These
two maternal factors are likely markers of maternal problem behaviors and circumstances that give rise to bad outcomes for her offspring rather than the causes per
se. For example, more aggressive young women are more likely to become teen
mothers and to drop out of school and are also more likely to be unresponsive parents. There is also evidence that women who begin childbearing early are more
likely to use harsh and erratic discipline. These mothers may also be more prone to
birth complications, which have been shown to be related to subsequent conduct
problems in the child (Arsenault et al. 2002; Raine et al. 1996). These findings suggest that the mothers themselves may be the agents of the intergenerational transfer of chronic physical aggression. The results are not nearly definitive about the
specifics of the transfer mechanism in terms of the separate and interactive roles of
biology, parenting practice (including the father), and the larger social environment. Notwithstanding, they do suggest that the intergenerational transfer mechanism may have profound consequences for the child and society at large.

Good marriages and trajectories of change in criminal offending (Laub, Nagin, and Sampson 1998)

The final example we summarize—Laub, Nagin, and Sampson (1998)—is as
notable for what it did not find as what it did find. This article further explored the
linkage between marriage and desistance that has been a central focus of the long-
time collaboration between John Laub and Robert Sampson (cf. Sampson and
Laub 1993; Laub and Sampson 2003). Figure 12 reports the trajectories that
emerged from the application of group-based trajectory modeling to the arrest
records from age seven to thirty-two of 480 men in Glueck and Glueck's (1950,
1968) delinquent sample. Observe that all four trajectories follow the classic
hump-shaped age crime curve, but only groups 3 and 4 peak prior to age twenty, as
is normally the case in the population average curve, whereas the peaks for groups
1 and 2 occur well past age twenty. Even more important, group 2 and especially

FIGURE 12
PREDICTED OFFENDING TRAJECTORIES

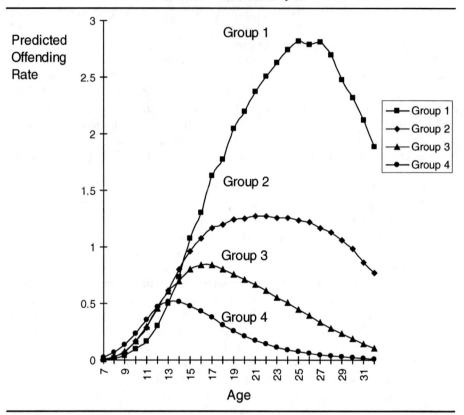

SOURCE: Laub, Nagin, and Sampson (1998).

group 1 have substantial predicted arrest rates at the close of the measurement period, age thirty-two.

Table 2 reproduces a key table from Laub, Nagin, and Sampson (1998). It reports group means on a variety of individual characteristics, behaviors, and life course outcomes. There are two prominent patterns in this table. One is the clear association between following a trajectory of desistance, namely trajectories 3 and 4, versus trajectories of persistence, namely, trajectories 1 and 2, and adult social bonds. Compared to the persisters, the desisters are significantly more likely to have quality marriages and to have stable jobs and are significantly less likely to be divorced or separated. By contrast, there is virtually no association between desister trajectory group status and individual and family differences in childhood. The absence of such associations makes it hard to argue that the correlation between adult social bonds and desistance is simply a reflection of long-standing individual differences that predict both desistance and quality adult social bonds.

TABLE 2

COMPARISON OF GROUP MEANS FOR SELECTED
CHARACTERISTICS, BY GROUP MEMBERSHIP

Characteristic	Groups 1 and 2	Group 3	Group 4
Individual differences in childhood			
Verbal IQ	5.63	5.49	5.44
Percentage extroverted	67.0	53.1	55.8
Percentage adventurous°	66.0	52.7	50.6
Percentage egocentric	12.3	15.9	9.7
Percentage aggressive	14.2	15.9	15.6
Percentage tantrums	44.3	41.4	34.4
Percentage difficult	55.8	60.9	57.9
Family differences in childhood			
Poverty	0.10	0.08	0.00
Family size°	6.00	5.34	5.23
Parental crime/alcohol abuse	2.06	1.94	2.04
Erratic discipline	0.13	−0.15	−0.08
Supervision	1.39	1.47	1.42
Attachment to family	3.07	3.13	3.10
Adolescent behavior			
Arrest frequency°	0.45	0.45	0.37
Unofficial delinquency°	15.6	14.0	13.6
Percentage attached to school°	21.6	35.9	39.7
Percentage early onset	15.4	14.1	9.6
Adult social bonds			
Percentage divorce/separation by age thirty-two°	38.5	18.9	10.3
Percentage "shotgun" marriage°	40.8	34.4	18.4
Percentage married by age thirty-two°	30.8	50.7	80.3
Quality of marriage at age thirty-two°	−2.01	−0.47	0.69
Job stability at age thirty-two°	−3.16	−1.37	0.50
Number of cases	106	220	154

SOURCE: Laub, Nagin, and Sampson (1998).
°Differences are jointly significant at $p < .05$ level.

This argument is far from sufficient for making the case that the bonds are the *cause* of the desistance. Notwithstanding, being able to plausibly rule out one important class of explanations is an important step forward, a step that was greatly facilitated by application of group-based modeling.

Guidelines for Choosing between Group-Based Trajectory Modeling and Standard Growth Curve Modeling

For what types of problems is the group-based approach more appropriate than standard growth curve modeling and for what types of problems is the standard approach a better fit? This is a question without a clear answer. Still, some guidelines are possible. One guideline relates to the adjective *growth* that modifies "curve modeling." The prototypical application of standard growth curve modeling involves a process in which population members follow a common developmental pattern of either increase or decline. Raudenbush (2001, 509) offered language acquisition as a quintessential example of such a process. Another good example is time spent with peers from childhood through adolescence (Warr 2002). Standard growth curve methods are well suited for analyzing such developmental phenomena because it is reasonable to assume that most individuals experience a common process of growth or decline, albeit at different rates. However, there are large classes of developmental phenomena for which the conception of a common growth process does not naturally fit. Raudenbush described the population differences for this class of problems as "multinomial," and for such problems he recommended a group-based approach as particularly appropriate. As noted earlier, Raudenbush used depression as an example.

The basis for Raudenbush's (2001) making a distinction between the developmental processes underlying language acquisition and depression is fundamental and cannot be overstressed. The former are appropriately analyzed by conventional analysis of variation; the latter are not. Because the vocabularies of all young children from normal populations increase with age, it is sensible to ask questions such as, What is the average growth curve of children's vocabulary over a specified age range? How large is the variation across children in their individual-level language acquisition growth curves? How do such "between-person" variations relate to factors such as the child's cognitive functioning and parental education? How are "within-person" changes in acquisition related to changes in interactions with primary caregivers due, for example, to parental conflict?

These questions are framed in the language of analysis of variance as reflected in the use of terms such as *within-person change* and "between-person change." This is only natural because standard growth curve analysis has its roots in analysis of variance. Like analysis of variance, growth curve analysis is designed to sort out factors accounting for variation about a population mean.

To meaningfully frame an analysis in the conceptual apparatus of analysis of variance requires that it be sensible to characterize population differences in terms of variation about the population mean. For processes such as language acquisition, the mean trend is, in fact, a sensible statistical anchor for describing individual variability. However, for many processes evolving over time or age, it is not. For example, it makes no sense to frame a statistical analysis of population differences in the developmental progression of attention deficit disorder (ADD) in terms of variation about the mean trajectory of ADD, because ADD is the exception, not the norm, within the general population. Other examples of evolving behavioral phenomena that are not properly described in terms of variation about a population mean are most forms of psychopathology and abuse of both licit and illicit drugs. More generally, a group-based approach to analyzing longitudinal data is usefully applied to phenomena in which there may be qualitatively different trajectories of change over age or time across subpopulations that are not identifiable ex ante based on measured characteristics such as gender or race.

The assumption that all individuals follow a process that increases or decreases regularly within the population may also be violated because there may not be a single explanation for the differences in the developmental trajectories of a subpopulation. As previously described, Nagin and Tremblay (2001b) found that a host of predictors involving the individual's psychological makeup and family circumstances distinguished individuals following low versus high trajectories of physical aggression in childhood. However, a comparison of two distinct subpopulations of high childhood trajectories—those following a trajectory of chronic aggression versus those who started childhood with high aggression but later declined—revealed that only two maternal characteristics distinguished these groups. Using standard growth curve modeling methods, it would have been very difficult to identify this important difference in variables that distinguished among trajectories of childhood physical aggression. Identification of such differences is far easier with a methodology that clusters individuals with similar developmental trajectories.

[T]rajectory groups, like all statistical models, are not literal depictions of reality. Rather, they are only meant as a convenient approximation.

A second guideline concerns the motivation for the analysis. One common aim of analyses of longitudinal data is to uncover distinctive developmental trends in the outcome variable of interest. For example, do sizable numbers of youths follow a trajectory of adolescent onset conduct disorder? The group-based approach is ideally suited for testing whether such distinctive patterns are present in the data. By contrast, another common aim of developmental studies is to test whether some identifiable characteristic or set of characteristics are associated with individual differences in trajectories of development. An example is whether trajectories of conduct disorder differ across sexes. For this type of problem, either approach may be most appropriate depending upon the specific objectives of the analysis. For example, if one were examining whether trajectories of number of sexual partners differed across sexes, standard growth curve modeling provides a natural starting point for framing the statistical analysis—a comparison of the mean trajectories for boys and girls. By contrast, if the objective were to distinguish whether there are distinctive predictors of distinctive developmental trajectories, the group-based approach is particularly well suited for this type of problem. Thus, the group-based approach lends itself to analyzing questions that are framed in terms of the shape of the developmental course of the outcome of interest, whereas either method may be most appropriate for analyzing questions framed in terms of predictors of the outcome's developmental course.[3]

A third guideline concerns the possibility of path dependencies in the response to turning point events such as marriage or to treatments such as hospitalization for a psychiatric disorder. Path dependencies occur when the response to a turning point event or treatment is contingent upon the individual's developmental history. For example, Nagin et al. (2003) found that the seeming impact of grade retention on physical aggression depended upon the child's trajectory of physical aggression. The subsequent physical aggression of children who had been following trajectories of little physical aggression or of chronic physical aggression appeared to be unaffected by the event of being held back in school. By contrast, the physical aggression of individuals who had been following trajectories of declining physical aggression seemed to be exacerbated. Such path dependencies are commonplace in the literature on human development (Elder 1985). Indeed, the possibility of path dependencies is a key rationale for longitudinal studies. The group-based trajectory model is well suited for identifying and testing whether the response to a turning point event or treatment is contingent upon the individual's developmental trajectory.

Laying out guidelines for the use of alternative statistical methods is a precarious exercise. Users naturally desire bright line distinctions. Yet bright line distinctions are generally not possible. The first guideline implies that developmental processes can be cleanly divided between those involving regular growth or decline and those that do not. The reality is that for many developmental processes, it is not possible to confidently make this distinction. The second guideline implies that the objective of an analysis can be classified as either identifying distinctive developmental trajectories or testing predictors of developmental trajectories. The reality is that most analyses have both objectives. Still a further complication is that standard growth curve modeling can be used to identify distinctive developmental trajectories for *predefined* groups (e.g., races or genders). The third guideline might be interpreted as implying that it is not possible to identify path dependencies with conventional growth curve models. This is not the case. Stated differently, both methods are designed to analyze change over time. The group-based method focuses on identification of different trajectory shapes and on examining how the prevalence of the shape and shape itself relate to predictors. By contrast, standard growth curve modeling focuses on the population mean trajectory and how individual variation about that mean relates to predictors. Thus, the alternative approaches are best thought of as complementary, not competing.

Concluding Remarks

Since its introduction less than twenty years ago, group-based trajectory modeling has had a significant and we believe salutary impact on the fields of developmental criminology and developmental psychopathology. In this article, we have attempted to summarize some useful contributions that were facilitated by the use of the methodology. These include illuminating important empirical regularities in the developmental course and origins of physical aggression, clarifying and testing taxonomic theories of the development of antisocial behavior, and clarifying the predictors and consequences of developmental trajectories.

The rapid growth in applications of group-based trajectory modeling stems at least in part from its usefulness in summarizing complexity. A hallmark of modern longitudinal studies is the variety and richness of measurements that are made about the study's subjects and their circumstances. Less often acknowledged is that this abundance of information is accompanied by a difficult companion—complexity. Commonly, researchers are confronted with the dilemma of how best to explore and communicate the rich set of measurements at their disposal without becoming so bogged down in complexity that the lessons to be learned from the data are lost on them and their audience. Group-based trajectory modeling does not solve the problem of balancing comprehensibility and complexity. However, it does improve a researcher's ability to identify, summarize, and communicate complex patterns in longitudinal data.

Notes

1. We also note that another important finding of the applications of trajectory modeling that included measurement into adolescence is that in all cases, a small group of chronics was identified. In a review by Moffitt (forthcoming) of evidence concerning her life-course persistent/adolescent-limited developmental taxonomy, she observed, "After ten years of research, what can be stated with some certainty is that the hypothesized life-course persistent antisocial individual exists, at least during the first three decades of life. Consensus about this group has emerged from all studies that have applied trajectory-detection analyses to a representative cohort sample having longitudinal repeated measures of antisocial behavior"

2. However, the offending behavior of the adolescent limited (AL) and high level chronic (HLC) individuals was not always significantly different than that of the low level chronics (LLCs) at these ages.

3. We thank Steven Durlauf and Wayne Osgood for pointing out this important distinction.

References

Anderson, John R.1980. *Cognitive psychology and its implications.* San Francisco: Freeman and Co.

Arseneault, Louise, Richard E. Tremblay, Bernard Boulerice, and Jean-Francois Saucier. 2002. Obstetrical complications and violent delinquency: Testing two developmental pathways. *Child Development* 73 (2): 496-508.

Blumstein, Alfred, Jacqueline Cohen, Jeffrey A. Roth, and Christy A. Visher, eds. 1986. *Criminal careers and "career criminals."* Washington, DC: National Academy Press.

Brame, Richard, Daniel S. Nagin, and Richard E. Tremblay. 2001. Developmental trajectories of physical aggression from school entry to late adolescence. *Journal of Child Psychology and Psychiatry* 42:503-12.

Brame, Richard, Daniel S. Nagin, and Larry Wasserman. Forthcoming. Exploring some analytical characteristics of finite mixture models. *Journal of Quantitative Criminology.*

Broidy, Lisa M., Daniel S. Nagin, Richard E. Tremblay, John E. Bates, Robert Brame, Kenneth A. Dodge,
David M. Fergusson, John L. Horwood, Rolf Loeber, Robert Laird, Donald Lynam, Terrie E. Moffitt,
Gregory S. Pettit, and Frank Vitaro. 2003. Developmental trajectories of childhood disruptive behaviors
and adolescent delinquency: A six site, cross national study. *Developmental Psychology* 39:222-45.

Bryk, Anthony S., and Stephen W. Raudenbush. 1987. Application of hierarchical linear models to assessing
change. *Psychology Bulletin* 101:147-58.

———. 1992. *Hierarchical linear models for social and behavioral research: Application and data analysis
methods.* Newbury Park, CA: Sage.

Burkhardt, Fredrick, and Sydney Smith. 1988. *The correspondence of Charles Darwin.* Vol. 4., 1847-1850.
Cambridge: Cambridge University Press.

Bushway, Shawn, Terence Thornberry, and Marvin Krohn. 2003. Desistance as a developmental process: A
comparison of static and dynamic approaches. *Journal of Quantitative Criminology* 19:129-53.

Cairns, Robert B., and Beverley D. Cairns. 1994. *Life lines and risks: Pathways of youth in our time.* New
York: Cambridge University Press.

Cairns, Robert B., Beverley D. Cairns, Holly J. Neckerman, Lynda L. Ferguson, and Jean-Louis Gariepy.
1989. Growth and aggression: 1. Childhood to early adolescence. *Developmental Psychology* 25 (2): 320-
30.

Caspi, Avshalom. 1998. Personality development across the life course. In *Handbook of child psychology,* 5th
ed., ed. N. Eisenberg and W. Daom. New York: Wiley.

Cloninger, Robert C. 1986. A unified biosocial theory of personality and its role in the development of anxiety
states. *Psychiatric Developments* 3:167-225.

———. 1987. A systematic method for clinical description and classification of personality variants. *Archives
of General Psychiatry* 44:573-88.

Côté, Sylvana, Tracy Vaillancourt, Ted Barker, Daniel S. Nagin, and Richard E. Tremblay. 2004. Continuity
and change in the joint development of physical and indirect aggression during early childhood. Working
Paper, University of Montreal, Canada.

Côté, Sylvana, Tracy Vaillancourt, John LeBlanc, Daniel S. Nagin, and Richard E. Tremblay. 2004. The development of physical aggression from toddlerhood to pre-adolescence: A nation wide longitudinal study.
Working Paper, University of Montreal, Canada.

Elder, Glen H., Jr. 1985. Perspectives on the life course. In *Life course dynamics,* ed. Glen H. Elder Jr. Ithaca,
NY: Cornell University Press.

Everitt, Brian S., and David J. Hand. 1981. *Finite mixture distributions.* London: Chapman & Hall.

Farrington, David P., and Donald J. West. 1990. The Cambridge Study in delinquent development: A prospective longitudinal study of 411 males. In *Criminality: Personality, behavior, and life history,* ed. Hans-
Jürgen Kerner and Günther Kaiser. New York: Springer-Verlag.

Furstenberg, Frank, Jeanne Brooks-Gunn, and S. Philip Morgan. 1987. Adolescent mothers and their children in later life. *Family Planning Perspectives* 19:142-51.

Glueck, Sheldon, and Eleanor Glueck. 1950. *Unraveling juvenile delinquency.* New York: Commonwealth
Fund.

———. 1968. *Delinquents and nondelinquents in perspective.* New York: Commonwealth Fund.

Goldstein, Harvey. 1995. *Multilevel statistical models.* 2nd ed. London: Edward Arnold.

Grogger, Jeffrey. 1997. Estimating the incarceration-related costs of early childbearing. In *Kids having kids,*
ed. Rebecca Maynard. Washington, DC: Urban Institute.

Haapasalo, Jaana, and Richard E. Tremblay. 1994. Physically aggressive boys from ages 6 to 12: Family background, parenting behavior, and prediction of delinquency. *Journal of Consulting and Clinical Psychology* 62:1044-52.

Haviland, Amelia, and Daniel Nagin. Forthcoming. Causal inference with group-based trajectory models.
Psychometrika.

Heckman, James, and Burton Singer. 1984. A method for minimizing the impact of distributional assumptions in econometric models for duration data. *Econometrica* 52:271-320.

Hindelang, Michael J., Travis Hirschi, and Joseph Weis. 1979. Correlates of delinquency: The illusion of discrepancy between self-report and official measures. *American Sociological Review* 44:975-1014.
Holyoak, Keith, and Barbara Spellman. 1993. Thinking. *Annual Review of Psychology* 44:265-315.
Human Capital Initiative Coordinating Committee on Reducing Violence. 1996. *Reducing violence: A research agenda*. Washington, DC: Author.
Jones, Robert, and Daniel S. Nagin. 2005. Advances in group-based trajectory modeling and a SAS procedure for estimating them. Working Paper, Carnegie Mellon University, Pittsburgh, PA.
Jones, Bobby L., Daniel Nagin, and Kathryn Roeder. 2001. A SAS procedure based on mixture models for estimating developmental trajectories. *Sociological Research and Methods* 29:374-93.
Kandel, Denise B. 1975. Stages in adolescent involvement in drug use. *Science* 190:912-14.
Kasen, Stephanie, Patricia Cohen, Andres E. Skodol, Jeffrey G. Johnson, Elizabeth Smailes, and Judith S. Brook. 2001. Childhood depression and adult personality disorder—Alternative pathways of continuity. *Archives of General Psychiatry* 58:231-36.
Kochanska, Grazyna. 1997. Multiple pathways to conscience for children with different temperaments: From toddlerhood to age 5. *Developmental Psychology* 33:228-40.
Lacourse, Eric, Daniel Nagin, Frank Vitaro, Michel Claes, and Richard E. Tremblay. 2003. Developmental trajectories of boys' delinquent group membership and facilitation of violent behaviors during adolescence. *Development and Psychopathology* 15:183-97.
Lagerspetz, Kirsti M., Kaj Bjorkqvist, and Tarja Peltonen. 1988. Is indirect aggression typical of females? Gender differences in aggressiveness in 11- to 12-year old children. *Aggressive Behavior* 14:403-14.
Laub, John H., Daniel S. Nagin, and Robert Sampson. 1998. Good marriages and trajectories of change in criminal offending. *American Sociological Review* 63:225-38.
Laub, John H., and Robert E. Sampson. 2003. *Shared beginnings, divergent lives: Delinquent boys to age 70*. Cambridge, MA: Harvard University Press.
Loeber, Rolf. 1991. Questions and advances in the study of developmental pathways. In *Models and integrations*, Rochester Symposium on Developmental Psychopathology, ed. D. Cicchetti and S. Toth. Rochester, NY: University of Rochester Press.
Loeber, Rolf, and Dale F. Hay. 1997. Key issues in the development of aggression and violence from childhood to early adulthood. *Annual Review of Psychology* 48:371-410.
MacCallum, Robert C., Cheongtag Kim, William B. Malarkey, and Janice K. Kiecolt-Glaser. 1997. Studying multivariate change using multilevel models and latent curve models. *Multivariate Behavioral Research* 32:215-53.
Markman, Ellen M. 1989. *Categorization and naming in children: Problems of induction*. Cambridge, MA: MIT Press.
McArdle, John J., and David Epstein. 1987. Latent growth curves within developmental structural equation models. *Child Development* 58:110-13.
McLachlan, Geoffrey, and David Peel. 2000. *Finite mixture models*. New York: Wiley.
Meredith, William, and John Tisak. 1990. Latent curve analysis. *Psychometrika* 55:107-22.
Moffitt, Terrie E. 1993. Adolescence-limited and life-course persistent antisocial behavior: A developmental taxonomy. *Psychological Review* 100:674-701.
———. Forthcoming. Life-course persistent versus adolescence-limited antisocial behavior. In *Developmental psychopathology*, 2nd ed., ed. D. Cicchetti and D. Cohen. New York: Wiley.
Moffitt, Terrie E., Avshalom Caspi, Nigel Dickson, Phil Silva, and William Stanton. 1996. Childhood-onset versus adolescent-onset antisocial conduct in males: Natural history from age 3 to 18. *Development and Psychopathology* 8:399-424.
Morash, Mary, and Lila Rucker. 1989. An exploratory study of the connection of mother's age at childbearing to her children's delinquency in four data sets. *Crime & Delinquency* 35:45-93.
Muthén, Bengt. 1989. Latent variable modeling in heterogeneous populations. *Psychometrika* 54:557-85.
Muthén, Linda K., and Bengt O. Muthén. 1998-2004. *Mplus user's guide*. 3rd ed. Los Angeles: Muthén & Muthén.
Nagin, Daniel. 1999. Analyzing developmental trajectories: Semi-parametric, group-based approach. *Psychological Methods* 4:39-177.

———. 2005. *Group-based modeling of development*. Cambridge, MA: Harvard University Press.

Nagin, Daniel S., David Farrington, and Terrie Moffitt. 1995. Life-course trajectories of different types of offenders. *Criminology* 33:111-39.

Nagin, Daniel S., and Kenneth C. Land. 1993. Age, criminal careers, and population heterogeneity: Specification and estimation of a nonparametric, mixed poisson model. *Criminology* 31:327-62.

Nagin, Daniel, Linda Pagani, Richard Tremblay, and Frank Vitaro. 2003. Life course turning points: A case study of the effect of school failure on interpersonal violence. *Development and Psychopathology* 15:343-61.

Nagin, Daniel S., and Richard E. Tremblay. 1999. Trajectories of boys' physical aggression, opposition, and hyperactivity on the path to physically violent and nonviolent juvenile delinquency. *Child Development* 70:1181-96.

———. 2001a. Analyzing developmental trajectories of distinct but related behaviors: A group-based method. *Psychological Methods* 6:18-34.

———. 2001b. Parental and early childhood predictors of persistent physical aggression in boys from kindergarten to high school. *Archives of General Psychiatry* 58:389-94.

———. 2002. Most fall but not all: Changes in physical aggression from childhood through adolescence. Working Paper, Carnegie Mellon University, Pittsburgh, PA.

———. 2005. Trajectory groups: Fact or fiction. Working Paper, Carnegie Mellon University, Pittsburgh, PA.

National Institute of Child Health and Development (NICHD) Early Child Care Research Network. 2004. Trajectories of physical aggression from toddlerhood to middle childhood. *Monograph of the Society for Research on Child Development* Serial no. 278, vol. 69, 4.

Osgood, Wayne D., Janet K. Wilson, Jerald G. Bachman, Patrick M. O'Malley, and Lloyd Johnson. 1996. Routine activities and individual deviant behavior. *American Sociological Review* 61:635-55.

Patterson, Gerald R., Barbara D. DeBaryshe, and Susan E. Ramsey. 1989. A developmental perspective on antisocial behavior. *American Psychologist* 44:329-35.

Pickles, Andrew, and Adriane Angold. 2003. Natural categories or fundamental dimensions: On carving nature at the joints and the rearticulation of psychopathology. *Development and Psychopathology* 15:529-51.

Piquero, Alex. 2004. What have we learned about the natural history of criminal offending from longitudinal studies? Paper presented at the National Institute of Justice, Washington, DC.

Pogarsky, Greg, Alan J. Lizotte, and Terence P. Thornberry. 2003. The delinquency of children born to young mothers: Results from the Rochester Youth Development Study. *Criminology* 41:101-38.

Raine, Adrain, Patricia Brennan, Bergitte Mednick, and Sarnoff Mednick. 1996. High rates of violence, crime, academic problem, and behavioral problems in males with both early neuromotor deficits and unstable family environments. *Archive General Psychiatry* 53:544-49.

Raudenbush, Stephen W. 2001. Comparing-personal trajectories and drawing causal inferences from longitudinal data. *Annual Review of Psychology* 52:501-25.

Reiss, Albert J., and Jeffrey A. Roth. 1994. *Understanding and preventing violence*. Vol. 4, *Consequences and control*. Washington, DC: National Academy Press.

Sampson, Robert J., and John. H. Laub. 1993. *Crime in the making: Pathways and turning points through life*. Cambridge, MA: Harvard University Press.

Thornberry, Terence P., Alan J. Lizotte, Marvin D. Krohn, Carolyn A. Smith, and Pamela K. Porter. 2003. Causes and consequences of delinquency: Findings from the Rochester Youth Development Study. In *Taking stock of delinquency: An overview of findings from contemporary longitudinal studies*, ed. T. Thornberry and M. D. Krohn. New York: Kluwer Academic.

Titterington, D. M., A. F. M. Smith, and U. E. Makov. 1985. *Statistical analysis of finite mixture distributions*. New York: Wiley.

Tremblay, Richard E. 2004a. The development of human physical aggression: How important is early childhood? In *Social and moral development: Emerging evidence on the toddler years*, ed. D. M. B. Hall, A. Leavitt, and N. A. Fox. New Brunswick, NJ: Johnson and Johnson Pediatric Institute.

———. 2004b. Why socialization fails? The case of chronic physical aggression. In *Causes of conduct disorder and juvenile delinquency*, ed. B. B. Lahey, T. E. Moffitt, and A. Caspi, 182-224. New York: Guilford.

Tremblay, Richard E., Christa Japek, Daniel Pérusse, Pierre McDuff, Michel Boivin, Mark Zoccolillo, and Jacques Montplaisir. 1999. The search for the age of "onset" of physical aggression: Rousseau and Bandura revisited. *Criminal Behaviour and Mental Health* 9:8-23.

Tremblay, Richard E., and Daniel S. Nagin. 2005. Aggression in humans. In *Developmental origins of aggression*, ed. Richard E. Tremblay, William W. Hartup, and John Archer. New York: Guilford.

Tremblay, Richard E., Daniel S. Nagin, Jean R. Séguin, Mark Zoccolillo, Philip D. Zelazo, Michel Boivin, Daniel Perusse, and Christa Japel. 2004. Physical aggression during early childhood: Trajectories and predictors. *Pediatrics* 114:e43-e50.

Truett, Jeanne, Cornfield Jerome, and Kannel William. 1967. A multivariate analysis of the risk of coronary heart disease in Framingham. *Journal of Chronic Diseases* 20:511-24.

Tyrka, Audrey R., Julia A. Graber, and Jeanne Brooks-Gunn. 2000. The development of disordered eating. In *Handbook of developmental psychopathology*, 2nd ed., ed. Arnold J. Sameroff, Michael Lewis, and Suzanne M. Miller. New York: Kluwer Academic/Plenum.

Wakschlag, Lauren S., Rachel A. Gordon, Benjamin B. Lahey, Rolf Loeber, Stephanie M. Green, and Bennett L. Leventhal. 2000. Maternal age at first birth and boys' risk for conduct disorder. *Journal of Research on Adolescence* 10:417-41.

Warr, Mark. 2002. *Companions in crime: The social aspects of criminal conduct*. New York: Cambridge University Press.

Willett, John B., and Aline G. Sayer. 1994. Using covariance structure analysis to detect correlates and predictors of individual change over time. *Psychological Bulletin* 116:363-81.

Developmental Trajectory Modeling: A View from Developmental Psychopathology

By
BARBARA MAUGHAN

Since its introduction just over a decade ago, developmental trajectory modeling has had a major impact in studies of childhood behavior problems as well as in studies of crime. This article explores some of the issues it raises from the perspective of developmental psychopathology. First, it notes debates over categorical versus dimensional approaches to the conceptualization and analysis of behavior and argues that in the current state of knowledge, much can be gained from exploring each. Second, it highlights heterogeneity in the behavioral manifestations of antisocial traits in childhood and suggests that trajectory modeling could productively be used to track trajectories in these differing aspects of child behavior problems. Third, it argues that though trajectories are typically analyzed in relation to age, a developmental approach requires that researchers "unpack" these associations to uncover the other aspects of development—biological, psychological, or social— that underlie the age trends they observe.

Keywords: categories; dimensions; heterogeneity; psychopathology; puberty

In their article, Nagin and Tremblay (2005 [this volume]) look back on just over a decade in which the application of a particular statistical technique—the group-based approach to trajectory modeling introduced by Nagin and Land in 1993—has had a major impact on developmental studies of crime. They conclude that that impact has been salutary, in part at least because the approach has added to the armory of techniques available to longitudinal researchers to render the complexities of their data more tractable. More important, as they illustrate persua-

Barbara Maughan is a member of External Scientific Staff of the UK Medical Research Council and a reader in developmental psychopathology at the Social, Genetic and Developmental Psychiatry Centre, Institute of Psychiatry, King's College London, United Kingdom. Her research has focused on psychosocial risks for behavioral and emotional problems in childhood and on continuities and discontinuities in disorder and problem functioning from childhood to adult life. She is editor, with Jonathan Hill, of Conduct Disorders in Childhood and Adolescence *(Cambridge University Press, 2001).*

DOI: 10.1177/0002716205281067

sively throughout their article, much of the appeal of their method lies in its capacity to explore models that assume that, rather than being continuously distributed in the population, trends in the developmental course of antisocial behavior—and so possibly in their etiology—differ for different subgroups of individuals.

The Albany Symposium was planned to address current debates in developmental criminology. My own background is in a related field: developmental psychopathology. Many of the issues that concern these two fields—the unfolding of troubling and troublesome behaviors across the life course and the factors that underlie those changing patterns—overlap. Richard Tremblay has made major contributions to both theorizing and research in developmental psychopathology, and investigators in child behavior are increasingly recognizing the applicability of Daniel Nagin's techniques to the phenomena they study. Alongside these many parallels, however, the two fields do show discernable differences in perspective and emphasis, arising in large part from their differing disciplinary roots and the particular historical contexts in which they emerged. Because I am much in sympathy with the arguments that Nagin and Tremblay present in their article, I will use this commentary not to discuss the specifics of their article in any detailed way but instead as an opportunity to reflect some of the issues they raise from the complementary perspective of developmental psychopathology. In particular, I will focus on three themes: first, categorical and dimensional approaches to the analysis of behavioral development; second, other aspects of heterogeneity in antisocial behavior; and third, some additional issues raised by the effort to take a developmental approach to the phenomena we study.

Categorical and Dimensional Models of Behavior

As Nagin and Tremblay set out in their article, the distinctive feature of the group-based approach to trajectory modeling derives from its assumption that there may be clusters or groupings of individuals within the population whose development on any given behavior of interest follows differing age-related patterns in its developmental course. In some instances, as they point out, the existence of such distinct groupings is already well established. In many others—including many of the phenomena of interest to criminologists and psychologists—it simply is not. Under such conditions of uncertainty, the availability of a range of statistical techniques that allow us to explore differing conceptual models is of major heuristic value.

The statistical issues raised by the group-based approach are discussed by other contributors to this volume. Here, I would like to look briefly at related debates on categorical and dimensional approaches to the conceptualization, measurement, and analysis of behaviors in the recent literature on developmental psychopathology (see, e.g., Sonuga-Barke 1998; Pickles and Angold 2003). The arguments here are more typically framed in terms of features defined at a single point in time and center on whether the phenomena we study are most appropriately characterized as discrete disorders or dimensionally distributed traits. In clinical practice, of course, categorical distinctions are a daily necessity: much of the clinician's work centers on decisions about whether any given individual requires treatment and, if so, which treatment is best suited to his or her particular needs. Much of the impetus for the development of the diagnostic classification systems now widely used in psychiatric research can be linked to these decision needs, with the aim of improving both the validity and reliability of clinical decision "rules." Categorical models are also argued to have other advantages: clearly specified categories can enhance communication, for example, and may provide a useful framework in which to examine interactions among hypothesized risks.

[M]any of the behaviors that we study are dimensionally distributed and do not show clear-cut points differentiating "normality" and "pathology."

Alongside these presses toward categorical models, however, there is also widespread recognition that many of the behaviors that we study are dimensionally distributed and do not show clear-cut points differentiating "normality" and "pathology." Commentators on these debates note that each model carries with it a variety of metatheoretical assumptions (Sonuga-Barke 1998) and that they have inevitable (and often self-reinforcing) implications for the ways in which we conduct research. Are these differing views resolvable on empirical grounds? In the psychopathology arena, one set of approaches designed to address this question are the taxometric procedures developed by Paul Meehl and his colleagues (Meehl 1995, 2004). These examine the covariation among indicators of a latent variable (such as a hypothesized disorder) and seek patterns indicative of latent categories ("taxa") or dimensions. A distinctive feature of this approach is its use of multiple procedures to assess whether a taxon exists and its reliance on consistency across these procedures in deriving conclusions. Empirical applications are still limited in number but have highlighted some interesting themes. In the "neurotic" domain, for example—in relation to phenomena such as anxiety and depression—current evidence provides most support for a dimensional view (Haslam 2003). In relation to personality functioning, including antisocial personality and psychopathy, emerging evidence points more in the direction of latent categories—although criminality per se has shown a dimensional distribution in a number of samples.

Analyses using item response models also found little evidence of nonnormality in the distribution of latent liability for adolescent delinquency or depressed mood (van den Oord, Pickles, and Waldman 2003). As a number of commentators have noted, however, such findings are not necessarily inconsistent with results—such as those provided by Nagin and Tremblay—that imply the identification of discrete groups. Latent groupings may differ in degree rather than in kind; the heuristic value of group-based approaches derives at least in part from their capacity to allow for direct tests of a range of hypothesized patterns of association. In our current state of knowledge, many commentators argue that we need to entertain both categorical and dimensional conceptions, and explore—and contrast—models and findings from each. The introduction of the group-based trajectory approach has added significantly to our capacity in this regard.

Heterogeneity in Antisocial Behavior

Though variations in course may be key pointers to heterogeneity in antisocial behavior—and ones that are especially salient from a developmental perspective—other features may also be important. In general, criminal career studies have identified only limited evidence of specialization in offending in adulthood (Piquero, Farrington, and Blumstein 2003). The developmental literature, by contrast, has highlighted a variety of distinctions that seem likely to carry important implications for our understanding of early developmental processes. At this stage, a variety of possible "contenders" have been identified, some based on differing behavioral manifestations of antisocial tendencies (such as Loeber's model of overt, covert, and authority conflict pathways—see Loeber et al. 1993), some on age at onset (Moffitt 1993), and some on associated features such as hyperactivity (see Rutter, Giller, and Hagell [1998] for a discussion of these and other possibilities). In their article, Nagin and Tremblay focus predominantly on one particular behavioral manifestation: physical aggression. The examples they cite form part of a wider program of studies through which, over time, they have carefully and elegantly charted the natural history of aggression across the first decades of life (see Tremblay 2000). Taken together, these studies have produced extensive evidence that the peak age for physical aggression is not—as had often been assumed—in the teens but, rather, early in childhood. The findings they assemble here suggest that that conclusion also holds for subgroups of children following quite different aggression trajectories; with few exceptions, the peak levels of aggression that the great majority of children are likely to display are already evident in the preschool years.

As Nagin and Tremblay highlight, this apparently simple conclusion has wide-ranging implications. First and foremost, it challenges the view that aggression is largely a *learned* behavior. Instead, their findings point to a quite different conclusion: that much aggression is likely to reflect an innate tendency that most children *unlearn* (or learn to control) early in childhood. This insight has major ramifications for theoretical models of the development of aggression and for the types of environmental processes that may contribute to its maintenance. It also carries implications for research. If the origins of aggression lie early in development, environmentally oriented risk research also needs to focus its attention there. In terms of process, if the typical pattern is one in which most young children are helped to control aggressive tendencies over the toddler period, more may be learned at this stage from exploring failures in proactive parenting—the strategies that most parents use to anticipate and circumvent young children's behavior problems (Gardner, Sonuga-Barke, and Sayal 1999)—than from focusing on the coercive processes that have proved so productive in understanding exacerbations in troublesome behavior later in childhood.

Do other forms of childhood antisocial behavior follow similar age trends? Perhaps surprisingly, systematic evidence of this "natural history" kind is still quite limited for indicators of nonaggressive conduct problems, but some pointers are beginning to emerge. Useful illustrations come from our own recent studies of age trends in the prevalence of the two main childhood antisocial disorders defined by the psychiatric classification systems: Conduct Disorder (CD) and Oppositional Defiant Disorder (ODD). Figure 1 shows overall rates of CD by age, using data from an epidemiologic study of more than ten thousand five- to fifteen-year-olds conducted recently in the United Kingdom (Meltzer et al. 2000). Although the data set did not include preschoolers, Figure 1 makes clear that from school entry onward, age trends in CD are quite different from those suggested by Nagin and Tremblay's findings on aggression. Instead, they conform much more closely to what might be expected if we extrapolate downward from the age-crime curve: CD (a strong predictor of later criminality) occurs at very low rates in early and middle childhood (especially in girls), then shows a sharp rise in prevalence for young people of both sexes with the approach of adolescence.

Criteria for CD include both aggressive and nonaggressive behaviors. Figure 2 shows what happens if we "unpack" these two contributory behaviors and examine age trends in each. The data here come from the Great Smoky Mountains Study (GSMS), a longitudinal study of psychiatric disorder in some fourteen hundred young people in a predominantly rural area of the southeastern United States (Costello et al. 1996). Figure 2 focuses on data for boys and on the key late childhood–early adolescent period when rates of CD as a whole appear to rise; data for the girls follow closely similar trends. As Nagin and Tremblay would anticipate, mean levels of aggression remain quite stable over this age period; instead, it is the nonaggressive behaviors (including both "covert" behaviors such as lying and stealing and "status offenses" such as truancy) that account for the sharp rise in overall rates of conduct problems in the early teens.

We return later to consider what this might imply in terms of contributory risks. Before that, we look briefly at trends in the other main antisocial diagnosis of childhood: ODD. As its name suggests, this disorder is characterized by a pattern of negativistic, defiant, and disobedient behaviors. The fourth edition of the *Diagnostic and Statistical Manual of Mental Disorders* (*DSM-IV*; American Psychiatric Association 1994) suggests that it usually becomes evident before age eight, and that in a significant proportion of cases it is a developmental antecedent to CD;

FIGURE 1
RATES OF CONDUCT DISORDER (CD) BY AGE
AND GENDER (1999 U.K. NATIONAL SURVEY)

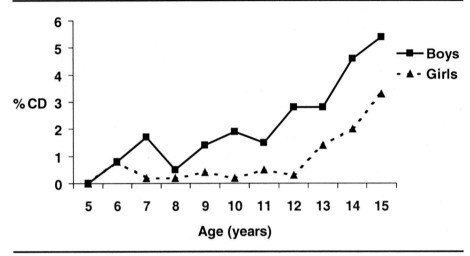

SOURCE: Maughan et al. (2004). Reproduced by agreement with the *Journal of Child Psychology and Psychiatry*.

FIGURE 2
AGE TRENDS IN ADOLESCENT CONDUCT PROBLEMS
(BOYS: GREAT SMOKY MOUNTAINS STUDY)

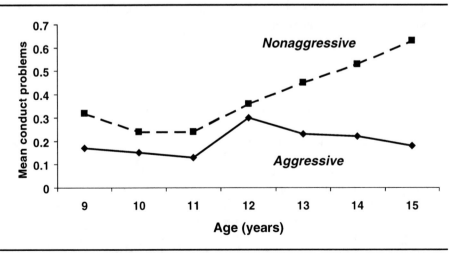

SOURCE: Rowe et al. (2004). Reprinted from *Biological Psychiatry*, vol. 55, p. 549. Copyright (2004) by the Society of Biological Psychiatry. Used with permission.

indeed, the presumption of developmental precursor status is so strong that a separate diagnosis of ODD is not made in *DSM-IV* if a child meets criteria for CD. This exclusion clause has meant that, following conventional diagnostic procedures, it is difficult to determine age trends in severe oppositional behaviors because many children who show them are as it were "creamed off" into a CD category. To get around that problem, we mapped age trends in ODD in the U.K. national data set irrespective of whether the young people involved met criteria for CD. Figure 3 shows the results. Once again, of course, we lack data for the preschool period, which may be especially important here. From school entry onward, however, these data suggest that age trends in ODD follow a quite different pattern from either of the behaviors considered thus far. Where physical aggression declines with age, and nonaggressive conduct problems increase, the prevalence of severe oppositional behaviors shows remarkable stability across childhood and early adolescence. We might speculate that where rates of both aggressive and nonaggressive conduct problems are sensitive to developmentally related changes in the child, or in his or her environment, oppositionality may be more akin to a more stable temperamental trait.

Taken alone, of course, these findings only provide beginning pointers to likely sources of heterogeneity in childhood antisocial behavior. It is unclear at this stage how far they map on to other proposed distinctions such as Moffitt's (1993) developmental taxonomy; evidence (including findings from genetic studies) that antisocial behavior associated with hyperactivity/attention deficits may form a distinct subtype (Rutter, Giller, and Hagell 1998); and studies suggesting, for example, that callous unemotional traits mark out a further important subgroup of antisocial individuals (Viding 2004). Investigations designed to provide explicit links between these differing models would be of considerable importance. Nagin and Tremblay's work on aggression provides a model for the type of detailed, systematic focus on well-characterized phenotypes that will form the building blocks for such efforts.

Developmental Perspectives
on Antisocial Behavior

The central aim of the Albany Symposium was to discuss issues in *developmental* criminology. Le Blanc and Loeber (1998) described this approach as involving two main areas of study: first, the development and dynamics of offending over age; and second, the identification of explanatory or causal factors that predate or co-occur with behavioral development and affect its course. In their article, Nagin and Tremblay provide numerous examples of the contribution of the group-based trajectory approach to each of these domains of inquiry. Their work has clearly cast important light on the developmental dynamics of antisocial behaviors and has also highlighted a variety of theoretically meaningful factors that differentiate among trajectory groupings and, in so doing, give pointers to likely risk. As their work also

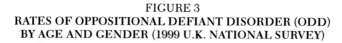

FIGURE 3
RATES OF OPPOSITIONAL DEFIANT DISORDER (ODD)
BY AGE AND GENDER (1999 U.K. NATIONAL SURVEY)

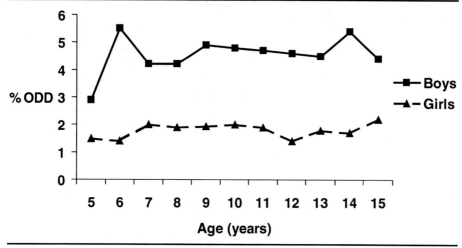

SOURCE: Maughan et al. (2004). Reproduced by agreement with the *Journal of Child Psychology and Psychiatry*.

illustrates, however, tracking the dynamics of behavior raises a further, equally important developmental issue: why some behavioral trajectories vary so strikingly with age. To address this question, we need to turn to a different type of covariate, reflecting not preconditions for offending, but instead other aspects of individual development or social context that co-occur with observed changes in behavior and may help understand variations over age.

Many years ago, Michael Rutter (1989) argued that although age is the developmentalist's fundamental variable, it is also highly ambiguous. Taken alone, chronological age rarely gives any direct insights into changes in the individual, or in his or her environment or experiences, which might account for the trends in behavior that we observe. For a developmental approach—one that aims to link knowledge of behavioral change with development in other aspects of individuals' lives—Rutter argued that we need to "unpack" age into its constituent elements. He suggested a variety of possibilities here. First, age may index changes in social experience: leaving school, becoming a gang member, starting work, or moving into a committed adult relationship are all examples of experiences known to hold implications for antisocial behavior. Second, age may index *duration* of exposure to environmental risks, or to the cumulating consequences of prior behavioral difficulties. Third, in terms of individual characteristics, chronological age may index changes in cognitive level; and fourth, it may reflect variations in biological maturity.

Following the logic of Rutter's (1989) argument, substituting one or more of these alternative metrics for chronological age may cast further light on developmental processes associated with age-related change in antisocial behavior and crime. The criminological literature already contains important illustrations of the value of this approach. Sampson and Laub's work on turning points in the adult life course and their links with desistance from offending are among the best known (Sampson and Laub 1993; Laub and Sampson 2003), though we should note here their more recent view that such adult experiences inevitably reflect not only broader developmental processes but also individual variability and the likelihood of selection effects (Sampson and Laub 2005 [this volume]). In our own recent work, we have been exploring a different example: how far some of the known changes of the adolescent years might illuminate the sharp rise in overall levels of offending reflected in the age-crime curve, in age-trends in CD, and—in a more nuanced way—in some of the specific trajectory groupings identified in Nagin and Tremblay's work (see, e.g., Rowe et al. 2004).

Adolescence is marked by dramatic changes in a plethora of aspects of individual development—biological, cognitive, and emotional—that may have relevance for behavioral change; in addition, it heralds major changes in the nature of young people's relationships and in the contexts in which they spend their time. I focus here on just two of these areas: pubertal maturation and affiliations with deviant peers. Puberty itself, of course, is a highly complex process, involving both physiological and hormonal changes and their biological and social sequelae. In girls, there is now considerable evidence that the *timing* of puberty is important for behavioral development: girls who mature earlier than their peers have consistently been found more likely than on-time or late maturers to be involved in norm-breaking, substance use, and externalizing and delinquent behaviors (Graber et al. 1997). Effects of this kind are generally attributed not to the biological changes of puberty but instead to social/psychological processes whereby early maturing girls are more likely to be exposed to stressors or to affiliate with older (and so probably more deviant) peers.

In addition, however, the onset of puberty is associated with a range of changes in arousal, motivation, and emotion. Recent evidence suggests, for example, that early adolescent increases in sensation seeking and in reckless behaviors are more strongly associated with pubertal stage than with chronological age and that sensitivity to social status increases in adolescence in line with hormonal change (Steinberg 2004). Importantly, other emerging findings suggest that these pubertally driven changes are initiated well before adolescent brain maturation (associated with the development of regulatory competencies and the calibration of risk and reward) is complete. The result has been likened to starting an engine at full throttle with an unskilled driver at the wheel. Are aspects of these changes implicated in changing levels of involvement in antisocial activities? We made some beginning explorations of this question for boys in the GSMS data set, which, alongside measures of aggressive and nonaggressive conduct problems, included indicators of pubertal stage, markers of hormone levels, and indicators of the extent of boys' association with deviant peers (Rowe et al. 2004). Our particular interest was in the possibility of interactions between these features and whether associations between antisocial behaviors and the biological changes of puberty might vary with features of boys' social context.

FIGURE 4
AGE TRENDS IN TESTOSTERONE LEVELS
(BOYS: GREAT SMOKY MOUNTAINS STUDY)

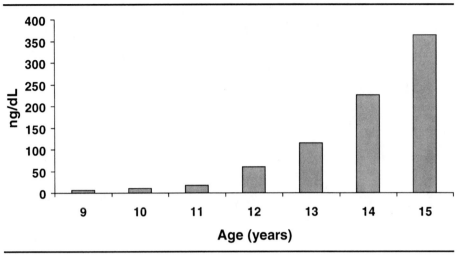

Several aspects of the findings were of interest. First, although age-related increases in nonaggressive conduct problems (Figure 2) did vary with our markers of physical development in adolescence (pubertal stage), chronological age proved the stronger predictor. Second, as numerous other studies have found, affiliations with deviant peers also increased strongly with age and contributed independently to the analyses. And third—rather against our initial expectations—testosterone levels also contributed to the prediction of *non*aggressive (but not aggressive) conduct problems. Figure 4 gives some indication of the massive changes in mean circulating testosterone levels that occur in early adolescence in boys. In the main, of course, testosterone has been assumed to relate to aggression, though findings in adolescent samples have been somewhat mixed. In addition, commentators have noted that testosterone may be less related to aggression per se than to achieving or maintaining dominance within a social group. To explore this possibility, we examined interactions between testosterone levels and our indicators of peer deviance.

Figure 5 illustrates the results, using categorical measures of peer deviance and hormone levels (analyses based on continuous measures, and controlled for age, showed a similar effect). We classified the boys into three groups according to their levels of exposure to peer deviance (those with nondeviant, possibly deviant, and definitely deviant peers) and also into three testosterone groupings (low, medium, and high). Figure 5 shows mean levels of nonaggressive conduct problems for the cross-classification of these groups. As it suggests, variations in conduct problems were unrelated to testosterone levels for boys with nondeviant or possibly deviant peers; in the subgroup reporting definite peer deviance, however, rates of

FIGURE 5
TESTOSTERONE, NONAGGRESSIVE CONDUCT PROBLEMS,
AND DEVIANT PEERS (BOYS: GREAT SMOKY MOUNTAINS STUDY)

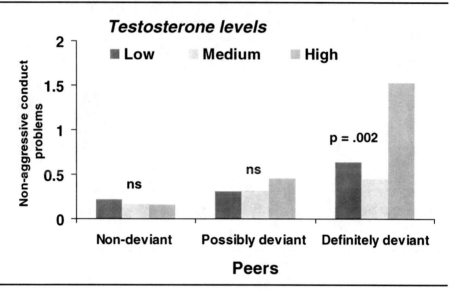

nonaggressive conduct problems were markedly elevated for boys in the high testosterone group. Taken alone, of course, these findings cannot confirm the direction of these effects: high testosterone levels may contribute to risk for antisocial behavior in the teens, but it is also plausible that behavior affects hormone levels. What they do suggest, however, is the potential value of attempts to disambiguate markers of chronological age into what are likely, at any given stage of development, to be indicators of the more specific developmental processes associated with patterns of behavioral change. Adolescence provides almost an embarrassment of possibilities here, at least some of which have already-established metrics. Exploring these alternative metrics constitutes one of the next steps in developmental studies in both criminology and psychopathology; integrating them in a trajectory modeling framework may offer the possibility of important future advance.

Conclusions

Although both criminology and the disciplines concerned with psychopathology have long evinced a concern with developmental issues, this has come much more prominently to the fore in recent years. A developmental perspective offers major advantages but, along with them, raises key challenges. Foremost among those is the need to match our conceptualizations with appropriate methodological tools.

In proposing group-based approaches to trajectory modeling, and in illustrating their application to key issues in the field, Nagin and Tremblay have done much to advance those ends. Their article here provides just a flavor of their contribution to date; it seems set to influence our two domains of enquiry for many years to come.

References

American Psychiatric Association. 1994. *Diagnostic and statistical manual of mental disorders*. 4th ed. Washington, DC: American Psychiatric Association.

Costello, E. Jane, Adrian Angold, Barbara J. Burns, Dalene K. Stangl, Daniel L. Tweed, Alaattin Erkanli, and Carol M. Worthman. 1996. The Great Smoky Mountains Study of Youth: Goals, design, methods, and the prevalence of DSM-III-R disorders. *Archives of General Psychiatry* 53:1129-36.

Gardner, Frances, Edmund Sonuga-Barke, and Kapil Sayal. 1999. Parents anticipating misbehaviour: An observational study of strategies parents use to prevent conflict with behaviour problem children. *Journal of Child Psychology and Psychiatry* 40:1185-96.

Graber, Julia A., Peter M. Lewinsohn, John R. Seeley, and Jeanne Brooks-Gunn. 1997. Is psychopathology associated with the timing of pubertal development? *Journal of the American Academy of Child and Adolescent Psychiatry* 36:1768-76.

Haslam, Nick. 2003. Categorical versus dimensional models of mental disorder: The taxometric evidence. *Australian and New Zealand Journal of Psychiatry* 37:696-704.

Laub, John H., and Robert J. Sampson. 2003. *Shared beginnings, divergent lives: Delinquent boys to age 70*. Cambridge, MA: Harvard University Press.

Le Blanc, Marc, and Rolf Loeber. 1998. Developmental criminology updated. *Crime and Justice: A Review of Research* 23:115-98.

Loeber, Rolf, Phen Wung, Kate Keenan, Bruce Giroux, Magda Stouthamer-Loeber, Welmoet B. Van Kammen, and Barbara Maughan. 1993. Developmental pathways in disruptive behavior. *Development and Psychopathology* 5:101-32.

Maughan, Barbara, Richard Rowe, Julie Messer, Robert Goodman, and Howard Meltzer. 2004. Conduct disorder and oppositional defiant disorder in a national sample: Developmental epidemiology. *Journal of Child Psychology and Psychiatry* 45:609-21.

Meehl, Paul E. 1995. Bootstrap taxometrics: Solving the classification problem in psychopathology. *American Psychologist* 50:266-75.

———. 2004. What's in a taxon? *Journal of Abnormal Psychology* 113:39-43.

Meltzer, Howard, Rebecca Gatward, Robert Goodman, and Tamsin Ford. 2000. *Mental health of children and adolescents in Great Britain*. London: The Stationery Office.

Moffitt, Terrie, E. 1993. Adolescence-limited and life-course persistent antisocial behavior: A developmental taxonomy. *Psychological Review* 100:674-701.

Nagin, Daniel S., and Kenneth C. Land. 1993. Age, criminal careers, and population heterogeneity: Specification and estimation of a nonparametric, mixed Poisson model. *Criminology* 31:327-62.

Nagin, Daniel S., and Richard E. Tremblay. 2005. What has been learned from group-based trajectory modeling? Examples from physical aggression and other problem behaviors. *Annals of the American Academy of Political and Social Science* 602:82-117.

Pickles, Andrew, and Adrian Angold. 2003. Natural categories or fundamental dimensions: On caring nature at the joints and the rearticulation of psychopathology. *Developmental Psychopathology* 15:529-51.

Piquero, Alex, David P. Farrington, and Alfred Blumstein. 2003. The criminal career paradigm. *Crime and Justice: A Review of Research* 30:359-506.

Rowe, Richard, Barbara Maughan, Carol Worthman, E. Jane Costello, and Adrian Angold. 2004. Testosterone, conduct disorder and social dominance in boys: Pubertal development and biosocial interaction. *Biological Psychiatry* 55:546-52.

Rutter, Michael. 1989. Age as an ambiguous variable in developmental research: Some epidemiological considerations from developmental psychopathology. *International Journal of Behavioral Development* 12:1-34.

Rutter, Michael, Henri Giller, and Ann Hagell. 1998. *Antisocial behavior by young people*. Cambridge: Cambridge University Press.

Sampson, Robert J., and John H. Laub. 1993. *Crime in the making: Pathways and turning points through life*. Cambridge, MA: Harvard University Press.

———. 2005. A life-course view of the development of crime. *Annals of the American Academy of Political and Social Science* 602:12-45.

Sonuga-Barke, Edmund J. S. 1998. Categorical models of childhood disorder: A conceptual and empirical analysis. *Journal of Child Psychology and Psychiatry* 39:115-33.

Steinberg, Lawrence. 2004. Risk taking in adolescence—What changes and why? *Annals of the New York Academy of Sciences* 1021:51-58.

Tremblay, Richard E. 2000. The development of aggressive behaviour during childhood: What have we learned in the past century? *International Journal of Behavioral Development* 24:129-41.

van den Oord, Edwin J. C. G., Andrew Pickles, and Irwin D. Waldman. 2003. Normal variation and abnormality: An empirical study of the liability distributions underlying depression and delinquency. *Journal of Child Psychology and Psychiatry* 44:180-92.

Viding, Essi. 2004. Annotation: Understanding the development of psychopathy. *Journal of Child Psychology and Psychiatry* 45:1329-37.

How Do We Study "What Happens Next"?

By
STEPHEN W.
RAUDENBUSH

Applications of group trajectory modeling summarize individual histories in a language that is broadly accessible to clinicians. This strength depends on the belief that a population consists, at least roughly, of a small number of subgroups whose members display similar records of behavior. In this view, the purpose of longitudinal research is to reveal the unfolding of essential differences between groups. The author offers an alternative view, in which historical records of personal behavior reflect a continuous interplay between individual action and environmental intervention. This interplay generates, for each participant, a myriad of potential trajectories. Rather than smoothing over this complexity with a small number of trajectory classes, the author proposes models that allow personal and environmental contributions to generate appropriate developmental complexity. The author illustrates this alternative approach using two examples: children's learning during the elementary years and effects of age and history on violent offending.

Keywords: longitudinal research, latent class models; hierarchical linear models

I've been cussed and discussed,
Talked to and talked about,
Lied to and lied about,
Held up and hung up
And doggone nigh murdered,
And the only reason I'm hangin' around here
    now
Is to see what in the heck is going to happen
    next.

—"Talking Hard Luck,"
New Lost City Ramblers, 1961, Vol 3.[1]

Stephen W. Raudenbush is the Lewis-Sebring Distinguished Service Professor, Department of Sociology and the College, University of Chicago. He develops, tests, and applies statistical methods for studying individual change and the effects of social settings such as schools and neighborhoods on change. He is further interested in methods for validly assessing social organization in neighborhoods, classrooms, and schools. In addition, he has coauthored a series of articles on experimental design in education and an authoritative book on analytic methods for multilevel data.

DOI: 10.1177/0002716205280900

Longitudinal research generates individual records of behavior. Longitudinal researchers summarize and compare these records with the aim of generalizing about how people change, why they change, and why people vary in their "trajectories," that is, in their personal summaries of recorded behavioral change. But records of observed behavior are artifacts of a flow of social action unfolding in continuous time: a person's actions generate social reactions, and social interventions trigger varied individual responses. Indeed, a key purpose of longitudinal research is to generate knowledge that can support effective social interventions. In essence, we want to know "What happens next?" Given a person's past behavior, what interventions does that person experience and how does that person respond?

Keeping in mind that behavioral trajectories reflect the interplay between environmental interventions and individual action, how do we understand the contribution of group-based trajectories as articulated by Daniel Nagin and summarized nicely in his article with Richard Tremblay (2005b [this volume]) titled "What Has Been Learned from Group-Based Trajectory Modeling? Examples from Physical Aggression and Other Problem Behaviors."

A key question emerging in this review is whether trajectory groups actually exist. If they do, then group-based trajectory modeling is clearly an ideal modeling approach. But if they do not, and if instead the notion of a finite set of trajectory groups represents an approximation to a more complex developmental reality, we must ask what insight is gained and also what is lost in this kind of approximation.

Emerging from this review is the conclusion that trajectory group analysis, in practice, has drawn attention to individual variation in development by evoking vivid typologies of great appeal to clinicians. What is lost is the notion of development as an ongoing interplay between individual action and social intervention. Given the great variation in personal predispositions, environmental interventions, and personal responses, such an interplay would presumably produce enormous variation in trajectories of behavior. This complexity would become ever more obvious as additional data are collected. In place of such a chaotic, transactional notion of development, trajectory group modeling, in practice, has encouraged a more static and lawful picture of development. In this view, additional time-series observations reveal ever more clearly the true underlying essence of group differences. These differences are presumably immanent in persons at the outset of the study, but a clear picture of them cannot emerge until enough experience has been accumulated to reveal the true type or group to which a person belongs. Such an image entails the belief that additional data will clarify the "true" membership of persons in trajectory-group classes rather than generating ever more varied trajectories of development.

The contrast between these two notions of development becomes clear when one considers how to study "what happens next." I shall use examples from studies of time-varying treatments in education and age and history effects in criminology to illustrate this contrast. These examples suggest that, at least for a substantial number of interesting persons, trajectory groups cannot be real and that the developmental reality that they might approximate must become ever more complex as time goes on. This limits the utility of the group trajectory approximation in studying "what happens next."

Some Benefits of Group Trajectory Modeling

As a quantitative methodologist, Dan Nagin is unusual in having immersed himself in some of the central problems of social science, as exemplified especially in his work with Richard Tremblay on the development of physical aggression in children and adolescents. He has carefully developed the method of group trajectory modeling to illuminate key developmental questions, incorporating the insights of his critics and colleagues in his methodology. His work thus serves as a model for methodological innovation in social science.

A key question emerging in this review is whether trajectory groups actually exist. . . . [I]f they do not, . . . we must ask what insight is gained and also what is lost in this kind of approximation.

A key strength in the applications of this method to date is that they summarize individual differences in ways that are broadly accessible to clinicians and researchers alike. It is not surprising that the language of trajectory group modeling maps directly to the language of practitioners. The modeling approach is retrospective; rather than using available observables to predict later observations, the approach allows types ("trajectory groups") to emerge from already collected data and then correlates group membership with prior covariates. This procedure is akin to clinical practice: the practitioner takes retrospective reports of behavior from patients and then classifies the patient for the purpose of treatment. Treatment decisions are generally discrete (to treat or not to treat; to treat with regime A versus regime B), so discrete classifications or typologies map nicely to treatment alternatives. While similar to clinical practice in this regard, group trajectory modeling is more sophisticated than clinical diagnosis in a key way: the approach quantifies uncertainty about the diagnoses by assigning posterior probabilities to membership in each group. For example, Nagin and Tremblay (1999) collected aggression data on youth from six to fifteen and discerned four groups: "low," "moderate declining," "high declining," and "chronic." Associated with each youth was a posterior probability of membership in each group. Thus, while treatment decisions for chronics would perhaps differ from treatment decisions for the other groups (those who are already declining or low in aggression), the approach appropriately attaches uncertainty to the designation of any youth as chronic, opening up a useful discussion of risks associated with treating a misclassified case.

The language of group trajectory modeling places a number of applications on a common footing by facilitating readily interpretable comparisons. For example, the fraction of chronics in different subpopulations or geographic areas is interesting. And the approach calls attention to small but important subgroups such as the chronics. The population prevalence and subsequent development of chronics is particularly salient in criminology because a comparatively small number of people commit a comparatively large fraction of crimes.

These benefits would seem to depend on the underlying assumption that distinct groups of essentially similar persons exist that differ substantially from other groups in ways that are relatively stable over historical time and space. Otherwise, estimating the population prevalence of the groups and comparing these prevalences over time and space would not be useful. Where does Nagin stand on the question of whether trajectory groups actually exist?

Do Trajectory Groups Exist?

In application, the trajectory groups are typically taken as real or as good approximations to truly distinctive subsets of persons. Thus, in comparing their approach to now-standard growth curve modeling, Nagin and Tremblay (2005b, 84) write, "Group-based trajectory modeling takes a qualitatively different approach to modeling individual differences. Rather than assuming that the population distribution of trajectories varies continuously across individuals, . . . it assumes that there may be clusters or groupings of distinctive developmental trajectories." Yet the authors also write, "One use of finite mixture models is to approximate a continuous distribution" (84).

If, however, the distribution of growth curves is truly continuous, there are no "distinctive" trajectories. So the question, "Do groups exist?" has evoked two quite different answers, apparently depending on the purpose of the application. However, a reading of important applications of the method to date indicates an adherence to the notion that the distinctive trajectories do indeed exist, and much of the appeal of the approach appears rooted in this assumption. The following claim from Nagin and Tremblay (2005b, 94) is typical in supporting the assertion that the "logic-in-use" of the method requires that groups are real: "The two largest trajectory groups . . . combined to account for 65.8 percent of the population" while the "high chronic group" is "6.6 percent" of the population.

Moreover, applications make the claim that formal statistical modeling strengthens our confidence in the validity of the group structure identified in a given study. Thus, we read that model fit tests can distinguish "real structural differences" between groups from random variation. Nagin and Tremblay (2005b, 101) assert, "Because the childhood and adolescent onset trajectories are the product of a formal statistical model, there is a firmer basis for their reality than if they had been constructed based on subjective classification rules."

In sum, although group membership can be used as an approximation to a continuous distribution, emerging from influential applications is the finding that groups so identified reflect real structural differences, that groups are distinctive, that group differences can be distinguished from random variation, and that because they are represented in a formal statistical model, there is a firm basis for making inferences about them. In short, groups exist.

However, when we read "Developmental Trajectory Groups: Fact or Fiction" (Nagin and Tremblay 2005a), an interesting methodological commentary as opposed an application, a very different picture emerges. Indeed, the authors identified "three major misconceptions" in the growing literature of applications of group-based trajectory analysis. The first misconception is "that individuals actually belong to a trajectory group." The authors cited the danger of such "reification" and asserted that "the risk of reification is particularly great when the groups are identified using a statistical model." The authors warned that "reification creates the impression of immutability." From this paper, it would appear that groups should not be regarded as real and that group-based modeling has as its sole purpose a statistical approximation to a more complex reality, and that the fact that formal statistical models are used to test for numbers and composition of groups, rather than "providing a firmer basis for making inferences about them," actually *increases* the risk of reification.

As this methodological paper (Nagin and Tremblay 2005a) noted, a major empirical problem emerges if one assumes that stable groups do exist and that formal statistical modeling can identify group membership. Under those conditions, predictions of future behavior would be highly accurate, and members of each group would exhibit the same or very similar future outcomes. In fact, predicting future violent behavior, for example, is difficult. The paper clarified for the nontechnical reader how the group-based methodology accounts for the apparently continuous (or at least semicontinuous) distribution of outcomes that social scientists tend to observe in practice:

1. Each person has a probability of being in each group.
2. Each group has a distinctive trajectory.
3. The expected trajectory for a given person is the sum of products of the probability of being in each group multiplied by the outcome implied by that group's trajectory.
4. Because the probabilities vary continuously over persons, the ensemble of expected outcomes is thus a comparatively smooth continuum, consistent with observable data.

The model does require that people belong to a finite number of groups, and it does require that every member of a group have exactly the same trajectory. Yet we know that future outcomes in social science typically display large variation, much larger than can be accounted by measurement error. This contradiction is resolved by a key feature of the model: group membership is uncertain, and this uncertainty generates the observable variation.

A key problem with this solution is that scientific uncertainty is required to account for human variation! Given a comparatively small number of groups, an increase in scientific knowledge would then require humans to display less variation than they do. Alternatively, under conditions of ever increasing scientific knowledge, the number of groups would have to grow virtually without bound to account for observable variation. But the supposition of an extremely large number of groups would rob the approach of the key source of its broad appeal, namely, the correspondence between the parsimonious typologies celebrated in the applications and the perspectives of clinicians who categorize patients to facilitate treatment decisions.

The scientific question that must be asked is whether the hypothetical existence of "latent" (that is, unobservable) groups helps make better predictions of future behavior than does a model that does *not* require such groups to exist. An alternative model might be a random effects model (Laird and Ware 1982; see review by Raudenbush 2001) also known as a "latent growth curve model" (see Singer and Willett 2003 for a review) or by a semicontinuous model (Olsen and Schafer 2001).

Perhaps we are better off assuming continuously varied growth a priori and therefore never tempting our audience to believe in the key misconception that groups of persons actually exist. We would then not have to warn them strongly against "reification" of the model they have been painstakingly convinced to adopt.

Why Are Groups Empirically Unstable?

Eggleston, Laub, and Sampson (2004) have found that as one collects more longitudinal data on criminal behavior and reestimates the group trajectory model, the numbers of groups and their composition change substantially. Their sample is a high-risk sample. Presumably, one would find greater stability in a sample representative of the larger population because many people in a normative sample could be relied upon never to commit a serious crime.[2] Presumably, a comparatively stable group of nonoffenders could then be identified. However, the high-risk sample is especially important in studying a central question in criminology— the timing and correlates of desistance from crime—and the question of whether group trajectory methods are helpful in this case has been contentious. Why are the number and composition of groups so unstable as more data are collected?

A simple explanation, and one that avoids the expletive, is that "shift happens." A high-risk boy's parents marry or get divorced; the family does or does not move to a new neighborhood or school that does or does not expose that boy to different kinds of peers. This boy commits a crime and does or does not get arrested, does or does not go to jail, does or does not get counseling. As an adult, this man does or does not get a good job or lose that job to downsizing, does or does not meet a powerful and loving woman, who, as Laub and Sampson (2003) documented, has the capacity of diverting her man from associating with past co-offenders. Such varied experiences presumably have the cumulative capacity to fragment a set of seemingly similar biographies into the apparently chaotic array of trajectories that social scientists actually observe when they look hard over time at behavior. In sum, what looks like a distinctive group at one point in time has the capacity to degenerate into a cacophony of personal histories as one continues to gather data.

Why are the number and composition of groups so unstable as more data are collected? A simple explanation, and one that avoids the expletive, is that "shift happens."

This capacity of "what happens next" to spoil an appealingly simple typology need not be a cause of social scientific despair. A key aim of social science is to subject "what happens next" to rational social control, helping, for example, to increase the likelihood of desistance from crime. The fact that society's big and little interventions have effects that complicate what we observe must be regarded as a good thing to anyone who pursues this aim. And "waiting around to find out what happens next" becomes a strong rationale for doing longitudinal research.

Development as revealed essence

In contrast, Nagin and Tremblay (2005a, 18) articulated a completely different rationale for longitudinal research: "The *raison d'etre* for continued data collection in prospective longitudinal studies is that the phenomenon under study has yet to unfold entirely. The uncertainties in trajectory group membership documented by Eggleston et al. (2004) give testimony to the importance of continued tracking and measurement until the phenomenon under study has fully unfolded."

So the purpose of data collection in this view is not to examine how the social world's myriad interventions deflect human behavior, but rather to reveal the essence of deep underlying group differences in development, that is, to progressively correct the misassignments of persons to groups made with more limited data.

This notion of new data "revealing the essence of group differences" is clear in Nagin and Tremblay's (2005a, 18) interpretation of their earlier (1999) comparison of group trajectory results from their study of boys from six to thirteen to the results of the analysis of the same boys after data are added for ages fourteen to fifteen:

> The only important difference between the two models is that, without the ages 14 and 15, the small chronic group has yet to emerge with sufficient clarity for statistical identification.

Development as chaos

In my view, more refined groups are not waiting to be revealed as we collect more data. Instead, life is a big interrupted time-series experiment with countless interventions creating countless potential branches of development. People do vary in important underlying ways that affect the environments to which they are exposed and that also affect their responses. But people also have capacity to learn from their varied experiences and to become agents of their own development. So the multiplicity of underlying predispositions combined with the multiplicity of interventions and responses creates trajectories that, while technically discrete, become uncountable and apparently chaotic, often well approximated by a continuous distribution. How, then, do we model "what happens next" in a way that allows for ever increasing cumulative variation in development over repeated observations?

How Do We Model "What Happens Next"?

To say that development is chaotic should not discourage us from formulating and testing explanatory models. Below, I draw on three examples to illustrate a modeling approach constructed from the interplay between underlying individual differences, time-varying interventions, and time-varying outcomes.

Value-added analysis in education

The educational career of an elementary school child illustrates in a familiar context the interplay between individual differences and time-varying interventions in generating developmental complexity. The outcome is reading achievement, measured on the same nearly continuous scale at the end of each school year. Children vary in their initial status at some initial time, L. They also vary in their expected learning rates given exposure to equally effective learning environments. This interpersonal variation is illustrated in Figure 1. For simplicity, child i's expected development, given "average" teachers, is described by a straight line plus random measurement error:

$$Y_{ti} = \pi_{0i} + \pi_{1i}(t - L) + e_{ti}.$$

FIGURE 1
SELECTION MODEL

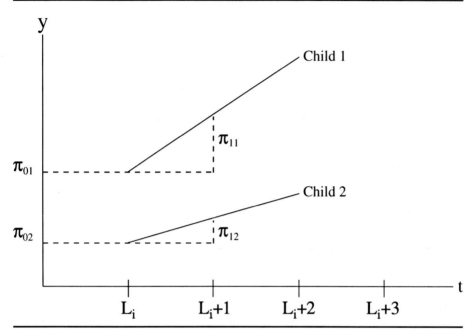

NOTE: π_{0i} = initial status of student i; π_{1i} = annual growth rate given "average" teachers. So π_{0i}, π_{1i} are governed by selection, not value added.

Here Y_{ti} is the reading achievement of child i at time t, π_{0i} is the "initial status" of that child (that is the status of the child at some time L designated as "initial"), and π_{1i} is the annual growth rate that child would experience if exposed to a sequence of "average" teachers. In Figure 1, we say that, as compared to child 2, child 1 has both a higher initial status ($\pi_{01} > \pi_{02}$) and a faster rate of growth ($\pi_{11} > \pi_{12}$) given average teachers.

However, children in fact experience teachers who differ uniquely from one another, as illustrated in Figure 2. Here child i experiences a better than average teacher in year $L + 1$, and that child's outcome is elevated by that teacher's "value added" of $\upsilon_1 > 0$ so that this child experiences growth $\pi_{1i} + \upsilon_1$ during year $L + 1$. In a similar vein, that child experiences an extremely good teacher in year $L + 2$ and a reasonably good teacher in year $L + 3$. The cumulative result of experiencing these good teachers is that, in Figure 2, child i is much more advanced in reading than would have been the case had that child experienced "average" teachers. Indeed, the cumulative benefit according to this very simple model is $\upsilon_1 + \upsilon_2 + \upsilon_3$.

In contrast, consider how the same child would have fared had that child experienced three straight ineffective teachers (Figure 3). Of course, all intermediate

FIGURE 2
VALUE-ADDED MODEL: AN EXAMPLE OF A FORTUNATE STUDENT

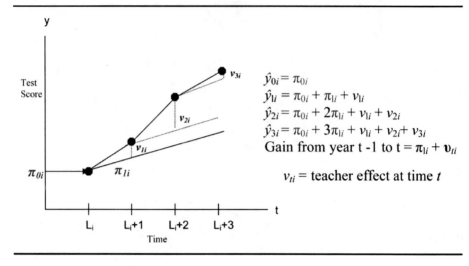

$\hat{y}_{0i} = \pi_{0i}$
$\hat{y}_{1i} = \pi_{0i} + \pi_{1i} + v_{1i}$
$\hat{y}_{2i} = \pi_{0i} + 2\pi_{1i} + v_{1i} + v_{2i}$
$\hat{y}_{3i} = \pi_{0i} + 3\pi_{1i} + v_{1i} + v_{2i} + v_{3i}$
Gain from year t −1 to t = $\pi_{1i} + \upsilon_{ti}$

v_{ti} = teacher effect at time t

FIGURE 3
VALUE-ADDED MODEL: AN EXAMPLE OF AN UNFORTUNATE STUDENT

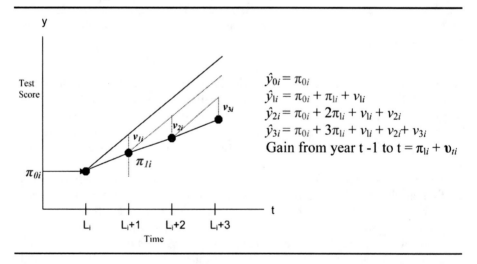

$\hat{y}_{0i} = \pi_{0i}$
$\hat{y}_{1i} = \pi_{0i} + \pi_{1i} + v_{1i}$
$\hat{y}_{2i} = \pi_{0i} + 2\pi_{1i} + v_{1i} + v_{2i}$
$\hat{y}_{3i} = \pi_{0i} + 3\pi_{1i} + v_{1i} + v_{2i} + v_{3i}$
Gain from year t −1 to t = $\pi_{1i} + \upsilon_{ti}$

possibilities could have arisen (e.g., one bad teacher, two good teachers), yielding, for any child, a very large number of potential trajectories over just three years of schooling.

Imposing prior probability distributions on individual differences π_{01}, π_{02} and teacher effects υ_t yields a remarkably parsimonious model that can generate, for any child, vast potential developmental variation over a few time points. The model can readily be made more complex as needed: characteristic growth can be nonlinear and effects of prior teachers can be allowed to decay over time (McCaffrey et al. 2004). Researchers have indeed found substantial variation in teacher effects (Wright, Horn, and Sanders 1997). These findings are not consistent with the notion that collecting data prospectively will reveal with increasing clarity a finite number of distinct trajectories.

Age and history in trajectories of offending

It is universally known in demography that a longitudinal study of a single cohort confounds age and history: "As I grow older, time marches on." Violent crime declined precipitously in Chicago and many other U.S. cities during the late 1990s, even as new cohorts of children were becoming adolescents, an age interval during which the propensity to commit violent crimes increases quite rapidly. How can we separate these two competing temporal trends, and what implication, if any, does this exercise have for trajectory modeling?

A research design that samples and follows multiple cohorts has potential to separate age and history effects under a key identifying assumption: that controlling measured covariates removes the effect of any compositional differences between the cohorts other than age and history. Let us accept this assumption without further elaboration to simplify key issues in trajectory modeling.

In 1995, the Project on Human Development in Chicago Neighborhoods (PHDCN) began collecting baseline data on about three thousand young people in four cohorts aged nine, twelve, fifteen, and eighteen. These young people were assessed again two years later when they were about eleven, fourteen, seventeen, and twenty. Figure 4a displays the fitted trajectories for violent offending for Hispanic males in each cohort, holding constant gender, immigration status, socioeconomic status, family structure, impulsivity, and cognitive skill (based on IQ and reading tests) (see Raudenbush, Johnson, and Sampson [2003] for details). The fitted trajectories for cohorts 9 and 12 were roughly consistent with past theory and research on the age-crime curve. Specifically, the expected propensity to offend increased substantially between nine and eleven and even more sharply between twelve and fourteen, just as expected in the age-crime literature. Contrary to past work on age and crime, however, cohort 15 displayed higher offending rates at age fifteen than at age seventeen. Moreover, the eighteen-year cohort experienced a very precipitous decline in violent offending between eighteen and twenty, much sooner than would be expected in light of past research. How can these seemingly anomalous findings be explained?

The within-subject trajectories of Figure 4a reflect the combined effects of age and history rather than pure effects of age. Under the assumption that demographic controls are adequate, the between-subject age-crime curve reflects only the effect of age. These between-subject age-crime curves are traced in Figure 4b.

FIGURE 4
(A) CHANGE IN THE PROBABILITY OF OFFENDING OF RESPONDENTS
BETWEEN WAVE 1 AND WAVE 2; (B) CHANGE IN THE PROBABILITY OF
OFFENDING OF RESPONDENTS BETWEEN WAVE 1 AND WAVE 2 WITH
CROSS-SECTIONAL AGE-CRIME CURVES SUPERIMPOSED FOR EACH WAVE

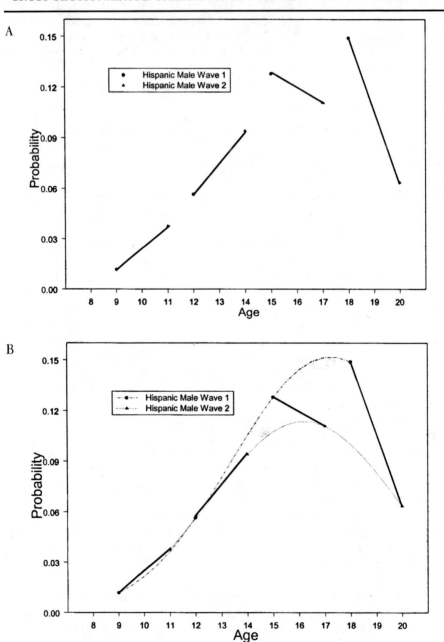

We see that the fitted between-subject age-crime curve in 1995 corresponds in shape to prior research on age and crime, as does the between-subject age-crime curve in 1997. However, the 1997 curve is globally displaced downward, consistent with the sharp drop in violent crime in Chicago over this time interval. Under the model assumptions, the vertical distance between the two age-crime curves at any age is the effect of history. The within-cohort trajectories result from the combined effects of age and history.

The central point in this sketch of PHDCN findings is not that key identifying assumptions or even the approach to measuring violent crime are correct. Rather, the exercise clarifies how a growth-curve model for multiple cohorts can, in principle, reconcile the combined effects of age and history on within-subject change. As in the case of value-added analysis in education, the interplay between age and historical events should, in theory, produce complexities in interpersonal trajectories that can only increase as cohorts and waves of data collection are added. The apparent solution is not to smooth over this complexity by imposing a small number of trajectory classes but rather to incorporate measured contributions of demography, age, and history in models that generate the appropriate developmental complexity.

Notes

1. Smithsonian Folkways Recordings, F2398. Used with permission.

2. A semicontinuous model (Olsen and Schafer 2001) or a zero-inflated Poisson regression model (Lambert 1992) might then be a useful alternative to either a group-based trajectory model or a random effects model. Trajectories would vary nearly continuously among a small high-risk group while a larger nonoffending group would not generate any serious crimes even over many waves of observation.

References

Eggleston, Elaine, John Laub, and Robert Sampson. 2004. Methodological sensitivities to latent class analysis of long-term criminal trajectories. *Journal of Quantitative Criminology* 20 (1): 1-42.

Laird, Nan, and James Ware. 1982. Random-effects models for longitudinal data. *Biometrika* 65 (1): 581-90.

Lambert, Diane. 1992. Zero-inflated Poisson regression, with an application to defects in manufacturing. *Technometrics* 34 (1): 1-14.

Laub, John H., and Robert J. Sampson. 2003. *Shared beginnings, divergent lives: Delinquent boys to age 70.* Cambridge, MA: Harvard University Press.

McCaffrey, Daniel F., J. R. Lockwood, Daniel Koretz, Thomas A. Louis, and Laura Hamilton. 2004. Models for value-added modeling of teacher effects. *Journal of Educational and Behavioral Statistics* 29 (1): 67-101.

Nagin, Daniel, and Richard Tremblay. 1999. Trajectories of boys' physical aggression, opposition, and hyperactivity on the path of the physically violent and non-violent juvenile delinquency. *Child Development* 70:1181-96.

———. 2005a. Developmental trajectory groups: Fact or fiction? Occasional paper distributed prior to the inaugural Albany Symposium on Crime and Justice, State University of New York at Albany.

———. 2005b. What has been learned from group-based trajectory modeling? Examples from physical aggression and other problem behaviors. *Annals of the American Academy of Political and Social Science* 602:82-117.

Olsen, Maren K., and Joseph L. Schafer. 2001. A two-part random-effects model for semicontinuous longitu-
    dinal data. *Journal of the American Statistical Association* 96 (454): 730-45.
Raudenbush, Stephen. 2001. Comparing personal trajectories and drawing causal inferences from longitudi-
    nal data. *Annual Review of Psychology* 52:501-25.
Raudenbush, Stephen, Christopher Johnson, and Robert Sampson. 2003. A multivariate, multilevel Rasch
    model for self-reported criminal behavior. *Sociological Methodology* 33 (1): 169-211.
Singer, Judith D., and John B. Willett. 2003. *Applied longitudinal data analysis: Modeling change and event
    occurrence.* New York: Oxford University Press.
Wright, S. Paul, Sandra Horn, and William Sanders. 1997. Teacher and classroom context effects on student
    achievement: Implications for teacher evaluation. *Journal of Personnel Evaluation in Education* 11:57-67.

RESPONSE

Further Reflections on Modeling and Analyzing Developmental Trajectories: A Response to Maughan and Raudenbush

By

DANIEL S. NAGIN
and
RICHARD E. TREMBLAY

In this article, the authors respond to the Raudenbush and Maughan commentaries elsewhere in this volume. Stephen Raudenbush's principal criticism of the group-based trajectory model is that it reifies the idea that people follow a small number of immutable trajectories of behavior. This criticism reflects a fundamental misunderstanding of the statistical role of trajectory groups. Trajectory groups describe the trajectory of behavior that has actually occurred; that behavior is not reified but real. There is nothing in a trajectory group model that asserts the behavior pattern is permanent, that no intervention can change it, or that it will continue beyond the time period of the observed data. The question of whether a group-based trajectory model or a hierarchal linear model can provide a better statistical representation of change is an empirical rather than philosophic question. The answer will undoubtedly be context-specific. Barbara Maughan's comments were cast as reflections from a developmental psychopathology perspective. The authors are in complete agreement with Maughan's observations about the importance of using diverse methods in studying developmental psychopathology and of unpacking the developmental trajectories of the constituent components of antisocial behavior. The authors would only add that the developmental origins of these behaviors should be studies from as early in life as possible.

Introduction

We want to begin by thanking Barbara Maughan and Steven Raudenbush for taking the time from their busy schedules to prepare commentaries on our work. That they would do this is in itself a great compliment.

The focus of the Maughan commentary (2005 [this volume]) is substantive. She offers insightful observations on the implications of our ongoing research program on the developmental origins

NOTE: We thank Ray Paternoster, Paul Rosenbaum, and Lowell Taylor for their comments and insights. The research reported in this article has been supported by the National Science Foundation (NSF; SES-99113700), the National Institute of Mental Health (RO1 MH65611-01A2), Québec's CQRS and FCAR funding agencies, Canada's NHRDP and SSHRC funding agencies, and the Molson Foundation.

DOI: 10.1177/0002716205281232

of physical aggression on several long-standing issues in developmental psychopathology. The Raudenbush commentary (2005 [this volume]), on the other hand, focuses on the methodology—group-based trajectory modeling—that has supported much of our research on physical aggression. Because of this fundamental difference in focus, we address these commentaries separately.

Response to Raudenbush Commentary

Critical commentary on a statistical methodology typically focuses on how and why the methodology results in faulty statistical inferences. Thus, we are heartened that a methodologist of Steve Raudenbush's stature took no exception to the substantive conclusions that have been obtained with group-based trajectory modeling. We are also gratified by his view that the method has illuminated key developmental questions. Combined with Barbara Maughan's praise for the substantive contributions that have emerged from the method's application, we are pleased by the conclusion of two leading scholars, one versed in development and the other in methodology, that our decade-long collaboration has made a difference.

Raudenbush's principal criticism seems to be philosophical, namely, that the costs of using trajectory groups to approximate a more complex underlying reality generally exceed the benefits. We disagree with Raudenbush's framing of the criticism. Bertrand Russell (quoted in Auden and Kronenberger 1966) once observed, "Although this may seem a paradox, all exact science is dominated by the idea of approximation." We agree. For our purposes here, we reframe Russell's observation as, "All statistical models involve approximation." The issue of approximation error is properly framed in comparative, not absolute, terms: how do the costs and benefits of alternative approximations comparatively stack up against one another? The Raudenbush critique focuses exclusively on his perceptions of the shortcomings of group-based trajectory modeling. As we discuss below, however, the issues he raises apply to all statistical methods, including hierarchal linear modeling (HLM).

Raudenbush has played an influential role in developing and applying HLM. Indeed, his contributions to its advancement are properly described as seminal. Not surprisingly, he advocates the virtues of HLM for studying development. Our article in this volume, as well as Nagin's writings elsewhere (Nagin 2005), lay out the key distinction between growth curve modeling in the HLM tradition and group-based trajectory modeling. This distinction turns on the issue of how to model differences across individuals in their developmental trajectories. No validated theory in the social or behavioral sciences proscribes the exact parametric form of the distribution of developmental trajectories across population members. Instead the distribution must be approximated. Following in a long tradition in nonparametric and semiparametric statistics, the group-based trajectory approach adopts the modeling strategy of approximating this unknown distribution by a finite number of points of support (aka trajectory groups). In contrast, HLM assumes that the population distribution of trajectories can reasonably be approximated by parameters drawn from a specific continuous distribution function, usually the multivariate normal.

Which is a better approach to modeling population differences in the course of development? It is our position that there is no unequivocal answer to this question. The answer to which method is preferable will depend upon the specific problem setting and on matters of taste concerning the most effective way of communicating statistical findings. Indeed, in the article that appears in this volume, the closing message of the section on guidelines for choosing between the two methods expressly states, "Laying out guidelines for the use of alternative statistical methods is a precarious exercise. Users naturally desire bright line distinctions. Yet bright line distinctions are generally not possible" (Nagin and Tremblay 2005, 112). Thus, we believe that in choosing between these two methods, users must make choices based on their strengths and vulnerabilities relative to the problem they are analyzing.

Raudenbush, however, argues that the HLM that he outlines in the closing section of his commentary is a better statistical approach to modeling change than group-based trajectory modeling. This conclusion seems to be based on the premise that the group-based approach has several important vulnerabilities that are not shared by the HLM approach. The logic of his argument seems to be that (1) the group-based model requires every member of a group to have exactly the same trajectory, (2) trajectory groups are empirically unstable, and (3) a finite number of groups "waiting to be revealed as we collect more data" cannot possibly explain the diversity of developmental paths present in the data. The essence of our response to Raudenbush on these issues is as follows: trajectory groups describe the trajectory of behavior that has actually occurred; that behavior is not reified but real. There is nothing in a trajectory group model that asserts the behavior pattern is permanent, that no intervention can change it, or that it will continue beyond the time period of the observed data.

Concerning the first argument, Raudenbush (2005) states,

> [The model] requires that every member of a group has exactly the same trajectory. . . . A key problem with this solution is that scientific uncertainty is required to account for human variation! Given a comparatively small number of groups, an increase in scientific knowledge would then require humans to display less variation than they do. (p. 136)

The statement that the model requires every member of a trajectory group to follow exactly the same trajectory misrepresents the model and is no more true than the statement that in the HLM framework all individuals follow their trajectories in lockstep. In both models the trajectory parameters describe trajectories *on average* (i.e., in expectation). The structure of both types of models allow for random variation around this average according to some assumed random variable such as the Poisson function. Raudenbush is correct in stating that in the group-based model such individual variation is centered on a finite number of groups. Consequently, the model is only an approximation of a more complex underlying reality. However, simulations studies reported in Brame, Nagin, and Wasserman (forthcoming) and Nagin (2005) suggest that the approximation error is small. As we have already noted, the HLM framework is also an approximation. The Raudenbush commentary is silent on HLM's approximation error relative to this same, more complex reality.

The Raudenbush commentary also describes the trajectory groups as empirically unstable. Here, he is referring to a study by Eggleston, Laub, and Sampson (2004) that examined the effect on the shapes and sizes of trajectory groups of adding successively more time periods of longitudinal data. Specifically, using the Gluecks' (Glueck and Glueck 1950) data for which they have arrest records on individuals from ages seven to seventy, Eggleston and colleagues estimated a series of group-based trajectory models in which the trajectories extended over ever longer periods of time. In a response, Nagin (2004) pointed out the changes in sizes and shapes of trajectory groups were not surprising because all statistical models are characterizations of collected data, not of yet-to-be collected data. Nagin's commentary also pointed out that the Eggleston, Laub, and Sampson analysis was a demonstration of the vulnerabilities associated with extrapolating a model outside of the range of data upon which it is estimated. This vulnerability is not unique to group-based trajectory models but generic to all statistical methods. Had HLM been applied to these same data measured over successively longer periods of time, equivalent instabilities would have been observed. Specifically, as more periods of data were added, the parameters describing both the population and individual-level trajectories would have changed in ways that were statistically equivalent to the changes that were observed with the group-based model. One difference, however, might be that the changes would have been less apparent within an HLM-based model. We do not count this as a benefit: in statistics at least, transparency is a virtue, not a vice.

Finally, the Raudenbush commentary argues that a finite number of groups "waiting to be revealed as we collect more data" cannot possibly explain the diversity of developmental paths present in the data. This argument is encapsulated in the title of the commentary: "How Do We Study 'What Happens Next'?" We disagree with his position for at least three reasons. First, the description of trajectory groups as paths "waiting to be revealed" is a caricature of the statistical role of trajectory groups. As we have repeatedly emphasized, the trajectory groups are a device for approximating the distribution of trajectories that *have* happened, not that *will* happen. The group-based trajectories are no more paths waiting to be revealed or, as Raudenbush also asserts, "immanent in persons at the outset of the study" than are the individual-level trajectories based on random effects that underlay HLM. They are simply summaries of data already collected—just like the trajectories of HLM. Second, the Raudenbush argument seems to be implying that covariates, such as marital status or participation in therapeutic interventions, cannot be embedded in group-based trajectory models. This is incorrect; see, for example, chapter 7 of Nagin (2005) or Nagin et al. (2003). Even more important, Haviland and Nagin (forthcoming) described an approach based on group-based trajectory modeling for making more confident inferences about the causal effect of turning point events and interventions in observational data. One of the great advantages of this approach is that it provides trajectory-group-specific estimates of the treatment effect in addition to the population average treatment effect. In so doing, the approach allows the magnitude of the causal effect estimate to vary as a function of developmental history. A firmer statistical basis for making valid causal inference is surely central to modeling "what happens next." Third, we point out that the question of what modeling strategy will best predict "what happens next" is an empirical question. The Raudenbush commentary simply asserts that HLM will predict better than the group-based model. This conclusion does not follow from the structure of the models as suggested by the commentary, and the commentary provides no empirical evidence in support of this assertion. Our own prediction is that the outcome of such an empirical test will depend on the problem context and be heavily affected by the specification of both types of models.

[N]othing in a trajectory group model . . .
asserts the behavior pattern is permanent,
that no intervention can change it,
or that it will continue beyond
the time period of the observed data.

We earlier stated that transparency is a virtue, not a vice. A model should be faithful to the observed data, but it should also aid understanding; it must be judged by both an empirical and a cognitive standard. Does the model fit the data? Does the model clarify the data? Raudenbush claims that HLMs are empirically better than trajectory groups but—surprisingly given that this is an empirical claim—he offers no evidence in support of this claim. He does not claim that HLMs provide greater clarity, and we think they do not. Organizing data according to trajectory groups has several important transparency virtues. These virtues are not limited to clinicians and practitioners as suggested by the commentary but also extend to researchers. As we note in the conclusion of our article in this volume (Nagin and Tremblay 2005), the abundance of data in modern longitudinal studies is accompanied by a difficult companion—complexity. Trajectory groups are powerful devices for organizing this complexity. They suggest that people have exhibited one of a few types of internally consistent behavior, they identify those types of behavior, and they group the study subjects by the types of behavior they exhibit. Such a typography facilitates understanding, and what is better understood is more open to critical discussion, to correction when in error, and to further elaboration.

One could, for instance, send an ethnographer out to meet a few members of each group and to construct a narrative account of the experiences of these individuals, thereby providing a qualitative expansion and check on a quantitative model. In a different but related context, Rosenbaum and Silber (2001) did something along these lines. Nothing comparable is facilitated by HLMs.

We earlier observed that trajectory groups describe the trajectory of behavior that has actually occurred; that behavior is not reified but real. We now add that this is also true of HLMs. We also observed that nothing in a trajectory group model asserts the behavior pattern is permanent, that no intervention can change it, or that it will continue beyond the time period of the observed data. Again, this is also true of HLMs. For these reasons, we close by repeating an earlier admonition. We do not advocate the primacy of group-based statistical modeling compared to HLM. We also caution readers against accepting arguments for the primacy of any other statistical method including HLM. The complexity of studying developmental trajectories is too great to be left to any one statistical method.

Response to Maughan Commentary

Barbara Maughan's comments on our article were cast as reflections from a developmental psychopathology perspective. These reflections are particularly useful for the community of developmental criminologists because in many ways developmental criminology and developmental psychopathology are inquiries into the same behavioral phenomenon but from a different intellectual tradition. The framing of research questions is often affected by the professional discipline the analysis is attempting to inform. Developmental criminologists are responding to justice systems' classifications of what constitutes criminal behavior, whereas developmental psychopathologists attempt to inform the mental health systems' classifications of healthy and sick individuals.

We agree with most of Maughan's comments and use them here as an opportunity to reflect further on the sorts of research questions that will help us better understand human development. We have already argued for the importance of methodological diversity in the study of developmental trajectories. Thus, readers should not be surprised that we are in complete agreement with her conclusion that the preferred way of dealing with the issue of categorical and dimensional models of behavior is to test both approaches with specific problems. In most cases, different methods with a shared core logic, such as group-based trajectory modeling and HLM, will lead to the same conclusion. When results differ, researchers should pause and try to ascertain what they imply about the strengths and weakness of the alternative methods.

Maughan's commentary also has important implications for the question, "What is antisocial behavior?" We especially agree with her comments concerning the importance of unpacking the concept of antisocial behavior. The evidence she cites of the differing developmental trajectories of aggressive conduct disorder, nonaggressive conduct disorder, and opposition nicely illustrate our admonition that the terms "criminal" and "antisocial" behavior comprise very diverse behaviors that may have very different developmental trajectories.

If understanding development is important for understanding causes, then one important task of longitudinal research is to trace the development of each type of antisocial and criminal behavior. The task is not an easy one. First, as just noted, there are numerous forms of antisocial behaviors. Second, as we have shown (Tremblay et al. 2004), the developmental precursors of behaviors that have come to be called criminal often start early in life. Furthermore, as Laub and Sampson (2003) have shown, these behaviors can continue until old age. By piecing together a patchwork of results from different longitudinal studies, we can get an idea of the general trends from womb to tomb (see Tremblay 2003b).

As illustrated by Nagin (2004, 2005), trajectories can change substantially as data points are added. This is true not only for data that trace development forward into life but also for data tracing behavior back over the earliest stages of life. Thus, we were gratified by Maughan's praise for our efforts to trace back into the life course the onset of physical aggression. The pursuit of this empirical question led us to the startling conclusion that the onset of physical aggression often coincides with the physical capacity to aggress and the availability of an appropriate target. For twins, these two events may indeed occur very early in life—prior to birth in the close confines of the mother's womb.

We believe that our work on the development of physical aggression is an object lesson in the power of description, a much maligned activity in modern research. Simple descriptions can speak volumes about the viability of causal hypotheses. As the Maughan commentary points out, the finding that physical aggression starts in infancy and peaks during toddlerhood runs counter to the hypotheses that the onset of physical aggression is caused by violence in the media, by peer relations during the school years, or by puberty. Such "causal" factors may sustain the behavior or increase its frequency, but it cannot be claimed that it causes the onset.

Maughan asks whether other forms of childhood antisocial behavior follow similar age trends as physical aggression. The data she presents in Figure 1 suggests that antisocial behaviors that are nonaggressive follow a different pattern. These behaviors include damage to property, deceitfulness and theft, and violation of rules (e.g., staying out late, running away, and truancy from school). The rationale that led to the aggregation of the nonaggressive behaviors is probably that they do not involve physically aggressing another human being. However, this does not imply that each of the behaviors that make up nonaggressive conduct disorder all develop in the same way. Validation of the assumption of a common developmental trend requires descriptive data from early childhood onward.

For example, some of the nonaggressive behaviors involve rule violations such as staying out late or truancy. Such behaviors are clearly age-contingent and cannot be manifested until early adolescence. However, it still may be a mistake to think of their "adolescent onset" outside of a longer developmental perspective. While preschool children cannot be truant, stay out late, or run away from home, they often run away from their parents or the day care staff and do things they very well know they should not do. Another example is theft. While we do not know of good developmental data on theft during early childhood, observational studies of conflicts among preschool children starting in infancy show that most physically aggressive interactions are linked to fights for objects. Children spontaneously take the property of others, and those who are in possession of the property will defend it with all their strength. We need to understand the developmental linkage between the forceful taking of property by toddlers and analogous behaviors by adolescents and adults called theft and robbery. It is a mistake for science and public policy to assume that the "onset" of the latter types of legally prohibited behaviors has no connection to the onset of the former categories of behaviors that some would argue are only inconsequential reflections: "children being children."

To understand the development of antisocial behaviors, we need to rethink what we mean by oppositional, antisocial, delinquent, and criminal behaviors (see Tremblay 2003b). To aid in the rethinking of these concepts, it will be helpful to have descriptive data on the development of each of the behaviors that are presumed to be "antisocial." From a developmental perspective, behaviors should be aggregated only if they have the same developmental trajectories. Once we know the development of the antisocial behaviors, then we can start looking at the development of other correlates such as hyperactivity and callousness toward others to create subcategories of antisocial development. Up to now, we have been debating categories of antisocial behavior based on data at only one or two points in time.

We also agree with Maughan's suggestion that to understand variation over age in antisocial behavior we need to study other aspects of individual development and social context that co-occur with observed changes in antisocial behavior. It is our position, however, that these variables should not displace age as the main covariate. The four covariates proposed by Maughan (social experience, duration of exposure to environmental risks, changes in cognitive level, and variations in biological maturity) need to be studied with reference to age, not instead of age. Time is a defining feature of human life rather than an outcome of development. Furthermore, similar to race and sex, it is not a variable that can be manipulated. Indeed, because race and sex are the outcomes of genes, in principal they can be manipulated, whereas the passing of time is totally beyond human control.

The four variables suggested by Maughan all vary with age because they depend on age. To sort out whether they are causes or consequences of antisocial behavior, we need to study them with reference to age. Unless an experimental approach is used to control for the development of all pertinent dimensions in the years that preceded the start of the study, studies that aim to understand the causes of any behavior from a developmental perspective need to start as close as possible to conception. For example, the effects of puberty and testosterone shown in Maughan's Figure 2 could be the consequence of the effect of preschool antisocial behavior on pubertal development. We could even hypothesize that in utero testosterone affected brain development, which in turn affected self-control during the preschool years, and which in its turn affected pubertal development.

In short, to "unpack" age, we must have a long-term developmental perspective for each of the dimensions we are examining. We need joint developmental trajectories from a correlational perspective to describe development, but we also need experiments to test causal hypotheses. It is clear that both developmental criminology and developmental psychopathology are far from this ideal. Most studies have focused on adolescents or elementary-school-aged children.

---

*In short, to "unpack" age, we must have
a long-term developmental perspective for
each of the dimensions we are examining.*

We end with the following parable, adapted from Tremblay (2003a), to describe one of the main problems with the methodology used by developmental criminologists and psychopathologists to understand, what they appear to believe is the "whole" *life-course* development of antisocial behavior.

Once upon a time there was a big debate among Swiss geographers concerning the topography of the United States as one travels from the West Coast to the East Coast. They decided to send their best members to measure exactly the ups and downs, as one travels different routes, from the West Coast to the East Coast of the United States.

Now, it would take too much time to explain why, but their flight from Geneva to San Francisco was diverted to Denver. They had a long discussion whether they should try to get to San Francisco to start their survey, or start from Denver. For reasons of time and cost they decided to start from Denver. They reasoned that the distance from San Francisco to Denver was only a small part of the total distance from the Pacific to the Atlantic. After a few years of hard work, they came back to the Geography Academy in Switzerland. They described the mountains, the valleys, and the plains one had to travel depending on which road was taken from Denver to the Atlantic.

It looked very much like the results of trajectory analyses presented in the articles in this issue of *The Annals*. It was shown that some routes had to go up over many mountains, others had only a few ups and downs, and still others had almost none. But there were two clear conclusions: first, all roads have to come down to get to sea level; second, it was crystal clear that there were no mountains in the United States that were half as high as those in Switzerland!

This parable reminds us that if we start at age seven to study the life-course development of physical attacks against others (violent crimes), or study taking things away from others (property crimes), we are in Denver standing with our back to the Rocky Mountains and the Great Divide. Criminologists and psychopathologists need to take the early years seriously.

References

Auden, W. H., and L. Kronenberger, *The Viking book of aphorisms*. New York: Viking.

Brame, Richard, Daniel S. Nagin, and Larry Wasserman. Forthcoming. Exploring some analytical character-istics of finite mixture models. *Journal of Quantitative Criminology*.

Eggleston, Elaine P., John H. Laub, and Robert J. Sampson. 2004. Methodological sensitivities to latent class analysis of long-term criminal trajectories. *Journal of Quantitative Criminology* 20:1-26.

Glueck, Sheldon, and Eleanor Glueck. 1950. *Unraveling juvenile delinquency*. New York: Commonwealth Fund.

Haviland, Amelia, and Daniel S. Nagin. Forthcoming. Causal inference with group-based trajectory models. *Psychometrika*.

Laub, John H., and Robert J. Sampson. 2003. *Shared beginnings, divergent lives: Delinquent boys to age 70*. Cambridge, MA: Harvard University Press.

Maughan, Barbara. 2005. Developmental trajectory modeling: A view from developmental psychopathology. *Annals of the American Academy of Political and Social Science* 602:118-30.

Nagin, Daniel S. 2004. Response to "Methodological sensitivities to latent class analysis of long-term criminal trajectories." *Journal of Quantitative Criminology* 20:27-35.

———. 2005. *Group-based modeling of development*. Cambridge, MA: Harvard University Press.

Nagin, Daniel S., Linda S. Pagani, Richard E. Tremblay, and Frank Vitaro. 2003. Life course turning points: The effect of grade retention on physical aggression. *Development and Psychopathology* 15:343-61.

Nagin, Daniel S., and Richard E. Tremblay. 2005. What has been learned from group-based trajectory mod-eling? Examples from physical aggression and other problem behaviors. *Annals of the American Acad-emy of Political and Social Science* 602:82-117.

Raudenbush, Stephen W. 2005. How do we study "what happens next"? *Annals of the American Academy of Political and Social Science* 602:131-44.

Rosenbaum, Paul R., and Jeffrey H. Silber. 2001. Matching and thick description in an observational study of mortality after surgery. *Biostatistics* 2:217-32.

Tremblay, Richard. E. 2003a. Age, crime, and human development: Looking for the highest peaks with our back to the Rockies. Paper presented at the Presidential Plenary, ASC annual meeting, Denver, CO.

———. 2003b. Why socialization fails? The case of chronic physical aggression. In *Causes of conduct disor-der and juvenile delinquency*, ed. B. B. Lahey, T. E. Moffitt, and A. Caspi, 182-224. New York: Guilford.

Tremblay, Richard E., Daniel S. Nagin, Jean R. Séguin, Mark Zoccolillo, Philip D. Zelazo, Michel Boivin, Daniel Perusse, and Chista Japel. 2004. Physical aggression during early childhood: Trajectories and pre-dictors. *Pediatrics* 114:e43-e50.

SECTION THREE

Multiple Patterns
of Offending

Explaining Multiple Patterns of Offending across the Life Course and across Generations

By
TERENCE P. THORNBERRY

Four general topics are discussed in this article. The first section uses data from the Rochester Youth Development Study to explore the development of antisocial careers across the life course. The second section presents interactional theory's explanation of offending. The theory recognizes that antisocial careers can begin at any point, from childhood through adulthood, and identifies causal influences associated with varying ages of onset. It then offers an explanation for changing patterns of offending. The third section presents an intergenerational extension of the theory, focusing specifically on the major pathways that mediate the impact of a parent's own adolescent antisocial behavior on the chances that his or her children will also show antisocial behavior. The final section tests key parts of this intergenerational theory using data from the Rochester Intergenerational Study. Adolescent antisocial behavior has indirect effects on a child's early delinquency, mediated by the disruption it causes to the parent's development and his or her subsequent style of parenting.

Keywords: interactional theory; onset; persistence; desistance; late bloomers; Rochester Youth Development Study; Rochester Intergenerational Study

The advent of developmental, life-course theories of delinquency is perhaps the most important advance in theoretical criminology during the latter part of the twentieth century.

Terence P. Thornberry is director of the Research Program on Problem Behavior at the Institute of Behavioral Science and a professor of sociology at the University of Colorado. He is also the principal investigator of the Rochester Youth Development Study, an ongoing panel study begun in 1986 to examine causes and consequences of delinquency and other forms of antisocial behavior. He is an author or editor of ten books, including Taking Stock of Delinquency: An Overview of Findings from Contemporary Longitudinal Studies *and* Gangs and Delinquency in Developmental Perspective. *The latter received the American Society of Criminology's Michael J. Hindelang Award for Most Outstanding Contribution to Research in Criminology in 2003. His research interests focus on understanding the development of delinquency and crime over the life course.*

DOI: 10.1177/0002716205280641

Driven in part by the empirical insights of descriptive longitudinal studies, in part by theoretical dissatisfaction with traditional models, and in part by a burgeoning interdisciplinary approach to the study of crime and delinquency, developmental models have greatly expanded the reach of our understanding of crime and delinquency. While traditional theories typically focused on behaviors occurring in adolescence and early adulthood, developmental models cover the full life course, from infancy to old age. An earlier preoccupation with the causes of delinquency has been replaced with a lively consideration of both the causes and consequences of offending and of how delinquency is interwoven with human development. Even the parameters of delinquent behavior to be explained have changed, from a simple consideration of prevalence (who does it) and frequency (how much do they do) to a consideration of onset, duration, escalation, desistance, and other aspects of delinquent careers.

In addressing these issues, developmental criminology presents a broad, generative research agenda, and, especially in light of its relative youthfulness, it is hardly surprising that developmental criminology has generated its own discontents. Indeed, there is currently considerable debate about such issues as the value of ontogenetic versus sociogenetic perspectives, taxonomic versus general theories, and monothematic versus integrated models. There is also disagreement about whether to restrict the outcome to only criminal behavior or to focus on a broader concept of antisocial behavior that includes delinquency, crime, and analogous behaviors. How these issues are resolved is likely to shape the field of developmental criminology for the foreseeable future.

In the remainder of this article, I would like to address some of these issues and to expand the reach of developmental models from the perspective of interactional theory. With respect to the first topic, I will identify what I think are some of the core issues that all life-course models should address and then present interactional theory's approach to them. With respect to the second topic, I will begin to incorporate an understanding of intergenerational influences into the explanation of antisocial behavior.

Core Issues

As is true of all theories, developmental theories of delinquency are designed to explain a variety of aspects of the phenomenon of interest. Some of these aspects are central, that is, the theory has to offer an explanation for them; others are more peripheral, adding to the scope of the theory. To my mind, the most central aspects that developmental theories should explain involve patterns of onset, course, and desistance.

NOTE: I would like to thank Shawn Bushway, David Huizinga, and Daniel Nagin for helpful comments on this article.

Onset of offending

Onset, of course, involves the fundamental question of etiology: why do only some members of a population engage in delinquent and criminal behavior? Obviously, any theory of delinquency has to offer a clear, compelling explanation of onset in this sense.

I view the trajectory method as a convenient way of describing a more complex phenomenon by dividing it into smaller descriptive units.

Developmental theories have an additional challenge though, namely, to account for the age of onset of offending. Longitudinal studies demonstrate that age of onset is distributed over a substantial portion of the early stages of the life course, from toddlerhood (Tremblay et al. 2004) to early adulthood (Eggleston and Laub 2002). Developmental theories need, first, to offer a conceptualization of age of onset, how variable it is, and whether its variability is discrete or continuous. However conceived, they need, second, to offer an explanation for why people begin to offend when they do. That is, what are the causal processes that will lead one person to initiate delinquent activity at age eight and another at age sixteen? Do these causal factors differ only in magnitude, are there different causal factors at play at different developmental stages, or are both of these processes at play?

Course

Those who offend do so at different levels. Some dabble or experiment in offending, committing relatively few offenses over relatively short periods. Others become persistent, chronic offenders, continuing to offend over long portions of their life. And potentially, there is a dizzying array of other patterns—for example, intermittent involvement—between these extremes. A developmental model should include a conceptualization of the course of offending with respect to such questions as whether there is a tight or loose association between age of onset and the length of criminal careers and whether that association is discrete or continuously distributed.

Analytically, two causal issues are raised. The first is simply to account for persistence. What are the processes that maintain offending for some offenders and lead some offenders to escalate in terms of frequency and seriousness? The second concerns a causal explanation of the association between age of onset and the persistence of offending. In particular, given the generally observed negative correlation between these variables (Krohn et al. 2001), why are offenders who start early somewhat more likely to persist longer?

Desistance

Most offenders cease to offend at some point in their life course. Developmental theories should include an explanation of the social and psychological processes that lead to desistance. In addressing this topic, there should be an explicit consideration of whether desistance occurs suddenly, as in the notion of "cease and desist," or whether it unfolds as a more gradual developmental process. Second, developmental theories should address whether the causes of desistance are simply the reverse of those associated with onset, a different set of influences entirely, or some combination of these influences. Developmental models should also explain the link between age of onset and both the likelihood and timing of desistance.

Although there are obviously other questions that a developmental theory of delinquency can address, I view these as the core ones from which the others derive. In the following sections, I discuss how interactional theory attends to each of them. I begin with a discussion of more descriptive or epidemiological hypotheses, for example, how onset is distributed and the expected strength of the association between onset and persistence. Following that, I turn to more substantive hypotheses about the causal processes associated with onset, course, and desistance.

Epidemiological Hypotheses

Interactional theory is designed to explain involvement in general antisocial behavior and delinquency. Tolan, Guerra, and Kendall (1995, 515) defined antisocial behavior as "a spectrum of behavior usually marked by aggression but representing transgressions against societal norms. . . . Antisocial behavior can range from relatively innocuous but obnoxious behavior such as tantrums and oppositional behavior to the most socially and criminally offensive acts." The manifestations of antisocial behavior vary over the life course (Patterson 1993), and during childhood and adolescence they center on delinquency and substance use.

Onset

Based on this definition, interactional theory offers the following expectations about onset. First, offending is relatively commonplace; that is, a substantial majority of the population will be involved in antisocial behavior. Second, although some involvement in offending is common, relatively few offenders will have extensive criminal careers. Extensiveness includes such dimensions as frequency, duration, seriousness, and, especially, the co-occurrence of these dimensions. Few offenders will be persistently and frequently involved in serious offenses.

Third, onset is continuously distributed across the age distribution, from child-hood at least through early adulthood. Offending can start earlier or later, but onset is not divided into neat patterns of "early starters" and "late starters" as hypothe-sized by taxonomic theories (Moffitt 1993; Patterson, Capaldi, and Bank 1991).

Fourth, this conception of onset introduces an important pattern of behavioral change: late bloomers or late onset. The life-course concept of "off-time" transi-tions (Elder 1997) applies to offending trajectories as it does to other life-course trajectories. Thus, precocious, age-normative, and late onset are all possible—indeed, expected.

Course

Those who initiate offending can experience a wide range of different careers during their period of active involvement. Some careers will be of short duration, almost of an episodic nature, while others will be quite persistent. Some persistent careers will involve high-frequency offending, others low-level sporadic offending. Yet other careers will be intermittent. Put differently, offending patterns do not emerge in a uniform pattern, unfolding in a similar shape over the life course as implied by ontogenetic models (e.g., Gottfredson and Hirschi 1990). Interactional theory is a sociogenetic model of human development in which the human organism always remains open and responsive to changing social environments (Dannefer 1984).

Although the course of offending careers takes on varying shapes, these patterns are not random. There are systematic linkages among aspects of careers. For exam-ple, age of onset and persistence are inversely correlated, and those who start ear-lier are likely to offend longer. Given its sociogenetic underpinnings, however, interactional theory hypothesizes that the magnitude of this association is, at best, moderate and that "these two dimensions of antisocial careers are to a substantial degree independent" (Thornberry and Krohn 2001, 302). This hypothesis, too, is different from ontogenetic models where early starters become life-course persis-tent offenders and late starters are adolescence-limited (Moffitt 1993; Patterson, Capaldi, and Bank 1991). Our view is quite different: onset is not destiny. Regard-less of when one starts, careers can take on different lengths and shapes, depending on later aspects of life-course development.

Desistance

Finally, most offenders desist, that is, change their behavior from some active involvement in offending to a zero or near-zero rate that persists across time. While someone who commits one or two offenses and then stops has technically desisted, there is actually little if any behavioral change in such a case. For desistance to be meaningful both theoretically and in terms of policy, we assume that there has to be some nontrivial level of offending from which one can desist (see also Bushway et al. 2001). For similar reasons, an individual does not have to remain at a zero offending rate to be considered a desistor. Occasional or sporadic relapses—as in the former alcoholic who falls off the wagon but quickly climbs back on—do not negate the more fundamental change in an offending career from active to inactive that the concept of desistance is meant to capture.

Interactional theory views desistance as composed of two developmental processes. The first reflects the downward movement from the peak level of involvement to the start of noninvolvement. The second process reflects the maintenance of behavior at a zero or near-zero level of offending. We do not assume that a person who has attained some period of nonoffending will automatically remain at that level. Conformity as well as deviance requires maintenance, and the causal forces associated with the downward movement to zero and those associated with maintenance at zero may or may not be the same.

While desistance can occur suddenly, as when an addict quits cold turkey, the more typical pattern is a gradual movement away from offending as the person's environmental and interactional patterns change. Thus, interactional theory does not anticipate sharp turning points that quickly deflect offending trajectories from high levels to zero.

Also, given the last hypothesis presented in the previous section about persistence, we expect some association between the timing of onset and the timing of desistance. Those who start earlier are likely to stop later, but even some of those who have the earliest entry into active offending will desist and do so relatively quickly. Desistance is not determined by age of onset and stable characteristics associated with onset; desistance is more likely a product of changing life circumstances.

Overview

In sum, interactional theory anticipates a complex pattern of linkages between the onset and course of criminal careers. It does not anticipate only two major types of offenders or a strong correlation between onset and persistence. On the contrary, criminal careers unfold in a variety of patterns or shapes, and the central task before developmental criminology is to describe and account for them. One analytic strategy for describing them is mixture models, such as the group-based trajectory model developed by Nagin and Land (1993). I turn now to a discussion and application of that approach.

Offending Trajectories

Nagin and Land's (1993) trajectory approach is designed to summarize developmental patterns of behavior, including criminal behavior. Substantively, this technique describes the relationship between levels of offending and age. It models onset, when offending behavior begins; varying levels or amplitudes of offending, without severe restrictions on the shape or number of inflection points; and when offending stops, assuming it does within the observation period. This technique does not constrain the pattern of offending to be the same for all individuals. The "mixture" part of the mixture model searches for different patterns of offending by identifying individuals who cluster together such that their developmental pattern of offending is relatively homogeneous within groups and different across groups. Importantly, the technique does not insist that there be different shapes to the trajectories, and there is no a priori reason to expect that the model will generate a set of results that are biased toward either ontogenetic or sociogenetic models, or toward early starter/late starter theories versus general theories. The method is agnostic with respect to these issues. Indeed, for different outcomes covering different developmental stages, the technique has recovered both ontogenetic patterns (e.g., Broidy et al. 2003) and sociogenetic patterns (e.g., Bushway et al. 2001). Similarly, this approach is capable of finding one group or multiple groups. Previous applications of the technique have identified between two and eight groups (Piquero 2004; Thornberry et al. 2004). Different measures of the outcome and different exposure times account in part for the different outcomes.

First, theories need to account for why some people offend and others do not. Second, they need to account for why some start earlier and others start later.

While the trajectory approach has these advantages, it is not without limitations. Indeed, there have been several recent critical assessments of this technique (Bauer and Curran 2003, 2004; Eggleston, Laub, and Sampson 2004). Perhaps the most central question is whether the trajectory groups—the individuals sharing a similar offense history—represent discrete groups with different etiologies or whether they reflect more dense areas from a single underlying distribution.

Although there is currently no definitive resolution to this issue, I view the trajectory method as a convenient way of describing a more complex phenomenon by dividing it into smaller descriptive units. Doing so provides a method for empirically assessing the epidemiological hypotheses presented earlier. First, the trajectory method simultaneously describes criminal careers in terms of onset, course, and desistance. That is, each trajectory group describes when offending starts, when or if it ends, and its level or rate in between. Second, the technique models the interrelationships between these core dimensions by identifying varying patterns of offending, the so-called groups. While it does not model these interrelationships as a continuous function, the trajectory method approximates it by identifying patterns of offending that depict the variety of interrelationships. These patterns have strong descriptive and analytic value, especially when it is recalled that neither their number nor shape is predetermined by the technique.

While these core dimensions of criminal careers are continuously distributed, that does not imply that they are evenly distributed or that all values along the distribution are equally likely. Continuous distributions can be—and many are—multimodal. Age of onset offers a good illustration.

Onset occurs at all ages from childhood through at least early adulthood. Nevertheless, onset can group or clump along this underlying distribution for a number of developmental reasons. For example, transitions from elementary to middle school and from middle to high school—and the differing social environments those changes represent—can spur (or retard) onset. The onset of puberty, which is itself continuously distributed albeit over a shorter period, can also produce local changes in the rate of onset. But those spurts in onset do not mean that the population is divided into discrete onset groups. Age of onset still reflects a continuous distribution; however, it is a multimodal one. If these hypotheses are correct, then the emergence of multiple "groups" or trajectory patterns is precisely what one would expect to find.

In several analyses, we have used the trajectory technique to describe patterns of offending for sample members of the Rochester Youth Development Study (RYDS) (e.g., Bushway, Thornberry, and Krohn 2003; Thornberry et al. 2004). Figure 1 presents the model from the analysis in Thornberry et al. (2004). The frequency of annual offending is measured by the general delinquency index, a thirty-two-item self-report inventory covering behaviors ranging from petty theft and simple assault to armed robbery and aggravated assault (see Thornberry, Krohn, et al. 2003). In this case, the analysis is restricted to the male members of the Rochester sample; the same substantive conclusions would be obtained if trajectories based on the full sample were used (see Bushway, Thornberry, and Krohn 2003). The Rochester study is based on a general community sample representing the full range of risk found in an urban setting.

Consistent with the epidemiological hypotheses presented earlier, we see that offending is rather commonplace in the Rochester sample. The low-level offender group constitutes 29.7 percent of the sample. Of this group, however, only 19 percent report no offending; the remainder offend at a very low, sporadic rate across the age span. Thus, 94 percent of the total sample self-report some involvement in delinquent behavior by their early twenties, and 70 percent report more than only sporadic involvement. At the other extreme, persistent, chronic offending is relatively rare; only 6.9 percent fall into the highest group.

Second, we expect age of onset to be continuously distributed across age, not divided into two broad categories, early and late. Figure 2 presents this distribution for the full sample of males in the Rochester study. There is no sharp break or disjunction in the distribution that would lead to the identification of two distinct groups of early starters versus late starters. Also, although onset is continuous, it is not smoothly or evenly distributed. For example, there is a sharp jump from ages six to seven, near the beginning of school, then onset drops slightly, followed by a

FIGURE 1
TRAJECTORIES OF CRIMINAL OFFENDING,
ROCHESTER YOUTH DEVELOPMENT STUDY, MALES ONLY (*N* = 647)

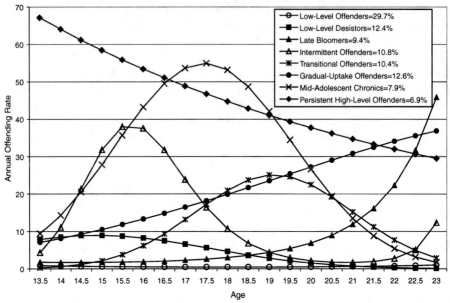

smooth increase from ages nine through twelve, followed by a large increase at ages thirteen and fourteen.

The continuous nature of onset is also reflected in the pattern of onset for the trajectory groups (Figure 1). The members of the low-level offender group who do offend have the latest age of onset with a mean of 15.1; only 17 percent began before age 13. In contrast, the mean age of onset for the persistent high-level offenders is 9.4, and 84 percent of them began before age 13. Onset for the other groups is arrayed between these extremes.

The trajectory method also identifies a late bloomer group, an offending pattern that is fundamentally at odds with ontogenetic perspectives. Late bloomers constitute 9.4 percent of the population and have very low offending rates up to age seventeen or eighteen. At that point, their level of offending increases rapidly, and by the end of the observation period they exhibit the highest offending rates, equivalent to those of the persistent high-level offenders. The presence of an offending pattern that blossoms after the age-normative period of early adolescence to midadolescence and that leads to serious adult careers has also been observed in more static analyses (e.g., Eggleston and Laub 2002; Wolfgang, Thornberry, and Figlio 1987) and in Figure 2 where 10 percent of the males in the Rochester study first report offending at age eighteen or beyond.

FIGURE 2
AGE OF ONSET OF OFFENDING FOR MALES
IN THE ROCHESTER YOUTH DEVELOPMENT STUDY

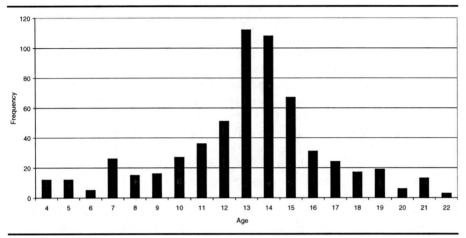

The patterns of offending identified in this analysis also demonstrate the modesty of the correlation between age of onset and persistence. This can be seen in any number of comparisons. Consider the midadolescent chronic offenders and the intermittent offenders. They have a similar average age of onset (12.6 and 11.9, respectively) and early careers, up to age 16, that are nearly identical. Yet as compared to the intermittent offenders, the midadolescent chronic offenders are much more persistent, reach a higher peak rate (55 vs. 38), and only approach nonoffending at the end of the observation period. A comparable pattern reflecting similarity with respect to onset and differences with respect to persistence can be seen for the gradual uptake offenders and the low-level desistors. The same conclusion can be reached by reversing the comparison. The late bloomers and the persistent high-level offenders both exhibit persistent, high-rate offending from the late teens onward but have vastly different patterns of onset.

Perhaps the most obvious and most important observation from Figure 1 is the presence of eight groups with diverging patterns of offending. It is not easy to reconcile these results with either taxonomic or ontogenetic models. First, patterns of offending do not divide neatly into two dominant groups, early starters and late starters à la Patterson, Capaldi, and Bank (1991) or Moffitt (1993). This, of course, follows from the previous point concerning the modest link between onset and persistence. Second, patterns of offending do not unfold in the same maturational pattern, mimicking the age-crime curve but at different levels à la Gottfredson and Hirschi (1990). Offending patterns crisscross in a variety of ways, a result perfectly consistent with sociogenetic models.

Turning to issues of desistance, we see two groups that conform to our definition—movement from some nontrivial level of offending to a persistent zero or near-zero rate. The first group is labeled low-level desistors and the second inter-mittent offenders. (The latter also exhibits an upswing in the last year, but the data are quite sparse at that point.) In neither instance is there a sharp or sudden drop in offending. For both, there is a more gradual decline from the peak to a near-zero rate.

Also, in both cases desistance appears to involve two developmental processes: the first is the gradual drop from the peak to near zero and the second is the mainte-nance of nonoffending. For example, the low-level desistors exhibit a gradual drop from ages 14.5 to 19.5 and then a persistent near-zero level from ages 20 to 23.

Finally, the process of desistance occurs at numerous ages, not just at the transi-tion from adolescence to adulthood as implied by the population age-crime curve. That curve is in fact an average of several curves, and whether that average reflects the actual behavior of a sizeable portion of the population is an empirical question. In the present case, desistance appears to begin at age 15 for the low-level desistors, 16 for the intermittent offenders, 17.5 for the midadolescent chronics, and 19 for the transitional offenders (assuming the latter two patterns remain near zero). Interestingly, all of this movement toward desistance occurs before one is likely to see the impact of marriage, work, and family, the typical explanations for desistance (Laub and Sampson 2003). This suggests that traditional explanations may be more focused on the *maintenance* of desistance, the second developmental process, than with the factors that *generate* desistance, the first developmental process.

An Interactional Theory of Offending

If the onset of offending is in fact continuously distributed, then the theoretical task before developmental criminology is twofold. First, theories need to account for why some people offend and others do not. Second, they need to account for why some start earlier and others start later. In addressing these questions, I draw heavily on the interactional model I recently developed with Marvin Krohn.[1] Fuller statements can be found in Thornberry and Krohn (2001, 2005); here I present a somewhat abbreviated version of the theory.

To begin, I discuss the initiation of offending in four broad developmental stages: the preschool years, childhood, adolescence, and late adolescence/emerg-ing adulthood. I do not view these stages as having sharp boundaries; rather, as indicated above, they are areas or regions of the more gradual, continuous process of human development.

Only a small portion of the population initiates antisocial behavior during toddlerhood and the preschool years (Krohn et al. 2001). These children are some-what more likely than others to persist in delinquency, especially serious delin-quency, over long portions of the life course. Their precocious onset is explained by the interaction of individual characteristics, ineffective parenting, and position in the social structure. The strongest influence is likely to be the family environment created by their parents. These parents are likely to exhibit a variety of parenting deficits that reflect their inability to monitor and supervise their children, to provide guidance in the development of problem-solving skills, to reward prosocial behavior, and to effectively punish antisocial behavior. In these families, parent-child interactions are characterized by low affective ties and involvement as well as explosive and physical disciplinary styles. In addition to being reared in adverse family environments, these children are also more likely than average to have negative temperamental qualities and neuropsychological deficits such as higher rates of negative emotionality, activity level, impulsivity, and poorer emotion regulation skills (Bates, Maslin, and Frankel 1985; Grolnick, Bridges, and Connell 1996; Shaw et al. 1996).

Consistent with the core premise of interactional theory, the child's negative characteristics and the parent's inept parenting styles become causally interwoven. Bidirectional influences between the child's temperamental qualities and the parent's child management style can be observed as early as toddlerhood. Young children with negative temperamental qualities are more subject to parental hostility, criticism, irritability, and coercive responses (Rutter and Quinton 1984; Zahn-Waxler et al. 1990). In turn, ineffective parenting creates maladaptive, coercive, and uncontrolled responses in the child (Belsky, Woodworth, and Crnic 1996; Shaw and Bell 1993). The combination of negative child characteristics and an adverse family context increases the odds that parent and child will develop a coercive style of interaction (Patterson, Reid, and Dishion 1992) and that the child will develop persistent patterns of oppositional and aggressive behavior (Shaw et al. 2003).

These individual and familial influences exist in a broader social context and, to a substantial degree, are brought about by that context. Children who initiate antisocial behavior during the preschool years are likely to be born to families experiencing severe structural adversity: chronic poverty, welfare dependence, residence in areas of concentrated poverty, and, especially, the co-occurrence of these attributes. Structural adversity increases parental stress and reduces social capital, which, in turn, increases poor family management skills and ineffective parenting (Belsky, Woodworth, and Crnic 1996; Conger et al. 1994). Indeed, Patterson, Reid, and Dishion (1992, 105) found that "social disadvantage makes the most significant contribution of any listed contextual variable to disruptions in parenting practices." The impact of structural adversity on negative temperamental qualities is less fully understood, although several studies show a significant positive association (Moffitt 1996; Prior et al. 1989; Simons et al. 1993; Stott 1978). Tibbetts and Piquero (1999) found that neuropsychological risk and disadvantaged environments interact to predict early onset offending.

For a sizable portion of the population, involvement in antisocial behavior and delinquency begins during the elementary school years, from about ages six through twelve. Onset is less common at the lower end of this age range and becomes more common as the individual approaches adolescence (see Figure 2). Thus, after a period of avoiding antisocial behavior during the preschool years, the behavior of these children changes and they begin some period of involvement in antisocial behavior and delinquency.

It is unlikely that their antisocial behavior is caused by the intense coupling of difficult temperament, ineffective parenting, and structural adversity just discussed. If those attributes are, in fact, present and intensely coupled, there would be little to inhibit the onset of antisocial behavior until the school-age years.

If these attributes are uncoupled, however, the causal forces that generate antisocial behavior weaken and the onset of antisocial behavior is likely to be delayed. For example, not all children with negative temperamental qualities are born into distressed families living in disorganized neighborhoods. The resources available to more advantaged families reduce the behavioral consequences of the child's difficult temperament, at least until he or she starts school and expands his or her peer relationships. Once the child reaches school and broadened social networks, however, the consequences of difficult temperament, for example, attention problems in school and rejection by peers, are likely to emerge and to increase the chances of antisocial behavior.

Although negative temperamental qualities play some role in generating antisocial behavior at these ages, interactional theory looks to the social environment, especially structural adversity and ineffective parenting, as the more likely point of origin. Three dimensions of parenting—attachment, monitoring, and discipline—are particularly important. First, children who experience cold, brittle relationships with their parents are freer to deviate as they are less controlled by parental desires and expectations. Second, poor monitoring also increases behavioral freedom and reduces the chances that parents will notice and respond appropriately to the child's behaviors by rewarding prosocial behavior and punishing antisocial behavior. Finally, harsh, erratic, physical discipline promotes coercive exchanges within the family and provides an environment for the child to learn antisocial behavioral patterns. Family effects are particularly strong at these ages as the child, lacking full autonomy, is more tightly enmeshed in the family environment. As noted earlier, parents living under conditions of structural adversity are more apt to exhibit these types of poor family management styles.

As the children age and move toward the upper end of this developmental stage, they confront new developmental challenges, and the mix of causal influences related to onset expands. Two arenas are particularly important: school and peer relations. First, one of the major developmental tasks of childhood is to succeed in school, both academically and behaviorally. Unfortunately, both structural adversity and ineffective parenting reduce the likelihood of doing so. Low commitment to school and low attachment to teachers weaken a major source of social control, and these variables have long been linked to higher rates of delinquency (Hirschi 1969; Krohn and Massey 1980). Second, structural adversity, ineffective parental monitoring, and school failure also increase access to deviant opportunity structures and involvement in deviant peer networks, which provide a strong learning environment for antisocial behavior.

In general, ineffective parenting, weak social bonds, and abundant deviant opportunities are likely to produce the initiation of antisocial behavior during the childhood years. As the strength of these deficits increases, delinquent behavior is likely to emerge at younger ages. As the strength of these deficits diminishes, however, that is, as bonding increases and deviant opportunities decrease, age of onset will increase and move toward the modal age of onset that occurs during early adolescence.

Up to this point, we have discussed the origins of early onset offending; while the age of onset varied from toddlerhood through childhood, it was always, to some extent, "off-time" or precocious. We now turn to the stage of age-appropriate or age-normative onset, from early adolescence to midadolescence, roughly from ages twelve to sixteen. After avoiding antisocial behavior throughout childhood, the behavior patterns of these adolescents change as they initiate delinquency and other problem behaviors. What accounts for this change? As was true at younger ages, characteristics and behavior of children, style of parenting, and environmental influences interact to produce delinquency during the teenage years. The content of these causal influences, however, is developmentally specific to adolescence.

The major developmental task of adolescence is establishing age-appropriate autonomy (Conger 1991; Cooper, Grotevant, and Condon 1983). Adolescents are increasingly expected to make their own decisions, to be more responsible for those decisions as they prepare to enter the adult world. With this added responsibility come expectations of more independence. Young adolescents seek distance from parents, teachers, and, more generally, adult authority. Their emerging physical, sexual, and social maturity provides the human capital needed for increased independence. Yet the attainment of autonomy does not increase at the same rate, often creating tension between parents and children. Conger (1991) suggested that the successful development of such autonomy relies on the processes of both separation and continued connectedness. Whereas adolescents must have sufficient freedom from parental authority to make decisions about their lives, they still need guidance and support from their parents. Balancing the need for adolescent autonomy with the concern for parental monitoring of attitudes, behaviors, and decisions is a crucial determinant of behavioral outcomes (Gecas and Seff 1990; Steinberg and Morris 2001). Some parents fail to provide adequate monitoring in response to their children's demands for independence, generating too much freedom and a sense of drift (Matza 1964); other parents fail to reduce or temper their monitoring to reflect the child's rightful need for increased independence, thereby generating anger and alienation. Either parental response increases the probability of delinquency. Although these young adolescents are never entirely alienated from parents and teachers, distance is created in these relationships.

While family effects are important in generating onset during adolescence, peer effects are dominant. As adolescents seek autonomy, especially if there is tension or conflict with their parents, they gravitate toward each other for their primary social networks. In large part, peers replace parents, or at least are added to parents, as major sources of rewards and approval of behavior (Gecas and Seff 1990). But since age-graded peers are going through the same process of searching for autonomy at roughly the same time, adolescent peer groups are closed to adult authority while valuing behaviors that demonstrate rebellion from adult authority (Cohen 1955; Stinchecombe 1964).

One consequence is that the peer culture encourages and reinforces problem behaviors—deviant lifestyles, experimentation with alcohol and drug use, and involvement in minor forms of delinquency. Much of this behavior involves precocious behavior typically reserved for adults, for example, smoking, drinking, and sexual relations; and much of it is, in Albert Cohen's (1955, 25) apt phrase, "non-utilitarian, malicious, and negativistic." While clearly delinquent, this behavior typically involves less serious forms of delinquency, and involvement in the most serious forms—for example, armed robbery, burglary, heroin use—is not very common.

I hypothesize that as the age of onset increases, the strength of the causal factors associated with antisocial behavior diminishes.

Structural adversity also plays a role at this stage, especially for youngsters who were buffered at earlier ages from its negative consequences by strong prosocial bonds. Poor parents often do not have the resources to provide alternative activities that could keep their adolescent children away from problematic influences; for example, "disadvantaged parents are less able to counteract negative peer pressures than middle-class parents" (Ambert 1997, 101). This effect may be particularly acute for adolescents who live in single-parent families and those who live in disorganized areas because of the richness of deviant opportunity structures that are available.

Although the onset of delinquency is most common during midadolescence, some careers start after this "normative" period, that is, during late adolescence and into what Arnett (2000) has recently labeled emerging adulthood. This pattern of offending differs fundamentally from the late starters as described in typological theories (e.g., Moffitt 1993; Patterson, Capaldi, and Bank 1991). These theories define late starters as a residual category: anyone who is not an early starter is a late starter. Defined in this way, the group is actually composed of two types of offenders: the large group of age-normative starters that we just discussed and a small group of truly late starters. I reserve the terms *late onset* and *late bloomers* for those who begin frequent offending at ages beyond the modal onset years of adolescence. (See Figure 1 for an illustration.)

Late bloomers present an intriguing pattern of offending. Why, after successfully traversing most of the adolescent years when offending is quite common, do they initiate and then continue serious offending? Accounting for this pattern is made more difficult by the fact that it is an underresearched area (Eggleston and Laub 2002).

Late onset offending is explained by a combination of developmental challenges, individual characteristics, and structural position. Prior to this period, involvement in delinquency is either nonexistent or exceedingly rare for late bloomers because of strong social control by family and school. Being enmeshed in prosocial networks controls antisocial behavior and reduces involvement in deviant peer networks, keeping these youth on the straight and narrow.

Emerging adulthood, however, is a volatile period of increasing freedom and independence. As Arnett (2000, 475) has noted, "Emerging adults can pursue novel and intense experiences more freely than adolescents because they are less likely to be monitored by parents and can pursue them more freely than adults because they are less constrained by [adult] roles." Behavioral freedom is evident in several domains. For example, emerging adults are likely to experience a variety of living arrangements—with roommates, in dorms or barracks, cohabiting, or alone—but without the controlling influence of parents or spouse. These are also the ages of great transiency between school, multiple jobs, college, unemployment, and leisure (Rindfuss 1991). In addition, they are the ages of peak involvement in a variety of risky behaviors such as unprotected sex with multiple partners; alcohol, drug use, and binge drinking; and risk-taking activities such as driving while intoxicated (Arnett 2000).

Youth who also suffer from individual deficits, such as low cognitive ability and poor academic performance, are more susceptible to this increased freedom and more likely to become ensnared in increasingly risky and antisocial behaviors. This explanation is consistent with the few studies that have explicitly examined late bloomers. Nagin, Farrington, and Moffitt (1995) found that late bloomers had low IQs (at ages eight to eleven) and did poorly in school during early adolescence. During adolescence, however, they were buffered from the effects of these deficits by a supportive family and school environment. In addition, we found that of the eight trajectory groups in the Rochester sample (Figure 1), the late bloomers have the lowest rates of structural adversity during early adolescence (Thornberry et al. 2004). Once the freedom and instability of emerging adulthood is confronted, however, deficits in human capital become a serious disadvantage for acquiring meaningful employment and, in turn, establishing a quality relationship with a partner. Accordingly, Sampson and Laub (1993) examined those who began offending at later ages and found that job instability and low marital attachment measured during emerging adulthood are related to late offending.

In addition to losing the protection of the family and the controlling environment of school, those with human capital deficiencies are vulnerable to other causal influences. Two seem particularly potent. First, involvement in other problem behaviors, especially alcohol and drug use, may contribute to both the onset of antisocial behavior at these ages and its relatively serious nature (Rutter, Giller, and Hagell 1998; Sampson and Laub 1993). Alcohol use and difficulties in making the transition to adult statuses continue to interact to increase the probability of continuing criminal offending. Consistent with this explanation, we found in the Rochester study that late bloomers experience significantly more life stressors than nonoffenders (Thornberry et al. 2004). Second, for late bloomers, both their difficulty in adjusting to the instability of emerging adulthood and their elevated substance use increase the chances of association with deviant peers. And as at younger ages, antisocial peer networks both reinforce problem behaviors and seal off involvement in prosocial roles and networks.

Explaining Continuity and Change in Delinquent Careers

Life-course theories also need to account for continuity and change in antisocial behavior and the relationships between onset, on one hand, and both continuity and change, on the other. Some offenders exhibit high levels of continuity in antisocial behavior over the life course, and as noted earlier, people who start earlier are somewhat more likely to persist than those who start later. Nevertheless, there is also a substantial amount of change in offending over time. Many early onset offenders stop offending, and many later onset offenders are persistent. What accounts for these varying patterns of continuity and change in antisocial behavior?

Individuals with the earliest onset of antisocial behavior are likely to have multiple, interwoven causal factors—especially structural adversity, ineffective parenting, and negative temperamental characteristics—and few offsetting assets. In contrast, as the causal factors become uncoupled and less extreme and as offsetting assets increase, the age of onset of offending increases. These characteristics also offer an explanation for patterns of continuity and change.

Continuity in offending

Two developmental processes help to account for the higher level of continuity for offenders with earlier ages of onset. The first stems from the stability of the causal factors themselves across the life course. If, as argued above, early onset offending is caused by exposure to multiple deficits and more extreme levels of those deficits, it is reasonable to assume that the stronger the deficits are, the more stable they are likely to be over time. For example, families experiencing extreme levels of structural adversity do not easily or often escape that adversity, and the development of children raised in those families is constantly compromised. Similarly, there is continuity across time in ineffective parenting styles (Patterson, Reid, and Dishion 1992) and in negative temperamental traits (Caspi, Bem, and Elder 1989; Moffitt, Lynam, and Silva 1994).

The stability of these attributes offers a partial explanation of the negative relationship between age of onset and continuity of offending (Figure 3). Since more extreme deficits are needed to bring about early onset offending and since more extreme deficits are themselves more likely to be stable, these deficits will remain in place to continue causing antisocial behavior over time. And since the strongest deficits are associated with the earliest ages of onset, this source of continuity is likely to be greatest for offenders with earlier rather than later onsets.

FIGURE 3
THE STABILITY OF CAUSAL INFLUENCES

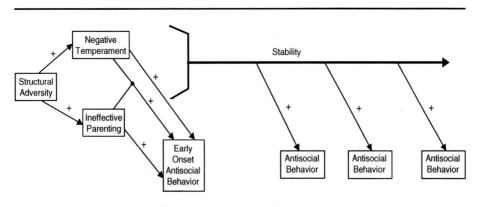

The second process that accounts for continuity concerns the developmental consequences of antisocial behavior, especially more serious forms of antisocial behavior. A basic premise of interactional theory is that antisocial behavior becomes embedded in a series of mutually reinforcing causal loops over time. Thus, antisocial behavior can have severe negative consequences for many aspects of a child's development, both weakening social bonds and strengthening antisocial influences (Figure 4).

Persistent antisocial behavior will continue to elicit coercive responses from the parent as the child ages (Lee and Bates 1985). In addition, children who have learned coercive behavioral styles in the family are apt to extend them to external settings such as peer relationships and school behavior. "There is now substantial evidence that aggressive children are likely to be rejected by their peers" (Coie and Dodge 1998, 828) and that rejected children lose the positive influence of prosocial peers in acquiring social and behavioral competencies (Coie et al. 1992; Ladd 1990). Aggressive children are also at risk for school failure (Patterson, Reid, and Dishion 1992). The coercive training they received in the family and the rejection by peers increase the chances of early academic adjustment problems. There is substantial evidence that isolation in deviant peer networks, coercive behavioral styles, and academic failure, all brought on in part by earlier antisocial behavior, lead to continuing involvement in delinquency during adolescence.

As these youth age, they are ill-prepared to meet the developmental challenges of adolescence and to prepare themselves for adult life. In a series of papers using the Rochester data, we have shown that delinquent behavior reduces social bonds (Jang and Smith 1997; Krohn et al. 1995; Thornberry et al. 1991), increases affiliation with deviant peers and fosters deviant belief systems (Krohn et al. 1996; Thornberry et al. 1994), and disrupts orderly and timely transitions to adult roles (Krohn, Lizotte, and Perez 1997; Thornberry, Smith, and Howard 1997).

FIGURE 4
MODEL OF CONTINUITY IN ANTISOCIAL BEHAVIOR

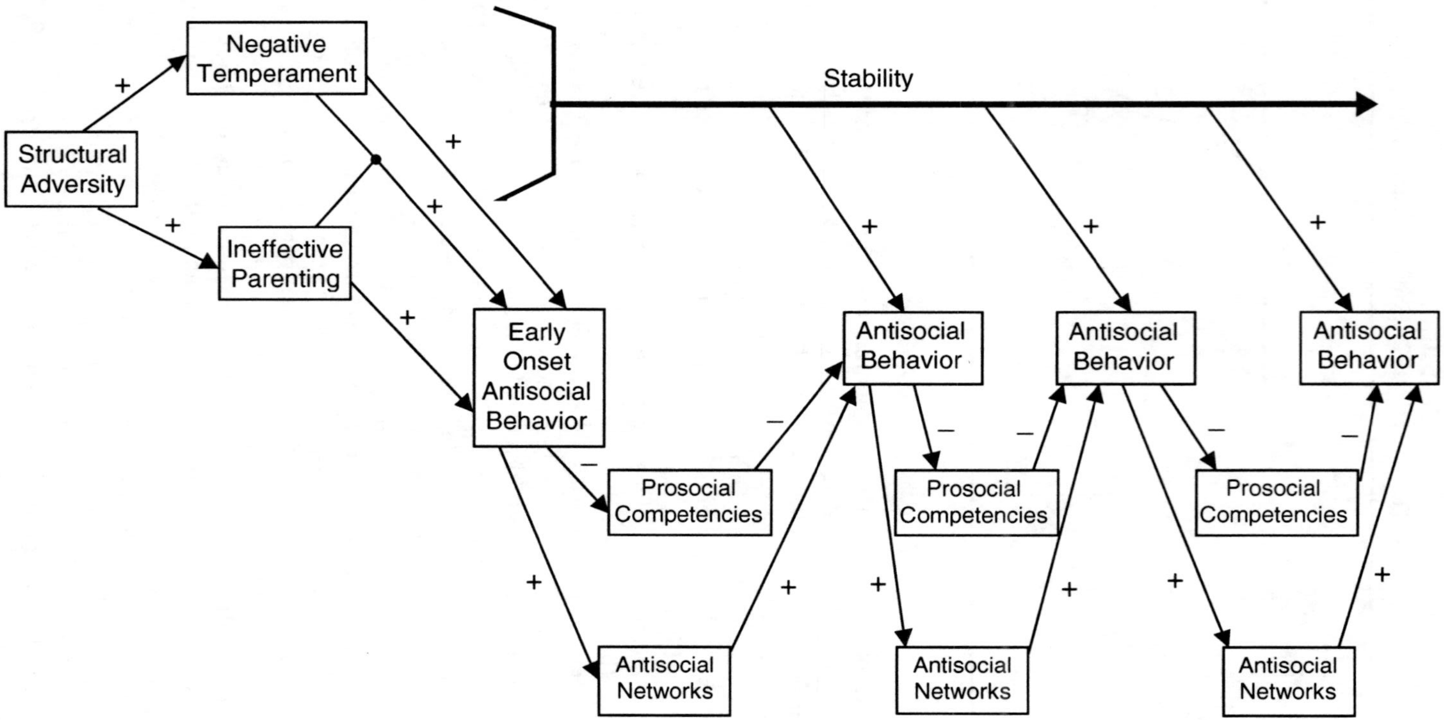

In brief, we hypothesize that individuals who initiate antisocial behavior at very young ages are more likely than average to persist because the causal factors are likely to remain in place and because early involvement in antisocial behavior generates cumulative and cascading consequences in the person's life course. These processes are most likely to be evident for youngsters with a precocious onset; hence the general correlation between childhood onset and more persistent careers.

As the age of onset increases to include individuals who initiate offending during early adolescence to midadolescence—the larger, more age-normative group—there is a stronger tendency toward shorter careers. For reasons discussed in the next section on desistance, this is likely to be the modal response. But even for these offenders, there are noticeable levels of persistence, as shown earlier in Figure 1. Some of these age-normative-onset individuals continue to commit crimes well into their early adult years. Indeed, Moffitt (2002) has recently observed that many of her adolescence-limited offenders continued to commit crimes at age twenty-six. Why, if they do not have multiple and extreme deficits, would they continue to offend into their early adult years?

Continuity for later onset offenders is most likely due to the reciprocal consequences of their behaviors and their association with deviant peers. For some youth, delinquent behavior can have adverse consequences that serve as obstacles to a successful transition to adulthood. This may be particularly true if youth are also involved in heavy alcohol or drug use (Jessor, Donovan, and Costa 1991; Krohn, Lizotte, and Perez 1997; Newcomb and Bentler 1988). These behaviors jeopardize their performance in conventional arenas such as school, the workplace, and establishing a quality relationship with a significant other. Failure to make successful transitions in these arenas increases the probability of continued offending. An additional consequence of offending is the solidifying of ties with deviant others (Krohn et al. 1996; Thornberry et al. 1994). For those later onset offenders who become enmeshed in extremely deviant social networks, especially street gangs, offending is likely to continue beyond the teenage years (Thornberry, Krohn, et al. 2003).

Up to this point, we have argued that the level of continuity in offending is likely to be highest for those who start earliest and to gradually diminish for those who start later, especially those who start in midadolescence. For late bloomers whose antisocial careers emerge in late adolescence or emerging adulthood, however, we hypothesize that this general relationship is reversed and that the level of continuity in offending increases. In other words, there is a U-shaped distribution between age of onset and the level of continuity in offending.

Late bloomers are hypothesized to have deficits in human capital that had been camouflaged by the strong protective factors of family and school during adolescence. Once removed from the protective cocoon of those arenas and exposed to the greater openness and freedom of emerging adulthood, however, these deficits in human capital make successful transitions to adult roles more difficult. Problems in acquiring stable, meaningful work and quality relationships with significant others are likely to increase, thus making continuity in offending a more likely outcome. These problems are exacerbated by the use of alcohol and drugs.

To summarize, earlier onset offenders are more likely to continue offending because of the stability in the strength of the causal forces that led to their early onset and the negative consequences of that behavior. As age of onset increases, offenders are less likely to have these serious interlocking deficits and therefore are less likely to experience continuity in offending. If they do continue to offend, it is more likely due to the consequences of their offending behaviors, especially becoming enmeshed in deviant social networks. Late bloomers, on the other hand, are somewhat more likely to continue offending because their deficits in human capital make adjustment to the independence and freedom of emerging adulthood exceedingly difficult to handle. That reaction, especially if accompanied by substance use, increases the difficulty of making successful transitions to adult roles. Continuing economic and relationship problems, combined with the use of alcohol and drugs, is likely to lead to offending well into the adult years for the late bloomers.

Change in offending

There are two basic patterns of behavioral change with respect to antisocial behavior. The first, movement from some sustained period of nonoffending to involvement in offending, has already been discussed in our explanation for offending that emerges later in the life course, most notably, with respect to late bloomers. In this section, we concentrate on the second pattern of change, from some sustained period of offending to nonoffending.

Although some offending careers are marked by high levels of continuity, there is also a substantial degree of change represented both by de-escalation—substantial reductions in the rate of offending—and by desistance (Bushway, Thornberry, and Krohn 2003; Loeber and LeBlanc 1990). Three developmental processes are hypothesized to account for this type of change.

First, I hypothesize that as the age of onset increases, the strength of the causal factors associated with antisocial behavior diminishes. That is, the causal factors are less numerous, less extreme, and less intertwined. Because of that, they are also less likely to be highly stable over time. Families do experience upward mobility and move to new neighborhoods and better schools; parental stressors such as family conflict, depression, and drug use can be ameliorated; and bonds between parents and children can improve. Interactional theory hypothesizes that as the person's social environment changes, so too will the person's behavior, regardless of age or age of onset. Thus, changes in causal factors potentially provide turning points in the person's life-course trajectories and in their antisocial behavior. These changes are more likely if the causal factors themselves are less extreme, and therefore, they are more likely to occur for later onset offenders.

Indeed, this developmental process is particularly salient in accounting for the high rates of desistance observed for those who initiate offending during the age-normative period of early to midadolescence. A large part of the impetus for their offending was generated by a specific developmental challenge of adolescence—the search for identity and autonomy. As that search unfolds, tension between parent and child and involvement in deviant peer groups often follow, increasing the likelihood of delinquency. As the challenges of adolescence are successfully met, and identity and autonomy are gained, the motivation for rebellion and deviance subside. To be sure, this transition does not happen for all, but it is the modal outcome in most societies. The dissipation of a developmentally specific motivating factor is a special case of the instability of causal factors.

The second process associated with the movement away from active offending is that the causal factors that give rise to the initial antisocial behavior are not intensely coupled. There are many youth with deficits in some areas, say a distressed family, who have compensating assets in other areas, say intelligence and school performance. The deficits they do experience put them at risk for delinquency, but the offsetting assets reduce the chances that they will have long, persistent antisocial careers. More generally, these youngsters have a richer set of protective factors, in part brought about by the somewhat less tenuous social position of their families (see Rutter 1987; Smith et al. 1995; Werner and Smith 1992). Again, consistent with our explanation for onset, the presence of offsetting assets is more likely as the age of onset increases.

Third, given the presence of protective assets, these youth are less likely to experience strong negative consequences brought about by feedback effects from delinquent behavior. Although the negative consequences of delinquency will find fertile soil in areas in which deficits already exist (the distressed family in our example), they will also find resistance in areas of resilience (school performance in our example). Thus, it is less likely that the various life-course trajectories will become interwoven to create an amplifying loop toward increasing involvement in antisocial careers. As with the other processes, this is less likely to happen for the earlier onset offenders because of the strength and coupling of causal factors in their case. Even there, however, some earlier onset offenders can be expected to have protective factors (e.g., high IQ) that may have been camouflaged by deficits in other domains. Those protective factors may enable even some early onset offenders the opportunity to change the course of their lives.

When these developmental processes are evident, youth are more likely to successfully complete the developmental challenges of adolescence and are better prepared to make on-time, successful transitions to adulthood, especially in the areas of family formation and stable employment. Attachment to partner and children and commitment to work and conventional activities create new social bonds and social capital to control behavior. They also alter social networks away from antisocial and toward prosocial venues (see Warr 1998). The reciprocal relationships between prosocial trajectories in family and work and trajectories of antisocial behavior now serve to maintain low or zero levels of offending.

Prosocial Careers

Just as a small portion of the population persists in offending across the life course, a small portion manages to avoid involvement in delinquency entirely. To establish a persistent pattern of prosocial behavior, conditions in childhood must either prevent the development of predispositions to antisocial behavior or be able to compensate for those predispositions so that they do not lead to antisocial behavior. Social and economic circumstances well above those characterized as indicative of structural adversity play a key role in generating conforming behavior early in the life course. Although having the economic means to provide for one's family does not preclude the possibility of having children with antisocial behavior, it does reduce the risk. A secure financial position reduces parental levels of stress and antisocial behavior, thereby increasing the probability that they will exhibit more appropriate parenting behaviors. They are also likely to have the human and social capital to ameliorate or correct the developmental consequences of any early temperamental difficulties such as oppositional behavior.

The intergenerational model reminds us that parenting styles are not randomly distributed in the population; nor do they arrive de novo at the birth of a child.

The strong bond to the family and the absence or control of negative temperamental qualities set the stage for continuity of prosocial behavior. Serious antisocial behavior is not part of the behavioral repertoire of these children, and therefore, such behavior cannot generate adverse effects on family life, peer relationships, and school success. Indeed, the prosocial behavior exhibited by these children serves to increase the strength of the child's ties to conventionality. Parents respond to the good behavior of their children by rewarding them, exhibiting more affection and greater involvement (Gecas and Seff 1990). Teachers favor children who are attentive and interested in their schoolwork. Children tend to establish friendship ties with peers who behave in similar ways (Kandel 1978), thus establishing a social network that constrains behavior toward conformity (Krohn 1986).

The pattern of relationships established in the early years not only increases ties to conventionality, but as these children enter adolescence, they are less likely to have access to deviant social networks and learning environments. The boundaries of social groupings that are formed in adolescence are often hard to penetrate (Schwendinger and Schwendinger 1985). Thus, prosocial youth are encapsulated in a prosocial cocoon facilitating their continued conformity. The increased demand for autonomy that characterizes adolescence results in decisions between alternative prosocial activities rather than between prosocial and antisocial behavior.

These youth are also more likely to have developed the necessary human and social capital to successfully meet the challenges of the transition to adulthood. Not burdened with the same level of structural adversities, poor school records, and deviant labels that beset the youth who are involved in antisocial behavior, they are less buffeted about by the openness and independence of emerging adulthood. These individuals, having successfully met the developmental challenges of adolescence, have the human and social capital to make smooth, on-time transitions to adulthood and to avoid the late onset of antisocial behavior.

Intergenerational Extensions

In all developmental theories of antisocial behavior, including the interactional theory just presented, parent characteristics and behaviors play a prominent explanatory role. The family's level of structural adversity, which in a sense is a parent characteristic, and ineffective parenting behaviors are basic causes of the onset and maintenance of delinquency. While central to all developmental theories, parental characteristics are themselves treated in a surprisingly nondevelopmental manner. The child's antisocial behavior is explained by the parent's contemporaneous statuses and style of parenting with relatively little concern for the developmental origins of those parenting behaviors or with whether an understanding of the parent's own earlier development would add to our ability to explain the onset and course of the child's antisocial behavior. The life-course concept of "linked lives" (Elder 1998) suggests, however, that intergenerational influences may well contribute to the explanation of behavior patterns. As Elder (1985, 40) noted, "Each generation is bound to fateful decisions and events in the other's life course."

An intergenerational perspective on antisocial behavior leads to the investigation of two key questions. First, does a parent's own involvement in adolescent antisocial behavior generate risk for his or her children to also become involved in antisocial behavior? And second, if it does, what are the mediating processes that link the generations in this fashion? Successfully addressing these questions will extend our understanding of the origins of a focal individual's antisocial behavior.

Intergenerational linkages

There is a common assumption, in both popular and scientific writings, that crime "runs in families." That is, a parent's history of antisocial behavior increases the odds that his or her children will also be at risk for involvement in antisocial behavior. Although generally assumed, little empirical evidence based on prospective data from multiple generations actually tests it. Moreover, the available studies suggest that the picture is actually more complicated than the common view would have it. While studies support a general theme of intergenerational continuity in antisocial behavior, there is also a strong subtheme of intergenerational discontinuity. That is, some antisocial parents have children who avoid antisocial behavior, and some parents who themselves were not antisocial have children who are.

These findings suggest that intergenerational models need to account for processes that lead both to behavioral similarity as well as to what might be called intergenerational resilience. Although both patterns are important, in the interest of space I only address issues of intergenerational continuity in the remainder of this article. The central question is, What are the mediating processes that lead from a parent's own involvement in adolescent antisocial behavior to an elevated risk of involvement in antisocial behavior on the part of his or her children?

Intergenerational models

The previous section offered a general theory of one generation's antisocial behavior. Let us call them generation 2, or G2. Their behavior was heavily influenced by their parents, that is, the members of generation 1, or G1. The question before us now is how G2's adolescent development influences generation 3, or G3.

The full explanation of how G2's involvement in antisocial behavior influences G3's involvement is obviously complex. Explanations range from genetic models in which there is direct transmission of risk from parent to child, to shared environment models in which the behavioral similarity is spurious, produced by each generation responding in similar ways to similar environmental stimuli. Elaborating the full range of these possible influences is beyond the scope of this article. The current approach is more focused: it examines the intergenerational implications of the interactional theory of antisocial behavior presented in the previous section.

Intergenerational continuity

An overview of the conceptual model for examining intergenerational continuity in antisocial behavior is presented in Figure 5. As a point of departure, the first three boxes, or conceptual clusters, present a very abbreviated version of the theoretical argument presented above. Briefly, G1 family characteristics, including structural adversity, weak bonding to and involvement with the family, ineffective parenting behaviors, and drug use all increase the likelihood of antisocial behavior on the part of G2. These G1 attributes are also likely to reduce the formation of prosocial bonds and social capital.

In the interest of space, I will not fully discuss grandparental effects, that is, the effect of G1 on G3. G1 characteristics and behaviors can directly impact G3 problem behaviors and have an indirect effect via the causal processes in Figure 5. Although not detailed in the current discussion, the full intergenerational model incorporates G1 influences on G3, as we will see in the empirical data to be presented shortly.

Returning to G2's adolescent development, antisocial behavior and prosocial bonds become reciprocally interwoven over the life course to create behavioral trajectories toward (or away from) extensive involvement in problem behaviors (Angold, Costello, and Erkanli 1999; Jang and Smith 1997; Thornberry et al. 1994). To illustrate, youth with low commitment to and success in school are more apt to be delinquent and to use drugs (Bryant et al. 2003; Jessor 1976), and their antiso-

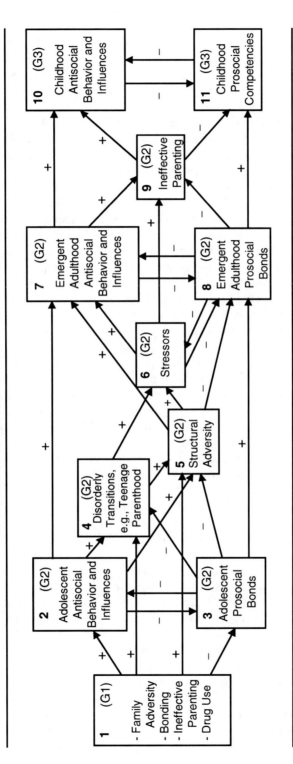

FIGURE 5

A GENERAL CONCEPTUAL MODEL FOR UNDERSTANDING
THE INTERGENERATIONAL TRANSMISSION OF RISK

NOTE: G2 and G3 are second and third generation, respectively.

181

cial behavior is likely to further erode school success (Fergusson and Horwood 1997; Mensch and Kandel 1988). Youth who are antisocial often associate with deviant peers (Kandel 1978; Kaplan, Martin, and Robbins 1984); those peer associations are likely to increase future antisocial behavior (Krohn et al. 1996; Newcomb and Bentler 1986).

Although the origins of delinquency and related problem behaviors contribute to the intergenerational transmission of risk, the *consequences* of delinquent careers are even more central. Delinquency, especially frequent and serious delinquency, has been shown to have systemic effects on the person's later development and transitions to adult roles (Ellickson et al. 1998; Kandel and Logan 1984; Krohn, Lizotte, and Perez 1997; Newcomb and Bentler 1987). Interactional theory uses these negative consequences to build an explanation for intergenerational continuity. The more extreme the person's involvement in delinquency and drug use, the greater these negative consequences are likely to be (Thornberry and Krohn 2001, 2005) and the greater the intergenerational transfer of risk. Conversely, there is little reason to assume that brief, experimental forays into antisocial behavior by G2 will have serious long-term consequences for either generation.

As shown in Figure 5, adolescents who have low prosocial bonds and who are heavily involved in antisocial behavior and in deviant social networks are less likely to have successfully completed the developmental tasks of adolescence and more likely to make early and unsuccessful transitions to adult statuses (Jessor, Donovan, and Costa 1991; Krohn, Lizotte, and Perez 1997; Newcomb and Bentler 1986). Particularly important to intergenerational study is the transition to parenthood; adolescent drug use and antisocial behavior increase the likelihood of becoming a teen parent (Amaro and Zuckerman 1992; Elster, Lamb, and Tavare 1987; Thornberry, Smith, and Howard 1997). In turn, early parenthood often has negative consequences for both the young parent and that parent's children (Furstenberg, Brooks-Gunn, and Morgan 1987; Hardy et al. 1998; Pogarsky, Lizotte, and Thornberry 2003).

Less successful adolescent development and disorderly transitions are both related to elevated levels of structural adversity during the early adult years (Capaldi and Stoolmiller 1999; Furstenberg, Brooks-Gunn, and Morgan 1987). Structural adversity increases stressors such as depression, financial stress, aversive life events, and partner conflict (Conger and Elder 1994; McLoyd 1990). In turn, structural adversity and stressors reduce the young adult's formation of prosocial bonds and social capital, leading to less stable employment patterns, lower rates of marriage, and more unstable partner relationships (Conger et al. 1992; Rutter et al. 1994). Adversity and stress increase involvement in problem behaviors, and they also increase exposure to antisocial influences during emerging adulthood (Capaldi and Stoolmiller 1999; Day and Leonard 1985; Kaplan, Johnson, and Bailey 1986). As is true at earlier ages, prosocial bonds and antisocial influences become reciprocally interwoven over time. For example, unemployment and marital instability increase involvement in crime and substance use. In turn, that involvement in antisocial behavior further erodes the chances of accomplishing a smooth transition to these adult roles.

In addition, for both prosocial and antisocial trajectories, there are stability effects reflecting intragenerational stability in behavior over time, for example, from adolescent antisocial behavior to antisocial behavior during the early adult years (Caspi and Elder 1988; Kandel et al. 1986; Krohn, Lizotte, and Perez 1997). Although not modeled in Figure 5 to reduce its complexity, there is also evidence of intergenerational continuity from G1 to G2 in many of these domains. For example, there is similarity across adjacent generations with respect to early parenthood (Jaffee et al. 2001), poverty (Rodgers 1995), stressors (Conger et al. 1994), and substance use (Costello et al. 1999).

The developmental processes discussed up to this point have intergenerational consequences for G3 children. Some of those effects are direct, for example, G2 antisocial behavior to G3 antisocial behavior. Parents who continue to be involved in antisocial behavior, for example, substance use or partner violence, increase their child's exposure to antisocial norms and reinforcements and serve as models for antisocial behavior. Although these effects can affect the G3 child directly, the dominant pathway is indirect, mediated by family processes like family conflict, hostility, and especially by the quality of parenting (Patterson, Reid, and Dishion 1992).

Less effective parenting styles include low affective ties and involvement with G3, inconsistent monitoring and standard setting, and explosive physical disciplinary styles. We saw earlier how these parenting behaviors are intimately linked to the onset and course of the child's antisocial behavior. The intergenerational model reminds us that parenting styles are not randomly distributed in the population; nor do they arrive de novo at the birth of a child. As shown in Figure 5, they are systematically related to the parent's own growth and development, including earlier involvement in antisocial behavior and the consequences wrought by that antisocial behavior. Parents exhibiting low prosocial competencies and high involvement in antisocial behavior during adolescence are less well prepared to succeed during the somewhat volatile period of emerging adulthood. As a result, these parents are more likely than others to be stressed, to continue antisocial behaviors and drug use, and to have weak prosocial bonds, all of which lead to poorer family management skills (Conger et al. 1984; Dishion, Patterson, and Reid 1985; Lahey et al. 1984).

And this, in a sense, brings us back to the starting point of interactional theory. The onset of G3 childhood antisocial behavior and the formation of prosocial competencies are directly influenced by current G2 antisocial behavior patterns, G2 level of prosocial bonds and social capital, and G2 parenting style. The latter is likely to be the most powerful and proximate influence (Conger et al. 1992; Patterson, Reid, and Dishion 1992), mediating the effect of many of the prior variables. The long-term consequences of this constellation for the child's development, including antisocial careers, were laid out in the previous section.

The conceptual model just discussed focuses exclusively on patterns of intergenerational continuity in behavior. That is, it identifies at least some of the mediating processes by which a parent's involvement in antisocial behavior is likely to increase the risk that his or her children will also engage in antisocial behavior. Two cautionary notes are in order. First, as noted earlier, there are likely to be other mediating pathways (e.g., genetic effects) that need to be incorporated into a fuller explanation (see Thornberry, Krohn, and Lizotte 2005). Second, our focus on continuity addresses only part, albeit the dominant part, of intergenerational linkages. There are clear patterns of discontinuity as well (Thornberry, Freeman-Gallant, et al. 2003; Thornberry, Krohn, and Freeman-Gallant forthcoming) that need to be considered. Adolescent antisocial behavior does not lead ineluctably to the negative consequences portrayed in Figure 5. As noted in the earlier discussion of interactional theory, for some individuals behavioral change (e.g., desistance) occurs, and that change can generate different intergenerational implications. Thus, the model as Figure 5 should not be viewed as the entire story.

Gender differences

The intergenerational model just presented discusses general processes that link the lives of parents and children with respect to antisocial behavior. In brief, parents who were extensively involved in antisocial behavior as adolescents, especially if they have weak prosocial bonds and competencies, face a host of developmental deficits as they enter adult roles, including parenthood. Those deficits increase structural adversity and stress and reduce the likelihood of developing effective parenting styles, thereby increasing their children's risk for antisocial behavior. Although the basic processes presented in Figure 5 apply to both G2 mothers and fathers, the strength of some relationships will vary by G2 gender.

Some mediating pathways are likely to be more dominant for G2 mothers. Perhaps the most important one concerns parenting behaviors. In American culture, mothers are cast as the primary parent, and "norms are stricter on the centrality and endurance of the mother-child dyad" (Doherty, Kouneski, and Erickson 1998). Fathers are more likely to play a secondary role; the father-child relationship is less enduring and more strongly shaped by contextual influences, especially relations with the child's mother (Cox et al. 1989; Doherty, Kouneski, and Erickson 1998; Furstenberg and Cherlin 1991). Given the centrality of the parenting role for women, I hypothesize that parenting styles will more fully mediate the impact of adolescent antisocial behavior for G2 mothers than for G2 fathers.

A second pathway likely to be stronger for G2 mothers involves assortative mating and partner conflict. Partnering with an antisocial individual has a stronger synergistic effect on problem behaviors and drug use for women than for men (Moffitt et al. 2001, 2002; Taylor, McGue, and Iacono 2000). In turn, parental antisocial behavior has been shown to be related to less effective parenting and, via that, to behavior problems for the child (Patterson, Reid, and Dishion 1992).

Third, adolescent problem behaviors are somewhat more likely to lead to internalizing problems, especially depression, for females than for males (McGee and Baker 2002; Moffitt et al. 2001; Silverthorn and Frick 1999). Thus, depression, which also increases poor parenting (Simons et al. 1999), is apt to be a stronger mediator for mothers than for fathers.

While the pathways that transmit risk from G2 mothers to their offspring seem to run more strongly through internal states and family processes, the more potent

FIGURE 6
INTERGENERATIONAL MODEL
OF ANTISOCIAL BEHAVIOR TO BE ESTIMATED

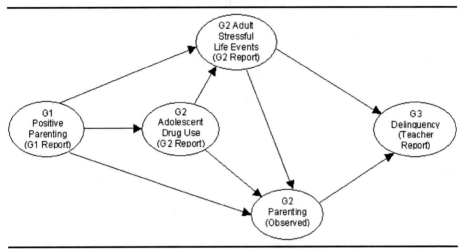

NOTE: G1-G3 are first through third generation, respectively.

pathways for fathers appear to be external to the family. Of particular importance are adjustment to work and stable employment careers (Moffitt et al. 2002). "Difficult, ill-tempered boys may experience problems in the adult domain most central to men's lives: work" (Elder, Caspi, and Downey 1986, 329). Curtailed employment opportunities and income have a particularly negative impact on fathering, leading to reduced father involvement and less effective parenting styles (Conger et al. 1993; McLoyd 1990; Thomson, Hanson, and McLanahan 1994).

Contact and involvement are also likely to be stronger mediators for fathers than for mothers. While mother involvement is almost a constant, father involvement, including living with the child, varies widely. It is influenced both by their prior problem behaviors (Jaffee et al. 2001; Smith et al. forthcoming) and the quality of their relationship with G3's mother (Furstenberg and Cherlin 1991; Parke 1996). The impact of father involvement on G3's problem behaviors is conditioned by their own antisocial behavior. For highly antisocial G2s, father absence decreases G3's antisocial behavior, but father presence increases G3's antisocial behavior (Jaffee et al. 2003; Thornberry and Krohn 2003).

Testing the model

Finally, I would like to present some preliminary results from the Rochester Intergenerational Study, an extension of the RYDS, which test key parts of this conceptual model. The estimated model (Figure 6) focuses on the mediating paths that link a parent's drug use during adolescence with his or her child's involvement in delinquency during childhood. For this analysis, the G3 children were between six and fifteen years of age, with an average age of about nine.

Consistent with the intergenerational theory just presented, the impact of the grandparent, G1, on the grandchild, G3, is hypothesized to be entirely indirect, mediated by G1's influence on G2's development. G1 positive parenting reduces the likelihood that G2 will be an adolescent drug user and, both directly and indirectly via adolescent drug use, impacts G2 life stressors during emerging adulthood. In addition, there is a direct transfer of parenting styles from G1 to G2, as well as indirect effects via the paths just discussed.

G2 adolescent drug use has indirect effects on G3 delinquency via the lifecourse disruption it causes for G2. Adolescent drug users, for the reasons laid out in the previous theory, are likely to experience greater levels of stress during emerging adulthood and are likely to exhibit ineffective styles of parenting once they become parents. These factors, in turn, increase the likelihood of G3 delinquent behavior during childhood.

The model in Figure 6 provides a strong test of these intergenerational processes. First, it is based on multimethod/multiagent measurement. G1 parenting is based on G1 interviews and includes scales of attachment and consistency of discipline. G2 drug use and life stressors are measured from the G2 interviews. The RYDS drug use index measures the frequency of the use of nine drugs ranging from marijuana to heroin and, in this analysis, covers use at ages 14.5 to 16.5. The stressful life events measure is a nine-item count of life stressors such as poverty, homelessness, and single-parenthood experienced during the first four years of the intergenerational study, when the G2 parents were in their early twenties to midtwenties. G2 parenting is based on videotaped observations of the G2-G3 dyad. Positive parenting is the sum of seven subscales (e.g., warmth/support, prosocial, positive parenting) and negative parenting of eleven subscales (e.g., hostility, angry coercion, harsh discipline), all measured by the Iowa Family Interaction Rating Scales (Melby et al. 1998). Finally, G3 delinquency is based on teacher reports using the Teacher Report Form developed by Achenbach (1991).

Second, the data cover a fifteen-year time span from when G1 parenting was measured until the measurement of the outcome, their grandchild's delinquency. Third, relying on the generality of the observational measures, we test models for warm, supportive parenting and for hostile, negative parenting, separately.

For the theoretical reasons presented above, results are presented separately for G2 mothers and G2 fathers. In the latter case, the sample is restricted to "supervisory fathers," fathers who either live with the child or have frequent contact in which they provide child care. In other analyses, we have not found significant linkages between G2 and G3 behavior for fathers with little or no contact; hence this sample restriction.

We begin by presenting the results for the G2 mothers and their families (Figure 7). The impact of G1 parenting on G3 delinquency is, as expected, mediated by its impact on G2 development. First, there is some evidence of intergenerational continuity in parenting style between mothers and daughters. G1 positive parenting is

FIGURE 7
INTERGENERATIONAL MODEL FOR G2 MOTHERS (*N* = 139)

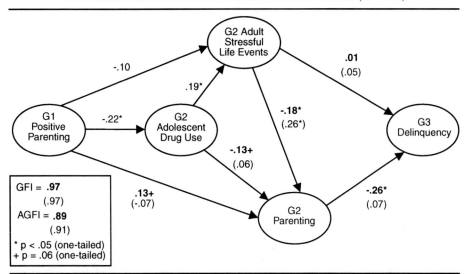

NOTE: Positive parenting model in bold; negative parenting model in parentheses. G1-G3 are first through third generation, respectively. GFI = generalized fit index; AGFI = adjusted generalized fit index.

positively related to G2 positive parenting (.13; *p* = .06). The more important influence of G1 parenting is indirect, via its impact on adolescent drug use.

Positive parenting by G1 reduces G2 drug use during adolescence. Adolescent drug use increases the likelihood of experiencing stress during emerging adulthood. In turn, stressors have a significant impact on G2 parenting, reducing warm, nurturing parenting and increasing hostile, negative parenting. There is also a direct association between adolescent drug use and positive parenting styles (−.13; *p* = .06).

Interestingly, the only significant influence on G3 delinquency is G2 positive parenting. When G2 mothers fail to provide warm, nurturing parenting to their children, those children are significantly more likely to be delinquent as reported by their teachers. And as we just saw, G2 parenting style is influenced by their earlier development and the parenting they received from G1. Negative parenting by these G2 mothers, however, is not linked to G2 delinquency; nor is it systematically related to the earlier variables.

The results for G2 supervisory fathers (Figure 8) offer an intriguing contrast. First, for G2 fathers it is the negative aspects of parenting—hostile, irritable reactions to the child—that are significantly related to G3 delinquency, not positive parenting. Second, negative life events have a significant direct impact on G3 delinquency, as well as an indirect impact via G2 negative parenting. These pater-

FIGURE 8
INTERGENERATIONAL MODEL FOR G2 SUPERVISORY FATHERS (*N* = 126)

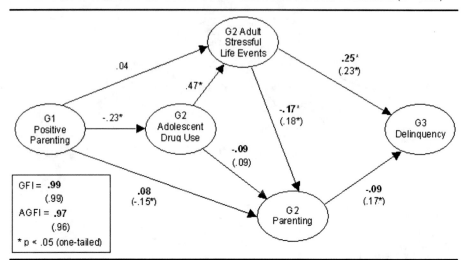

NOTE: Positive parenting model in bold; negative parenting model in parentheses. G1-G3 are first through third generation, respectively. GFI = generalized fit index; AGFI = adjusted generalized fit index.

nal characteristics are related to their earlier development, especially adolescent drug use. G2 fathers who used drugs are more apt to experience later stress, and that in turn leads to ineffective parenting styles.

In addition, the grandparent also has an indirect effect on these G3 children. First, there is some transfer of parenting styles across the generations. Grandmothers who exhibit positive style of parenting are less likely to have sons who exhibit hostile, negative parenting. G1 positive parenting also reduces adolescent drug use, and as we saw, that has important indirect influences on G3 delinquency.

Discussion

These intergenerational results have a number of interesting implications for understanding the origins of delinquency. I will close by briefly discussing four of them.

First, some intergenerational transfer of risk for antisocial behavior is evident in the Rochester study. The children of G2 parents who have higher levels of adolescent drug use are more apt to engage in delinquency, as reported by their teachers. This impact is mediated by some of the life-course consequences of adolescent drug use identified in our conceptual model.

Second, parent characteristics and behaviors, of both G2 fathers and G2 mothers, are obviously important in understanding the origins of delinquency. The nature of these effects are somewhat gender-specific, however. For mothers, failure to provide a warm, nurturing parenting environment increases the likelihood that their children will engage in delinquency. For the fathers, however, it is financial stress and harsh, negative parenting that influence their children's development. This pattern is consistent with dominant aspects of gender roles in American society. Mothers are expected to be more centrally involved in raising their children and in providing a nurturing environment; failure to do so creates risk for their children. Fathers are expected to be more centrally involved in work and career, and stress in this environment increases risk for their children both directly and via its impact on harsh, explosive parenting. Investigating these gender differences is an important task for future research, as is a fuller understanding of father effects, an unfortunately underinvestigated topic.

Third, these results also indicate that parenting behaviors are systematically related to earlier aspects of the parent's own development. The style of parenting for both mothers and fathers is produced in part by the style of parenting they received from G1 and by their earlier behavior patterns, such as adolescent drug use. Intergenerational studies have just begun to identify these earlier influences and their relative importance. An understanding of these origins will be quite helpful for the design of effective parenting programs.

Finally, the impact of "parenting" is not confined solely to the impact of parents. Grandparents also appear to have a role to play in creating risk (or resilience), for their grandchildren. Part of that effect is indirect, as evidenced in this analysis. But part of it can be direct, as seen in some of our other analyses (Thornberry, Krohn, and Freeman-Gallant forthcoming). Incorporating grandparental influences will also enhance our understanding of the origins and development of delinquent careers.

Conclusion

The onset of antisocial behavior and delinquency can occur at any age from childhood through, at least, the early adult years. And whenever it emerges, it can lead to careers of varying duration. As a result, development criminology is faced with a rather daunting challenge: to identify and explain these varying patterns of offending without grossly oversimplifying them. In the previous pages, I present interactional theory's perspective on these issues, including a systematic incorporation of intergenerational influences. No doubt this explanation will ultimately prove to be inadequate, but hopefully it will contribute in some measure to our growing understanding of the origins, course, and consequences of antisocial behavior.

Note

1. I would like to express my appreciation for Marv's theoretical insights and contributions to this joint effort.

References

Achenbach, Thomas M. 1991. *Manual for the teacher's report form and 1991 profile.* Burlington: University of Vermont Department of Psychiatry.

Amaro, Honalee, and Barry D. Zuckerman. 1992. Psychoactive substance use and adolescent pregnancy: Compounded risk among inner-city adolescent mothers. In *Adolescent stress: Causes and consequences,* ed. Mary Ellen Colten and Susan Gore. Hawthorne, NY: Aldine de Gruyter.

Ambert, Anne-Marie. 1997. *Parents, children, and adolescents: Interactive relationships and development in context.* New York: Haworth Press.

Angold, Adrian, E. Jane Costello, and Alaattin Erkanli. 1999. Comorbidity. *Journal of Child Psychology and Psychiatry* 40:57-87.

Arnett, Jeffrey J. 2000. Emerging adulthood: A theory of development from the late teens through the twenties. *American Psychologist* 55:469-80.

Bates, John E., Christine A. Maslin, and Karen A. Frankel. 1985. Attachment security, mother-child interaction, and temperament as predictors of behavior-problem ratings at three years. *Monographs of the Society for Research in Child Development* 50:167-93.

Bauer, Daniel J., and Patrick J. Curran. 2003. Distributional assumptions of growth mixture models: Implications for overextraction of latent trajectory classes. *Psychological Methods* 83:338-63.

———. 2004. The integration of continuous and discrete latent variable models: Potential problems and promising opportunities. *Psychological Methods* 91:3-29.

Belsky, Jay, Sharon Woodworth, and Keith Crnic. 1996. Troubled family interaction during toddlerhood. *Development and Psychopathology* 8:477-95.

Broidy, Lisa M., Daniel S. Nagin, Richard E. Tremblay, John E. Bates, Bobby Brame, Kenneth A. Dodge, David Fergusson, John L. Horwood, Rolf Loeber, Robert Laird, Donald R. Lynam, Terrie E. Moffitt, Gregory S. Pettit, and Frank Vitaro. 2003. Developmental trajectories of childhood disruptive behaviors and adolescent delinquency: A six-site, cross-national study. *Developmental Psychology* 39:222-45.

Bryant, Alison L., John E. Schulenberg, Patrick M. O'Malley, Jerald G. Bachman, and Lloyd D. Johnston. 2003. How academic achievement, attitudes, and behaviors relate to the course of substance use during adolescence: A 6-year, multiwave national longitudinal study. *Journal of Research on Adolescence* 13:361-97.

Bushway, Shawn D., Alex R. Piquero, Lisa M. Broidy, Elizabeth E. Cauffman, and Paul Mazerolle. 2001. An empirical framework for studying desistance as a process. *Criminology* 39:491-515.

Bushway, Shawn D., Terence P. Thornberry, and Marvin D. Krohn. 2003. Desistance as a developmental process: A comparison of static and dynamic approaches. *Journal of Quantitative Criminology* 19:129-53.

Capaldi, Deborah M., and Mike Stoolmiller. 1999. Co-occurrence of conduct problems and depressive symptoms in early adolescent boys: III. Prediction to young-adult adjustment. *Development and Psychopathology* 11:59-84.

Caspi, Avshalom, Daryl J. Bem, and Glen H. Elder Jr. 1989. Continuities and consequences of interactional styles across the life course. *Journal of Personality* 57:375-406.

Caspi, Avshalom, and Glen H. Elder Jr. 1988. Emergent family patterns: The intergenerational construction of problem behavior and relationships. In *Relationships within families: Mutual influence,* ed. Robert A. Hinde and Joan Stevenson-Hinde. Oxford: Oxford University Press.

Cohen, Albert. 1955. *Delinquent boys.* New York: Free Press.

Coie, John D., and Kenneth A. Dodge. 1998. Aggression and antisocial behavior. In *Handbook of child psychology,* vol. 3, ed. William Damon and Nancy Eisenberg. New York: Wiley.

Coie, John D., John E. Lochman, Robert Terry, and Clarine Hyman. 1992. Predicting early adolescent disorder from childhood aggression and peer rejection. *Journal of Consulting and Clinical Psychology* 60:783-92.

Conger, John J. 1991. *Adolescence and youth: Psychological development in a changing world.* 4th ed. New York: HarperCollins.

Conger, Rand D., Katherine J. Conger, Glen H. Elder Jr., Frederick O. Lorenz, Ronald L. Simons, and Les B. Whitbeck. 1992. A family process model of economic hardship and adjustment of early adolescent boys. *Child Development* 63:526-41.

Conger, Rand D., and Glen B. Elder 1994. *Families in troubled times: Adapting to change in rural America.* Hillsdale, NJ: Aldine de Gruyter.

Conger, Rand D., Xiaojia Ge, Glen H. Elder Jr., Frederick O. Lorenz, and Ronald L. Simons. 1994. Economic stress, coercive family process and developmental problems of adolescents. *Child Development* 65:541-61.

Conger, Rand D., Frederick O. Lorenz, Glen H. Elder Jr., Ronald L. Simons, and Xiaojia Ge. 1993. Husband and wife differences in response to undesirable life events. *Journal of Health and Social Behavior* 34:71-88.

Conger, Rand D., John A. McCarty, Raymond K. Lang, and Benjamin B. Lahey. 1984. Perception of child, child-rearing values, and emotional distress as mediating links between environmental stressors and observed maternal behavior. *Child Development* 55:2234-74.

Cooper, Catherine R., Harold D. Grotevant, and Sherri M. Condon. 1983. Individuality and connectedness in the family as a context for adolescent identity formation and role-taking skill. In *Adolescent development in the family*, ed. Harold D. Grotevant and Catherine R. Cooper. San Francisco: Jossey-Bass.

Costello, E. Jane, Alaattin Erkanli, Elizabeth Federman, and Adrian Angold. 1999. Development of psychiatric comorbidity with substance abuse in adolescents: Effects of timing and sex. *Journal of Clinical Child Psychology* 28:298-311.

Cox, Martha J., Margaret T. Owen, Jerry M. Lewis, and V. Kay Henderson. 1989. Marriage, adult adjustment, and early parenting. *Child Development* 60:1015-24.

Dannefer, Dale. 1984. Adult development and social theory: A paradigmatic reappraisal. *American Sociological Review* 49:100-116.

Day, Nancy, and Kenneth E. Leonard. 1985. Alcohol, drug use and psychopathology in the general population. In *Substance abuse and psychopathology*, ed. Arthur I. Alterman. New York: Plenum.

Dishion, Thomas J., Gerald R. Patterson, and John B. Reid. 1985. Parenting practices in the etiology of child drug use: Implications for treatment and prevention. Paper presented to the NIDA Technical Review Committee on Adolescent Drug Abuse: Analysis of Treatment and Research, Washington, DC.

Doherty, William J., Edward F. Kouneski, and Martha F. Erickson. 1998. Responsible fathering: An overview and conceptual framework. *Journal of Marriage and the Family* 60:277-92.

Eggleston, Elaine P., and John H. Laub. 2002. The onset of adult offending: A neglected dimension of the criminal career. *Journal of Criminal Justice* 30:603-22.

Eggleston, Elaine P., John H. Laub, and Robert J. Sampson. 2004. Methodological sensitivities to latent class analysis of long-term criminal trajectories. *Journal of Quantitative Criminology* 20:1-26.

Elder, Glen H., Jr. 1985. Perspectives on the life course. In *Life course dynamics*, ed. Glen H. Elder Jr. Ithaca, NY: Cornell University Press.

———. 1997. The life course and human development. In *Handbook of child psychology*, vol. 1, *Theoretical models of human development*, ed. Richard M. Lerner. New York: Wiley.

———. 1998. The life course as developmental theory. *Child Development* 69:1-12.

Elder, Glen H., Jr., Avshalom Caspi, and Geraldine Downey. 1986. Problem behavior and family relationships: Life course and intergenerational themes. In *Human development and the life course: Multidisciplinary perspectives*, ed. Aage Sorensen, Franz Weinert, and Lonnie Sherrod. Hillsdale, NJ: Lawrence Erlbaum.

Ellickson, Phyllis L., Khanh Bui, Robert Bell, and Kimberly McGuigan. 1998. Does early drug use increase the risk of dropping out of high school? *Journal of Drug Issues* 28:357-80.

Elster, Arthur B., Michael E. Lamb, and Jane Tavare. 1987. Association between behavioral and school problems and fatherhood in a national sample of adolescent fathers. *Journal of Pediatrics* 11:932-36.

Fergusson, David M., and John L. Horwood. 1997. Early onset cannabis use and psychosocial adjustment in young adults. *Addiction* 92:279-96.

Furstenberg, Frank F., Jr., Jeanne Brooks-Gunn, and S. Philip Morgan. 1987. *Adolescent mothers in later life.* Cambridge: Cambridge University Press.

Furstenberg, Frank F., Jr., and Andrew Cherlin. 1991. *Divided families: What happens to children when parents part.* Cambridge, MA: Harvard University Press.

Gecas, Viktor, and Monica A. Seff. 1990. Social class and self-esteem: Psychological centrality, compensation, and the relative effects of work and home. *Social Psychology Quarterly* 53:165-73.

Gottfredson, Michael R., and Travis Hirschi. 1990. *A general theory of crime.* Stanford, CA: Stanford University Press.

Grolnick, Wendy S., Lisa J. Bridges, and James P. Connell. 1996. Emotion regulation in two-year-olds: Strategies and emotional expression in four contexts. *Child Development* 67:928-41.

Hardy, Janet B., Nan M. Astone, Jeanne Brooks-Gunn, Sam Shapiro, and Therese L. Miller 1998. Like mother, like child: Intergenerational patterns of age at first birth and associations with childhood and adolescent characteristics and adult outcomes in the second generation. *Developmental Psychology* 34:1220-32.

Hirschi, Travis. 1969. *Causes of delinquency.* Berkeley: University of California Press.

Jaffee, Sara R., Avshalom Caspi, Terrie E. Moffitt, Alan Taylor, and Nigel Dickson. 2001. Predicting early fatherhood and whether young fathers live with their children: Prospective findings and policy reconsiderations. *Journal of Child Psychology and Psychiatry* 42:803-15.

Jaffee, Sara R., Terrie E. Moffitt, Avshalom Caspi, and Alan Taylor. 2003. Life with or without father: The benefits of living with two biological parents depend on the father's antisocial behavior. *Child Development* 74:109-26.

Jang, Sung Joon, and Carolyn A. Smith. 1997. A test of reciprocal causal relationships among parental supervision, affective ties, and delinquency. *Journal of Research in Crime and Delinquency* 34:307-36.

Jessor, Richard. 1976. Predicting time of onset of marijuana use: A developmental study of high school youth. *Journal of Consulting and Clinical Psychology* 44:125-34.

Jessor, Richard, John E. Donovan, and Frances M. Costa. 1991. *Beyond adolescence: Problem behavior and young adult development.* Cambridge: Cambridge University Press.

Johnston, Lloyd D., Patrick M. O'Malley, and Jerald G. Bachman. 1985. *Use of licit and illicit drugs by America's high school students, 1975-1984.* Rockville, MD: National Institute of Drug Abuse.

Kandel, Denise B. 1978. Homophily, selection and socialization in adolescent friendships. *American Journal of Sociology* 84:427-36.

Kandel, Denise B., Mark Davies, Daniel Karus, and Kazuo Yamaguchi. 1986. The consequences in young adulthood of adolescent drug involvement. *Archives of General Psychiatry* 43:746-54.

Kandel, Denise B., and John A. Logan. 1984. Patterns of drug use from adolescence to young adulthood: I. Periods of risk for initiation, continued use, and discontinuation. *American Journal of Public Health* 74:660-66.

Kaplan, Howard B., Robert J. Johnson, and Carol A. Bailey. 1986. Self-rejection and the explanation of deviance: Specification of the structure among latent constructs. *American Journal of Sociology* 92:384-411.

Kaplan, Howard B., Steven S. Martin, and Cynthia Robbins. 1984. Pathways to adolescent drug use: Self-derogation, peer influence, weakening of social controls, and early substance use. *Journal of Health and Social Behavior* 25:270-88.

Krohn, Marvin D. 1986. The web of conformity: A network approach to the explanation of delinquent behavior. *Social Problems* 33:581-93.

Krohn, Marvin D., Alan J. Lizotte, and Cynthia M. Perez. 1997. The interrelationship between substance use and precocious transitions to adult statuses. *Journal of Health and Social Behavior* 38:87-103.

Krohn, Marvin D., Alan J. Lizotte, Terence P. Thornberry, Carolyn Smith, and David McDowall. 1996. Reciprocal causal relationships among drug use, peers, and beliefs: A five-wave panel model. *Journal of Drug Issues* 26:405-28.

Krohn, Marvin D., and James L. Massey. 1980. Social control and delinquent behavior: An examination of the elements of the social bond. *Sociological Quarterly* 21:529-43.

Krohn, Marvin D., Terence P. Thornberry, Lori Collins-Hall, and Alan J. Lizotte. 1995. School dropout, delinquent behavior, and drug use: An examination of the causes and consequences of dropping out of school. In *Drugs, crime, and other deviant adaptations: Longitudinal studies*, ed. Howard B. Kaplan. New York: Plenum.

Krohn, Marvin D., Terence P. Thornberry, Craig Rivera, and Marc LeBlanc. 2001. Later delinquency careers. In *Child delinquents: Development, intervention, and service needs*, ed. Rolf Loeber and David P. Farrington. Thousand Oaks, CA: Sage.

Ladd, Gary W. 1990. Having friends, keeping friends, making friends, and being liked by peers in the classroom: Predictors of children's early school adjustment. *Child Development* 61:312-31.

Lahey, Benjamin B., Rand D. Conger, Beverly M. Atkeson, and Frank A. Treiber. 1984. Parenting behavior and emotional status of physically abusive mothers. *Journal of Consulting and Clinical Psychology* 52:1062-72.

Laub, John H., and Robert J. Sampson. 2003. *Shared beginnings, divergent lives: Delinquent boys to age 70.* Cambridge, MA: Harvard University Press.

Lee, Carolyn L., and John E. Bates. 1985. Mother-child interaction at two years and perceived difficult temperament. *Child Development* 56:1314-25.

Loeber, Rolf, and Marc LeBlanc. 1990. Toward a developmental criminology. In *Crime and justice: An annual review of research*, vol. 11, ed. Michael Tonry and Norval Morris. Chicago: University of Chicago Press.

Matza, David. 1964. *Delinquency and drift*. New York: John Wiley.

McGee, Zina T., and Spencer R. Baker. 2002. Impact of violence on problem behavior among adolescents: Risk factors among an urban sample. *Journal of Contemporary Criminal Justice* 18:74-93.

McLoyd, Vonnie. 1990. The impact of economic hardship on black families and children: Psychological distress, parenting, and socioemotional development. *Child Development* 61:311-46.

Melby, Janet N., Rand D. Conger, Ruth Book, Martha Rueter, Laura Lucy, Daniel Repinski, Shauna Rogers, Barbara Rogers, and Laura Scaramella. 1998. *The Iowa Family Interaction Rating Scales*. 5th ed. Ames: Iowa State University Institute for Social and Behavioral Research.

Mensch, B. S., and Denise B. Kandel. 1988. Dropping out of high school and drug involvement. *Sociology of Education* 61:95-113.

Moffitt, Terrie E. 1993. "Life-course-persistent" and "adolescence-limited" antisocial behavior: A developmental taxonomy. *Psychological Review* 100:674-701.

———. 1996. The neuropsychology of conduct disorder. In *Readings in contemporary criminological theory*, ed. Peter Cordella and Lawrence J. Siegel. Boston: Northeastern University Press.

———. 2002. Males on the life-course-persistent and adolescence-limited antisocial pathways: Follow-up at 26 years. *Development and Psychopathology* 14:179-207.

Moffitt, Terrie E., Avshalom Caspi, Honalee Harrington, and Barry J. Milne. 2002. Males on the life-course-persistent and adolescence-limited antisocial pathways: Follow-up at age 26 years. *Development and Psychopathology* 14:179-207.

Moffitt, Terrie E., Avshalom Caspi, Michael Rutter, and Phil Silva. 2001. *Sex differences in antisocial behavior: Conduct disorder, delinquency, and violence in the Dunedin Longitudinal Study*. New York: Cambridge University Press.

Moffitt, Terrie E., Donald R. Lynam, and Phil A. Silva. 1994. Neuropsychological tests predict persistent male delinquency. *Criminology* 32:101-24.

Nagin, Daniel S., David P. Farrington, and Terrie E. Moffitt. 1995. Different types of offenders. *Criminology* 33:111-39.

Nagin, Daniel S., and Kenneth C. Land. 1993. Age, criminal careers, and population heterogeneity: Specification and estimation of a nonparametric, mixed Poisson model. *Criminology* 31:327-62.

Newcomb, Michael D., and Peter M. Bentler. 1986. Cocaine use among young adults. *Advances in Alcohol and Substance Abuse* 6:73-96.

———. 1987. Changes in drug use from high school to young adulthood: Effects of living arrangement and current life pursuit. *Journal of Applied Developmental Psychology* 8:221-46.

———. 1988. *Consequences of adolescent drug use: Impact on the lives of young adults*. Newbury Park, CA: Sage.

Parke, Ross D. 1996. *Fatherhood*. Cambridge, MA: Harvard University Press.

Patterson, Gerald R. 1993. Orderly change in a stable world: The antisocial trait as a chimera. *Journal of Consulting and Clinical Psychology* 61:911-19.

Patterson, Gerald R., Deborah Capaldi, and Lew Bank. 1991. An early starter model for predicting delinquency. In *The development and treatment of childhood aggression*, ed. Debra J. Pepler and Kenneth H. Rubin. Hillsdale, NJ: Lawrence Erlbaum.

Patterson, Gerald R., John B. Reid, and Thomas J. Dishion. 1992. *Antisocial boys*. Eugene, OR: Castalia Press.

Piquero, Alex R. 2004. Taking stock of developmental trajectories of criminal activity over the life course. Unpublished manuscript.

Pogarsky, Greg, Alan J. Lizotte, and Terence P. Thornberry. 2003. The delinquency of children born to teenage mothers: Results from the Rochester Youth Development Study. *Criminology* 41:1249-86.

Prior, Margot, Ann Sanson, Raeleen Carroll, and Frank Oberklaid. 1989. Social class differences in temperament ratings by mothers of preschool children. *Merrill-Palmer Quarterly* 35:239-48.

Rindfuss, Ronald R. 1991. The young adult years: Diversity, structural change, and fertility. *Demography* 28:493-512.

Rodgers, Joan R. 1995. An empirical study of intergenerational transmission of poverty in the United States. *Social Science Quarterly* 76:178-94.

Rutter, Michael 1987. Psychological resilience and protective mechanisms. *American Journal of Orthopsychiatry* 47:316-31.

Rutter, Michael, Henri Giller, and Ann Hagell. 1998. *Antisocial behavior by young people*. Cambridge: Cambridge University Press.

Rutter, Michael, Richard Harrington, David Quinton, and Andrew Pickles. 1994. Adult outcome of conduct disorder in childhood: Implications for concepts and definitions of patterns of psychopathology. In *Adolescent problem behaviors: Issues and research*, ed. Robert D. Ketterlinus and Michael E. Lamb. Hillsdale, NJ: Lawrence Erlbaum.

Rutter, Michael, and David Quinton. 1984. Parental psychiatric disorder: Effects on children. *Psychological Medicine* 14:853-80.

Sampson, Robert J., and John Laub. 1993. *Crime in the making: Pathways and turning points through life*. Cambridge, MA: Harvard University Press.

Schwendinger, Herman, and Julia S. Schwendinger. 1985. *Adolescent subcultures and delinquency*. Westport, CT: Praeger.

Shaw, Daniel S., and Richard Q. Bell. 1993. Developmental theories of parental contributors to antisocial behavior. *Journal of Abnormal Child Psychology* 21:35-49.

Shaw, Daniel S., Miles Gilliom, Erin M. Ingoldsby, and Daniel S. Nagin. 2003. Trajectories leading to school-age conduct problems. *Developmental Psychology* 39:189-200.

Shaw, Daniel S., Elizabeth B. Owens, Joan I. Vondra, Kate Keenan, and Emily B. Winslow. 1996. Early risk factors and pathways in the development of early disruptive behavior problems. *Development and Psychopathology* 8:679-99.

Silverthorn, Persephanie, and Paul J. Frick. 1999. Developmental pathways to antisocial behavior: The delayed-onset pathway in girls. *Development and Psychopathology* 11:101-26.

Simons, Ronald L., Jay Beaman, Rand D. Conger, and Wei Chao. 1993. Childhood experience, conceptions of parenting, and attitudes of spouse as determinants of parental behavior. *Journal of Marriage and the Family* 55:91-106.

Simons, Ronald L., Kuei-Hsiu Lin, Leslie C. Gordon, Rand D. Conger, and Frederick O. Lorenz. 1999. Explaining the higher incidence of adjustment problems among children of divorce compared with those in two-parent families. *Journal of Marriage and the Family* 61:1020-33.

Smith, Carolyn A., Marvin D. Krohn, Rebekah Chu, and Oscar Best. Forthcoming. African American fathers: Myths and realities about their involvement with their firstborn children. *Journal of Family Issues*.

Smith, Carolyn A., Alan J. Lizotte, Terence P. Thornberry, and Marvin D. Krohn. 1995. Resilient youth: Identifying factors that prevent high-risk youth from engaging in delinquency and drug use. In *Delinquency and disrepute in the life course*, ed. John Hagan. Greenwich, CT: JAI.

Steinberg, Laurence, and Amanda S. Morris. 2001. Adolescent development. *Annual Review of Psychology* 52:83-110.

Stinchcombe, Arthur L. 1964. *Rebellion in a high school*. Chicago: Quadrangle Books.

Stott, Denis H. 1978. Epidemiological indicators of the origins of behavior disturbance as measured by the Bristol Social Adjustment Guides. *Genetic Psychology Monographs* 97:127-59.

Taylor, Jeanette, Matt McGue, and William G. Iacono. 2000. Sex differences, assortative mating, and cultural transmission effects on adolescent delinquency: A twin family study. *Journal of Child Psychology and Psychiatry* 41:433-40.

Thomson, Elizabeth, Thomas L. Hanson, and Sara S. McLanahan. 1994. Family structure and child well-being: Economic resources versus parent socialization. *Social Forces* 73:221-42.

Thornberry, Terence P., Shawn Bushway, Marvin D. Krohn, and Alan J. Lizotte. 2004. Accounting for behavioral change. Paper presented at the annual meeting of the American Society of Criminology, Nashville, TN, November.

Thornberry, Terence P., Adrienne Freeman-Gallant, Alan J. Lizotte, Marvin D. Krohn, and Carolyn A. Smith. 2003. Linked lives: The intergenerational transmission of antisocial behavior. *Journal of Abnormal Child Psychology* 31:171-84.

Thornberry, Terence P., and Marvin D. Krohn. 2001. The development of delinquency: An interactional perspective. In *Handbook of youth and justice*, ed. Susan O. White. New York: Plenum.

———. 2003. Intergenerational patterns of drug use. Presentation to staff at the Division of Epidemiology, Services, and Prevention Research, National Institute on Drug Abuse, Rockville, MD, July.

———. 2005. Applying interactional theory to the explanation of continuity and change in antisocial behavior. In *Integrated developmental and life course theories of offending advances in criminological theory*, vol. 14, ed. David P. Farrington. Piscataway, NJ: Transaction.

Thornberry, Terence P., Marvin D. Krohn, and Adrienne Freeman-Gallant. Forthcoming. Intergenerational roots of early onset substance use. *Journal of Drug Issues.*

Thornberry, Terence P., Marvin D. Krohn, and Alan J. Lizotte. 2005. Intergenerational influences on risk for substance use and associated health risk. Proposal submitted to the National Institute on Drug Abuse, National Institutes of Health, Rockville, MD.

Thornberry, Terence P., Marvin D. Krohn, Alan J. Lizotte, Carolyn A. Smith, and Kimberly Tobin. 2003. *Gangs and delinquency in developmental perspective.* New York: Cambridge University Press.

Thornberry, Terence P., Alan J. Lizotte, Marvin D. Krohn, Margaret Farnworth, and Sung Joon Jang. 1991. Testing interactional theory: An examination of reciprocal causal relationships among family, school, and delinquency. *Journal of Criminal Law and Criminology* 82:3-35.

———. 1994. Delinquent peers, beliefs, and delinquent behavior: A longitudinal test of interactional theory. *Criminology* 32:47-83.

Thornberry, Terence P., Carolyn A. Smith, and Gregory J. Howard. 1997. Risk factors for teenage fatherhood. *Journal of Marriage and the Family* 59:505-22.

Tibbetts, Stephen G., and Alex R. Piquero. 1999. The influence of gender, low birth weight, and disadvantaged environment in predicting early onset of offending: A test of Moffitt's interactional hypothesis. *Criminology* 37:843-78.

Tolan, Patrick H., Nancy G. Guerra, and Philip C. Kendall. 1995. Introduction to special section: Prediction and prevention of antisocial behavior in children and adolescents. *Journal of Consulting and Clinical Psychology* 63:515-17.

Tremblay, Richard E., Daniel S. Nagin, Jean R. Seguin, Mark Zoccolillo, Philip D. Zelazo, Michel Boivin, Daniel Perusse, and Christa Japel. 2004. Physical aggression during early childhood: Trajectories and predictors. *Pediatrics* 114:e43-e50.

Warr, Mark. 1998. Life-course transitions and desistance from crime. *Criminology* 36:183-216.

Werner, Emmy E., and Ruth S. Smith. 1992. *Overcoming the odds: High risk children from birth to adulthood.* Ithaca, NY: Cornell University Press.

Wolfgang, Marvin E., Terence P. Thornberry, and Robert M. Figlio. 1987. *From boy to man, from delinquency to crime.* Chicago: University of Chicago Press.

Zahn-Waxler, Carolyn, Ronald J. Iannotti, E. Mark Cummings, and Susan Denham. 1990. Antecedents of problem behaviors in children of depressed mothers. *Development and Psychopathology* 2:271-91.

Making Sense of Crime and the Life Course

By
D. WAYNE OSGOOD

This article reflects on the progress of research on developmental and life-course criminology, comments on the status of some unresolved issues, and offers recommendations for the future. The first sections relate these articles and the current status of the field to two themes from the criminal careers debate of the 1980s and 1990s: generalization versus disaggregation as approaches to advancing science and continuous versus categorical conceptions of variation in criminal careers. The article also discusses the use of the growth curve models that are so prominent in developmental and life-span research, emphasizing the aspects of change that they do and do not capture, pointing out implications of that limitation for the need for expanding theories and models of change, and explaining the simple steps needed to enhance growth curve models to accomplish that purpose.

Keywords: life course; developmental criminology; growth curves; trajectories; criminal careers; crime; delinquency

I am honored to have been asked to comment on Terry Thornberry's article as well as on the broader set of issues raised by all three lead articles. In 1992, Sampson and Laub could reasonably lament that criminologists paid little attention to any age period other than adolescence, but since then developmental and life-course studies of crime have become one of the liveliest and most prominent areas of research in this field. The lead articles demonstrate this well, as

D. Wayne Osgood is a professor in the Crime, Law and Justice Program of the Department of Sociology at Pennsylvania State University, and he is a member of the MacArthur Research Network on Transitions to Adulthood and of the National Consortium on Violence Research. His research focuses on delinquency and other deviant behaviors of adolescence and early adulthood as well as quantitative methods for criminological research. He has published substantive research on peers and delinquency, time use and deviance, criminal careers, the generality of deviance, and biology and crime, and he has written methodological articles concerning multilevel models for longitudinal research, scaling self-reported delinquency, and limited and discrete dependent variables.

DOI: 10.1177/0002716205280383

Sampson and Laub follow former teen offenders to age seventy, Nagin and Tremblay trace origins of offending to the second year of life, and Thornberry examines influences on offending across three generations. As is so evident in the work of these influential scholars, there is much to celebrate in the field's progress, and their articles provide an occasion for reflecting on where we have come from and where we should be going.

My comments fall into two sections. In the first, I will relate these articles to themes from the criminal careers debate of the late 1980s and early 1990s. Doing so will prove useful both for illuminating the progress that has been made on the fundamental issue of whether parsimony or disaggregation is the most productive approach for developing useful life-course explanations and for reminding us of an important issue on which there has been a tacit, but in my view premature, resolution. The second section concerns methodological issues. Growth curve and trajectory models have come to be the primary tools for studying offending over age spans, and I will comment on the aspects of change that these methods do and do not capture. From these observations, I will draw implications about how reliance on those methods has influenced which questions we tend to ask about crime over the life course. I will encourage readers to broaden their use of these methods to study the process of change rather than just its predictors, which also provides a means to test explanations of the age-crime curve.

Themes from the Great Debate

The criminal careers debate began with Gottfredson and Hirschi's (1986) forceful challenge to the criminal career paradigm of the National Research Council's Panel on Research on Criminal Careers (Blumstein et al. 1986). This challenge initiated a lengthy exchange among these authors (Blumstein, Cohen, and Farrington 1988a, 1988b; Gottfredson and Hirschi 1988), accompanied by solicited commentaries from other leading figures (Hagan and Palloni 1988; Tittle 1988), all of which enticed additional authors to join the conversation (Rowe, Osgood, and Nicewander 1990; Greenberg 1991), in turn provoking further response and commentary (Barnett et al. 1992; Greenberg 1992; Land 1992; Osgood and Rowe 1994). I view the debate as a watershed event that stimulated the growth of research on crime and the life course by highlighting critical intellectual challenges and suggesting a variety of approaches for addressing them.

The criminal careers debate did not end in resolution but rather reverberates still in continuing waves of research. Naturally, as time passes the debate's core articles gradually lose their places on reading lists in favor of newer work, and the debate itself has receded from the preoccupations of the field. Yet as I read this set of articles, I found it useful to reflect on the current state of developmental and life-course criminology in light of some issues from the debate.

The criminal careers debate and the mission of science

I found the life-course aspects of Thornberry's interactional theory (2005 [this volume]; Thornberry and Krohn, forthcoming) especially interesting in light of the contrasting views of the mission of science that emerged as the essential point of contention across the iterations of the criminal careers debate. Gottfredson and Hirschi advocated general principles and parsimony as the best means of advancing knowledge while Blumstein and colleagues promoted disaggregation to isolate an essential coherence underlying the diversity of crime. The criminal career paradigm characterized an individual's offending over the life course in terms of several parameters, including participation, frequency, age of onset, and age of termination. Blumstein, Cohen, and Farrington (1988a, 1988b) saw this disaggregation as having great value because there may be different causal processes for each parameter. Gottfredson and Hirschi (1988) argued that it is more fruitful to explain crime in general, as most criminological theories attempt to do, which would parsimoniously account for all of the career parameters as well.

My forays into the criminal career debate with my friend David Rowe (Osgood and Rowe 1994; Rowe, Osgood, and Nicewander 1990) offered a conceptual and statistical framework for empirically testing the relative merit of these two positions. We proposed translating Gottfredson and Hirschi's position into a framework in which a single, latent propensity to offend generates the various parameters of the criminal career paradigm. Evidence that this model accounted for relationships between those parameters would support their position, while evidence that it did not would support the criminal career paradigm.

A weak point of the criminal career paradigm was that it offered no theory to lend substance to Blumstein and colleagues' claim that there would be different causes for the various career parameters. Though not explicitly built on the career paradigm, Moffitt's (1993) developmental taxonomy in many ways filled this bill with its interesting and coherent portrayal of separate causal processes producing distinct patterns of offending over the life course. Notably, her theory made predictions contrary to uniform explanations, such as that adolescent limited offenders would commit just as many offenses in the midteens as life-course persistent offenders, that preteen measures of offending would predict adult crime better than would more recent late-teen measures, and that life-course persistent offenders' high offense rates would not regress toward the mean. The distinctiveness of her position is also evident in comparison to Patterson and Yoerger's (1993, 1997). Though age of onset is the key predictor of long-term offending in both, Patterson and Yoerger (1997) viewed late-onset offending as stemming from lower levels of the same causal factors, rather than from entirely different causal processes.

Thornberry does not present interactional theory as taking a stance on the issue of unified versus disaggregated theory. I find that it embodies a productive one, however, and I commend it to others as a model for developing life-course theory. Interactional theory treats criminal career features such as onset, frequency, and duration as phenomena worthy of attention but not as deriving from separate causal processes. The theory instead unites them through a unified explanation, thereby using a parsimonious and general framework to give serious attention to the phenomena highlighted by the criminal career paradigm.

Thornberry and Krohn (forthcoming) built this unifying position around the simple idea that offending at all ages is the result of the total magnitude of all relevant causal forces. Thornberry notes that this stance meshes with the developmental principle of equifinality, which is that many potential combinations of influences can produce the same result. I would also add that it matches the conception of propensity in the Rowe and Osgood framework.

Thornberry follows and extends Sampson and Laub's (1993) life-span developmental orientation through careful attention to the age-graded relevance of the key causal factors. In interactional theory, this varying relevance is largely due to age differences in the levels of the causal variables. For instance, poor parenting is a prominent cause of early-onset offending because children are exposed to varying parental skills quite early, while peer delinquency is tied to late-onset offending because it is rare to have many delinquent friends until early adolescence. The age difference in causal contribution is because the levels rather than causal impacts of these factors vary with age. Thus, this parsimonious framework would also predict that heavy exposure to delinquent peers at an exceptionally young age could engender early-onset offending and a radical shift from good to bad parenting could produce late-onset offending.

Thornberry wisely reserves the possibility that a variable's causal impact would change with age for exceptional cases when that is justified by a strong life-course argument. A good example is the prediction that early neuropsychological deficits will become more consequential as youth move from adolescence to adulthood. Thornberry reasons that strong parental guidance can no longer compensate for these weaknesses after youth leave home to face alone the challenges of employment and family formation.

In contrast with the criminal career paradigm's call for separate explanations for the onset and duration of offending, interactional theory also takes a unified approach to explaining the stability of offending and its association with age of onset. Making good use of the idea that offending is a product of the total causal force, Thornberry accounts for stability of offending through the combination of stable causes and the correlation of earlier causes with later ones. Thus, neuropsychological deficits and poor parenting engender early onset because they are present early, and this offending is likely to persist both because there is relatively little change in either factor and because both contribute to later influences such as school failure. Interestingly, though these predictions of interactional theory are largely consistent with Moffitt's (1993) account, Thornberry's unified treatment leads him to subtle but important differences. Specifically, he views age of onset as a continuous variable of modest predictive power rather than the key marker for a typology of persistent versus short-term offending. Note that his position is in essential agreement with Hirschi and Gottfredson's (1983) argument that the correlation between continuity and age of onset is not itself of causal significance but rather arises only because early onset is rare (and thus reflects high causal force or propensity) and offending is relatively stable.

I have a few suggestions for modest alterations in the current presentation of interactional theory that I think tighten its consistency around the features of its general explanatory approach that I find especially appealing. The first is to avoid the "risk factor" approach of dichotomizing continuous variables, such as converting an extensive measure of parenting skills to poor versus adequate parenting. This commonplace practice may be useful for simplifying practitioners' diagnostic inventories or for aiding communication to nonscientific audiences. Yet for scientific purposes, ignoring differences of degree seems a poor match to interactional theory's emphasis on total causal force and attention to stability and change in causal variables. I would also recommend that Thornberry rethink the position that extreme levels of causal factors are inherently stable and therefore produce stable offending. The ubiquitous tendency for regression to the mean implies that this is especially unlikely, and the position strikes me as logically unnecessary as well. A simpler and plausible position would be that when risk is extreme, even a moderate improvement is likely to leave sufficient causal force to produce continued offending. Weekly child abuse is a definite improvement over daily, but it is still highly problematic.

In 1992, Sampson and Laub could reasonably lament that criminologists paid little attention to any age period other than adolescence, but since then developmental and life-course studies of crime have become one of the liveliest and most prominent areas of research in this field.

Finally, I would encourage Thornberry and all other developmental and life-span criminologists to be wary of the difficulties inherent in the criminal career concept of participation, which is the distinction between being an active offender at any time or not. This simple idea underlies all of the criminal career parameters, but its meaning is entirely dependent on the choice of a measure of offending. The striking differences between the distributions of age of onset presented in this volume by Thornberry (concentrated in early adolescence) and by Nagin and Tremblay (concentrated in toddlerhood) illustrate this dependence. I find the contrast interesting and informative precisely because it is interpretable in light of the different criteria for offending that each uses to define onset. The lesson is that key topics such as onset, desistance, and continuity of offending are not clear-cut unitary phenomena. Rather, meaningful theory and research on each necessarily rests on a somewhat arbitrary choice of what we will and will not count as offending. I recommend two steps in acknowledgement of this fact. First, scholars should be explicit about these choices and give attention to the likely consequences of having made one choice rather than another. Second, we should follow Thornberry's lead in seeking unifying explanations that make sense of the differences in results produced by alternative offense criteria.

In praise of shades of gray

Are there just a few different types of offenders, or is involvement in crime a continuous dimension permitting fine distinctions among people at many different levels? This contrast between categorical and continuous conceptions of crime is a theme from the criminal careers debate that is visible in the three lead articles of this volume. Early empirical work modeling criminal careers typically assumed offenders fell into only a few different groups, each essentially homogeneous and categorically different from the others and from nonoffenders (e.g., Blumstein, Farrington, and Moitra 1985). Some critics of the criminal careers paradigm took issue with this approach. They argued that this assumption was arbitrary and made little theoretical sense, and they offered evidence that a model assuming a continuous distribution could fit the frequency distributions of various measures of offending at least as well as models that assumed discrete groups (Rowe, Osgood, and Nicewander 1990; Greenberg 1991).

Since the early 1990s, two developments in the field have given impetus to categorical approaches to developmental and life-course criminology. First, the developmental taxonomies of Moffitt (1993) and Patterson and Yoerger (1993) provided strong theoretical statements supporting distinct types of offenders, thus filling a major gap in the early criminal career research. These theories proved enormously influential, leading researchers to a wide variety of interesting research questions that directly or indirectly concerned offender types.

The second spur to categorical approaches was methodological. Nagin and Land's (1993) statistical model of offense trajectories provided a flexible means of empirically distinguishing groups of individuals with different patterns of offending over time. By enabling individual-level analyses, suitably acknowledging the probabilistic nature of offending, and allowing researchers to relate explanatory variables to offense patterns, their approach resolved the major shortcomings of earlier models of criminal careers (Land 1992). Since their original article, Nagin and colleagues have enhanced their method in many ways so that it is now applicable to a wide range of research problems (e.g., Nagin 2005).

Though these advances have placed the categorical position at the forefront of developmental and life-course criminology, the matter is not wholly resolved. Tensions remain between typological theory and the empirical findings. On one hand, many trajectory typology studies (e.g., Nagin and Land 1993) have found evidence of the groups hypothesized by Moffitt (1993): long-term, high-rate trajectories that match life-course persistent offenders; and late-onset, short-term trajectories that

match adolescent limited offenders. On the other hand, virtually all of these studies identify additional groups not hypothesized by Moffitt or Patterson, such as
low-rate chronic offenders and late-onset but long-term offenders. Theory may
have motivated the search for groups, but this method is atheoretical and exploratory, akin to factor analysis and cluster analysis. As a result, this line of research has
produced unexpected findings that leave a gap between theory and research.

Also, the use of categorical research approaches does not require accepting the
view that offenders actually fall into discrete and homogeneous groups. Nagin has
repeatedly stressed the heuristic value of his method for capturing the diversity of
individual paths over time, regardless of whether the underlying reality is one of
discrete groups or continuous differences (Nagin 2005; Nagin and Tremblay 2005
[this volume]; Nagin and Land 1993). Because there is no empirical means of testing which of these is the case, he has warned against treating estimated groups as
indicative of a more concrete reality. Instead, the strengths of the method are the
pragmatic virtues of a readily understandable format for communicating the complexity of pathways in crime and the freedom from assuming specific statistical distributions (such as the normal distribution standard for random effects models).

Thornberry's article in this volume not only demonstrates this pragmatic stance
about the categorical research approach but also shows the continuing relevance of
the earlier debate about categorical versus continuous conceptions of individual
differences in offending over time. Though Thornberry makes many of his key
points through a trajectory group analysis of the Rochester Youth Development
Study data, he clearly states that the groups are a simplified representation of a
more continuous underlying reality. Indeed, his support for a continuous rather
than categorical position looms large in his theoretical stance on a central issue for
developmental criminology. This exposition of his interactional theory stresses his
reasons for viewing age of onset as a continuous basis for differentiating pathways
in offending, in contrast to Moffitt's (1993) treatment of age of onset as the key
marker differentiating her two types of offenders.

I have always found continuous conceptions more appealing, and I have been
uncomfortable with the growing prominence of the categorical perspective.
Despite the heuristic appeal of the categorical approach, I would like to weigh in
on the topic by arguing that there are important reasons to emphasize that there
are many shades of gray between the white and black of saints and serial killers.

Early criminological research relied almost exclusively on categorical conceptions, typically of criminals or delinquents distinguished by official records versus
everyone else. The first major self-report studies of the 1950s and 1960s (Short and
Nye 1958; Gold 1967) revolutionized the field by documenting that illegal behavior was far more widespread than generally assumed. The dichotomy between
offenders and everyone else seemed woefully inadequate if the typical citizen
would be counted as an offender, so these findings cast doubt on most of the field's
prior evidence. A widespread response was to call for studying delinquent behavior

rather than delinquents (e.g., Gold and Petronio 1980), in other words, to move to a continuous conception recognizing widely varying degrees of involvement in crime.

Skepticism about the categorical distinction between official delinquents and normal youth also fueled major juvenile justice reforms of the 1970s (Empey 1982). If a large share of the youth apprehended and processed through the juvenile justice system were little different from many who were not, then there was little justification for intrusive intervention in their lives. Labeling theory, which had gained in popularity from these same findings, took the argument a step further in claiming that the actions of the justice system often engendered further delinquency rather than reducing it.[1] These positions supported the widespread adoption of the reform agenda of diversion, deinstitutionalization of status offenders, decarceration, and due process for juveniles (Empey 1982).

From this history, I draw several lessons about why it is important that developmental and life-course criminologists give greater prominence to continuous conceptions of offending rather than unreservedly adopting a categorical approach, even if only for heuristic purposes. A continuous perspective is helpful on scientific grounds because it brings attention to the role of measurement criteria in defining what does and does not count as crime and as being an offender. For instance, comparisons among trajectory typology studies reveal that the proportions of samples classified as nonoffenders, low-rate or short-term offenders, and high-rate or long-term offenders is very much dependent on the underlying offense measure (e.g., self-report, any arrests, or felony convictions). Furthermore, my reading of the literature suggests that, despite Nagin's admonitions, many scholars will treat groupings from these analyses as reflecting a deeper reality underlying the original data. Such reification is evident, for example, in Bushway et al.'s (2001) strategy of treating high probability of membership in certain groups as better evidence of desistance than an individual's own offense data.

While I hold no illusion that criminologists are a driving force behind justice policy in the United States today, we should be mindful of the policy implications that can flow from categorical versus continuous conceptions of crime. The 1970s policies of restraining the justice system, supported by the rise of a more continuous view of crime, stand in stark contrast to the ever-increasing punitiveness of the system since that time. As I see it, that punitiveness stands on a foundation of viewing offenders as the "other," wholly and categorically distinct from good people like ourselves. Yet it is notable that so many of our religious traditions take the opposite position, calling for practices such as atonement, contrition, and confession to encourage adherents to recognize that no one is free from fault, and casting doubt on the appropriateness of retribution given these shortcomings ("let he who is without sin cast the first stone"). For all these reasons, I would encourage criminologists to think through their own stance on categorical versus continuous distributions of offending. I find considerable merit in emphasizing the shades of gray.

Methodological Issues

What growth curves do and do not contribute to the study of change

My comments on methodological issues concern the role of growth curve models, which appear in all three of the lead articles of this volume and which have become so important in developmental and life-course studies in general. These models depict change across a longitudinal series of observations on an outcome measure such as annual arrest data or self-report offending from each wave of a panel study. Early work on this approach emphasized its value as an alternative measure of change that resolved difficult issues concerning reliability and bias in standard measures (Rogosa, Brandt, and Zimowski 1982). Growth curve models compactly summarize each person's set of observations in terms of an individual-level regression of the outcome on age or time, typically as a polynomial function. Growth curve analyses provide results in the form of (1) a mean growth curve that characterizes the overall pattern of change, (2) a characterization of the amount and form of variation across individual growth curves, and (3) a regression model that captures the relationships of individual characteristics to differences in growth curves.

Thornberry does not present interactional theory as taking a stance on the issue of unified versus disaggregated theory. I find that it embodies a productive one, however, and I commend it to others as a model for developing life-course theory.

Standard growth curve methods include random coefficient, multilevel regression models (Raudenbush and Bryk 2002; Goldstein 1995) and the structural equation modeling of latent growth curves (McArdle and Epstein 1987). These methods are conceptually equivalent in most respects, but each offers variations the other does not. Though distinctive in several ways, Nagin and Land's (1993) trajectory grouping method is definitely a form of growth curve model as well. Like the other methods, theirs is built on a polynomial model of individual change over time. It differs by placing greater emphasis on individual differences in the growth curves, which it captures categorically by grouping individuals (in contrast to the continuous, normal distributions assumed in other approaches).

Though growth curve models are very useful in many respects, they provide a view of individual change that is restricted in a way that has important conceptual ramifications. Figure 1 illustrates this limitation with the data and corresponding growth curves across grades 7 through 11 for three individuals' self-reported delinquency.[2] The upper portion of Figure 1 plots the raw data, while the lower overlays the raw data with fitted quadratic growth curves.[3] For the individual represented by the solid line and diamonds, the correspondence between the raw data and growth curves is close every year, so the growth curve faithfully tracks the major shifts in offending over time. The correspondence is much weaker for the other two individuals. For instance, the growth curve for the person represented by the dashed line and squares indicates a slowly rising offense rate from grades 7 through 10, followed by a large increase to grade 11. That curve is entirely inconsistent with this person's substantial increase in offending at grade 8 and sizable decrease at grade 10. There are similar discrepancies for the third person.

Growth curves necessarily reflect only a portion of within-individual change because a polynomial function is constrained to be smooth and to have a limited number of changes in course. Though my quadratic model fits three parameters to only five data points, it entails sufficient constraints that the growth curves fail to reflect short-term changes in offending. The change score interpretation assumes that the growth curve reflects all meaningful change, and variance around the curve is random noise, a view that would be tenable only if that variance were no larger than the error of measurement. I suspect this is rarely the case, for in my experience the varying slopes of growth curves typically account for less than half of all within-individual variation. Thus, it is highly unlikely that the typical growth curve model will capture all meaningful change and far more likely that a good deal of it remains in the discrepancies between raw data and growth curves illustrated in Figure 1.

This limitation of growth curve models is not really a shortcoming of these very useful methods, but understanding it is critically important for properly interpreting the results they provide and for appreciating the need for additional conceptual approaches and analytic tools. The primary issue for interpretation is to realize that growth curves do not fully capture individual change, but instead they are more abstract summaries of general trends, smoothed according to the constraints of the statistical model. Appreciating that growth curves do not reflect the full reality will save us from unjustified inferences, such as interpreting level growth curves as indicating that individuals are highly consistent in their offending from year to year. As Figure 1 demonstrates, the orderliness of growth curves reflects the form of the mathematical model, not the orderliness of individual change, which is likely to be chaotic by comparison. Once again, the issue is reification. Growth curves are useful summaries of the more consistent aspects of patterns of change, but they are only a partial picture, not some deeper reality.

FIGURE 1
FIVE YEARS OF SELF-REPORTED OFFENDING FOR THREE INDIVIDUALS

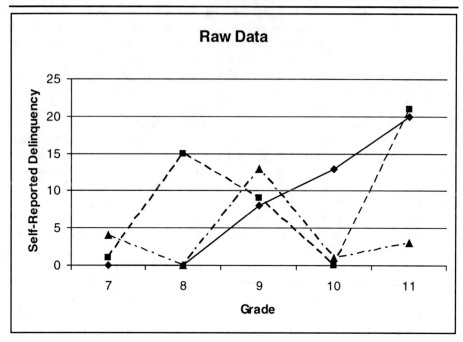

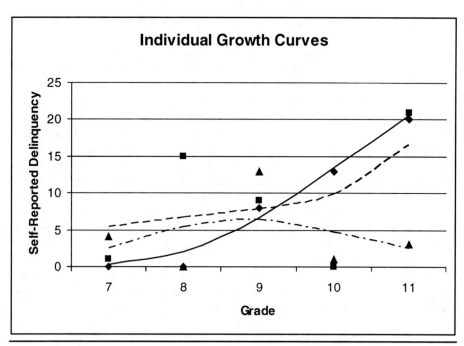

Moving beyond growth curves

We must also understand that there is more to explaining change than accounting for individual differences in growth curves. If much of the variation around those curves represents genuine change, then it is worthy of our attention as well. Furthermore, this short-term variation clearly cannot be explained by the type of theory often offered for growth curves. Because growth curves summarize the entire pattern of change over an extended period, many scholars find it appealing to explain them in terms of early experiences (such as childhood socialization) or unchanging characteristics (such as stable traits). Statistical models of growth curves are well-suited to this approach because they permit unchanging individual characteristics to serve as explanatory variables for the parameters of the growth curves (e.g., Raudenbush and Bryk 2002).

In their article in this volume, Sampson and Laub challenge this presumption that offense trajectories represent the predetermined unfolding of tendencies or causal forces lying far back in the past. They argue instead that trajectories or growth curves are "being continually socially produced over time" (p. 42). This alternative is especially well-suited to the shorter-term fluctuations around the growth curves, for how would unchanging characteristics or long-past experiences account for a brief period of high-rate offending or desistance? Logic dictates that these less enduring changes in offending would instead be tied to changes in experience and life circumstances. Taking seriously the task of explaining short-term as well as long-term patterns of change gives further support to Sampson and Laub's argument that developmental criminology has placed too much emphasis on early experience and personality and too little emphasis on ongoing processes of change.

Available theory also gives good reason for turning our attention to studying the effects of changing experience on offending. For instance, getting married and finding meaningful employment are prominent sources of reform in Laub and Sampson's age-graded social control theory, and they test this idea by assessing the relationship of these events to within-person change in offending (2003; Sampson and Laub 2005). Moffitt's and Thornberry's theories include many propositions about how changes in life circumstances will be associated with increases and decreases in offending at various ages, sometimes in ways that depend on enduring personal characteristics. No doubt many more hypotheses about effects of changes in experience could be derived from the standard set of criminological theories, such as social learning and strain. Indeed, it is surprising that so few studies in developmental and life-span criminology have taken this approach to testing theoretical propositions about which variables should explain change (see Osgood et al. [1996] for an example).

If growth curve models are not adequate for studying effects of life experience, what methods are needed? Interestingly, the multilevel regression methods used for growth curve analysis are also well-suited to this task. We only need to loosen the growth curve conceptual framework by adding time-varying explanatory variables, as in the following example:

$$Y_{i,t} = \beta_{0,i} + \beta_{1,i}\text{Age}_{i,t} + \beta_{2,i}\text{Age}_{i,t}^{2} + \beta_{3,i}X_{i,t} + e_{i,t}.$$

Here β_3 will reflect the association between the time-varying explanatory variable $X_{i,t}$ and individual-level change on the outcome, while $\beta_{1,i}$ and $\beta_{2,i}$ will capture the systematic age-related change not accounted for by that variable. This approach has proved effective in Horney, Osgood, and Marshall's (1995) research on the relationship of current life circumstances to monthly variation in offending and in Laub and Sampson's analyses of the contribution of marriage and employment to offending (2003; Sampson and Laub 2005).

This statistical model also provides the means for addressing one of the most interesting research questions in developmental and life-course criminology: what accounts for the age-crime curve? In their well-known article on age and crime, Hirschi and Gottfredson (1983) made the audacious claim that social and psychological factors could not account for the age-crime curve. Though most criminologists clearly disagree, few have risen to the challenge of attempting to prove them wrong (though see Osgood et al. 1996 and Warr 1993). Multilevel regression analyses with time-varying explanatory variables provide the means for testing explanations of the relationship of age and crime. All that is required is to compare the above equation with one that excludes the time-varying explanatory variable, and the degree to which that variable explains the age trend will be indicated by reductions in $\beta_{1,i}$ and $\beta_{2,i}$ and the corresponding flattening of the age curve.

How to Make Sense of Crime and the Life Course

As I compare the developmental criminology of today to that of twenty years ago, I find considerable progress on the problem of how to make sense of crime and the life course. Many of the challenges of the criminal careers debate have been met. Researchers now routinely conduct research meeting the standards then called for as future goals (e.g., Land 1992), and scholars too numerous to list have responded to Tittle's (1988) challenge to develop meaningful theories of offending over the life course. As the present set of articles and commentaries demonstrates, much has been learned, the standards have risen, and new challenges and controversies await. I will end by offering a few summary comments of my views about how best to enhance our ability to make sense of crime and the life course.

My first recommendation is to strive for cohesive and unifying theory that integrates various aspects of offending over time, and I have pointed to features of Thornberry's interactional theory as an exemplary strategy for doing so. From my view, without such a unifying framework, the accumulating mass of evidence about disparate features of criminal careers (e.g., LeBlanc and Loeber 1998; Piquero, Farrington, and Blumstein 2003) seems of limited theoretical or practical value. Second, I would encourage researchers in this area to keep in mind the possibility (and I would even say likelihood) that there are not just a few types of criminal careers but rather that differences in offense patterns over time vary continuously, perhaps on several important dimensions. Though there can be heuristic value in the simplicity of typologies, there is also theoretical and policy importance in appreciating the shades of gray.

In the methodological realm, I have argued that we will make better sense of crime and the life course if we recognize that, though they are quite useful, growth curve models of all types present a simplified and therefore incomplete picture of individual change over time. They must be interpreted for what they are, summaries of certain general patterns in the data consistent with a particular statistical model, rather than as somehow representing a deeper reality beyond the original observations. Furthermore, the discrepancies between growth curves and short-term change point to the need for research on the effects of changing life experience, which can be captured by augmenting growth curve models with time-varying covariates. Finally, models with time-varying covariates enable us to address one of the most interesting and important challenges of research on crime and the life course, namely, explaining the age-crime curve.

Notes

1. The more extreme forms of labeling theory claimed that the concepts of crime and deviance were entirely social constructions, essentially unrelated to individual differences in behavior (e.g., Becker 1963; Kitsuse 1962). Hirschi (1973) argued that such claims were built on word games rather than evidence and that this position hampered empirical progress. Fortunately, Hirschi's view has won out in the long run.

2. These data come from the national evaluation of the G.R.E.A.T. (Gang Resistance Education and Training) program (Esbensen et al. 2001). The measure is similar to Thornberry's: a seventeen-item self-report delinquency inventory that asks respondents to report how many times they committed each offense in the past six months, scored as a sum across items, each capped at a maximum of twelve. The three cases shown here are essentially random, chosen only for having similar rates of delinquency and having different enough patterns that they are readily visible in the same graph. I assure readers that the correspondence between data and individual growth curves is typical.

3. These individual growth curves come from a Poisson hierarchical linear modeling (HLM) analysis that included random linear and squared terms for grade and a fixed cubic term. These graphed curves are individual fitted rather than empirical Bayes (for which discrepancies would be even larger).

References

Barnett, Arnold, Alfred Blumstein, Jacqueline Cohen, and David P. Farrington. 1992. Not all criminal career models are equally valid. *Criminology* 30:133-40.

Becker, Howard S. 1963. *Outsiders*. New York: Free Press.

Blumstein, Alfred, Jacqueline Cohen, and David P. Farrington 1988a. Criminal career research: Its value for criminology. *Criminology* 26:1-36.

———. 1988b. Longitudinal and criminal career research: Further clarifications. *Criminology* 26:57-74.

Blumstein, Alfred, Jacqueline Cohen, Jeffrey A. Roth, and Christy Visher, eds. 1986. *Criminal careers and career criminals*. Vol. 1. Washington, DC: National Academy Press.

Blumstein, Alfred, David P. Farrington, and Soumyo Moitra. 1985. Delinquency careers: Innocents, desisters, and persisters. *Crime and Justice: An Annual Review of Research* 6:187-219.

Bushway, Shawn, Alex Piquero, Lisa Broidy, Elizabeth Cauffman, and Paul Mazerolle. 2001. An empirical framework for studying desistance as a process. *Criminology* 39:491-515.

Empey, LaMar T. 1982. *American delinquency: Its meaning and construction*. Rev. ed. Homewood, IL: Dorsey Press.

Esbensen, Finn-Aage, D. Wayne Osgood, Terrance J. Taylor, Dana Peterson, and Adrienne Freng. 2001. How great is G.R.E.A.T.? Results from a longitudinal quasi-experimental design. *Criminology and Public Policy* 1:87-115.

Gold, Martin. 1967. Undetected delinquent behavior. *Journal of Research in Crime and Delinquency* 3:27-46.

Gold, Martin, and Richard J. Petronio. 1980. Delinquent behavior in adolescence. In *Handbook of adolescent psychology*, ed. Joseph Adelson. New York: Wiley.

Goldstein, Harvey. 1995. *Multilevel statistical models*. 2nd ed. London: Arnold.

Gottfredson, Michael, and Travis Hirschi. 1986. The true value of Lambda would appear to be zero: An essay on career criminals, criminal careers, selective incapacitation, cohort studies, and related topics. *Criminology* 24:213-34.

———. 1988. Science, public policy, and the career paradigm. *Criminology* 26:37-56.

Greenberg, David F. 1991. Modeling criminal careers. *Criminology* 29:17-46.

———. 1992. Comparing criminal career models. *Criminology* 30:141-47.

Hagan, John, and Alberto Palloni. 1988. Crimes as social events in the life course: Reconceiving a criminological controversy. *Criminology* 26:87-100.

Hirschi, Travis. 1973. Procedural rules and the study of deviant behavior. *Social Problems* 21:159-73.

Hirschi, Travis, and Michael Gottfredson. 1983. Age and the explanation of crime. *American Journal of Sociology* 89:552-84.

Horney, Julie, D. Wayne Osgood, and Ineke Haen Marshall. 1995. Criminal careers in the short-term: Intra-individual variability in crime and its relation to local life circumstances. *American Sociological Review* 60:655-73.

Kitsuse, John. 1962. Societal reaction to deviant behavior: Problems of theory and method. *Social Problems* 9:247-56.

Land, Kenneth C. 1992. Models of criminal careers: Some suggestions for moving beyond the current debate. *Criminology* 30:149-55.

Laub, John H., and Robert J. Sampson. 2003. *Shared beginnings, divergent lives: Delinquent boys to age 70*. Cambridge, MA: Harvard University Press.

LeBlanc, Marc, and Rolf Loeber. 1998. Developmental criminology updated. *Crime and Justice: A Review of Research* 23:115-98.

McArdle, J. J., and David Epstein. 1987. Latent growth curves within developmental structural equation models. *Child Development* 58:110-33.

Moffitt, Terrie E. 1993. Adolescence-limited and life-course-persistent antisocial behavior: A developmental taxonomy. *Psychological Review* 100:674-701.

Nagin, Daniel S. 2005. *Group-based modeling of development*. Cambridge, MA: Harvard University Press.

Nagin, Daniel S., and Kenneth C. Land. 1993. Age, criminal careers, and population heterogeneity: Specification and estimation of a nonparametric, mixed Poisson model. *Criminology* 31:327-62.

Nagin, Daniel S., and Richard E. Tremblay. 2005. What has been learned from group-based trajectory modeling? Examples from physical aggression and other problem behaviors. *Annals of the American Academy of Political and Social Science* 602:82-117.

Osgood, D. Wayne, and David C. Rowe. 1994. Bridging criminal careers, theory, and policy through latent variable models of individual offending. *Criminology* 32:517-54.

Osgood, D. Wayne, Janet K. Wilson, Jerald G. Bachman, Patrick M. O'Malley, and Lloyd D. Johnston. 1996. Routine activities and individual deviant behavior. *American Sociological Review* 61:635-55.

Patterson, Gerald R., and Karen Yoerger. 1993. Developmental models for delinquent behavior. In *Crime and mental disorder*, ed. Sheilagh Hodgins. Newbury Park, CA: Sage.

———. 1997. A developmental model for late-onset delinquency. In *Motivation and delinquency*, vol. 44 of the Nebraska Symposium on Motivation, ed. D. Wayne Osgood, 119-77. Lincoln: University of Nebraska Press.

Piquero, Alex R., David P. Farrington, and Alfred Blumstein. 2003. The criminal career paradigm. *Crime and Justice: A Review of Research* 30:359-506.

Raudenbush, Stephen W., and Anthony S. Bryk. 2002. *Hierarchical linear models*. 2nd ed. Thousand Oaks, CA: Sage.

Rogosa, David, David Brandt, and Michele Zimowski. 1982. A growth curve approach to the measurement of change. *Psychological Bulletin* 92:726-48.

Rowe, David C., D. Wayne Osgood, and Alan W. Nicewander. 1990. A latent trait approach to unifying criminal careers. *Criminology* 28:237-70.

Sampson, Robert J., and John H. Laub. 1992. Crime and deviance in the life course. *Annual Review of Sociology* 18:63-84.

———. 1993. *Crime in the making: Pathways and turning points through life*. Cambridge, MA: Harvard University Press.

———. 2005. A life-course view of the development of crime. *Annals of the American Academy of Political and Social Science* 602:12-45.

Short, James F., Jr., and F. Ivan Nye. 1958. Extent of unrecorded juvenile delinquency: Tentative conclusions. *Journal of Criminal Law and Criminology* 49:296-302.

Thornberry, Terence P. 2005. Explaining multiple patterns of offending across the life course and across generations. *Annals of the American Academy of Political and Social Science* 602:156-95.

Thornberry, Terence P., and Marvin D. Krohn. Forthcoming. Applying interactional theory to the explanation of continuity and change in antisocial behavior. In *Integrated developmental and life course theories of offending: Advances in criminological theory*, vol. 14, ed. D. P. Farrington. Piscataway, NJ: Transaction.

Tittle, Charles R. 1988. Two empirical regularities (maybe) in search of an explanation: Commentary on the age/crime debate. *Criminology* 26:75-85.

Warr, Mark. 1993. Age, peers, and delinquency. *Criminology* 31:17-40.

Explaining Patterns of Offending across the Life Course: Comments on Interactional Theory and Recent Tests Based on the RYDS-RIS Data

By
JANET L. LAURITSEN

This article assesses "interactional theory" and recent developmental research based on that theory. The author argues that the unique contributions of interactional theory would be enhanced by greater formalization of the theory and comparisons of the theory's hypotheses to other developmental and criminological theories. Patterns of offending across the life course would be better understood if more longitudinal data sets were made accessible to investigators with other perspectives and areas of expertise.

Keywords: interactional theory; longitudinal data; assessment

In 1987, a conference was held at the University at Albany to debate one of the critical issues facing criminologists at the time—theoretical integration. Participants were asked to take seriously the notion that criminology had reached a theoretical standstill and that perhaps the best way to advance our understanding of crime would be to develop integrated theoretical models capable of capturing "the entire range of relevant causal variables" (Liska, Krohn, and Messner 1989, 4). Despite a great deal of disagreement over the costs and benefits of integrated models (e.g., compare Hirschi 1989 and Elliott 1985), there was agreement about how the results of such efforts should be judged. Like all theories, the models should be assessed according to their level of empirical support, their ability to organize accumulated knowledge and promote new research agendas,

Janet L. Lauritsen is a professor in and chairperson of the Department of Criminology and Criminal Justice at the University of Missouri–St. Louis. Her current research examines how methodological research and social and political factors influence the measurement of criminal victimization and how individual, family, and community factors are related to the risk of violent victimization among women, men, and adolescents. She is currently a visiting research fellow at the Bureau of Justice Statistics and chair of the Committee on Law and Justice Statistics of the American Statistical Association.

DOI: 10.1177/0002716205280152

and their precision in the derivation of unambiguous hypotheses (Liska, Krohn, and Messner 1989).

Nearly two decades have passed, and the topic of theoretical advances in criminology once again was the focus of a conference at the University at Albany. This time the task was to critically assess various manifestations of "developmental" criminology—a perspective described by Thornberry (2005 [this volume], 156) as "perhaps the most important advance in theoretical criminology during the latter part of the twentieth century." In this article, I examine "interactional theory" and recent research based on that theory as presented by Thornberry (2005) and Thornberry and Krohn (2005). I view interactional theory as a broad attempt at theoretical integration; thus, my assessment relies, in part, on the debates at the earlier conference and on longstanding discussions about the role of theory in empirical research and the bearing of empirical research on theory (see Messner, Krohn, and Liska 1989; Merton 1967). The article begins with comments about interactional theory and follows with an evaluation of recent empirical tests of the model using data from the Rochester Youth Development Study (RYDS). This assessment is followed by a discussion of how the value of RYDS and other longitudinal data could be maximized by making them more widely available to the research community. The article concludes with a call for renewed attention to the challenges associated with theoretical integration and formalization and to the potential consequences of how we go about our studies of crime and delinquency. My goal is to motivate discussion about how best to move theory and research forward in ways that would broaden our understanding of crime across the life course.

Interactional Theory

According to Thornberry and Krohn, there are three fundamental aspects of interactional theory (2005, 187). The first is that the theory takes a "life-course" perspective. By this, the authors mean that they view delinquency involvement as something that "unfolds over time; for most people it has an onset, duration, and, for most offenders, a termination." Explaining this behavior at various ages (increasingly summarized in the form of trajectories) requires linking antisocial behavior patterns to other trajectories in life, such as family, school, and work experiences. Interactional theory predicts a mixture of causes that differ depending on one's age and reflect successes or failures in previous developmental stages.

The second premise of the theory is that delinquency and "many of its causes often become involved in mutually reinforcing causal loops as delinquent careers unfold" (Thornberry and Krohn 2005, 188). In other words, delinquency and its causes "interact" with each other, often resulting in greater (or lesser) levels of offending. For instance, ineffective parenting may lead to delinquency involvement, which, in turn, may result in parental responses that further increase the occurrence of delinquent behaviors.

The third key premise of the theory is that the multiple causes of delinquency vary in their magnitude across persons due to the presence of "offsetting assets" or protective factors. Thornberry and Krohn (2005, 189) referred to the variation in causal factors as the concept of proportionality of cause. This concept asserts that "as the magnitude of the causal force increases, the person's involvement in crime (a) becomes more likely and (b) increases in severity." An illustration of this concept is contained in a hypothesis about the age of onset of antisocial behavior: "we hypothesize that early onset is associated with the strength of the causal force associated with delinquency. Individuals with the earliest onset of antisocial behavior are likely to have multiple, interwoven causal factors—especially structural adversity, ineffective parenting, and negative temperamental characteristics—and few offsetting assets" (p. 196).

[I]t is not clear exactly how interactional theory differs from other theories that also strive to understand these nonrecursive mechanisms.

In addition to the three main premises, interactional theory includes other assertions and hypotheses. For instance, early involvement in antisocial behavior is the result of what is described as "the intense coupling of structural, individual, and parental influences, that is, when the causal force associated with childhood antisocial behavior is near a maximum" (Thornberry and Krohn 2005, 190). Childhood onset of delinquency is said to be "strongly associated with growing up in families and neighborhoods characterized by poverty and disorganization" (ibid., 191). "Age-appropriate" or a "normative" onset of offending appears to be a reflection of increased peer influences, decreased parental supervision, and associations with peers who want to demonstrate rebellion from adult authority (ibid., 194). Finally, "late starters"—defined as those who "begin frequent offending at ages beyond the modal onset years of adolescence"—are hypothesized to have lower intelligence and academic competence but were not affected by these traits earlier because they had a supportive family and school environment (ibid.).

Space limitations prohibit descriptions and assessments of the factors that are related, according to interactional theory, to the stability of and desistance from delinquency. Readers are encouraged to consult recent sources for hypotheses about these aspects of crime and delinquency (e.g., Thornberry and Krohn 2005; Thornberry 2005). I use the main premises of interactional theory and its assertions about the onset of offending behavior to illustrate some of the strengths and weaknesses of the theory as one begins to operationalize and test the theory's main hypotheses. What insights are provided by interactional theory compared to other theories or perspectives, and what are the challenges faced by researchers who want to use this theory to guide research?

I begin with the first premise—that the theory takes a "life-course" perspective on antisocial behavior, delinquency, and crime. This premise instructs the researcher to consider delinquent behaviors not simply as isolated events but rather as age-specific occurrences with causes that are expected to vary depending on an individual's age or stage of development. This premise strongly suggests that researchers must have longitudinal or age-specific data on offending and its proposed causes to fully understand crime from an interactional perspective. Generally speaking, this premise is not unique to interactional theory, as the need for longitudinal data has appeared in discussions of many other theoretical perspectives (e.g., Elliott, Huizinga, and Ageton 1985; Moffitt 1993; Sampson and Laub 1993). To judge which model might be preferred, the researcher could begin by looking at how the various perspectives differ in their claims about the nature of offending patterns.

It is not clear whether interactional theory differs from other theories seeking to understand delinquency patterns over time. However, Thornberry and colleagues distinguished interactional theory from Moffitt's (1993) findings about the number of generalized pathways in offense involvement. In a set of "epidemiological hypotheses," Thornberry (2005, 159) noted that age of onset and persistence of offending are inversely correlated but that "interactional theory hypothesizes that the magnitude of this association, is, at best moderate." The statement indicates that interactional theory will provide a more satisfactory starting point as long as the correlation is greater than zero but less than very strong. In addition, rather than expect age of onset to be a determinant of one's life-course involvement (e.g., persistent versus adolescence-limited), interactional theory expects there to be a need for more than two categories to describe general patterns of offense involvement.[1] It appears, then, that one distinction between the two perspectives has to do with expectations about the strength of the association between age of onset and length of involvement in offending. The other distinction is how best to *describe* the phenomenon that is to be explained.

The second major premise of interactional theory—that delinquency and its causes may interact in a nonrecursive way over time—is an important insight that theorists should consider as they develop and refine their theoretical models.[2] Labeling, symbolic interactionist, and defiance theories (e.g., Lemert 1972; Matsueda and Heimer 1997; Sherman 1993) similarly hypothesize that there is a dynamic relationship between delinquency and social control efforts. But it is not clear exactly how interactional theory differs from other theories that also strive to understand these nonrecursive mechanisms. Clarification of the differences would help researchers compare and test the insights offered by interactional theory to those outlined in labeling, symbolic interactionist, and defiance theories.

The third key premise of the theory is that variation exists in the magnitude of causal factors across persons (the concept of proportionality of cause). Recall that from this premise, Thornberry and Krohn (2005, 196) "hypothesize that early onset is associated with the strength of the causal force associated with delinquency." It is difficult for me to see how this statement might be falsified through research. Thornberry and Krohn also stated that early onset of delinquency is expected to be the result of "multiple, interwoven causal factors—especially structural adversity, ineffective parenting, and negative temperamental characteristics—and few offsetting assets" (p. 196). Although potential factors are provided in this hypothesis, it is not clear what research findings (other than a complete set of null findings) would constitute a falsification of this hypothesis. Would interactional theory be damaged by research that showed that structural adversity and ineffective parenting, but not temperamental differences, were associated with early age offending? Earlier theories (such as social disorganization, cultural deviance, social control, etc.) have also provided hypotheses about these relationships, but the causal mechanisms of those hypotheses vary considerably from one another. If interactional theory, or any new theory, seeks to replace earlier criminological theories, the theorist must show how the hypotheses can be distinguished from earlier models.

[T]he models do not incorporate family composition and the additional parenting that likely takes place in two-parent homes or homes with another adult living with the child.

When the first delinquent act occurs at later ages, interactional theory proposes a different set of relevant factors. For example, "age-appropriate" offending is affected by increased peer influences, decreased parental supervision, and a peer culture that encourages rebellion from adult authority in the form of minor deviance such as drinking, smoking, and sexual activity (Thornberry and Krohn 2005, 194). During adolescence, then, interactional theory appears to incorporate hypotheses from social control, subcultural, and social learning theories. Late starters, who begin frequent offending after adolescence, are hypothesized to have "reduced human capital, especially lower intelligence and academic competence" but were not affected by these traits earlier because they had a supportive family and school environment (ibid.). This discussion suggests that social control factors in the form of schools and parents are no longer present and that the effects of these deficits make it more difficult for the individual to obtain "meaningful employment" or a "quality relationship with a partner." This also "may make those with human capital deficiencies more vulnerable to the influence of deviant friends" (ibid., 195). Thus, offending that waits until adulthood to begin appears to be a reflection of certain individual-level traits (e.g., lower intelligence), social control, and social learning processes. But here as well, researchers need greater clarification as to whether interactional theory would be damaged by research that found little association between the interaction of early social control and lower intelligence and late onset. In other words, what hypotheses constitute crucial tests of the theory, and how do the causal mechanisms of the theory differ from earlier traditional theories and other life-course perspectives?

In many ways, interactional theory is very ambitious in that it attempts to provide a comprehensive understanding of crime across the life course and organize knowledge about delinquency and its consequences. It offers plausible accounts of how various empirical findings about offending at different ages might be interpreted. Some of these interpretations are consistent with other criminological theories, such as Hirschi's (1969) social control theory and Sampson and Laub's (1993) age-graded theory of social control. Some interpretations appear to be drawn from social learning and other perspectives (e.g., a youth subculture that encourages status offending). In this sense, interactional theory appears to be an attempt at theoretical integration most similar to the types described as "side-by-side" and "end-to-end" integration (Hirschi 1979; Liska, Krohn, and Messner 1989). If this is the case, then more discussion is needed about how the contradictory premises and assumptions of these component theories have been reconciled.

However, in its current formulation, I do not believe that "interactional theory" is a theory per se but, rather, a broader orientation to studying crime across the life course. The validity and superiority of this orientation compared to other theories could more easily be assessed if the following issues were considered. First, the unique claims of interactional theory could be made more apparent by greater formalization. All theories are composed of definitions of the phenomenon to be explained; propositions; hypotheses; and, whether acknowledged or not, underlying assumptions about human nature and society and oftentimes about the phenomenon itself. Granted, this may seem like an old-fashioned view of theory, but without attention to this structure, it is very difficult for a researcher to use the theory to organize data collection, test specific or crucial hypotheses, or examine the theory's logical coherence and assumptions. Two decades ago, Jim Short (1985, 63) noted that "criminology remains a . . . largely descriptive discipline" in part because of the lack of sufficient attention to the formal aspects of theoretical development. Without formalization, empirical assessments of hypotheses, propositions, and assumptions are difficult; data collection efforts may be insufficient or too scattered; and scientific progress is less likely (Bernard 1990).

Second, although the theory appears ready to explain the distinct phenomena of "antisocial behavior," "delinquency," and "crime," and the levels of these behaviors joined together, end to end in the form of trajectories, it is not clear how a researcher should determine what behaviors do or do not need to be included when operationalizing these concepts. Although it *may* be relatively easy for researchers to agree on definitions of "crime" and "delinquency," this is less likely to be true for early "antisocial behavior" on the part of preschoolers and young children. If a definition for antisocial behavior were offered, it would allow for broader tests of the theory in other places or eras, hence determining its scope and generalizability. It would also help researchers develop and test new methodologies that try to incorporate and blend childhood, adolescent, and adult indicators into a single life-course trajectory when the component measures at various stages differ. The measurement issues associated with studying individual change across these stages are complex and have not yet been fully resolved (e.g., Lauritsen 1999; Jang 1999).

Third, greater clarification is needed for determining how some hypotheses might be falsified. For example, Thornberry and Krohn (2005, 185) stated, "We hypothesize that among early starters some offenders will persist, but many others will desist, a hypothesis that is consistent with Robins' original observation. Similarly, we hypothesize that among later starters some offenders will desist relatively quickly, but others will persist in their offending." It seems to me that the only way this statement could be falsified is if every "early starter" is identical in age of onset and length of persistence. The same could be said for "later starters." But since we already know from prior research that this is not the case, the likelihood of falsifying these two hypotheses is practically zero. It appears that these statements might be better thought of as descriptions of the phenomenon to be explained rather than as hypotheses.

Fourth, greater clarification is needed to determine what kinds of evidence would falsify key hypotheses involving the relationships between various factors and offending. As noted earlier, several factors are noted to be associated with delinquency, such as temperament, intelligence, academic competence, parenting skills and supervision, structural location, neighborhood poverty and deprivation, school environment, and peers—in other words, all of the traditional correlates of the past century. Of course, a variety of competing explanations have been offered to account for these correlates, and many of them have their own weaknesses with respect to empirical support and formalization. But the main challenge of any theory is whether it provides a more satisfactory explanation than other theories purporting to account for the same phenomena and relationships. Without details such as those just noted, it is difficult to make the kinds of empirical assessments that could determine whether interactional theory should be preferred to other developmental or traditional theories of delinquency.

Empirical Tests

Interactional theory is most closely associated with the research of Terry Thornberry, Marvin Krohn, Alan Lizotte, Carolyn Smith, and others and with the RYDS—a prospective longitudinal study of one thousand high-risk youth from Rochester, New York, that began in 1988. In that year, approximately one thousand seventh and eighth graders and their primary caretakers (i.e., their mothers) were selected and interviewed every six months for a total of nine waves. A second phase produced three additional annual interviews, so that by age twenty-two, adolescents had been interviewed a total of twelve times, and their parent eleven times. The retention rate across the two phases of the study is very impressive—around 86 percent. As far as I could determine, analyses using these data have been the basis for at least three books, fifteen book chapters, forty articles, a dozen Office of Juvenile Justice and Delinquency Prevention reports, and a dozen or more dissertations—an impressive scholarly output, to be sure.

Adolescent childbearing is not randomly distributed across youth, and so the cases on which these analyses are based are selected according to the correlates of teen childbearing.

The full body of empirical work is not, of course, reviewed here. I use results presented in this volume and in a recent article (Thornberry et al. 2003) to illustrate some methodological and theoretical issues. These recent applications inform us that RYDS data collection has continued in the form of the Rochester Intergenerational Study (RIS). In 1999, the researchers began following the oldest children born to the original cohort. By this time, some of the original cohort of seventh and eighth graders had had children of their own. These three generations—the original youth (designated generation 2 or "G2"), their G1 parent, and their G3 children form the samples for the analyses in these models.

The purpose of the new data collection is stated as follows: "Despite the plausibility of intergenerational continuities in behavior, there is surprisingly little research that prospectively traces the life course of adjacent generations to see if parents who are antisocial also have children who are antisocial. There is even less information about the causal processes that might account for any observed level of intergenerational continuity" (Thornberry et al. 2003, 171). Many of the previous studies examining the intergenerational transmission of antisocial behavior are described as "methodologically weak" because they (1) rely on a single source of data for information about the subject, the subject's parent(s), or the subject's children; (2) rely on reports about behavior that are retrospective; (3) have sample sizes that are small; or (4) use nonrandom samples selected on the basis of involvement in antisocial behavior. The authors summarize past literature as incapable of "providing firm conclusions about the intergenerational transmission of antisocial behavior" (ibid., 176) and use the RYDS and RIS data because it is prospective; relatively large in size; and the data about G1, G2, and G3 subjects come from unique sources and do not suffer from the potential problem of what the authors refer to as "common method variance" distortion.

Thornberry et al. (2003) and Thornberry (2005) also examined whether intergenerational continuities in antisocial behavior vary across gender. Three hypotheses (not derived from "interactional theory" as far as I can determine) are directly stated: (1) "that the level of intergenerational continuity in antisocial behavior is stronger for G2 fathers than for G2 mothers"; (2) "that parenting styles more fully mediate the impact of adolescent antisocial behavior for G2 mothers than for G2 fathers"; and (3) "that the direct link from G1 parenting style to G2 parenting style is stronger for G2 mothers than for fathers" (Thornberry et al. 2003, 174-75). Results are presented in G2 gender-specific path models designed to assess variation in early antisocial behavior (Thornberry et al. 2003) and delinquency (Thornberry 2005) among G3 youth.

The meaning of all statistical analyses is found in the details, so discussion of some of the measures and how they might influence the interpretation of results is necessary. In Thornberry et al. (2003), the primary dependent variable is a measure of early antisocial behavior composed of the answers to thirty-three items from the Child Behavior Check List (CBCL) in which G3's other care giver (OCG) was asked how often the child engages in behaviors such as hostility, aggression, and disobeying rules. Rather than rely on answers provided by the G2 parent, the researchers interviewed a person designated as the OCG—"the person who, in addition to the RYDS parent, is primarily responsible for raising the child" (p. 177). If G2 is the father of G3, 94 percent of the OCG reporters are the mother of G3. But if G2 is the mother of G3, then just more than one-third of OCGs are the father of G3. The remaining OCGs are grandmothers, partners of the mother, or other relatives. This sample was reduced by 25 percent because it was decided that OCG reports of G3's early antisocial behavior should be gathered only from OCGs who spent at least one hour with the child in the month prior to the interview.[3] In these models, the paths from G2 adolescent delinquency and G2 parenting of G3 are estimated controlling for G2 financial stress, G1 family poverty, and G1 parenting of G2.

From the analyses of the G2 fathers, we learn that G2 parenting of G3 is significantly associated with G3's early antisocial behavior and that much of the correlation between the father's delinquency as an adolescent and his child's early antisocial behavior is mediated by the father's parenting measure. That finding is consistent with past research. The results for G3 mothers also find that the parenting style of G2 mothers is significantly associated with G3's early antisocial behavior, and the intergenerational continuity between the G2 mother's adolescent delinquency and her child's behavior is mediated by parenting style. It is difficult to assess the effect size of these coefficients, however, since means and standard deviations for the original measures are not provided. In addition, G1 parenting was not significantly related to female G2's level of delinquency in adolescence, suggesting that parenting might not be a very important factor for explaining adolescent delinquency among the G2 girls.[4]

In Thornberry (2005), the primary dependent variable is a delinquency measure obtained from teacher reports when the G3 children were somewhat older (six to fifteen years). The variables included in this model are somewhat different from the model just described. Although some of the variables are measured in different ways, they include G2 parenting of G3, G2 adolescent drug use, G2 adult stressful life events, and G1 parenting of G2. The results for G2 males are based on a sample using a more restrictive definition of fathers than the previous study (i.e., those who spend more time with their children) and suggest that fathers who display higher levels of negative parenting have children with higher levels of delinquency but that fathers' adolescent drug use has no direct effect on G3's delinquency. For G2 mothers, the results also show no significant effects of adolescent drug use on children's delinquency and that mothers with higher levels of positive parenting have children with significantly lower delinquency levels.

I believe that one of the best ways to move forward with studies of crime and delinquency is to make the data accessible to other researchers.

These details are provided so that measurement and model specification issues that are critical to assessing theoretical hypotheses can be discussed. In my view, neither set of models appears to be specified to the extent necessary for advancing our understanding of family influences on early antisocial behavior or childhood delinquency. Consequently, they are also insufficient for determining whether causal mechanisms vary by gender. Past research has demonstrated that it is important to control for other dimensions of family life, including G2's family composition, marital status, and other aspects of family functioning (Loeber and Stouthamer-Loeber 1986), if the purpose of the research is to assess the influence of specific parenting behaviors or attitudes. Most important, the models do not incorporate family composition and the additional parenting that likely takes place in two-parent homes or homes with another adult living with the child. Nor do the models include measures of time spent with other caregivers such as teachers or day care professionals. Thus, what appears to be a reflection of G2 parenting (or gender differences in G2 parenting) might represent other correlates of the family.

In addition, although a measure of "negative parenting" is included in the second set of models, these measures are based on in-home videotaped interactions that may be unlikely to capture the full range of important parent-child dynamics, such as child abuse and neglect (Widom and Maxfield 2001).

Interpretation also is made problematic by the lack of other control variables representing important aspects of the child's life. Without control variables for correlates such as school environment, time spent with delinquent peers, peer victimization, or residing in a highly disadvantaged area, it is likely that the effects associated with parenting are overestimated. Model specification and other methodological problems make it easy to overestimate family influences (see also Rowe 1994).

Even if the findings here persisted when other variables were included in the models, the generalizability of these findings to other families and children must be made very carefully, not simply because the original sample involves high-risk youth from one city or because the sample cannot assess potentially important period effects. Rather, by virtue of their age, the G3 children used in the first set of models were born when the G2 mother or father was a teenager, and most of the G3 children in the second set of models appear to have been born to teens. Adolescent childbearing is not randomly distributed across youth, and so the cases on which these analyses are based are selected according to the correlates of teen childbearing.

In their conclusions, the authors acknowledge that more work needs to be done and that understanding the causal mechanisms underlying intergenerational continuity is a complex task. I agree. Left unsaid are the consequences of these results for interactional theory itself. For reasons outlined earlier, it is not clear to me, for example, whether the lack of a direct effect of G2 father and mother's adolescent drug use on G3's childhood delinquency has any consequences for the theory. And given the theory's emphasis on the life course and interactional processes, it would seem necessary to include these dimensions in the model (e.g., incorporate G3's early antisocial behavior in the analyses of G3 childhood delinquency or include information about earlier nonrecursive outcomes in both sets of models).

Moving Forward

What implications do these results have for the theory, and together, what do the theory and research suggest about the next phase of research? These are difficult questions to answer. It is not clear whether the theory is in need of revision or whether the theory in its current form provides the kind of guidance that makes it possible to state what hypothesis should be assessed next or what specific issue is most important to resolve before moving on. Thornberry et al. (2003, 182-83) noted in their discussion that a variety of other factors should be considered, including some that are noted here. But the list is not prioritized in a way that would direct the next set of hypotheses and accompanying research.

Many theories offer suggestions about the same relationships studied here, and one could argue that even without theory, a good criminologist should be able to offer detailed suggestions about future analyses based on the state of the research literature. But after studying this issue, I found it difficult to use the theory and these findings to develop a subsequent research agenda. One reason for this is that it is very difficult to know what kinds of models the RYDS and RIS data can assess because the data are not accessible to many researchers. The instruments from the intergenerational study or, for that matter, from the earlier phases have not been published. So detailed suggestions—the types that are most helpful to researchers and that researchers often provide to each other when they have years of experience working with the same data sets—cannot be offered. This situation puts RYDS-based research at a disadvantage compared to other research projects that rely on data that have been used by a broader community of scholars working from alternative perspectives.

Of course, the RYDS data are not alone in this regard. One likely reason the RYDS data have not been made available to the wider research community is concern about maintaining and protecting respondent confidentiality. This is an extremely important and legitimate issue. In my own research on violent victimization using National Crime Victimization Survey (NCVS) data that include area identifiers for the subjects' place of residence, I learned that it is not easy to convince those entrusted with data collection to release the results of those efforts for research purposes. More than two decades of resistance by the Census Bureau and the Bureau of Justice Statistics were overcome when Al Blumstein and Jan Chaiken (then director of the Bureau of Justice Statistics) negotiated a strategy that would permit access to the data and ensure that there would be no disclosure of subjects' identities. Granted, this resulted in some rather extraordinary protocols such as obtaining "sworn status" from the Census Bureau, submitting research proposals detailing statistical models and purpose, traveling to secure data facilities managed by the Census Bureau, having output screened prior to removal from the secure facility, and obtaining research funds to pay for these social control mechanisms. But this has been worth it to me and to other researchers because it was the only way to use national data to study a variety of important issues about crime and victimization.

A variety of approaches now exist that can be used to ensure that subjects' identities are not divulged and that guarantees of confidentiality are maintained. The National Institutes of Health (NIH) have developed a workbook that outlines how sensitive data can be shared with legitimate researchers—*especially* unique data resources that would be difficult or impossible to replicate because of their costs, such as longitudinal data (NIH n.d.).

The two main strategies include restricting access to the data and restricting access to certain information in the data set. The former is the approach I experienced. Typically, this involves stipulating who can access the data (e.g., legitimate researchers at universities with institutional review board approval), the conditions under which access can be granted, and signed assurances about the use, presentation, and transference of the data. The second approach goes under various names but essentially involves removing identifying items from the data set. This includes the obvious, such as name and date of birth, but it can also include removing or blocking variables with very low prevalence rates that might lead to the identification of an individual. There are now cadres of statisticians who specialize in data de-identification or redaction techniques.

It is not clear which of the above strategies would work best with the RYDS data. I offer these suggestions because I believe that one of the best ways to move forward with studies of crime and delinquency is to make the data accessible to other researchers. Given the reported level of detail and very high response rates, these data are most likely loaded with research possibilities that could further our understanding of crime and delinquency if they were opened up to additional perspectives and areas of expertise. To be sure, the RYDS publication record is impressive, but there are only so many hours in a research team's day. I encourage those responsible for making this decision to make data from the first two phases of the project accessible. Phase 1 covered 1988 to about 1992, and Phase 2 was completed in 1997. The NIH Office of Extramural Research nicely summarizes the benefits of this strategy:

> Sharing data reinforces open scientific inquiry, encourages diversity of analysis and opinion, promotes new research, makes possible the testing of new or alternative hypotheses and methods of analysis, supports studies on data collection methods and measurement, facilitates the education of new researchers, enables the exploration of topics not envisioned by the initial investigators, and permits the creation of new datasets when data from multiple sources are combined. (NIH n.d.)

A second reason I found it difficult to use interactional theory to guide future research has already been stated: the theory is a broad attempt to integrate a variety of theories under one life-course framework. Many of the empirical relationships are discussed using social control terminology, but some discussions suggested social learning or subcultural hypotheses. If theoretical integration is the goal, then it is important that attention be paid to the broader issues that have challenged these efforts (Liska, Krohn, and Messner 1989).

Third, I find it difficult to use the theory and findings discussed above as a guide for future research because of the degree of formalization of the theory. In an article that takes stock of the scientific progress of criminology, Bernard (1990) argued that all theorists face several key tasks including constructing falsifiable predictions, analyzing existing theories and the relations between existing theories, and separating definitions from propositions. If interactional theory strives to be more than a framework or orientation, it must attend to these tasks as well. Bernard argued that theorists should devote most of their efforts to developing the logic for making precise statements about how their theory can be falsified (p. 331). By doing this, "theory can be viewed as an iterative, cumulative, developmental enterprise in which long-range progress is accomplished by a large number of small steps. It would allow a greater number of criminologists to contribute to theorizing and a greater variety of contributions from those criminologists" (p. 330).

My final comment involves a broader concern about how we, as researchers, decide when enough data have been gathered from our subjects. In qualitative research, observations and interviews typically are stopped when the data are said to be "saturated"—in other words, when relatively little new information is gained from additional interviews. Sometimes this occurs after twenty interviews, sometimes after one hundred—it depends on the research question and the judgment of the researcher. Quantitative research tends not to be structured in a way that forces us to pay much attention to this issue. The study of relatively rare events and complex causal processes requires large samples and many indicators of key concepts. Longitudinal research, including life-course research, can press these data demands even further.

Scientific and ethical concerns are handled, in part, by peer review processes and institutional review boards. From a scientific point of view, the concerns range from sample attrition and potential "panel fatigue" and testing effects (e.g., Lauritsen 1998; Thornberry 1989; Osgood et al., 1989) to spending valuable resources gathering more data that might be better spent on other scientific matters. But there are other potential empirical consequences, including the possibility that the research itself influences the lives of its subjects. By this I mean something beyond concerns about voluntary participation and consent. In the criminological classic, *The Jack-Roller*, Clifford Shaw (1966) took a close look at the how "Stanley" became a "chronic offender." He studied many aspects of Stanley's life history ranging from personality traits, to family and peer influences, to neighborhoods and opportunities and the transmission of cultural values. Years later, when Stanley was seventy-five years old, he stated in an interview with Snodgrass (1982, 171), "Now if anyone ever had an influence over me, it was Shaw." He appeared to mean this in a positive way. But the comment reminds us of the possibility that researchers, through their probing interviews and observations, might to some extent contaminate their own studies and affect their subjects in positive but also negative ways.

Plans for the third phase of RYDS data collection (i.e., the RIS study) are very ambitious. They include annual interviews with the (G2) subjects and their (G3) children for five more years; in-home videotaping of G2 parent–G3 child interactions during years 1, 3, and 5; more data from teachers, schools, and other agencies; and so on. As one of the most extensive delinquency data collection projects to date, it is critical to understand the methodological limitations of these data, such as potential testing effects, panel fatigue, and changes in the validity and reliability of measures. We also know relatively little about why the subjects do or do not continue to participate. Why would subjects, who have already participated in twelve interviews, continue extensive involvement for another five years? Perhaps the subjects enjoy participating, or perhaps they agree to do so because they are paid to participate or because they believe they are contributing to science. Alternatively, it may be the case that young American adults whose culture is inundated with reality TV shows, confessional talk shows, and unprecedented surveillance technology see nothing unusual with this request. For the sake of ongoing and future data collection, it is important to understand all of the limitations of longitudinal data.

These efforts would permit more sound interpretations of our findings and theories and help us determine how much data we should ask subjects to provide in the name of further research.

Notes

1. Interactional theory suggests that this epidemiological hypothesis would be falsified if it could be shown that there is a need for more than two general categories of offending across the life course. In his trajectory analyses based on males in the Rochester Youth Development Study (RYDS) data, Thornberry (2005 [this volume]) uses Figure 1 as evidence that interactional theory provides a more accurate characterization of the phenomenon than Moffitt's (1993) taxonomy. But these analyses must be considered incomplete because they do not contain information about offending before age thirteen. Furthermore, some might look at these eight trajectories and also see that there are two broad groups consisting of those with high levels of offending by age thirteen (perhaps "early starters") and those with low levels at age thirteen who appear to have waited until adolescence to begin their offending. Of the latter group, most appear to have minimal levels of involvement by age twenty-three. If data gathered after age twenty-three were to show that the "late bloomers" and the "gradual uptake offenders" decreased their offending relatively soon, and "persistent high-level offenders" maintained high offending levels, it might be the case that two broad categories provide adequate descriptions. This decision regarding the correct number to use should be based on the ultimate purpose of the typologies (e.g., predicting future offending versus adequately describing between-individual differences).

2. The term *interact* is not used in the statistical sense (e.g., the product of two independent variables) but rather to capture the sense of nonrecursive change.

3. It is also important to know whether the other care giver (OCG) assessments are highly correlated with the primary caregiver's assessments of the child. Obviously, the lower this correlation, the more difficult it is to interpret the meaning of the coefficient. The authors' justification for using OCG reports rather than primary caregiver reports was the possibility that "common method variance" was a potential problem. Perhaps this issue was resolved in previous research, but it is important to demonstrate the OCG reports are more valid and reliable than the parents' reports of these behaviors and that the results were not sensitive to who the OCG was. Research that triangulates different sources of delinquency data remains critically important to the field (see, e.g., Short 2002).

4. The authors focus their discussion of the findings on the similarities and differences across gender. They state: "The major point of similarity for G2 mothers and fathers is the immediate and powerful association of their parenting style on G3's early antisocial behavior" (Thornberry et al. 2003, 181). However, available information makes it impossible to determine whether these effects are "powerful." The coefficient suggests that for every one-unit increase in the combined affection/discipline index, there is a .33 standardized unit decrease in the thirty-three item subscale of the Child Behavior Check List (CBCL), as reported by the child's OCG. But because the means and standard deviations for the unstandardized variable are not provided, one cannot determine the kind of distinction that a standard unit difference represents. The authors also conclude that these results vary by G2 gender: "antisocial behavior plays a more central role in the model for fathers and parenting style plays a more powerful mediating role . . . for mothers" (ibid.). It is true that the coefficients from G2's adolescent delinquency to G3's early antisocial behavior differ—for G2 mothers, it was .11 (n.s.), while for G2 fathers it was .19 ($p < .05$, one-tail test). This difference in the coefficients was not tested for statistical significance. Given the sample size of the two groups, there is a good chance that this difference was not statistically significant.

References

Bernard, Thomas J. 1990. Twenty years of testing theories: What have we learned and why? *Journal of Research in Crime and Delinquency* 27:325-47.

Elliott, Delbert. 1985. The assumption that theories can be combined with increased explanatory power. In *Theoretical methods in criminology*, ed. Robert Meier. Beverly Hills, CA: Sage.

Elliott, Delbert S., David Huizinga, and Suzanne S. Ageton. 1985. *Explaining delinquency and drug use.* Beverly Hills, CA: Sage.

Hirschi, Travis. 1969. *Causes of delinquency.* Los Angeles: University of California Press.

———. 1979. Separate and unequal is better. *Journal of Research in Crime and Delinquency* 16:34-37.

———. 1989. Exploring alternatives to integrated theory. In *Theoretical integration in the study of deviance and crime: Problems and prospects*, ed. Steven F. Messner, Marvin D. Krohn, and Allen E. Liska. Albany: State University of New York Press.

Jang, Sung Joon. 1999. Different definitions, different modeling decisions, and different interpretations: A rejoinder to Lauritsen. *Criminology* 37:695-702.

Lauritsen, Janet L. 1998. The age-crime debate: Assessing the limits of longitudinal self-report data. *Social Forces* 77:127-54.

———. 1999. Limitations in the use of self-report data: A comment. *Criminology* 37:687-94.

Lemert, Edwin M. 1972. *Human deviance, social problems, and social control.* Englewood Cliffs, NJ: Prentice Hall.

Liska, Allen E., Marvin D. Krohn, and Steven F. Messner. 1989. Strategies and requisites for theoretical integration in the study of crime and deviance. In *Theoretical integration in the study of deviance and crime: Problems and prospects*, ed. Steven F. Messner, Marvin D. Krohn, and Allen E. Liska. Albany: State University of New York Press.

Loeber, Rolf, and Magda Stouthamer-Loeber. 1986. Family factors as correlates and predictors of juvenile conduct problems. In *Crime and justice: An annual review of research*, vol. 7, ed. Michael Tonry and Norval Morris. Chicago: University of Chicago Press.

Matsueda, Ross L., and Karen Heimer. 1997. A symbolic interactionist theory of role transitions, role commitments, and delinquency. In *Advances in criminological theory*, vol. 7, *Developmental theories of crime and delinquency*, ed. Terence Thornberry. New Brunswick, NJ: Transaction.

Merton, Robert K. 1967. *On theoretical sociology: five essays, old and new.* New York: Free Press.

Messner, Steven F., Marvin D. Krohn, and Allen E. Liska, eds. 1989. *Theoretical integration in the study of deviance and crime: Problems and prospects.* Albany: State University of New York Press.

Moffitt, Terrie E. 1993. "Life-course persistent" and "adolescence-limited" antisocial behavior: A developmental taxonomy. *Psychological Review* 100:674-701.

National Institutes of Health. N.d. NIH Data Sharing Policy and Implementation Guidance. http://grants.nih.gov/grants/policy/data_sharing/data_sharing_guidance.htm#goals (accessed June 1, 2005).

Osgood, Wayne D., Patrick O'Malley, Jerald Bachman, and Lloyd Johnston. 1989. Time trends and age trends in arrests and self-reported illegal behavior. *Criminology* 27:389-418.

Rowe, David C. 1994. *The limits of family influence: Genes, experience, and behavior.* New York: Guilford.

Sampson, Robert J., and John H. Laub. 1993. *Crime in the making: Pathways and turning points through life.* Cambridge, MA: Harvard University Press.

Shaw, Clifford R. 1966. *The Jack-Roller: A delinquent boy's own story.* Chicago: University of Chicago Press.

Sherman, Lawrence. 1993. Defiance, deterrence, and irrelevance: A theory of the criminal sanction. *Journal of Research in Crime and Delinquency* 30:445-73.

Short, James F., Jr. 1985. The level of explanation problem in criminology. In *Theoretical methods in criminology*, ed. Robert Meier. Beverly Hills, CA: Sage.

———. 2002. Unwinding: Reflections on a career. In *Lessons of criminology*, ed. Gilbert Geis and Mary Dodge. Cincinnati, OH: Anderson.

Snodgrass, Jon. 1982. *The Jack-Roller at seventy: A fifty-year follow-up.* Lexington, MA: Lexington Books.

Thornberry, Terence P. 1989. Panel effects and the use of self-report measures of delinquency in longitudinal studies. In *Cross-national research in self-reported crime and delinquency*, ed. Malcolm Klein. Dordrecht, the Netherlands: Kluwer Academic.

———. 2005. Explaining multiple patterns of offending across the life course and across generations. *Annals of the American Academy of Political and Social Science* 602:156-95.

Thornberry, Terence P., Adrienne Freeman-Gallant, Alan J. Lizotte, Marvin D. Krohn, and Carolyn A. Smith. 2003. Linked lives: The intergenerational transmission of antisocial behavior. *Journal of Abnormal Child Psychology* 31:171-84.

Thornberry, Terence P., and Marvin D. Krohn. 2005. Applying interactional theory in the explanation of continuity and change in antisocial behavior. In *Advances in criminological theory*. New Brunswick, NJ: Transaction.

Widom, Cathy Spatz, and Michael G. Maxfield. 2001. An update on the cycle of violence. National Institute of Justice Research in Brief, NCJ184894, February. Washington, DC: National Institute of Justice.

RESPONSE

The author's article on interactional theory and on intergenerational models presented at the Albany Symposium received comments from Wayne Osgood and Janet Lauritsen. They raised several issues concerning theory construction, empirically testing developmental and intergenerational models, and collecting longitudinal data. The present article responds to those issues, continuing the discussion of life-course theories of crime begun at the symposium.

Notes on Theory Construction and Theory Testing: A Response to Osgood and Lauritsen

By
TERENCE P. THORNBERRY

My paper on interactional theory received comments by Wayne Osgood and Janet Lauritsen. I would like to begin by responding to four issues raised in Osgood's thoughtful commentary.

First, I completely agree with Osgood's (2005 [this volume]) admonition to avoid a risk factor approach. I do have a tendency in my theoretical writings to use categorical terminology—e.g., good parenting versus bad parenting—in referring to causal influences. That is a heuristic device that I think, perhaps wrongly, more clearly portrays the causal dynamic. However in my empirical assessments of the theory I use continuous measures of these concepts, including parenting. I should, of course, be more consistent across theoretical and empirical writings.

Second, I did argue that extreme levels of causal factors are more stable than moderate levels, but I meant it precisely in the sense that Osgood describes. That is, for extreme deficits, even if change occurs, it is unlikely to move the person out of the portion of the distribution that causes delinquency. More moderate levels of these causal factors are more volatile and, in that sense, less stable.

Third, the most challenging issue Osgood raises concerns the definition of offending. When I first presented interactional theory, I was clearly focused on delinquency and crime. And in a sense, the Rochester Youth Develop-

NOTE: I would like to thank Marvin Krohn, Alan Lizotte, and Pamela Porter for helpful comments on this response.

DOI: 10.1177/0002716205280693

ment Study (RYDS) reified that conception as it was based on an adolescent sample and measured offending using a standard self-reported delinquency inventory. As the field of developmental criminology progressed and as we began the Rochester Intergenerational Study (RIGS) with children as young as two, that conception of offending seemed increasingly narrow. We extended interactional theory to account for behavior at younger ages, and this led to a stronger focus on general antisocial behavior in childhood, followed by delinquency in adolescence. The data in the RIGS are developmentally targeted and range from externalizing behaviors in childhood, through delinquency and drug use in adolescence, to crime in adulthood. As Patterson (1993) warned us, measuring the chimera of antisocial behavior over the life course is a daunting task. We tried to be sensitive to that in the measures we chose and created for the RIGS, but only time will tell how successful we were.

In the meantime, Osgood's concern is well-founded. While my theoretical conception of offending has expanded from the original presentation of interactional theory in 1987 to the one in this volume, the measures available for the original Rochester sample members are focused on delinquency and crime, limiting what one can say about trajectories of offending. Those limitations will be reduced once the intergenerational data are fully available.

Finally, I would like to concur with one of Osgood's basic points. Focusing on "shades of gray" and on "continuous conceptions of offending rather than unreservedly adopting a categorical approach" are fundamentally good things for developmental criminology. That is true for theoretical reasons, as I showed in my article, as well as for the policy and practice reasons that Osgood discussed. Oversimplifying the phenomenon to be studied in the name of parsimony leads to misspecified models and is likely to hamper rather than advance understanding. Antisocial behavior is a complex phenomenon, with many shades of gray, and we need to recognize and tackle that complexity.

Turning to Lauritsen's (2005 [this volume]) comments, I will respond to each of the three broad issues that she raises. They concern theory, empirical tests, and data.

Theoretical Issues

Lauritsen (2005) begins her critique by referring to the 1987 Albany Symposium on theoretical integration, citing the proceedings of that symposium and Hirschi's chapter in it. She claims that "interactional theory [is] a broad attempt at theoretical integration" (p. 213) and then critiques it for not satisfying some of the conditions of theoretical integration such as the reconciliation of "contradictory premises and assumptions" (p. 217).

Inexplicably, Lauritsen never refers to my own contribution to the 1987 Symposium also published in Messner, Krohn, and Liska (1989), where I very explicitly argue against integration as a theory construction strategy. I argue that integration

diverts attention . . . from the fundamental purpose of theory construction—the explanation of a particular phenomenon—to a secondary purpose—the reconciliation of differences found in previous theories in the hope that such reconciliation improves explanatory power. (Thornberry 1989, 56)

In its place, I argue for the value of theoretical elaboration.

In the process of elaboration, . . . the theorist is concerned with maximizing the explanatory power of a particular theory without the attendant concern of reconciling differences
across theories. . . . [T]he theorist is free to borrow or not borrow from competing theories,
and there is certainly no obligation to represent all, or even substantial portions, of the
competing theories in the elaborated model. (Thornberry 1989, 59-60)

Consistent with this view, interactional theory is guided by theoretical elaboration.
I have never presented it as an "integrated theory." It is hardly surprising, therefore, that interactional theory does not conform to the strictures of theoretical integration, an approach to theory construction that I find severely wanting.

Lauritsen's next point is that interactional theory shares common premises,
propositions, and hypotheses with other theories and therefore is not unique. This
concern evinces a profound misunderstanding of theory and theory construction.
First, "a theory is a *set of* logically interrelated *propositions* designed to explain a
particular phenomenon" (Blalock 1969, italics added). Thus, theories are distinguished by how their theoretical propositions are bundled together, that is, logically interrelated, and not by the inclusion of any particular proposition. It is hardly
surprising that theories attempting to explain the same phenomenon share concepts and propositions, especially since all of the theories mentioned by Lauritsen
derive from a common sociological perspective. Even so, the theories can be, and
are, distinguished one from another, and interactional theory from them, because
the *set of propositions* in each differs from the set in the others, notwithstanding
some degree of overlap.

Second, this concern over uniqueness is logically flawed as a criterion for judging the adequacy of any theory. If interactional theory overlaps to some extent with
labeling, control, learning, and so on, as Lauritsen correctly states, they, in turn,
logically overlap with interactional theory and, more important, with each other.
Thus they, and by extension all the theories of crime mentioned by Lauritsen,
should be found as wanting as interactional theory on this score. And that is precisely why this criterion is fallacious: it is nondiscriminating.

Even if one were to take it seriously, however, Lauritsen's application is wrong.
For example, she claims that interactional theory's focus on reciprocal causation
overlaps with the hypotheses of labeling, symbolic interactionist, and defiance theories (2005). That claim misses a fundamental distinction between interactional
theory and the other three. In the other theories, it is the societal reaction to delinquent behavior, that is, the label, that generates negative consequences for the
individual. Interactional theory deliberately shifted attention away from societal
responses and placed it on delinquent behavior. That is, involvement in delin-

quency is hypothesized to generate negative consequences for the individual, regardless of whether it is labeled. To know that societal reactions generate negative consequences does not show (or refute) that earlier behavior does; to show that earlier behavior does, does not show (or refute) that official labels do. These theories focus on different processes in their rightful concern with causal reciprocity. Thus, the causal overlap is found in Lauritsen's misreading of the theories, not in the theories.

Lauritsen also claims that interactional theory is not falsifiable. I disagree on several grounds. First, interactional theory is presented as a probabilistic theory of human behavior, consistent with the long tradition of social scientific theory construction (Blalock 1969). In this regard, interactional theory does not differ from any of the other criminological theories cited by Lauritsen. To illustrate, interactional theory hypothesizes that causal influences, such as low attachment to parents or association with delinquent peers, increase the probability or likelihood of subsequent delinquency. It seems abundantly clear to me that those hypotheses can be tested and falsified, using standard social science research methods. If these concepts are unrelated to delinquency (and suppressor effects are not at play), that evidence would be damaging to the theory. These are the ground rules for testing all other criminological theories, and it is entirely baffling to me to think that they would not apply to interactional theory or that I would have to explicitly state what is so obvious, that they do.

Second, the examples of "nonfalsifiable assertions" offered by Lauritsen are misleading. Her discussion of my hypothesis concerning the link between age of onset and the length of careers is illustrative. She claims that the hypothesis "that among early starters some offenders will persist, but many other will desist, . . . [and] that among later starters some offenders will desist relatively quickly, but others will persist in their offending" (2005, 218) is not falsifiable. Unfortunately, she takes that statement out of context. The full presentation of this hypothesis is as follows:

> Given its sociogenetic underpinnings, however, interactional theory hypothesizes that the magnitude of this association [between early onset and length of careers] is, at best, moderate. . . . This hypothesis, too, is different from ontogenetic models where early starters become life-course persistent offenders and late-starters are adolescence-limited (Moffitt 1993; Patterson, Capaldi, and Bank 1991). Our view is quite different: onset is not destiny. Regardless of when one starts, careers can take on different lengths and shapes, depending on later aspects of life-course development. (Thornberry 2005 [this volume], 160)

From this fuller statement, it is clear that I am contrasting expectations from two different types of developmental theories of delinquency: ontogenetic models (e.g., Moffitt 1993; Patterson, Capaldi, and Bank 1991) and sociogenetic models (e.g., Thornberry 2005). Thus, the real hypothesis is a comparative one—the contrast between these two types of developmental models—and that is clearly testable.

Third, there have been numerous efforts to falsify interactional theory, that is, there are numerous empirical studies of it—some with results consistent with the theory, some not (e.g., Jang 1999, 2002; Lee 2003; Scaramella et al. 2002; Thornberry, Lizotte, et al. 2003). Moreover, Lauritsen's particular claim of "nonfalsifiability" concerning ontogenetic versus sociogenetic models was actually tested in my article in this volume using trajectory analyses on the Rochester data. The results, at least by my reading, are inconsistent with ontogenetic models and consistent with sociogenetic models.

Finally, Lauritsen comments on the definition and measurement of delinquency, crime, and antisocial behavior over the life course. As noted in my response to Osgood, I agree that this is a difficult issue and one that needs to be considered more fully. Lauritsen goes on to say, however, "If a definition for antisocial behavior were offered . . . " (2005, 218), implying that I failed to define this key concept. In fact, both papers presented Tolan, Guerra, and Kendall's (1995) definition of antisocial behavior. Lauritsen is obviously free to criticize that definition if she wishes, but not to state that we failed to provide a definition.

Empirical Issues

Lauritsen (2005, 220) then discusses two empirical tests of the intergenerational model, noting that "the meaning of all statistical analyses is found in the details." I completely agree, so let us look at the details.

Her major point is that these tests are not complete because they do not control for all possible predictors of the outcome. Of course that is correct, both in this, and in all other statistical analyses. As is the case with all truisms, this assertion is both self-evident and uninformative. More to the point, though, my colleagues and I recognize and state clearly that these investigations test only part of the overall model:

> Testing the full range of these [intergenerational] influences is . . . beyond the scope of the present analysis. Our approach, therefore, is more focused. We start with a core part of interactional theory's model of antisocial behavior that has been shown to be predictive of delinquency and other problem behaviors within a generation. We then develop an intergenerational extension of that model and test it, using data from the Rochester study. (Thornberry, Freeman-Gallant, et al. 2003, 172; see also Thornberry 2005, 185)

This approach to model testing is quite common in developmental criminology where general models are tested in incremental, overlapping steps. Excellent examples can be found in the work of Conger et al. (1992); Elder, Caspi, and Downey (1986); Patterson, Reid, and Dishion (1992); and Sampson and Laub (1993). This strategy recognizes the reality of developmental models: conceptual models of behavior across the life course are complex, and it is unlikely that any data set can validly test the full model in one structural equation model.

But what would Lauritsen do? She would "control for other dimensions of family life, including G2's family composition, marital status, and other aspects of family function . . . additional parenting that likely takes place in two-parent homes or homes with another adult living with the child . . . time spent with other caregivers such as teachers or day care professionals" (2005, 221). In addition, she would control for "school environment, time spent with delinquent peers, peer victimization, or residing in a highly disadvantaged area" (2005, 222).

There are two fundamental problems with her approach. First, it is entirely atheoretical. There is no conceptual justification for this particular laundry list of variables. They represent Lauritsen's idiosyncratic view of "important" correlates and, as such, violate fundamental tenets of model specification (Blalock 1969).

It is hardly surprising that theories attempting to explain the same phenomenon share concepts and propositions . . .

Second, to include all these variables in one analysis would be statistically irresponsible. The intergenerational model presented in this volume contains five variables, eight structural paths, and sample sizes of 139 for mothers and 136 for fathers. Thornberry, Freeman-Gallant, et al. (2003) included six constructs, two with attached measurement models, nine structural paths, and sample sizes of 111 for mothers and 109 for fathers. Lauritsen would add *at least* ten other variables, generating an unspecified number of additional structural coefficients to be estimated. Even if a structural equation model of that complexity were to converge, the coefficients would not be meaningful. Based on our experience with these types of models and, more important, the formal power analyses we have conducted (e.g., Thornberry, Krohn, and Lizotte 2004), there is not adequate power to accurately estimate models as complex as the one envisioned by Lauritsen. Meaning is indeed in the details, and in this case, estimating a series of smaller models testing core parts of general developmental theories is a more valid way to build knowledge.

Lauritsen also criticizes our use of the child's other caregiver (OCG) and teacher as the measurement source for G3's (the third generation's) antisocial behavior. She claims that "it is also important to know whether the other caregiver assessments are highly correlated with the primary caregiver's assessments of the child. Obviously, the lower this correlation, the more difficult it is to interpret the meaning of the coefficient" (2005, 226, note 4). That is not at all obvious, and even a passing familiarity with the developmental literature in psychology and criminology would show that Lauritsen's critique misses the mark.

Numerous studies have shown that relying on the same reporter to measure both the independent and dependent variables can bias results. For example, highly antisocial parents often project their antisociality onto their reports of the child's behavior, inflating the reports; seriously depressed parents are unreliable reporters of their child's behavior because of their illness. Using different reporters or a mixture of interview and observational measures is a well-settled psychometric matter in developmental studies (see, e.g., Bank et al. 1990; Conger, Lorenz, and Wickrama 2004; Loeber et al. 1989; Lorenz et al. 1991; Patterson 1993) and, from a developmental perspective, a great strength, not a weakness, of our study. Also, the similarity of results I presented in these two analyses is strong evidence for construct validity.

Two other empirical issues should be mentioned. In commenting on Thornberry, Freeman-Gallant, et al. (2003), Lauritsen (2005, 220) complains that "it is difficult to assess the effect size of these coefficients . . . since means and standard deviations for the original measures are not provided." Apparently she missed Table 1 (Thornberry, Freeman-Gallant, et al. 2003, 178), which presents the means and standard deviations. Granted, I did not include them in this volume because of space limitations, but her comment was directed at the 2003 article.

Second, she claims that "it is not clear to me, for example, whether the lack of a direct effect of G2 father and mother's adolescent drug use on G3's childhood delinquency has any consequences for the theory" (2005, 222). Of course it does. The intergenerational model I presented above strongly and clearly argues that the G2 parent's adolescent antisocial behavior is *indirectly* related to G3 antisocial behavior via its disruption of G2's life-course development and subsequent impact on parenting style. The consequences are clear: these results are quite consistent with our mediational model.

Data Sharing and Data Collecting

Lauritsen's last area concerns data sharing and collection. With respect to the former, she states that the RYDS instruments have never been published. In their entirety that is true, but the full set takes up two shelves of my bookcase and are not exactly scintillating reading. We have, however, published many of the scales and indices from our earliest publications (e.g., Krohn et al. 1992; Lizotte et al. 1992) to the most recent (e.g., Thornberry, Freeman-Gallant, et al. 2003). Moreover, we have always shared our instruments with interested researchers and continue to do so.

The release of collected data is far more challenging, but not unique to the Rochester study; it applies to other contemporary longitudinal studies—those in Denver, Pittsburgh, and Seattle; Monitoring the Future; and others. There is obviously a reason for this: these projects collect a great deal of sensitive data that can easily be linked to individual participants, even if names and obvious identifiers (e.g., date of birth) are removed from the file. Identifying an individual participant violates pledges of confidentiality, human participants' protections, and a host of ethical and legal standards. Making the data more generally available in a way that does not incur these unacceptable costs has proven to be elusive. Lauritsen's comments imply that we have been insensitive to this issue and have not attempted to make the data available. In fact, the three projects of the Program of Research on the Causes and Correlates of Delinquency (PRCCD) began to release data in the late 1990s but realized that a general release would be imprudent. Since then, we have spent considerable time and effort working on strategies that would enable a broader release while protecting participants' rights.

The Checklist on Disclosure Potential of Proposed Data Releases, prepared by the Interagency Confidentiality and Data Access Group: An Interest Group of the Federal Committee on Statistical Methodology (Office of Management and Budget 1999), illustrates the problem. The Checklist provides guidance on when it is safe to release individual-level data files. When we apply the Checklist criteria to the projects of the PRCCD (Huizinga and Thornberry 2000), the results are worrisome.

To start, "All geographic areas identified *must* have at least 100,000 persons in the sampled area (according to latest Census or Census estimate)" (Office of Management and Budget 1999, 7). The Rochester sample is not based on a household survey of a geographic area; our population consists of only four thousand individuals, all seventh and eighth graders in Rochester public schools in 1988. Moreover, the sample of one thousand represents 25 percent of the population, further easing the likelihood of deductive or inadvertent discovery. Based on this general rule about population size, any general release of the Rochester data is extremely problematic.

The Checklist presents eleven conditions that increase the risk of individual disclosure, including such criteria as the sampling frame being provided by an outside source (e.g., a school), collection of longitudinal data, and having multiple respondents from the same household. If *any* of these conditions are met, disclosure risk is high and data release is problematic. The projects of the PRCCD failed on *all* eleven criteria (Huizinga and Thornberry 2000). The Rochester project and similar longitudinal projects collect the type of data that maximizes the likelihood of identifying individual participants and therefore makes the general release of the data most problematic.

The projects of the PRCCD continue to work on this, and we are now testing a Remote Access Data Center to enable qualified researchers to use the data. We appreciate the need and the desirability of making these data more generally available, but as Lauritsen (2005, 223) notes, "Maintaining and protecting respondent confidentiality . . . is an extremely important and legitimate issue." I agree, and until we are completely convinced that those primary ethical and legal concerns are met, it would be imprudent, at best, to release the data.

Lauritsen's final concern is about deciding when we have collected too much data from our participants. It is well known that the value of longitudinal, developmental projects is directly related to the length of the follow-up and the comprehensiveness of the data. Given this, her concern seems misplaced. Moreover, the Rochester project is no different from a host of other longitudinal projects in scope and duration. Would she stop all longitudinal studies?

But look at the facts. With the RYDS sample, we have conducted fourteen interviews, lasting usually sixty to seventy-five minutes, over the past seventeen years.

In the RIGS, we have conducted an additional six annual assessments, three of which included a twenty- to thirty-minute videotaped observational interview. All of our procedures are approved by the institutional review board and reapproved to meet current standards, including those to reduce respondent burden and fatigue. Participants are always "reconsented," reminded that participation is voluntary and that they can withdraw at any time. They generally do not object, as indicated by our excellent retention rates: 82 percent of the living participants in 2004. The few that do feel "saturated" tell us when we call to schedule an interview; we thank them for their help over the years and remove them from the study list.

[U]ntil we are completely convinced that . . . primary ethical and legal concerns are met, it would be imprudent, at best, to release the data.

Lauritsen is also concerned that studies such as the RYDS "through their probing interviews and observations, might to some extent contaminate their own studies and affect their subjects in positive but also negative ways" (2005, 225). By way of "evidence," she offers an analogy to Clifford Shaw's famous case study, *The Jack-Roller* (1966). Shaw spent endless amounts of time with one subject, "Stanley," over many years. That such an extensive experience could alter a research participant's behavior is plausible. To extend that finding to the Rochester study is not.

In contrast to Shaw's (1966) extensive and prolonged interviews, if we assume that all of our interviews lasted 75 minutes, then we have interviewed our participants for a total of 17.5 hours over 17 years. That means our interviews consumed 0.00012 percent (17.5/148,920 hours) of our participants' lives over this time period. Perhaps that brief intervention did have a profound impact on their life course; I doubt it.

One final point on Lauritsen's criticism that we collect too much data. Earlier, she criticized us for collecting too little: "measures . . . based on in-home-video-taped interactions . . . may be unlikely to capture the full range of parent-child dynamics, such as child abuse and neglect" (2005, 222). (I am well aware of this, which is why we also collect extensive interview data on parenting from multiple respondents, as well as data on maltreatment; they just were not used in the analysis presented in my article in this volume.) But the broader point is this: if I am to be criticized for collecting too little data on page 222 and too much data on page 225, I fear there is no way to satisfy this critic. So I shall stop.

References

Bank, Lew, Thomas J. Dishion, M. Skinner, and Gerald Patterson. 1990. Method variance in structural equation modeling: Living with "glop." In *Depression and aggression in family interaction*, ed. Gerald R. Patterson. Hillsdale, NJ: Lawrence Erlbaum.

Blalock, Hubert M. 1969. *Theory construction*. Englewood Cliffs, NJ: Prentice Hall.

Conger, Rand D., Katherine J. Conger, Glen H. Elder Jr., Frederick O. Lorenz, Ronald L. Simons, and Les B. Whitbeck. 1992. A family process model of economic hardship and adjustment of early adolescent boys. *Child Development* 63:526-41.

Conger, Rand D., Frederick O. Lorenz, and K. A. S. Wickrama. 2004. Studying change in family relationships: The findings and their implications. In *Continuity and change in family relations: Theory, methods, and empirical findings*, ed. Rand D. Conger, Frederick O. Lorenz, and K. A. S. Wickrama. Mahwah, NJ: Lawrence Erlbaum.

Elder, Glen H., Jr., Avshalom Caspi, and Geraldine Downey. 1986. Problem behavior and family relationships: Life course and intergenerational themes. In *Human development and the life course: Multidisciplinary perspectives*, ed. Aage B. Sorensen, Franz E. Weinert, and Lonnie R. Sherrod. Hillsdale, NJ: Lawrence Erlbaum.

Huizinga, David, and Terence P. Thornberry. 2000. The creation of public release data files by the projects of the OJJDP's program of research on the causes and correlates of delinquency. Unpublished report prepared for the Office of Juvenile Justice and Delinquency Prevention, U.S. Department of Justice.

Jang, Sung Joon. 1999. Age-varying effects of family, school, and peers on delinquency: A multilevel modeling test of interactional theory. *Child Development* 74:109-26.

———. 2002. The effects of family, school, peers, and attitudes on adolescents' drug use: Do they vary with age? *Justice Quarterly* 19:97-126.

Krohn, Marvin D., Susan B. Stern, Terence P. Thornberry, and Sung Joon Jang. 1992. The measurement of family process variables: The effect of adolescent and parent perceptions of family life on delinquent behavior. *Journal of Quantitative Criminology* 8:287-315.

Lauritsen, Janet L. 2005. Explaining patterns of offending across the life course: Comments on interactional theory and recent tests based on the RYDS-RIS data. *Annals of the American Academy of Political and Social Science* 602:212-28.

Lee, Sangmoon. 2003. Testing Thornberry's interactional theory: The reciprocal relations. Unpublished doctoral diss., Iowa State University, Ames.

Lizotte, Alan J., Deborah J. Chard-Wierschem, Rolf Loeber, and Susan B. Stern. 1992. A shortened child behavior checklist for delinquency studies. *Journal of Quantitative Criminology* 8:233-45.

Loeber, Rolf, Stephanie Green, Benjamin B. Lahey, and Magda Stouthamer-Loeber. 1989. Optimal informants on childhood disruptive behaviors. *Development and Psychopathology* 1:317-37.

Lorenz, Frederick O., Rand D. Conger, Ronald L. Simons, Les B. Whitbeck, and Glen H. Elder Jr. 1991. Economic pressure and marital quality: An illustration of the method variance problem in the causal modeling of family process. *Journal of Marriage and the Family* 53:375-88.

Messner, Steven F., Marvin D. Krohn, and Allen E. Liska. 1989. *Theoretical integration in the study of deviance and crime: Problems and prospects*. Albany: State University of New York Press.

Moffitt, Terrie E. 1993. "Life-course-persistent" and "adolescence-limited" antisocial behavior: A developmental taxonomy. *Psychological Review* 100:674-701.

Office of Management and Budget. 1999. Checklist on disclosure potential of proposed data releases. Unpublished report prepared by the Interagency Confidentiality and Data Access Group, Statistical Policy Office, Office of Information and Regulatory Affairs, Washington, DC.

Osgood, D. Wayne. 2005. Making sense of crime and the life course. *Annals of the American Academy of Political and Social Science* 602:196-211.

Patterson, Gerald R. 1993. Orderly change in a stable world: The antisocial trait as a chimera. *Journal of Consulting and Clinical Psychology* 61:911-19.

Patterson, Gerald R., Deborah Capaldi, and Lew Bank. 1991. An early starter model for predicting delinquency. In *The development and treatment of childhood aggression*, ed. Debra J. Pepler and Kenneth H. Rubin. Hillsdale, NJ: Lawrence Erlbaum.

Patterson, Gerald R., John B. Reid, and Thomas J. Dishion. 1992. *Antisocial boys*. Eugene, OR: Castalia Press.

Sampson, Robert J., and John Laub. 1993. *Crime in the making: Pathways and turning points through life*. Cambridge, MA: Harvard University Press.

Scaramella, Laura V., Rand D. Conger, Richard Spoth, and Ronald L. Simons. 2002. Evaluation of a social contextual model of delinquency: A cross-study replication. *Child Development* 73:175-95.

Shaw, Clifford R. 1966. *The Jack-Roller: A delinquent boy's own story*. Chicago: University of Chicago Press.

Thornberry, Terence P. 1989. Reflections on the advantages and disadvantages of theoretical integration. In *Theoretical integration in the study of deviance and crime: Problems and prospects*, ed. Steven F. Messner, Marvin D. Krohn, and Allen E. Liska. Albany: State University of New York Press.

———. 2005. Explaining multiple patterns of offending across the life course and across generations. *Annals of the American Academy of Political and Social Science* 602:156-95.

Thornberry, Terence P., Adrienne Freeman-Gallant, Alan J. Lizotte, Marvin D. Krohn, and Carolyn A. Smith. 2003. Linked lives: The intergenerational transmission of antisocial behavior. *Journal of Abnormal Child Psychology* 31:171-84.

Thornberry, Terence P., Marvin D. Krohn, and Alan J. Lizotte. 2004. Intergenerational transmission of risk for drug use. Proposal submitted to the National Institute on Drug Abuse, National Institutes of Health, Rockville, MD.

Thornberry, Terence P., Alan J. Lizotte, Marvin D. Krohn, Carolyn A. Smith, and Pamela K. Porter. 2003. Causes and consequences of delinquency: Findings from the Rochester Youth Development Study. In *Taking stock of delinquency: An overview of findings from contemporary longitudinal studies*, ed. Terence P. Thornberry and Marvin D. Krohn. New York: Kluwer Academic/Plenum.

Tolan, Patrick H., Nancy G. Guerra, and Philip C. Kendall. 1995. Introduction to special section: Prediction and prevention of antisocial behavior in children and adolescents. *Journal of Consulting and Clinical Psychology* 63:515-17.

SECTION FOUR

Final Thoughts

FINAL THOUGHTS

An Overview
of the
Symposium
and Some
Next Steps

By
ALFRED BLUMSTEIN

This article identifies some overarching issues raised at the Albany Symposium on Developmental Criminology, with particular focus on important issues in conflict. In developing theory in this very complex area, there is tension between a parsimonious theory with a limited number of constructs and richer description that tries to capture more critical features. It seems that one concept is too limiting. The debate over the benefits of identifying subgroups in a population will depend on the analytical context; those groups can be identified empirically (say, by trajectory analysis) or a priori theoretical conceptualization. There is a need for greater interaction across the variety of rich data sets and scholars' perspectives that could be facilitated with greater data sharing, particularly by bringing in new methodological skills. Also, there is a need for a developmental criminology forum to address some common agreed-upon questions with several of the rich data sets represented at the symposium.

Keywords: criminal careers; career length; desistance; offending frequency; offender groups; developmental criminology forum; age-crime curve; longitudinal data; theory testing

T his was a notable symposium, and its importance is reflected in the quality of the articles and commentary in this volume. There were some excellent presentations of the three principal papers, some challenging discussants, and some lively interaction. This came about

Alfred Blumstein is the J. Erik Jonsson University Professor of Urban Systems and Operations Research and former dean (from 1986 to 1993) at the Heinz School of Public Policy and Management of Carnegie Mellon University. He also directs the National Consortium on Violence Research (NCOVR). He has chaired National Academy of Sciences panels on research on Deterrent and Incapacitative Effects, on Sentencing, and on Criminal Careers. He is a fellow of the American Society of Criminology, was the 1987 recipient of the Society's Sutherland Award for "contributions to research," and was the president of the Society in 1991-1992. His research has covered many aspects of criminal-justice phenomena and policy, including criminal careers, sentencing, deterrence and incapacitation, prison populations, demographic trends, juvenile violence, and drug-enforcement policy.

DOI: 10.1177/0002716205281181

because the planners—John Laub and Rob Sampson—chose some excellent scholars to present the papers and chose some excellent critics to seek out the substantive and the methodological limitations of the papers. And the meeting organizers—Dean Julie Horney and Greg Pogarsky at the School of Criminal Justice at the University at Albany—provided a forum to address some key alternative approaches for the future of developmental criminology. The principal papers, by Sampson and Laub, Nagin and Tremblay, and Thornberry, provided the meat for the Albany Symposium on Developmental Criminology as well as the essential strength for this volume.

Sampson and Laub (2005b [this volume]) reported on what is undoubtedly the longest longitudinal series of criminal careers likely ever to be constructed. Laub and Sampson (2003) built on the work of Sheldon and Eleanor Glueck (1950), who assembled detailed records of five hundred boys confined to one of two juvenile reform schools in Massachusetts in the 1930s and followed them until they were thirty-one. Sampson and Laub then collected follow-up records of these individuals until they were into their seventies, noting who died and when and collecting their arrest histories since age thirty-one.[1] Their article reports on some of the rich analyses they were able to carry out with these time-extensive records.

The Nagin and Tremblay article (2005 [this volume]) focuses primarily on the group-based trajectory method developed by Nagin that has provided important insights into trajectories of offending patterns by being applied to richly developed longitudinal data collected on multiple cohorts by Tremblay. The strength of the method is that it approaches a set of individual trajectories in a statistically rigorous way in the same way that cluster analysis might approach a set of points in two-space—finding groups that resemble each other closely and then assigning each of the others to the group that it most closely resembles. This identifies a handful of aggregate groups, which are much easier to deal with analytically than hundreds of individual trajectories. Then one can seek to identify what characteristics distinguish the individuals constituting each of the groups, with a focus particularly on the most troublesome groups.

The Thornberry article (2005a [this volume]) reports on his research as part of one of the most innovative government ventures in supporting longitudinal research. Labeled the "Causes and Correlates" project, the Office of Juvenile Justice and Delinquency Prevention launched parallel projects in three cities (Rochester, Pittsburgh, and Denver) with common measures of delinquent acts. Beyond that initial similarity, the three projects proceeded in different ways to draw their samples, to investigate the origins of delinquency, and to study the delinquency and criminal careers of their subjects. Thornberry's work has emphasized his "interaction theory" and the insights it brings to an understanding of phenomena looking across the offending patterns of his subjects. He also has extended that

NOTE: The symposium was organized and sponsored by the School of Criminal Justice at the University at Albany. The National Consortium on Violence Research (NCOVR) was also a cosponsor, and I, as the director of NCOVR, was pleased that it could also serve as one of our research workshops.

work by exploring intergenerational transmission of delinquency by following not only their initial sample and the influence of their parents but also the children of the members of the initial sample.

Common Purposes in Using Longitudinal Data

All of these papers were concerned with the development of crime, what Barbara Maughan (2005 [this volume], 119) describes as "the unfolding of troubling and troublesome behaviors across the life course and the factors that underlie those changing patterns." To some degree, some of these issues could well be addressed in cross-sectional studies, taking a sample of individuals of diverse ages and asking them—or also their parents and teachers—about their offending, augmented by official arrest records. The richness of the information would certainly be less than in a longitudinal study, there would be significant recall errors, but if one tried to generate an age-crime curve (the rate of crime commission or arrest for various crime types as a function of age), it probably would not be very different from what would result from a longitudinal study.

But the strength of the longitudinal approach is the continuity of the same individuals tracked over time. That permits analysis of the developmental processes within particular individuals—each serving as his own control—that gives the longitudinal study its distinctive strength. Also, most important, the longitudinal study allows one to examine in detail the connections among what Thornberry (2005a) identifies as "onset, course, and desistance"—What are the factors that make some individuals start early, others later, and others not at all? What are the patterns of offending during the course of the criminal career—to what extent do individuals follow a pattern like the age-crime curve (starting at an early age, rising to a peak in the late teens, and then dropping rather slowly to almost zero at a late age), or are the patterns more jagged or perhaps even flat until desistance sets in? Or is there a gradual slowing down, but with desistance occurring much earlier for the large majority of offenders? And what factors affect the desistance process? Everyone seems to agree that a good wife and a good job are important considerations, but important individual selection factors are also at work here: some people would repel a potentially good wife and would not be hired for a good job. Another issue that is very important for policy purposes is measurement of the duration of the criminal career. Particularly important for shaping sentencing policy is information about the residual of a career after an individual is arrested, convicted, and awaiting sentencing.

The Search for Meaningful Theory

We all know that criminology is a complex field, both in terms of the wide variety of criminal behaviors of concern and the considerable variety of factors interacting to stimulate or inhibit criminal expression. In the search for meaningful theory, which underlies all research, a continuing tension exists between a desire for unity and parsimony on one hand and richness of elaboration on the other. The phenomena associated with crime and antisocial behavior are so diverse that theories that explain one aspect may be found wanting when they are applied to others. Also, the different sequence of phases of a criminal career from early childhood into adulthood can have very different antecedents, and it will be very difficult to bring them all under a single umbrella. Of course, one might try to define some sufficiently flexible constructs that are given a common name but have very different meanings at different stages. "Social control" is one such construct, but that must represent something quite different when exercised by a parent over a preadolescent than when exercised by a wife over her husband. On the other hand, if one tries to put into a grand theoretical framework all of the associations between individual characteristics, their parents' characteristics, and their peers' characteristics, and how each of these affects propensity to engage in different kinds of crime, one is left with lots of correlations but nothing as concise as one would like in a theory.

Also, any theory must be structured differently if it is to help describe the initiation of offending, reflecting the draw of offenders from a general population, compared to termination of offending, which reflects the distinction *among offenders* of those who stop as distinguished from those who continue. Any theory that tries to subsume both of these perspectives needs to recognize that the factors that contribute to initiation may be quite different from those that contribute to termination.

I am intrigued, for example, by Thornberry's (2005a) characterization of late bloomers as individuals with significant cognitive deficits who were protected from early initiation by parental controls but who find that their deficits later lead them into criminal activity as compensation for those deficits. This clearly reflects an interaction between cognitive deficits and quality of parenting. I presume that this insight derives from experiences with the Rochester Youth Development Study (RYDS) sample. But it is also interesting that no other longitudinal study seems to have captured this particular interaction. That new wrinkle certainly does not invalidate the earlier theories. At the same time, it is possible that it occurs only among the Rochester youth, so its failure to apply generally does not invalidate the totality of the rich but elaborate interactional theory. It serves as one interesting feature of Thornberry's largely descriptive theory.

One of the continuing demands of any theory is that it comport with empirical observation. One of the most insistent of those demands is that the theory help explain the classic age-crime curve, the relationship between the rate of crime commission and age. That relationship usually is demonstrated by a rapid rise from an early age to a peak, usually in the late teens, and then a relatively slower decline. In calling for that consistency, it is important to recognize that there are many age-crime curves, one for each crime type, and those relationships could change rather dramatically over time (see, for example, the dramatic changes in the age-crime curve for murder between 1985 and 1993 depicted in Fig. 2.5 in Blumstein 2000) and between countries. Some have argued that all these curves are "invariant" (see Hirschi and Gottfredson 1983), but whether these unimodal curves are indeed seen as the same or different depends on whether one is trying to cram many different phenomena into a single box or interested in identifying what factors contribute to the differences. In the former case, there is the benefit of parsimony but the risk of excessive simplification and missing crucial details, whereas in the latter case, there is the problem of finding more elaboration than can be dealt with in terms of important covariates and offending patterns. The Sampson and Laub article (2005b) falls into the former camp and the Thornberry article (2005a) into the latter, and that seems to highlight the desirability of pursuing both directions until we find some optimum mixture.

There are a number of problems in measuring career length—one is never sure when a career is terminated short of death.

Lauritsen (2005 [this volume]) raised the entirely reasonable issue of falsifiability in the context of the Thornberry (2005a) formulation of his interactional theory. As Popper (1963) has emphasized, a true scientific theory must have the potential for a test in which it can be falsified. Unfortunately, it is hard to find any theory in criminology or in criminological development that could survive such a test. Much too often, their predictions are vague (they may apply to some crime types and not to others); they rarely are met with certainty and so must countenance exceptions. Inevitably, as Thornberry (2005b [this volume]) points out in his rejoinder, they are taken as probabilistic statements, and so that leaves plenty of room for less than perfect prediction. Thus, the various theories must be seen as conjectures or descriptions that are often or mostly correct, but one could always find counterexamples where they do not hold. This, for example, pertains to the very interesting ideas put forth by Moffitt (1993) regarding the large number of individuals who have a turn at delinquency as adolescents and others who persist well beyond that period. It seems unreasonable to insist that the fact that many discontinue their offending before age seventy provides a contradiction of her theory. Rather, it should be seen as a concept that provokes finding further precision in its formulation rather than discarding an idea that could be developed more usefully. The median career of this sample lasts about twenty years from first to last arrest, which seems sufficient to be taken as the "life course" for many analytic purposes.

One important theme that pervades much theory development is the iterative effects that result from various experiences. Thornberry (2005a) highlights such effects in the self-reinforcing effects of early onset of delinquency as well as the self-reinforcing effects of prosocial activities. This opens the old question of whether an intervention by the juvenile or criminal justice systems labels an individual as "criminal," thereby causing him to act in accord with that label (an example of "state dependency") or whether his subsequent criminality is merely a manifestation of heterogeneity (i.e., he had a greater tendency or proclivity to engage in such acts, and that proclivity stimulated both the first arrest as well as the follow-on arrest).[2] Those issues have been addressed in some specific circumstances, and both perspectives undoubtedly pertain in any particular data set, perhaps to differing degrees. No broad general insights have been uncovered, and the issue is sufficiently important that it warrants continued pursuit in any longitudinal data analysis.

Career Length, Desistance, and Offending Frequency (λ)

One important feature of a criminal career that received scant attention at the symposium was the issue of career length. This characteristic is of major significance in policy decisions like judicial sentencing. If a career—more specifically the *residual* career after some criminal justice intervention—is reasonably short, then a long sentence will result in considerable "wastage" of prison space. The most likely response by legislatures to noteworthy criminal incidents is to impose mandatory sentences or to crank up the mandatory sentence that failed to prevent that incident. It would be most desirable to richly and credibly inform this process with strong empirical information on career duration. This measure is related reciprocally to the issue of desistance, which was discussed only in the context of factors contributing to desistance like a good marriage and a good job. But we have still seen little in the way of estimates of desistance rates or career lengths for various crime types at various ages.

One of the great values offered by the impressive data that Sampson and Laub (2005b) collected on the Glueck and Glueck (1950) men into their seventies is the wonderful opportunity it provides to study the duration of their careers. Thanks to their generosity in providing some processed data on the careers of their subjects,[3] my coresearchers and I were able to estimate the career lengths of various subgroups of the Glueck/Sampson and Laub cohort. There are a number of problems in measuring career length—one is never sure when a career is terminated short of death. Measuring career length as the time between the first and last recorded arrest, we found that these careers were relatively short, displaying a median of about 11.5 years for property offenses and 14.5 years for violent offenses. But many of the boys terminated early, so an examination of their "adult careers" (counting only from the time they reached the adult age of 17 in Massachusetts at the time) was 8.5 years for the career in property crimes and 12 years for the careers in violent crimes, the latter being a more severe offender group since basically all of the sample did property crimes, but only about a third of them did violent crimes also.[4]

One other important feature of this perspective on career length is the desirability of distinguishing the factors contributing to the decline of the age-crime curve following its peak. There is no question of that decline, as reflected in all three of the primary papers. It is of interest, however, to be able to distinguish how much of that decline is due to termination of the criminal careers and how much is attributable to slowing down of the offending frequency (or λ) of those still active. Those two effects are confounded in the Sampson and Laub (2005b) analyses and in the trajectories developed using the Nagin and Tremblay (2005) methods. It is entirely possible that different factors will affect the termination rate than those that affect the slowing down. In reviewing the data on adult careers, for example, we found that there was a sharp change—about a factor of five—in offending frequency λ during the first seven years of the career (λ for property crimes dropped from about 2.8 per year to about 0.5, and for violent crimes it dropped from about 1.7 to about 0.4). Then the careers of those who continued to be active continued for as long as forty years—and there was only a very slight decline in λ over that period. This issue is explored in more detail in the appendix. These results suggest a sharp change in the regime of offending between the first seven years of the adult career and the many more later years: offending frequency is high during the early years, then there is a fairly rapid decline, with a majority of the sample continuing to offend after that transition point; and they do so at a significantly reduced rate, and with that rate diminishing only slowly with age—quite a contrast with the much more rapid decline of the age-crime curve. This might suggest that the short-career offenders with the high rates are reflective of Moffitt's (1993) adolescent-limited group and the ones who continue beyond that seven-year transition period look like the life-course persistents, but with their persistence slowly diminishing as their careers gradually terminate. But making any such linkage would require much more detailed analysis of the characteristics of the individual offenders and their career patterns, not yet available in the data provided.

This discussion highlights some of the value in disaggregation of the criminal career parameters. If we keep them separate, some richer insights of the separate determinants might emerge. For example, if the sample was drawn from a general population (in contrast to most of the studies reported in this volume, which were drawn from a high-risk population), race would likely be a significant factor distinguishing those who participate in serious crime from those not participating, but not a significant factor affecting offending frequency. One would also expect cognitive skills to affect termination (as the offenders move into the legitimate labor force) and to have less effect on the offending frequency of those who stay active as offenders. Amalgamating these separate parameters into a single, presumably comprehensive, crime factor precludes being able to make those useful distinctions.

Identification of Offender Groups

One of the continuing debates without easy resolution in the field of developmental criminology is the value of grouping. There can be an inherent value in grouping if there is an interaction between membership in a particular group and, say, the effectiveness of one or more interventions: learning that some groups are amenable to the intervention and others not would be very helpful in making such assignments. Grouping may be done on theoretical grounds if there is some distinction among different groups that goes beyond the quantitative distinction of some small number of observable factors. The Moffitt (1993) characterization of the adolescent-limited and life-course persistent offender groups could derive from some theoretical distinction that appeared in the New Zealand boys as early as their twenties, well before the unfolding of the information about the Glueck and Glueck (1950) men into their seventies. Or the grouping could be done on empirical grounds as in the trajectory analysis developed by Nagin in Nagin and Land (1993) and many publications subsequently—and see especially Nagin (2005). The ultimate test of grouping should be based on whether there is a benefit in aggregating individuals into groups, and that will depend on the context of the analyses to be done.

There are some obvious advantages to finding intelligent groupings of the respondents to longitudinal surveys. If we could identify such useful groupings, then analyzing the characteristics and patterns of such groups could lead to theoretical insights that might well differ among the groups but would be more precisely formulated for each of the groups. Thornberry's (2005a) contrast between his late starters and early onsets, for example, would likely not have arisen had he not thought of them as distinct groups. Finding such groupings provides the means for analyzing interactions with various predictor variables or intervention approaches that may be high for one group and low for another. Thus, the value of any grouping will inevitably lie in the degree to which there is a homogeneity within the group in terms of some conceptual or operational similarity that does not prevail similarly with other groups. Nagin and Tremblay's (2005) trajectory groups may well display different risk factors or may respond differently to various kinds of interventions. It is interesting that Nagin and Tremblay (2001) found that members of one group of particular concern for their chronic offending were characterized by mothers with low education and early first childbirth. That was not the case with the other groups. That certainly suggests an intervention involving parenting training targeted at those mothers, which would be expected have an important effect in reducing offending, and enabling it to be done quite efficiently.

Need for Methodological Improvements

Most early work in criminology used analytic methods that were little more than bivariate correlations. There was an important advance with the introduction of richer multivariate regression models. In that format, there is a seductive appeal of being able to introduce an additional variable into the model that then enables the analyst to claim that that factor is "controlled for." But this ignores the possibility of a nonlinear effect of that variable, and especially the possibility of interaction effects of that variable with other included variables (a possibility that could certainly be incorporated into the model, but even that simple step is rarely done in most analyses). In this context, there is an important benefit in being able to identify subgroups of a population being studied because the appropriate model could be different with each of the identified groups. We typically find, for example, that models partitioned by race/ethnicity or by gender have different equations indicating the influence of various factors, and this kind of analysis could be much richer than including these characteristics only as single covariates.

Thus, the introduction of theoretically different groups or empirically based groups offers an even richer possibility because one such group may differ from others in terms of multiple observables and in terms of interactions with other covariates. This could be especially important in considering interventions, whose effects could well differ across groups. This approach is particularly interesting because there is a natural presumption that individuals partitioned into such groups may be responsive to similar interventions, and those in different groups

---

The phenomena associated with crime and antisocial behavior are so diverse that theories that explain one aspect may be found wanting when they are applied to others.

---

may be responsive to different interventions. Thus, it is understandable that we have seen widespread efforts to include such groups in a variety of longitudinal settings, not because these differences are certain but rather because there is a reasonable possibility that it may reveal insights that would not be evident in the normal course of analysis by applying a single model to all members of the sample. It is reasonable to expect that members of an identified group—however identified—will respond similarly to each other and differently from the response of members of other groups.

This urges a search for other means of identifying meaningful subgroups with these similar characteristics. The propensity scoring methods developed by Rosenbaum and Rubin (1983) provide another such approach. In some research I have conducted with Brian Wiersema, we tried to sort out the degree to which the higher rate of violence experienced by residents of public housing is a consequence of the individuals who inhabit public housing or something inherent about public housing. We developed a propensity score by a regression model of the characteristics of the public housing residents and applied that score to the nonrespondents of public housing to the National Crime Victimization Survey. This enabled us to identify those nonresidents who were most like the residents of public housing. We found that the higher the score of the comparison group, the more closely their violence experience matched the public housing residents, thereby suggesting that the difference in experience was attributable more to the characteristics of the residents and less to public housing as an institutional arrangement.

It is clear that there is a continuing need for new and diverse methodological approaches to address the needs of the rich array of longitudinal data that have already been collected. These improved methodological approaches are more likely to be developed by individuals with strong methodological skills, and these are not likely associated with the data-collection enterprises. The rich collection of research results generated by linking Daniel Nagin and his trajectory methods with the variety of longitudinal records collected by Richard Tremblay could well be replicated by building such linkages of other methodologically skilled analysts with the data maintained by other research groups.

Some of the discussion at the symposium was focused on the question of which methodological approach is more helpful, whether the choice be hierarchical linear modeling (HLM), regression models, trajectory models, or other new ones yet to become popular. I find this to be somewhat of a fruitless debate. It is not likely that any single method is found to be uniformly superior to any other in all circumstances and for all issues to be addressed. Each approach can provide distinctive benefits, and the utility of those benefits will depend on the context of the question being pursued, the nature of the available data, and the research approach being pursued. Developmental processes are complex and involve a large array of factors contributing to success or failure. Ideally, one should use a mixture of approaches and report the results that are most strongly supported rather than select the approach arbitrarily.

Providing Access to Longitudinal Data to a Broader Community of Researchers

One of the important issues raised by Janet Lauritsen (2005) is the need to provide access to the rich array of longitudinal data that have been collected to a wider community of researchers beyond those who have collected the data. Doing so would be totally consistent with one of the fundamental principles of science—replication of original findings is necessary to validate any research observations. That would be a more efficient use of the government and foundation resources that supported the collection. It would open the door to a wider range of theoretical conceptions and approaches than those that were stimulated by the original designers and investigators.

Of course, the interests of those original investigators have to be protected also. They invested significant time and effort—in many cases, a major portion of their careers—to collect and organize the data. Also, the original investigators made promises of confidentiality to the respondents, and the respondents' have very legitimate privacy concerns.

The major challenge is finding ways that resolve these competing concerns. In many cases, the initial investigators have made portions of their data accessible to colleagues who focused on a particular aspect of the longitudinal data. Indeed, some investigators (David Farrington is a striking example) have been most generous in this regard and have thereby expanded considerably the volume of publications based on their longitudinal data and enhanced the impact of their research. Most government funding agencies have an explicit policy encouraging data sharing, but they differ considerably in the degree to which that policy is enforced.

It would seem very reasonable to seek means of requiring the original investigators to provide greater access to the longitudinal data they collected, at least after some reasonable lead time of several years to give them the first opportunity to pursue issues of interest to them. They should be required to make public their data-collection instruments no later than three years after they first use them. Then they should be required to make their data available to other certified researchers no later than a reasonably few years after they were first collected. In light of the legitimate concerns about confidentiality, making the data available to the general public will usually not be reasonable. But this should not preclude providing access to legitimate research colleagues.

A limited number of researchers could be given access to the data in a variety of ways while protecting the confidentiality of the information contained there. As Lauritsen (2005) points out, that could be addressed by establishing an organization (perhaps involving the government funding agencies as well as representatives of the research community, including possibly professional associations like the American Society of Criminology) that would certify investigators who have a track record of appropriate skills and experience in working with longitudinal data and who would sign a strong confidentiality pledge to avoid seeking any individual identification. Also, the data records could be stripped of the obvious identifiers like name, precise address (although census tract would be important to establish information about neighborhood), and precise date of birth (although age is one of the most important variables and must be maintained). At the extreme, one could develop further protections by adapting a method used by the Census Bureau of requiring the new investigators to operate in a protected setting, with the data housed on computers in that special room and with an independent screener examining all data taken out of the room to ensure that it contains no confidential information. It should certainly be possible to identify individuals and procedures that can be fully confident of protecting the confidentiality of the personal information contained in the longitudinal data. It requires only a commitment on the part of the initial developers and their funding agencies to expand the number of investigators having the opportunity to pursue research on these data without compromising the rights of the initial investigators or the subjects involved.

Because the need for replication is an essential aspect of all science, professional journals should adopt a policy that requires making available a data set that permits independent replication of the findings in any article it publishes. That data set could be configured to protect the confidentiality of the individual respondents and to reveal only the information relevant to the tables or the analyses used in the article. This would contribute both to reanalysis to verify the original conclusions of the article as well as to introduce other approaches to analysis of the same data.

Next Steps and Some Key Questions

I believe that the Albany Symposium was an important event in nurturing a science of developmental criminology, with primary papers by leading scholars in early development and life-course development, in empirical methodology, and in theoretical framing. It benefited from some excellent discussants who raised important challenges to the primary papers, and the entire field benefits from the publication of those papers and the commentaries in this issue of the *Annals*.

Despite the excellence of the work and the content, there are still a number of disappointments. Each of the papers presented is a continuation of the important work the individual authors have been doing. One would hope that these important streams of research would join up in some ways so that the results would be stronger than that resulting from each of the authors alone. There was some joining in Thornberry's (2005a) use of trajectory methods, and that is certainly a desirable move in the right direction. It would be even better to see some greater mixture of integration across the various investigators. It would be desirable to see some cumulation by building on each other's—and other investigators'—work. Unfortunately we have seen much too little of that in criminology, although I suspect that as new methodologies appear and more people try them out, new insights are likely to result. I would find it attractive if more effort were directed at building on each other's work, perhaps by modification of the concepts or methods. I think that would be more constructive than discarding ideas with flaws and replacing them with different ideas with comparably large flaws but with new names and identities. These are important steps necessary to build a scientific community.

In this concluding section, I would like to offer some suggestions on where we might go next, both in institutional arrangements and in some substantive issues to be pursued.

The institutional arrangements involve seeking means to build an interacting research community that will share ideas and data, critique each other's work, and build a stronger science than any one alone will be able to do. The most noble attempt to achieve that goal was the Office of Juvenile Justice and Delinquency Prevention of the U.S. Department of Justice (OJJDP) effort in creating the "Causes and Correlates" program with three teams working in three sites but with some common agreed-upon measures of delinquency. While the individual studies have been enormously productive of published work, there have been very few products of the collaborative. Each of the constituent projects has been beset by serious funding problems, and so each has had to be very entrepreneurial in continuing its efforts, often in competition with its ostensible partners. The three teams come from different research traditions, and so each has built its instrument outside the common measures. Each team has understandably pursued its own research agenda rather than seeking cumulation with its partners. And of course, the academic reward system encourages such efforts that generate more publications rather than having to suffer the pains of collaboration with other less familiar data and less familiar colleagues. The collection of work that has resulted has been impressive, but the collaboration that was initially wished for is still more a dream than a reality, and so there is an important national need to find ways to develop that integrated research community.

One approach would be to organize under government sponsorship a "developmental criminology forum" composed of owners of longitudinal data sets, theorists with interesting questions to ask of these data, and methodologists who will propose new approaches to addressing those questions.[5] In establishing this forum, it would be important to provide support for a technical staff to deal with the many data-crunching problems with each of the constituent data sets, identifying comparability in the different data sets.

The participants should agree first on some key questions that they would like to see addressed with the strengths that come from multiple data sets and multiple disciplinary approaches. The issues chosen should be issues that represent current challenges to find ways to address them that will resolve important current controversies in the field. I would like to pose some that derive from discussion at the Albany Symposium for initial consideration by the forum when it meets.[6]

Perhaps the most intriguing is the challenge posed by Moffitt (1993) in her proposal for an adolescent-limited and life-course persistent grouping. Sampson and Laub (2005b) have shown some important limitations in her initial conceptualization, and it would be interesting to involve Moffitt with them and others to see if some more appropriate modification of that initial formulation comports better with the Glueck and Glueck (1950) data and the much longer careers they offer—so important because it truly does cover the full "life course"—and with other relevant data sets that go sufficiently far into maturity to offer a sufficient basis for test and modification (e.g., the Farrington [2003] London cohort now in their forties). A second effort I would like to see undertaken is the disaggregation of the effects of slowing down (reducing λ) compared to career termination after the peak age of offending as shown in the age-crime curve. The clustered trajectories all show the decline as does the age-crime curve, but it is important to separate a simple reduction in λ from those who do complete their careers either through experiencing their last crime or introducing a long interval until their next one.

A third effort I would like to see would focus on the nature of the dynamics of crime-type choice over the course of a criminal career. There are effects of age readiness (and strength and skill readiness as they age) at the early ages, possible effects of escalation as offenders move from the less risky to the more threatening (e.g., from burglary to robbery), and possible specialization as they move into more mature periods of offending and develop expertise in one type of offense or the other.

One final issue I would like to encourage is the issue raised in the interchange between Sampson and Laub (2005a [this volume]) and Gottfredson (2005 [this volume]) over the issue of marriage that Sampson-Laub emphasize as an important issue of desistance. Does marriage serve to change the individual (propensity) or reduce the opportunity (event reduction)? Since many of those marriages are likely to be unstable, one would think that a growth in offending between marriages associated with a reduction during marriage would provide evidence of event reduction. Alternatively, a discontinuous reduction in offending that continued between marriages would suggest a socialization effect on propensity. Of course, both of these effects could take place in any individual's career. Clarifying this issue would seem to be a task that is particularly well suited to a long-duration data set like that collected by Sampson and Laub.

These are just a few of the issues that I would like to see pursued, in part because they derive from the symposium and in part because the data sets that comprise the main papers are amenable to addressing these issues. I would like to see many more important issues pursued, including the issues raised earlier in this overview as well as the other issues raised by the articles and discussants throughout this volume. The major impediment at this time is the profound shortage of government funding to address such important issues. In an earlier time, there was reasonable funding from NIJ, NIMH, CDC, NSF, and a number of private foundations. One can only hope that the opportunity will once again return, and that it does not take another outbreak of violence to shake those funds loose.

Appendix
Some Preliminary Analyses of the Criminal Careers of the Glueck Men When Active

One approach to isolating offending patterns of the "active" offenders from the desisters is to study individuals only during the time they are "active." One approach to that is to examine their offending patterns between their first and last arrests. This is less than fully satisfactory because they may have desisted for an extended period of time and then reinitiated offending in only a minor way (what might be described as "intermittency"). Or that last arrest may have been made in error. Or their last arrest may have occurred just before they died and their career likely would have continued longer. Also, we cannot identify a criminal-career duration for individuals whose only offense or offenses were committed in just one year, so our analysis is based on those with arrests in at least two different years. Nevertheless, it is a reasonable approach to identifying the period of activity of each of the individuals in the sample.

Using data from the Sampson and Laub (2005b) re-creation of the criminal careers of the Glueck and Glueck (1950) men, we can develop estimates of the relationship between their offending frequency over their careers (which I define as mean aggregate lambda [MAL] or arrests per year over the duration of this "active" career). I present a graph of this relationship in Figure A1, with the property offenses depicted in the upper curve and the violent offenses (committed only by about 20 percent of the number committing property offenses) depicted in the lower curve.

I also begin the counts of career length with the "adult career," which started at age seventeen in Massachusetts at the time. The principal reason for focusing on this adult career is a concern that offending frequency during the juvenile years are distorted by

FIGURE A1
MEAN AGGREGATE LAMBDA (AVERAGE NUMBER OF ARRESTS
PER YEAR FOR INDIVIDUALS WITH THE SPECIFIED CAREER LENGTH)
VERSUS CAREER LENGTH (YEARS)

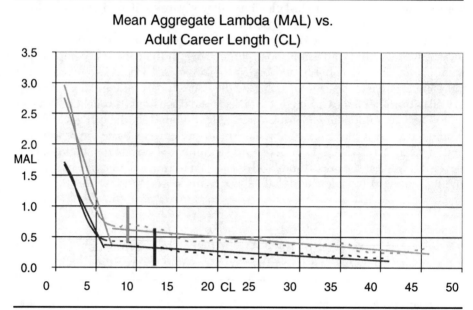

SOURCE: Data based on Sampson and Laub (2005b [this volume]) data of the criminal careers of Glueck and Glueck (1950) men. Values of MAL are doubly smoothed with three-point smoothing. Data provided by Elaine Eggleston Doherty.

NOTE: The upper curve represents property offenses, and the lower curve represents violent offenses. The vertical bars on each curve indicate the median career lengths for each offense type. The solid lines are the fitted linear trend lines during the two portions of each of the curves. Based on arrests at age seventeen ("adults") and beyond. Career length defined as the interval between first and last arrest for each crime type.

the selection effects that made it more likely that individuals with many arrests were more apt to have been committed to the reformatories from which the offender sample was drawn. By focusing on the adult careers, I examine the men in the sample without the contamination of this selection effect. Also, since essentially all the men whose MAL is measured in Figure A1 had already started their careers by age seventeen, then the measure of "career length" is reasonably close to age –17.

The first thing one might notice in Figure A1 is how different the graph is from the age-crime curve, even if one thinks of starting the age-crime curve at seventeen. The rate of decline is quite rapid in the early years of the career, and that decline is attributable to a "slowing down" not contaminated by the termination that is an important aspect of the age-crime curve in these later years. The second thing one notices is the relative flatness of the MAL curve after a rather sharply defined break point, a decline that is much slower than what occurs in the age-crime curve.

One of the interesting aspects of Figure A1 is what appears to be a two-regime phenomenon in the offending frequency of the Glueck men. Those with short careers seem to have an appreciably higher offending frequency over their short careers than those with more extended careers. There seems to be a sharp break at about six years for violent offenses and about seven years for property offenses. Before these break points, the frequency is appreciably higher (starting about 3 per year for property offenses and about 1.6 for violent offenses) and dropping rather sharply with career length (about 0.3 to 0.4 per year). After the break point, the mean annual frequency is small, is almost flat, declining slowly at a rate of about 0.01 per year, or a rate about 1/30th to 1/40th the rate of decline before the break point.

The median markers on Figure A1 indicate that almost half of the individuals who did property offenses (almost everyone in the sample did property offenses) had only short careers (ending at or before the break points), while about 30 percent of those with violent careers had the short careers. Among the property offenders, a full quarter are still active with more than an eighteen-year career length, and a full quarter of the violent offenders are still active with more than a twenty-year career length.

The existence of these two regimes suggests that there may be something quite different about the men with the short careers and those with the longer careers. This distinction may be seen as somewhat in the vein of the adolescent-limited (AL) and life-course persistent (LCP) distinction suggested by Moffitt (1993). But this distinction appears to be quite different from what motivated her classification. The LCP folks here are not necessarily much more aggressive during their early years—they are merely persistent for longer periods into the life course. And they are clearly not all persistent throughout the life course, but their termination rate after the break point is relatively slow.

Also, the termination rate during the adolescent years into the early twenties is relatively rapid, with almost half ending their careers by the break point. One possible explanation for the rapid decline of MAL in the short career length could be selective attrition of the highest-lambda individuals early in the career, leaving ultimately only the persisters with their low offending frequency. Alternatively, the rapid decline could be attributable to a more uniform slowing down.

Notes

1. The careers until age thirty-one accounted for time off the street in correctional institutions. That correction could not be made after age thirty-one.

2. See, for example, Nagin and Paternoster (2000).

3. Elaine Eggleston Doherty provided me with the processed data, and her help is much appreciated.

4. More detailed results will be available in Blumstein et al. (n.d.).

5. I understand that such a collaborative has already been established by the National Institute of Alcohol and Alcohol Abuse (NIAAA) of NIH to study developmental aspects of alcohol abuse.

6. A lengthy agenda is proposed by David Farrington (2005).

References

Blumstein, Alfred. 2000. Disaggregating the violence trends. In *The crime drop in America*, ed. Alfred Blumstein and Joel Wallman, chap. 2. Cambridge: Cambridge University Press.

Blumstein, Alfred, Elaine Eggleston Doherty, Benjamin Novak, John Laub, and Robert Sampson. N.d. Some criminal career analysis of the Glueck guys. Manuscript.

Farrington, David P. 2003. Key results from the first 40 years of the Cambridge Study in Delinquent Development. In *Taking stock of delinquency: An overview of findings from contemporary longitudinal studies*, ed. Terrence P. Thornberry and Marvin D. Krohn, 137-83. New York: Kluwer/Plenum.

———. 2005. Building developmental and life-course theories of offending. In *Advances in criminological theory*, vol. 15, *Taking stock: The status of criminological theory*, ed. F. T. Cullen, J. P. Wright, and K. R. Bevins. New Brunswick, NJ: Transaction.

Glueck, Sheldon, and Eleanor Glueck. 1950. *Unraveling juvenile delinquency*. New York: Commonwealth Fund.

Gottfredson, Michael R. 2005. Offender classifications and treatment effects in developmental criminology: A propensity/event consideration. *Annals of the American Academy of Political and Social Science* 602:46-56.

Hirschi, Travis, and Michael Gottfredson. 1983. Age and the explanation of crime. *American Journal of Sociology* 89:552-84.

Laub, John H., and Robert J. Sampson. 2003. *Shared beginnings, divergent lives: Delinquent boys to age 70*. Cambridge, MA: Harvard University Press.

Lauritsen, Janet L. 2005. Explaining patterns of offending across the life course: Comments on interactional theory and recent tests based on the RYDS-RIS data. *Annals of the American Academy of Political and Social Science* 602:212-28.

Maughan, Barbara. 2005. Developmental trajectory modeling: A view from developmental psychopathology. *Annals of the American Academy of Political and Social Science* 602:118-30.

Moffitt, Terrie E. 1993. Adolescence-limited and life-course-persistent anti-social behavior: A developmental taxonomy. *Psychological Review* 100:674-701.

Nagin, Daniel S. 2005. *Group-based modeling of development*. Cambridge, MA: Harvard University Press.

Nagin, Daniel S., and Kenneth C. Land. 1993. Age, criminal careers, and population heterogeneity: Specification and estimation of a nonparametric, mixed Poisson model. *Criminology* 31:327-62.

Nagin, Daniel S., and Raymond Paternoster. 2000. Population heterogeneity and state dependency: State of the evidence and directions for future research. *Journal of Quantitative Criminology* 16 (2): 117-44.

Nagin, Daniel S., and Richard Tremblay. 2001. Parental and early childhood predictors of persistent physical aggression in boys from kindergarten to high school. *Archives of General Psychiatry* 58:389-94.

———. 2005. What has been learned from group-based trajectory modeling? Examples from physical aggression and other problem behaviors. *Annals of the American Academy of Political and Social Science* 602:82-117.

Popper, Karl. 1963. Science as falsification. In *Conjectures and refutations*. London: Routledge and Keagan Paul.

Rosenbaum, Paul, and Donald B. Rubin. 1983. The central role of the propensity score in observational studies for causal effects. *Biometrika* 70:41-55.

Sampson, Robert J., and John H. Laub. 2005a. When prediction fails: From crime-prone boys to heterogeneity in adulthood. *Annals of the American Academy of Political and Social Science* 602:73-79.

———. 2005b. A life-course view of the development of crime. *Annals of the American Academy of Political and Social Science* 602:12-45.

Thornberry, Terence P. 2005a. Explaining multiple patterns of offending across the life course and across generations. *Annals of the American Academy of Political and Social Science* 602:156-95.

———. 2005b. Notes on theory construction and theory testing: A response to Osgood and Lauritsen. *Annals of the American Academy of Political and Social Science* 602:229-39.

The Complex Dynamics of the Onset, the Development, and the Termination of a Criminal Career: Lessons on Repeat Offenders to Be Drawn from Recent Longitudinal Studies in Criminology

By
HANS-JÜRGEN KERNER

John H. Laub and Robert J. Sampson, 2003. *Shared Beginnings, Divergent Lives. Delinquent Boys to Age 70.* Cambridge, MA: Harvard University Press. 347 pp. ISBN 0-674-01191-0.

Daniel S. Nagin, 2005. *Group-Based Modeling of Development.* Cambridge, MA: Harvard University Press. 212 pp. ISBN 0-674-01686-6.

Terence P. Thornberry, Marvin D. Krohn, Alan J. Lizotte, Carolyn A. Smith, and Kimberly Tobin, 2003. *Gangs and Delinquency in Developmental Perspective.* Cambridge: Cambridge University Press. 261 pp. ISBN 0-521-81439-1.

I.

Because it is considered general wisdom in criminology that criminal behavior tends to occur most extensively in the life period between early adolescence and early adulthood, most studies in criminology focus on this age period (Cline 1980; Weitekamp et al. 2000).

Hans-Jürgen Kerner, Dr.jur., is director of the Institute of Criminology and chair of Criminology, Juvenile Penal Law, Penal Procedure, and Corrections at the Faculty of Law at the University of Tübingen in Germany. Previously, he was a professor at the Universities of Bielefeld, Hamburg, and Heidelberg. He was a visiting professor/ fellow at the Universities of Southampton (United Kingdom), Peking (Peoples' Republic of China), Pennsylvania (United States), Melbourne (Australia), and Cambridge (United Kingdom). He is president of the German Foundation for Crime Prevention, president of the European Society of Criminology (2005-2006 term), and lifetime honorary president of the International Society for Criminology. He holds lifetime memberships with the ASC and the ACJS in the United States and is a member of numerous other scholarly associations. Formerly, he was a member of a Council of Europe research fellowship team on the state of organized crime in Europe (Strasbourg, France) and a judge at the Hanseatic High Court of Appeal, Criminal Law Division, State of Hamburg (Germany).

DOI: 10.1177/0002716205281245

This tendency is supported by the so-called age-crime curve depicting the rates of officially registered offenses. This curve has always shown a remarkably stable and skewed structure, much more so for male than female subjects. In its basic shape, not necessarily in every detail, it seems quasi-independent of the time period taken into consideration and of the kind of state or society concerned. The rates of the male population tend to rise sharply from around twelve years of age on, reach a peak or a certain plateau somewhere between seventeen and twenty-two years of age, fall rather sharply until twenty-five or thirty years of age, and then slowly "fade away" with the aging of the population concerned. The rates of the female population show a much less extended picture over the age groups, and the peak age is reached at least one age group earlier than it is reached by young men.

Gottfredson and Hirschi (1990) pointed explicitly and with strong emphasis to this stable structure in their "general theory of crime." They used it as proof of their "invariance" hypothesis of a stable distribution of peoples' differentially distributed propensity to crime (see also the discussion, with European references, in Mischkowitz 1993). Consistent with that hypothesis, the authors challenged the necessity, stressed by many other scholars, to look for the actual ties and bonds of individuals to their particular social contexts when studying why people diminish the intensity of their criminal acts or end their official criminal careers. Gottfredson and Hirschi used "low self-control" as a basic guiding concept. Low self-control is taken as a factor that can be observed in very early childhood. Once established, it does not change much during the later life course. Individuals with low self-control exhibit certain behavioral dispositions, which induce most criminal acts. Individuals with low self-control behave in distinctive ways. They are, inter alia, impulsive, insensitive, very body oriented, very risky, shortsighted, and spontaneous in their decision making. Gottfredson and Hirschi did not deny exogenous influences in the development of those particular personal properties or behavioral patterns. On the contrary, they stressed the importance of educational experiences in shaping eventual outcomes of stable dispositions. They pointed explicitly to the influence of ineffective (mostly parental) child-rearing practices in early childhood. Their approach posits, however, that "later on" nothing or at least not very much can be done to alter the degree of self-control an individual has after the first few years of his or her life.

What does this tell us about the shape of the age-crime curve and the possible real-life processes behind it? Gottfredson and Hirschi (1990) assumed the age-crime curve to be invariant across social and cultural conditions. None of the existing criminological factors or a combination of them seems able, along their path of arguing, to specifically explain the skewed distribution. Changes in circumstance and decisions do not account for the differences in crime rates between groups. One should not expect, therefore, to be able to intervene and considerably influ-

NOTE: This is a compressed review as integrated into a broader discussion of the relevant issues in the realm of criminal career, developmental, age-graded, and interactional paradigms in criminology.

ence the central direction of people's lives. What is decisive, then, are the consequences of a general change happening to people or emerging in their everyday life when they grow older. As offenders grow older, most of them, including those who have had serious juvenile criminal records, diminish their criminal activity.

Life-course approaches posit that (most) persons/offenders are never fully developed. According to them, early developments in life can be overturned, so to speak, by later developments caused by new life events and experiences.

The seeming discrepancy between the stability of the low self-control and a decline of officially registered rates of offending can be resolved by distinguishing, as Gottfredson and Hirschi (1990) did, between "criminality" and "crime." Criminality as a result and expression of low self-control is at most only marginally dependent on conditional factors and therefore represents a relatively stable difference between individuals. But low self-control is not a sufficient condition for criminal behavior to occur. Crime as an observable act is characterized by contingent constellations such as activation to criminal behavior or the opportunity to commit a particular offense. Moreover, crime as manifest criminal behavior is only one of many surface phenomena of a low self-control status. People may turn to another form of deviant behavior, or they may in the extreme case eventually live a very reduced way of life due to general burnout and become totally dependent on welfare or institutional care. Gottfredson and Hirschi's distinction between crime and self-control thus provides a device for solving one of the major empirical dilemmas of criminology: the fact that crime declines with age while differences in crime tendency across individuals remain stable over the life course. In other words, the frequency of individual offending can vary substantially throughout the life course, while the underlying low self-control does not have to change at all.

The books under review here are pivotal recent examples of a fundamentally different approach. The authors may not contest in principle what Gottfredson and Hirschi (1990) described as orientations, attitudes, and behavioral patterns characteristic of repeat, intense, or chronic offenders. Indeed, studies in many countries of the world report very similar descriptions, though the terms may vary in accordance with cultural traditions, linguistic particularities, professional terminologies, and the like. In Germany, for example, the founder of the Tübingen Criminal Behavior Development Study (TCBDS), Hans Goeppinger, introduced a whole series of predominantly behaviorally oriented criteria of similar extension when developing his method of so-called ideal typical comparative individual case analysis (*Methode der idealtypisch vergleichenden Einzelfallanalyse*; see Goeppinger 1983, 1985). And most recently, the results of the Wuhan Birth Cohort Study in China are in so many respects in line with what Western studies have found to be correlates and covariates of heavy offending among young people that one could become inclined to forget about the strong historical, economic, societal, and cultural differences that signify, let us say in simple terms, the pivotal capitalist United States on one side, and the pivotal communist Peoples' Republic of China on the other side (cf. Taylor et al. 2004; Friday et al. 2005).

The crucial point of divergence for those scholars opposing Gottfredson and Hirschi's (1990) scholarly contentions and other approaches stressing stable traits is not "the facts" so to speak but the "contextualizing" of those facts. Context always matters in that people/offenders are confronted with varying life conditions, essential experiences, stark life events, divergent personal contacts, different challenges, informal rewards and punishments, formal reactions to their (mis)deeds, and so on. Human behavior has to be considered within the relevant contexts, and these contexts vary through life. The varying conditions and circumstances are, on one hand, "objectively given." They confront an individual like an outer force. But on the other hand, they are also almost always "subjectively modified and transformed." To take effect within a person's mental system and behavioral outfit, they first have to be perceived and interpreted by the person alongside the "complex unity" of worldviews, value orientations, ingrained habits, and intrinsically related attitudes he or she holds at that point in the process of maturing and aging. Before dealing further with this issue, let us consider the relevance of early onset of delinquency for understanding further developments in life.

II.

Most modern societies do not attribute "criminality" in a formal sense to children. What a child means in terms of substantive criminal law is usually defined by the lower legal age of criminal responsibility. Internationally, this ranges widely from around seven to eighteen years of age, but with a modal range between twelve and fourteen years of age (cf. Newman 1999, 263-65). In a recent study on "modeling crime and offending" with large birth cohort data from England and Wales, John MacLeod (2003, 14) put forward a challenging hypothesis. He argued that the age-crime curve likely reflects the age dependency of societies' reaction to criminal behavior more than the age dependency of delinquent or criminal behavior itself. This cannot be discussed here in detail. His hypothesis does not invalidate the numerous studies that concentrate on early childhood problems and forms of child misbehavior anteceding later criminality, for example, the impressive work by Thornberry and Krohn (2003). It has potential serious implications, however, for some common assumptions in criminology, which are also the object of scrutiny in the three books reviewed here. Taken in a simple form, the first assumption is that such early signs of distortion "lead" in a causal way to later criminal behavior. The second assumption is that many repeat offenders, called for example "chronics" (in the United States) or *"Intensivtaeter"* (literally translated as intense offenders, in Germany), exhibit a comparatively strong tendency or "proneness" to commit forbidden acts, from delinquency in early childhood to criminality in adolescence and adulthood.

During the past decade, many, and sometimes very engaged, discussions have focused on Terrie Moffitt's (1993) now famous dual taxonomy of "adolescent limited offenders" on one hand and "life-course persistent offenders" on the other (see also Weitekamp and Kerner 1994). It is also at issue here with the reviewed books and has a lot of theoretical, conceptual, methodological, and substantial implications. In playing with words, one could argue in favor of Moffitt's approach that she seemingly did not and also recently does not speak of "life-*time*" persistent offenders. On the factual side, one could point at the following: when Moffitt was about to develop her taxonomy, the subjects she was drawing her ideas from belonged to the Dunedin (South New Zealand) birth cohort study. This study is surely one of the best pieces of longitudinal research ever undertaken in the world. However, at that point in time the cohort members were just about to reach early adulthood. So Moffitt's taxonomy was based, in analytical terms, on detailed observations of early periods of life, but inevitably just on mere assertive assumptions as to the later periods of adulthood. As time passes, we will learn whether the Dunedin panel subgroup of "life-course persisters" eventually exhibits the same pattern in officially registered crime as do the subjects of many other studies. The most explicit "counterpart" study is Sheldon and Eleanor Glueck's (1950) famous Boston study on reform school boys and matched nondelinquent boys out of the same neighborhoods and socioeconomic conditions, which was followed up and theoretically refined in a highly sophisticated manner by John H. Laub and Robert J. Sampson. And the pattern referred to is put in a condensed message: there is always change! Even the seemingly worst and behaviorally stubborn individuals experience possibilities to end their criminal careers. Most of them actually "take the chance" and try to use those opportunities to enter a law-abiding life. The "turning points" and "pathways" in their lives reflect substantial alterations in their behavior and attitudes over and above the general effect of aging that usually leads to "less of the same" as Gottfredson and Hirschi (1990) would posit. Sampson and Laub developed their approach in a couple of articles and then in their masterful book on pathways and turning points through life (Sampson and Laub 1993). They elaborated it further later on, and it culminates now in the reviewed book of 2003, which influenced much of the debate during the Albany symposium represented in this special issue of *The Annals*.

III.

Thornberry and colleagues join in with their book on gangs and delinquency. The subjects of their study are taken from the Rochester Youth Development Study. It is a longitudinal investigation of antisocial behavior that started in 1986. So its subjects have not yet reached the age of the still surviving members of the Glueck and Glueck (1950) "delinquent boys" born in the 1930s. The Rochester study encompasses twelve interview waves, representing the subjects' age span from 13 to 22. The authors concentrate their gang-related analysis on the first nine waves, however, which sets the subjects' upper age limit around 17.5 years. The reason is simple but nevertheless important: the limit is due to the fact that "the prevalence of gang membership drops very substantially at Wave 10" (p. 31). "Careers in gangs" tend to terminate rather early in young peoples' lives. The continuation of gang-related activity, in particular gang-related criminality, becomes a rare event after 18 years of age. The question is whether entering and leaving a youth gang are turning points that determine the length of criminal activity of the study subjects. The authors, due to the prospective longitudinal design of the Rochester project, were able to realize a large set of exact before and after comparisons. Their results bear a concise message they elaborated in chapter 6 of the book under the headline of "Gangs as a Facilitating Context for Delinquent Behavior." They report a strong, consistent gang facilitating effect among the young subjects:

> When male adolescents join gangs their behavior changes; delinquency, violence, drug selling, and—to a lesser extent—drug use increase. When they leave the gang, their behavior changes again; involvement in deviant behavior decreases, with the exception of involvement in drug selling. Indeed, the most consistent finding in this chapter is that gang members do *not* have significantly higher rates of general delinquency, violence, drug use, and drug selling than the nonmembers unless they are actively involved in the gang. (p. 120)

This empirical insight is not to be confounded, however, with the further question of whether former membership in youth gangs may exert long-term consequences on individuals. The authors could indeed find a couple of direct and indirect relations that resulted in higher crime rates up to the age of twenty-two years. In a couple of interesting equations, Thornberry et al. (pp. 176-78) show that it is not the membership in gangs as such, but rather the quality of membership, measured as "stability," that will significantly increase the odds of young men of getting arrested as adults. Then comes the mediating effect of the accumulated *number* of what they call "precocious transitions" or "off-time transitions" like dropping out of school, early pregnancy, teenage parenthood, early nest leaving, unstable employment patterns, and cohabiting (pp. 165-69). Earlier commitment to school has a continuously beneficial effect in early adulthood. All in all, the most enduring distorting effect comes from the "negative life events" (pp. 175, 177). This finding may become the object of further study. For example, Dutch scholars found, in a national representative longitudinal study of adolescents, that the effects of parental attachment and life events on juvenile acting out are mediated by any "emotional disturbance" from which young people are suffering (Overbeek et al. 2005).

This is a central theoretical focus of the "developmental perspective" followed by Thornberry and colleagues and by many other scholars in the recent decades of research and theorizing in criminology. In the core assumptions, this approach is very compatible with other types of age-graded interactional theories of delinquency and informal social control, one of them being the "life course criminology" of Laub and Sampson as developed to the full, at least in the principal components, in their 2003 book and in their Albany Symposium presentation enclosed in this special issue of *The Annals*.

IV.

In a nutshell, developmental or life-course dynamic theorists do not pretend that change always occurs in the life of persons, in particular among those persons heavily involved in crime. Indeed, they acknowledge explicitly that some persons exhibit very long-lasting patterns of misbehavior, and some even deliberately and decisively do so (cf. chap. 7 of Laub and Sampson 2003 under the headline "Why Some Offenders Persist"). They also do not contest the results of more traditionally offender-oriented studies that show that a high percentage of crimes committed, particularly violent and severe crimes, are attributable to repeat offenders (cf. the definite "setting of the issue" with the publication of the results of the first Philadelphia birth cohort study in 1972 by Wolfgang, Figlio, and Sellin). Thornberry and colleagues (chaps. 6-8) demonstrate that young "gang members" are responsible for the lion's share of severe offenses, especially for offenses with firearms, and some undoubtedly heinous crimes.

The central position is, however, that change for the better is the prevailing standard among offenders when sufficient time spans of life are taken into detailed consideration by appropriate approaches, methods, and techniques of research. "Heavy offenders," "chronics," "recidivists," or however else one may conceptually label them are not the "total others" lost forever. Whether they remain the same "persons" or "personalities" or "character types" throughout the life course is a question not to be wiped away easily or even deliberately denied on the outset. In the extreme, like with the so-called sociopaths, some offenders may pose strong and pertinent dangers for the society at large and for some particular vulnerable groups like little children in the case of sociopathic sex offenders. So it is of utmost importance not to confound those probably essentially different "kinds of people" committing potentially highly idiosyncratic "types of crime" with other persons who are deeply involved in living a criminal life, involving many different offenses, but who are not bound to these specific "inner" personality dimensions in need to be treated as such.

The central perspective of the life-course criminology and developmental approaches pertains to those offenders whose offenses may be more or less woven into personality development but not inevitably or invariably bound to stable personality "traits" or clinical deficit "syndromes" or, in more modern terms, genetic or neuropsychological "deficits" as aptly to be "diagnosed" and professionally "treated" in the core sense of that term by psychiatrists, clinical psychologists, sex therapists, and other specialists within or outside the correctional system. It seems to be a challenging endeavor in and for the coming years to delineate the true distinctive factors, behavioral patterns, inner drives, motives, and so on allowing to separate off in a theoretically convincing and practically fruitful manner such different offender groups: on one hand, the minority of offenders who "are" dangerous if not treated or in spite of treatment; on the other, the majority of offenders

---

In a nutshell, developmental or life-course dynamic theorists do not pretend that change always occurs in the life of persons, in particular among those persons heavily involved in crime.

---

who just "behave" (sometimes) in a dangerous way but are amenable to overcome this "behaviorally patterned stage of life." They may eventually reach a new base for their future living independently by learning from experience. It is to be assumed that something in this direction may lie behind phenomena of leaving a certain pathway of problematic behavior (e.g., drugs, gambling, extremely risk-taking outdoor activities, delinquency, and crime) without any visible or easily intelligible reason or substantial cause, which is referred to in epistemologically nominal terms like "spontaneous recovery" or "spontaneous resocialization." In the majority of cases, however, one surely would not dare to conceive of recovery or resocialization as representing a spontaneous event as such or having been generated by an isolated event. Here, one has to look instead for developmental pathways toward a positive end. Those pathways are highly complex and multidimensional real-life processes. Offenders actively and interactively pursue them with the sometimes rather unconscious and sometimes quite explicit aim of rebuilding their patterns of thinking, relating to others, and structuring their everyday behavior patterns in work and leisure time. By doing so, they manage, in part with the help from significant others that they now can emotionally accept or even ask for, to turn their lives away from crime and toward integration.

Even the very same or at least centrally comparable conditions during early life provide "options" at many "crossroads" that can be taken or overseen or deliberately avoided. And the reasons for acting in a certain way may vary at different points in the life course of the same individual/offender. The title of Laub and Sampson's book, *Shared Beginnings, Divergent Lives*, is quite fitting. The "Divergent Pathways of Troubled Boys" (chap. 1) who are now "old men" are being analyzed with the explicit substantial and theoretical aim to "make sense of lives" (p. 4). And that "sense" has as much to do with the sense offenders are making of their lives as it does with the sense the scholarly trained observer can gain intersubjectively when dealing with people instead of just "variables or risk factors." Putting it more simply: quantitative and qualitative approaches can and should not be considered conflicting but complementary attempts to grasp at parts of the "true meaning" of complex realities of persons, social relationships, ecological influences and constraints, and patterned "outcomes" of their particular conditions and interactions. Laub and Sampson address this concern for integrative approaches time and again in their book, with many impressive quantitative facts (calculations) and qualitative insights (narratives), especially in chapter 9 under the headline "Modeling Change in Crime."

V.

Such a modeling is based on certain assumptions about what the term *development* basically means, including some anthropological positions regarding our common *conditio humana* or, approximately translated from ancient Roman into modern English, the whole set of phylogenetic inheritance and ontogenetic experience of the humankind as such. Life-course approaches posit that (most) persons/ offenders are never fully developed. According to them, early developments in life can be overturned, so to speak, by later developments caused by new life events and experiences. Life-course approaches are, in general, open to the possibility and occurrence of permanent change among all people, with only a few exceptions due to genuinely pathological conditions.

Laub and Sampson stress this line of thinking in the beginning of their 2003 book in a deliberately sharp sequence of statements. They describe the core elements of the lives of Arthur and Michael, two men with very similar backgrounds as boys, who then developed "radically different adult lives." Laub and Sampson then set as the aim of their book to understand the lives of Arthur and Michael and many others like them stating: "More specifically we try to account for patterns of criminal offending and many other behaviors over the full life course of high-risk children" (p. 4).

Indeed, only a few studies provide data that cover the whole development of subjects from childhood to *late* adulthood. Earlier studies with life span data extending beyond thirty include the studies of Robins (1966); McCord (1978); Farrington (1994, 2003); Sampson and Laub with their first follow-up (1993); Kerner, Weitekamp, and Stelly (1995); Kerner et al. (1997); and Kaplan (2003). Promising, recently started studies, which are very sophisticated in design, will perhaps eventually cover the whole life span. They include the Rochester Youth

Development Study (e.g., Thornberry, Lizotte, et al. 2003), the Denver Youth Survey (e.g., Huizinga et al. 2003), the Pittsburgh Youth Study (e.g., Loeber et al. 2003), and the Seattle Social Development Project (e.g., Hawkins et al. 2003) in the United States; the Montreal Longitudinal and Experimental Study (e.g., Tremblay et al. 2003) in Canada; and the Dunedin Multidisciplinary Health and Development Study in New Zealand (e.g., Moffitt et al. 2001; Lahey, Moffitt, and Caspi 2003). But at present, the sample members are still in their early adult phase.

So all in all, the landscape of knowledge has remarkably improved compared with the situation some forty years ago. Nevertheless, many questions remain to be answered in a theoretically concise, methodologically stringent, and substantially convincing manner. This can aptly be shown by lining up some quotations in historical sequence of order.

Pointing to desistance from a criminal career as one of the least systematically researched phenomena in criminology, Reckless stated in 1972 (p. 211) that it is much easier to explain why an offender continues with his career rather than to understand why he stops the career.

In her review of criminal career research, Petersilia reached the following conclusion in 1980: "Little is known about how and when criminal career begins, or how long it is likely to last, why criminal careers persist, and why some persons abandon criminal careers early, others continue into adult crime, and still others begin crime careers late in life. . . . Little is known about the extent and types of crime committed at different stages of criminal careers" (p. 325).

Sampson and Laub themselves argued a bit more than a decade later (1995, 2) that "although desistance is a major component of the criminal career model it is the least studied process compared with research on onset, persistence, and escalation of offending." In their most recent book under review, they still consider the situation far from being optimal: "The question of behavioral change and stability within individuals over the life span is virtually uncharted territory in criminology and the social sciences at large" (p. 4).

Statements like these suggest therefore that this specific area in criminology continues to suffer from gaps. However, the most recent works contribute a remarkable amount of knowledge to fill at least parts of that gap. Laub and Sampson position their insights in the frame of a vividly formulated number of sentences aimed at sharpening the focal points of their otherwise elaborated theoretical approach:

> [We] reject several popular notions. For one, we reject the idea that childhood experiences such as early involvement in antisocial behavior, growing up in poverty, and woeful school performance are sturdy markers for predicting long-term patterns of offending. In a similar vein, we reject the notion that individual "traits" such as poor verbal skills, low self-control, and difficult temperament can explain long-term patterns of juvenile delinquents. From our perspective, in order to explain longitudinal patterns of offending, data are needed on childhood, adolescence, *and* adulthood experiences. (p. 4)

Thornberry et al., referring to groundbreaking earlier works like that of Glen Elder, posit accordingly that the life-course perspective emphasizes the importance of treating behavior as constantly evolving as various demands, opportunities, interests, and events impinge upon actors as they age. . . . Human development is not completed in childhood or even in adolescence; indeed, behavior that is initiated in adolescence can have important consequences for transitions to adulthood, and these transitions, in turn, can shape the course of adult development. Thus, within the life-course perspective, emphasis shifts from a focus on early socialization to one on the entire life-span. (p. 5)

VI.

The developmental and life-course approaches mostly rely on the concepts of "trajectories" and "transitions" when analyzing the pathways people follow in their lives and the turning points they are challenged with. Thornberry et al. (p. 5) refer in their own approach to Glen Elder, who defined a life course as an "interweave" of age-graded trajectories like family pathways or work careers, open to changing conditions and further options, and of short-term transitions occurring over the life span, like leaving school, entering the workforce, or leaving the workforce for retirement. There is, however, an intricate mixture of potential benefits and pitfalls with such an approach, dealt with by all three books under review here.

The potential benefits are aptly characterized by Thornberry et al. when explaining their variant of the life-course perspective. It seems worthwhile to quote them with an entire paragraph:

> Human development is viewed as explicitly multidimensional because people simultaneously move along different trajectories (e.g. family and school) as they age. Not everyone enters all developmental trajectories, however, and people can be characterized in terms of patterns of trajectories they do and they do not enter. Trajectories also become interlinked over time . . . , and entrance into some trajectories can impact movement along other trajectories. . . . A central theme of the life-course perspective is that the timing of transitions into or along trajectories has real behavioral consequences. Off-age transitions, especially precocious or early transitions, can create disorder in the developmental sequence and lead to later problems of adjustment because the person is less likely to be socially and psychologically prepared for the transition. (p. 5)

Conceptually speaking, trajectories and transitions seem to be powerful tools for gaining detailed and meaningful knowledge about peoples' lives. But how close to "real reality" can we come when those tools are administered in empirical research? Laub and Sampson address some of the problems in their "opening statements":

> We also reject the popular idea that offenders can be neatly grouped into distinct categories, each displaying a unique trajectory and etiology of offending. We believe such approaches reify the idea of offender groups and ignore the instability of categorization over time. Consistently with this belief, our aim is to examine criminal and deviant offending as a general process, with the goal of using both quantitative and qualitative data to explicate the pathways to persistent offending and desistance over the full life course. (pp. 4-5)

VII.

Daniel Nagin's very impressive and timely book on *Group-Based Modeling of Development* provides a systematic exposition of a group-based statistical method for analyzing longitudinal data. He explains what can be done with this method as compared to other statistical approaches, in particular standard growth curve modeling (pp. 4-10). The core advantage of the text is that it continually "binds" the attention of the reader back to the substantive issues. And the even bigger advantage for criminology is that many of the examples used in the book are real-life data, heavily taken from the field of actual research on delinquency, criminality, crime prevention, and crime control.

Nagin (chap. 9) explicitly tackles the danger of reification that lies in all kinds of group-based thinking and methods, including his own. He stresses the important issue that the method always requires an interplay of formal statistical criteria and subjective judgment for making a well-founded decision on the number of groups to include in the model (chaps. 4 and 9.2.1). The following sentences explicate the issue quite convincingly:

> The groups are intended as an approximation of a more complex underlying reality, the objective is not to identify "true" number of groups. Instead, the aim is to identify as simple a model as possible that displays the distinctive features of the population distribution of trajectories. The number of groups and the shape of each group's trajectory are not fixed realities. Both of these features of the full model may be altered by the size of the data set that is used for estimating the model. (p. 173)

Within these limits as defined by a genuine statistician himself, the new method demonstrates big advantages in assigning people to groups, which, if perhaps not fully "true," nevertheless can be considered as theoretically and practically useful approximations to a "real-world" phenomenon. This is due to a particular property: the method does not rely, as other methods do, on the assumption of the existence of developmental trajectories of a specific form before statistical data analysis begins; instead it allows the trajectories to emerge from the data themselves.

Nagin demonstrates the power of the method by administering it to a large Montreal study that tracked 1,037 young males. Among the assessments were annual self-reports, made from ages 11 to 17, about involvement with a delinquent gang in the past year. Had the otherwise highly useful method of growth curve modeling been applied, the result would have been a description of "the average probability trajectory of gang involvement at each age from 11 to 17, and an associated set of variance parameters measuring the population variability about this mean trajectory." With the method of group-based modeling three distinct categories were detected, among them two crossing lines of early high-level beginners at 11 with a gradual decrease until 17 and of low-level starters whose gang related behavior peaked at 17 (pp. 5-7).

Even more telling seems another example. Here Nagin applies his method to the West and Farrington (1977) Cambridge study subjects for their life period of ten to thirty-two. He does so with the explicit aim to test several predictions of Moffitt's (1993) two-group taxonomic theory, pertaining to the "adolescence limited" versus the "life-course persistent" offenders. It may be useful to remind the reader again here that the Dunedin study data set did, then, not cover yet a sufficiently expanded time period for allowing real long-term calculations. What are the results? Apart from a large group of nonoffenders or at most occasional offenders called "rare" (comprising 69.5 percent of all subjects), three distinct trajectory groups unfold with the method. One of these groups (12.4 percent) seems to fit rather nicely with the concept of "adolescent limited" offenders. But a second group called "low chronic" (12.2 percent) exhibits a trajectory not predicted by the twofold taxonomy; it follows a rather stable, long-lasting path of convictions. They do, however, remain at a very moderate or low level. The third group, called "high chronic" (5.9 percent) is, in Nagin's words, "similar in some respects to Moffitt's second group, the life-course persisters." That means, in other words, this group is also "dissimilar" in some other respects. It seems worth noting what the dissimilarities are precisely all about: the groups' convictions do show a "high-hump-shaped" trajectory, that is,

> The group is already actively engaged in delinquency at age 10. However, group members' frequency of antisocial behavior, at least as measured by conviction, is very age-dependent—a pattern that is not anticipated by Moffitt's theory. The trajectory rises until about 18 and then begins a steady decline. By age 30 it has dropped below its starting point at age 10 and is about equal to [the other] group, called low-chronic offenders. (pp. 13-14, underscored with impressive Figure 1.3)

VIII.

The message is unambiguous: offenders whose officially "recognized" criminal behavior is already declining after eighteen and coming to a level of ten-year-old boys at thirty or thirty-two can hardly be characterized as *lifetime* persistent offenders. For it is safe to assume that in general, or at least on the average, they will not reactivate their life in crime until forty, fifty, sixty, or even seventy in such a manner that it again reaches the late adolescence and early adulthood levels. The data in Laub and Sampson's work, covering the truly long life span from seven to seventy of their American research subjects, provide impressive evidence, in numbers and graphs, for that assumption (pp. 85-91, 256-71). The case histories of the originally four hundred German subjects of the Tübingen Criminal Behavior Development Study include ages over sixty; however, due to data protection issues and other shortcomings, the quantitative data set had to be cut off for full statistical analyses at the age of forty-six. The analysis of the history of convictions exhibits results highly similar in shape with those found among the British and the American subjects: here the higher-level persistent offenders show a peak in their officially "recognized" criminal behavior around twenty-three to twenty-five. The curve declines until thirty, then sharply drops down and oscillates around a further downward oriented trend line (Stelly and Thomas 2001, 119-25, with additional graphs). Returning to Moffitt's (1993) data, one may dare to posit that New Zealand subjects, many of whom are of European descent, are not extremely likely to exhibit dissimilar life-course trajectories in crime compared to their German, English, and American counterparts. Most of them are predicted to fade out of crime or to decisively stop their criminal behavior around their thirtieth birthday. However, one has to remain reluctant to altogether dismiss the concept of "life-*course*" persistent offenders as used by Moffitt. Perhaps it could be interpreted, within the theoretical framework of Gottfredson and Hirschi (1990) and the clinical data collected by Moffitt and her colleagues (2001) with the following modifications: many persons may exhibit a life*time* persistence of psychosocial problems and problematic behavioral patterns alike in different fields, but the "specific variant" of criminal offending may be concentrated on a limited part of their life *course*. This seems worthwhile to be followed up by further interdisciplinary research endeavors and related suitable theorizing.

The strong age dependency of official criminal careers nevertheless needs to be stressed, including the decline of seemingly chronic trajectories between approximately twenty-five and thirty-five years of age. Kerner (1996) was not able, in his rather comprehensive secondary analysis of prospective and quasi-prospective recidivism studies in Germany and beyond, to find any convincing exception. The publications that appeared since the termination of that study do not indicate a reverse trend at all.

IX.

I will finish this essay by extracting a few results of two German longitudinal studies in which I was intimately involved. The general purpose is to show that those German studies fit the picture gained from Anglo-American studies well. The specific purpose is more important, however: the results neatly underpin the validity of age-graded theories of criminality and informal social control as developed by the authors reviewed here. And they also neatly underpin the importance of the "turning points" for subjects who are about to desist from crime, as explicated so impressively and convincingly by Sampson and Laub, in their 1993 and 2003 books as well as in other diverse publications.

The first example is taken from the longitudinal Northrhine-Westfalia Youth Prison Release Study. Here, Kerner and Janssen (1996) analyzed the criminal careers of a representative cohort of roughly 500 subjects who had been sentenced to youth imprisonment in Northrhine-Westfalia (the largest state of the Federal Republic of Germany) and were released during the year 1960 at an average age of twenty. For 452 of the released young adults, the conviction records were made completely available over a follow-up period of twenty years. First, in following the traditional approach of recidivism studies, the authors could easily reproduce the common and, for many observers, frustrating picture of prevailing "failure." In the long run, more than 80 percent of the group assembled new convictions and sentences. Considered from this perspective, the continuation of a criminal career seems to be the norm for most serious offenders. Turning then to a conceptually different second approach, the authors decided to look at the data from an individualized and person-oriented diachronic perspective. In a step-by-step procedure, they checked the transition probabilities from one to the next conviction, in each step taking into account only those released persons that continued offending. Time at risk was controlled for. Figure 1 leads to the conclusion that desistance from crime happens after every single conviction. Seen from this perspective, desistance may not be the norm for every offender in the *short run* and on an *equal level*. But in the *long run*, it eventually emerges as the *standard result of a graded life course development*. From conviction to conviction, the number of persons continuing their criminal careers becomes smaller and smaller, and the percentage of desisters increases.

Additional theoretical considerations in terms of an "auto-dynamic process" of intensified recidivism gradually turned into a process of desistance indicated that aging was probably not *the* decisive force behind the developments (Hermann and Kerner 1988). Indeed, Britta Kyvsgaard (2003, 112-21) came to that conclusion when calculating the career influences of the age of onset, the age of recidivism, and the age of desistance with large Danish birth cohorts between ages fifteen and twenty-six. And John MacLeod's creative and meticulous calculations for the oldest, and therefore especially suitable, English and Welch birth cohort out of the Offenders-Index, that is, the 1953 birth cohort, led him to the conclusion that the whole development into and out of a criminal career could probably best be understood as an age-independent Poisson process where, in substance, the *life-choice decisions* of offenders to change plays a pivotal role (MacLeod 2003, chap. 12). The latter conclusion supports what Laub and Sampson (p. 280) explicate as "the power of human agency" (cf. also the histories of "going straight"; Maruna 2001). The conclusion is also in line with the term *cognitive resocialization*, which Kerner (1998) coined when filtering the core meaning out of the many narrative descriptions, considerations, and retrospective evaluations of life events of the subjects of the Tübingen Criminal Behavior Development Study. The term *cognitive* focuses attention on the idea that there was no quasi-mechanistic causal chain from "treatment units" or "interventions" to the "effect." On the contrary, those offenders who eventually returned to a normal, if not successful, civil life almost always emphasized voluntary actions enhancing their own, sometimes idiosyncratic, way out of crime. They either mentioned a clear decision to stop at once, or they explained that they started with a promise to themselves to change and this change developed gradually, sometimes with relapses, into a final "will" and the related personal "capacity" to eventually hold through.

The second example is taken from the follow-up study of the longitudinal Tübingen Criminal Behavior Development Study, which started in 1965 when the subjects were, on the average, twenty-five years old (for some details, cf. Weitekamp et al. 2000). To examine whether true changes during the life course occurred, we selected those subjects of the prison subsample who had already committed serious crimes up to twenty-five and had exhibited similarly shaped deviant careers. These 109 subjects (out of 200) were then checked to see whether

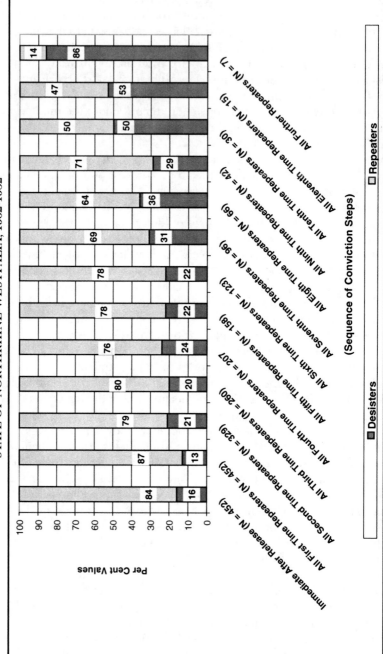

FIGURE 1
INDIVIDUALLY FOLLOWED UP CRIMINAL HISTORIES
OF FIVE HUNDRED YOUTH PRISON RELEASES IN GERMANY,
STATE OF NORTHRHINE-WESTFALIA, 1962-1982

SOURCE: The raw data for this figure were taken from the research study as, for example, depicted in Kerner and Janssen (1996).

FIGURE 2
PATHWAYS OUT OF CRIME AMONG ONE
OF TWO SUBGROUPS OF YOUNG EX-PRISONERS
(SIMILARLY HEAVY YOUNG CRIMINALS UP TO TWENTY-FIVE YEARS:
CHANGES IN LIFE PERIOD BETWEEN TWENTY-FIVE AND THIRTY-FIVE)

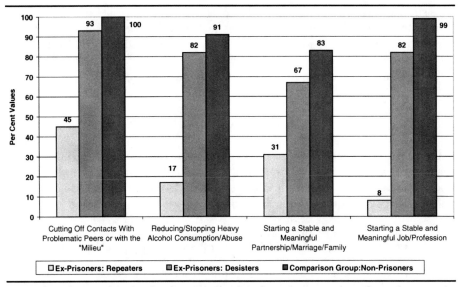

SOURCE: The raw data for this figure were taken from the research study as, for example, depicted in Weitekamp et al. (2000) and Stelly and Thomas (2001).

they continued their criminal career between the follow-up period between twenty-six and thirty-five, or turned to the committal of only minor offenses, or desisted fully from crime. The results showed some percentage differences in the characteristics of the subjects' family of origin, but these results were not statistically significant with regard to persistence or desistance.

It is clear that between the twenty-fifth and thirty-fifth years in the life of the Tuebingen study subjects, important changes were about to occur: desisters are largely successful up to the midforties to get rid of their alcohol-abusing habits; to break with their pals by avoiding further contacts to the downtown milieu; to find steady and often rewarding work; and to form stable, emotionally supportive, and even rewarding relationships in the form of partnerships, marriages, or even full families (cf. for the Glueck and Glueck [1950] subjects the relevant summary of Laub and Sampson, pp. 271-73). They exhibit a structure of living quite similar to the comparative group of two hundred men out of the normal population of the same counties of origin. As can easily be seen in Figure 2, the persisters could not substantially change their lifestyle in a positive way. When looking back into the offenders' lives, we also learned that a considerable part of them had started their repeat and chronic offending between the ages of nineteen and twenty-five without any sign of social disadvantages in early childhood and without exhibiting serious juvenile delinquency.

Consequently then, desistance occurred between twenty-five and thirty-five regardless of prior disadvantages (Stelly et al. 1998). We also found (Kerner et al. 1997) that neither early experience of socialization nor imprisonment experience were sufficient causal conditions for heavy alcohol consumption and abuse. This "noncausal linkage" became even more distinct after the criminal history was controlled for. The best theoretical approach to explain the relationship between alcohol and crime seems to be a milieu approach: a deviant lifestyle increases the probability of heavy alcohol consumption drastically, and vice versa.

X. Conclusion

What are the "lessons to be learned" as promised in this review essay's title? There is no clear-cut answer that will gain unanimous acceptance from all criminological scholars, not even full support by all adherents of developmental or life-course or interactionist perspectives. A few basic points, however, deserve to be stressed:

- Long-term longitudinal studies are the pivotal tool to enhance our understanding of what the commonly used terms of *variability* and *complexity* imply in substance for peoples' lives.
- Even if one of the "pathways to crime" as depicted in the literature apparently tends to lead to a (pre)determined result in the short run, one never could exclude or deny the possibility of an eventual considerable if not fundamental change to the normal or positive in the long run. Stark pieces of new evidence for that position can be drawn from the very recently published results of a carefully designed and theoretically refined longitudinal research study on three groups of serious young chronic offenders in California followed up by Ezell and Cohen (2005).
- Speaking in a more technical manner: one has always to remain aware that in the real world of human beings, it is not "variables" interacting with one another but individual men/women with other individual men/women with ever-changing situations under ever-changing structural conditions.
- Life histories of people may, to borrow a bit from the term coined by Norbert Elias (1939/2000) in his famous theory of civilization, be conceived of as a fluid movement over time of experientially linked "configurations" instead of "fixed constellations" or "straight lines." Therefore, any attempt to understand development in terms of linear cause-effect relationships or chains is doomed to fail.
- Even if quasi-mechanical naturalistic nonlinear causal linkages were assumed to exist "out there," we do not yet and probably never will have the scientific methods to perfectly depict those and, in any event, to firmly and accurately predict an individual's precise outcome.
- It may become possible, when further improving our already existing complex methods and models, to even better predict patterned outcomes for (large) groups of persons/offenders. Risk factor approaches follow aptly such a line of orientation. However, there is a danger to reify otherwise undoubtedly useful instruments. This danger inheres in the conceptual framework of any risk factor approach. It may lead scholars, and even more engaged practitioners and policy makers, to mistakenly interpret eventually certain descriptive group characteristics as durable personal properties: "populations at risk" may

so turn out to be seen as a collection of "risk-prone or risk-bearing persons" who "own" some trait or ingrained idiosyncratic predisposition to act (out).

- There is a tendency to overlook what I would like to call resistance already present as a kind of threshold in persons from their early life on or alternatively building up during the life course. This resistance relates to what is called resiliency in psychology. Such resiliency as seen among young people experiencing sometimes extreme adverse conditions of living seems still a rather vague concept in empirical terms, but nevertheless a very promising one in terms of "prognostics" (individual prediction). Let us think as an example of having found out that a certain group of people with twenty-five risk factors "produces" eventually some 40 percent of offenders as compared to another group of people with only five risk factors that produces only 15 percent of offenders. Well, after having neatly calculated the odds of the more heavily affected group, why do we not start a whole series of studies on exactly what enables those remaining 60 percent to withstand temptations, to master critical situations, and eventually to refrain from behaving criminal?
- Human agency surely plays a crucial role here, as time and again referred to in Laub and Sampson's 2003 book. This human agency is being connected, inter alia, to divergent value orientations of people (see recently Hermann 2003), to mental moral maps of people (see recently Palmer 2005), to patterns of preferences and commitment, and finally to choice (see recently Squires and Stephen 2005, 154-83, with young English subjects having been put under Antisocial Behaviour Orders). It seems worthwhile if not indispensable to follow such a line of inquiry in the future.

References

Cline, Hugh F. 1980. Criminal behavior over the life span. In *Constancy and change in human development*, ed. Orville Brim and Jerome Kagan. Cambridge, MA: Harvard University Press.

Elias, Norbert. 1939/2000. *The civilising process*. London: Blackwell. Originally published as *Ueber Prozesse der Zivilisation*, 2 vols. (Basel, Switzerland: Verlag Haus zum Falken).

Ezell, Michael E., and Lawrence E. Cohen. 2005. *Desisting from crime. Continuity and change in long-term crime patterns of serious chronic offenders*. Oxford: Oxford University Press.

Farrington, David P. 1994. Human development and criminal careers. In *The Oxford handbook of criminology*, ed. Mike Maguire, Rod Morgan, and Robert Reiner, 511-84. Oxford: Oxford University Press.

———. 2003. Key results from the first forty years of the Cambridge study in delinquent development. In *Taking stock of delinquency: An overview of findings from contemporary longitudinal studies*, ed. Terence P. Thornberry and Marvin D. Krohn, 137-84. New York: Kluwer Academic.

Friday, Paul C., Xin Ren, Elmar Weitekamp, Hans-Jürgen Kerner, and Terrance Taylor. 2005. A Chinese birth cohort: Theoretical implications. *Journal of Research in Crime and Delinquency* 42 (2): 123-46.

Glueck, Sheldon, and Eleanor Glueck. 1950. *Unraveling juvenile delinquency*. New York: The Commonwealth Fund.

Goeppinger, Hans. 1983. *Der Taeter in seinen sozialen Bezuegen. Ergebnisse aus der Tuebinger Jungtaeter-Vergleichsuntersuchung* [The offender in his social settings and relationships]. Berlin: Springer Verlag.

———. 1985. *Angewandte Kriminologie. Ein Leitfaden fuer die Praxis* [Applied criminology]. Berlin: Springer Verlag.

Gottfredson, Michael R., and Travis Hirschi. 1990. *A general theory of crime*. Stanford, CA: Stanford University Press.

Hawkins, J. David, Brian H. Smith, Karl G. Hill, et al. 2003. Understanding and preventing crime and violence: Findings from the Seattle Social Development Project. In *Taking stock of delinquency: An overview of findings from contemporary longitudinal studies*, ed. Terence P. Thornberry and Marvin D. Krohn, 255-312. New York: Kluwer Academic.

Hermann, Dieter. 2003. *Werte und Kriminalitaet. Konzeption einer allgemeinen Kriminali taetstheorie* [Values and criminal behavior. Elements of a general theory of criminality]. Opladen, Germany: Westdeutscher Verlag.

Hermann, Dieter, and Hans-Jürgen Kerner. 1988. Die Eigendynamik der Rueckfallkriminalitaet [On the auto-dynamics of recidivism]. *Koelner Zeitschrift fuer Soziologie und Sozialpsychologie* 40:485-504.

Huizinga, David, Anne Wylie Weiher, Rachele Espiritu, et al. 2003. Delinquency and crime: Some highlights from the Denver Youth Survey. In *Taking stock of delinquency: An overview of findings from contemporary longitudinal studies*, ed. Terence P. Thornberry and Marvin D. Krohn, 47-92. New York: Kluwer Academic.

Kaplan, Howard B. 2003. Testing an integrative theory of deviant behavior: Theory-syntonic findings from a long-term multi-generation study. In *Taking stock of delinquency: An overview of findings from contemporary longitudinal studies*, ed. Terence P. Thornberry and Marvin D. Krohn, 185-254. New York: Kluwer Academic.

Kerner, Hans-Jürgen. 1996. Erfolgsbeurteilung nach Strafvollzug [Evaluating the success of imprisonment]. In *Jugendstrafvollzug und Bewaehrung*, ed. Hans-Jürgen Kerner, Gabriele Dolde, and Hans-Georg Mey, 3-92. Bonn, Germany: Forum Verlag Godesberg.

———. 1998. Vom Ende des Rueckfalls: Probleme und Befunde zum Ausstieg von Wiederholungstaetern aus der sogenannten kriminellen Karriere [On the termination of recidivism: Problems and results on the ways of desisting from crime among repeat offenders]. In *Kriminologie und Strafrecht*, ed. Hans-Joerg Albrecht, Frieder Duenkel, Hans-Jürgen Kerner, Josef Kuerzinger, Heinz Schoech, Klaus Sessar, and Bernd Villmow, 141-76. Berlin: Duncker & Humblot.

Kerner, Hans-Jürgen, and Helmut F. Janssen. 1996. Rueckfall nach Verbuessung einer Jugendstrafe [Recidivism after serving a youth imprisonment term]. In *Jugendstrafvollzug und Bewaehrung*, ed. Hans-Jürgen Kerner, Gabriele Dolde and Hans-Georg Mey, 137-218. Bonn, Germany: Forum Verlag Godesberg.

Kerner, Hans-Jürgen, Elmar G. M. Weitekamp, and Wolfgang Stelly. 1995. From childhood delinquency to adult criminality: First results of the follow-up of the Tuebingen Criminal Behavior Development Study. *EuroCriminology* 8-9:127-62.

Kerner, Hans-Jürgen, Elmar G. M. Weitekamp, Wolfgang Stelly, and Jürgen Thomas. 1997. Patterns of criminality and alcohol abuse: Results from the Tuebingen Criminal Behavior Development Study. *Criminal Behavior and Mental Health* 7:401-20.

Kyvsgaard, Britta. 2003. *The criminal career. The Danish Longitudinal Study*. Cambridge: Cambridge University Press.

Lahey, Benjamin B., Terrie E. Moffitt, and Avshalom Caspi, eds. 2003. *Causes of conduct disorder and juvenile delinquency*. New York: Guilford.

Loeber, Rolf, David P. Farrington, Magda Stouthamer-Loeber, et al. 2003. The development of male offending: Key findings from fourteen years of the Pittsburgh Youth Study. In *Taking stock of delinquency: An overview of findings from contemporary longitudinal studies*, ed. Terence P. Thornberry and Marvin D. Krohn, 93-136. New York: Kluwer Academic.

MacLeod, John. 2003. A theory and model of the conviction process. In *Modelling crime and offending: Recent developments in England and Wales*, section C. Occasional Paper no. 80 of the Home Office. London: HMSO Research, Development and Statistics Directorate.

Maruna, Shadd. 2001. *Making good. How ex-convicts reform and rebuild their lives*. Washington, DC: American Psychological Association.

McCord, Joan. 1978. A thirty-year follow-up of treatment effects. *Journal of Personality and Social Psychology* 37:284-89.

Mischkowitz, Robert. 1993. *Kriminelle Karrieren und ihr Abbruch. Empirische Ergebnisse einer kriminologischen Langzeituntersuchung als Beitrag zur "Age-Crime-Debate."* Bonn, Germany: Forum Verlag Godesberg.

Moffitt, Terri E. 1993. Adolescence limited and life-course-persistent antisocial behavior: A developmental taxonomy. *Psychological Review* 100:674-701.

Moffitt, Terrie E., Avshalom Caspi, Michael Rutter, and Paul A. Silva. 2001. *Sex differences in antisocial behavior: Conduct, disorder, delinquency, and violence in the Dunedin Longitudinal Survey*. Cambridge: Cambridge University Press.

Newman, Graeme R., ed. 1999. *Global report on crime and justice*. New York: United Nations Office for Drug Control and Crime Prevention, Centre for International Crime Prevention.

Overbeek, Geertjan, Wilma Vollebergh, Rutger Engels, and Wim Meeus. 2005. Juvenile delinquency as acting out: Emotional disturbance mediating the effects of parental attachment and life events. *European Journal of Developmental Psychology* 2 (1): 39-46.

Palmer, Emma J. 2005. *Offending behaviour. Moral reasoning, criminal conduct and the rehabilitation of offenders.* Cullompton, UK: Willan Publishing.

Petersilia, Joan R. 1980. Criminal career research. In *Crime and justice: An annual review of research*, ed. Norval Morris and Michael Tonry, 321-79. Chicago: University of Chicago Press.

Reckless, Walter C. 1972. *The prevention of juvenile delinquency.* Columbus: Ohio State University Press.

Robins, Lee. 1966. *Deviant children grown up: A sociological and psychiatric study of sociopathic personality.* Baltimore: Williams & Wilkins.

Sampson, Robert F., and John H. Laub. 1993. *Crime in the making: Pathways and turning points through life.* Cambridge, MA: Harvard University Press.

———. 1995. Understanding variability in lives through time: Contributions of life-course criminology. *Studies on Crime & Crime Prevention* 4:143-59.

Squires, Peter, and Dawn E. Stephen. 2005. *Rough justice. Anti-social behaviour and young people.* Cullompton, UK: Willan Publishing

Stelly, Wolfgang, and Juergen Thomas. 2001. *Einmal Verbrecher—Immer Verbrecher?* [Once a criminal—always a criminal?]. Wiesbaden, Germany: Westdeutscher Verlag.

Stelly, Wolfgang, Juergen Thomas, Hans-Jürgen Kerner, and Elmar G. M. Weitekamp. 1998. Kontinuität und Diskontinuität sozialer Auffälligkeiten im Lebenslauf [Continuity and discontinuity of social problem behaviors in the life-course]. *Monatsschrift fuer Kriminologie und Strafrechtsreform* 81:104-22.

Taylor, Terrance J., Paul C. Friday, Xin Ren, Elmar G. M. Weitekamp, and Hans-Jürgen Kerner. 2004. Risk and protective factors related to offending: Results from a Chinese cohort study. *Australian and New Zealand Journal of Criminology* 37 (Suppl.): 13-31.

Thornberry, Terence P., and Marvin D. Krohn, eds. 2003. *Taking stock of delinquency: An overview of findings from contemporary longitudinal studies.* New York: Kluwer Academic.

Thornberry, Terence P., Alan J. Lizotte, Marvin D. Krohn, et al. 2003. Causes and consequences of delinquency: Findings form the Rochester Youth Development Study. In *Taking stock of delinquency: An overview of findings from contemporary longitudinal studies*, ed. Terence P. Thornberry and Marvin D. Krohn, 11-46. New York: Kluwer Academic.

Tremblay, Richard E., Frank Vitaro, Daniel Nagin, et al. 2003. The Montreal Longitudinal and Experimental Study: Rediscovering the power of descriptions. In *Taking stock of delinquency: An overview of findings from contemporary longitudinal studies*, ed. Terence P. Thornberry and Marvin D. Krohn, 205-54. New York: Kluwer Academic.

Weitekamp, Elmar G. M., and Hans-Jürgen Kerner, eds. 1994. *Cross-national longitudinal research on human development and criminal behaviour.* Dordrecht, the Netherlands: Kluwer Academic.

Weitekamp, Elmar G. M., Hans-Jürgen Kerner, Wolfgang Stelly, and Juergen Thomas. 2000. Desistance from crime: Life history, turning points and implications for theory construction in criminology. In *Social dynamics of crime and control. New theories for a world in transition*, ed. Susanne Karstedt and Kai-D. Bussmann, 202-27. Portland, OR: Hart Publishing.

West, Donald J., and David P. Farrington. 1977. *The delinquent way of life.* London: Heinemann.

Wolfgang, Marvin, Robert Figlio, and Thorsten Sellin. 1972. *Delinquency in a birth cohort.* Chicago: University of Chicago Press.

SECTION FIVE

Quick Read Synopsis

QUICK READ SYNOPSIS

Q
R
S

Developmental Criminology and Its Discontents: Trajectories of Crime from Childhood to Old Age

Special Editors: ROBERT J. SAMPSON
Harvard University
and JOHN H. LAUB
University of Maryland

Volume 602, November 2005

Prepared by Herb Fayer, Jerry Lee Foundation

DOI: 10.1177/0002716205281467

A Life-Course View of the Development of Crime

Robert J. Sampson, Harvard University;
and John H. Laub, University of Maryland

Background

In this article, the focus is on whether (and why) adolescent delinquents persist or desist from crime as they age. Three major issues are addressed:

- A life-course view of the idea of developmentally distinct groups that have unique causes. Contrary to predictions from developmental theory,
  - The authors find desistance from crime is the norm for all men and all crimes.
  - They also find little support for the idea that offender trajectory groups can be identified prospectively and that such offender groups are causally distinct.
- A revised life-course view of turning points, one that captures how people move in and out of various states over time.
- A life-course view that takes human agency and people's choices in life seriously.

Crime in the Making	In *Crime in the Making*, the authors used a theoretical framework to explain childhood antisocial behavior, juvenile delinquency, and crime in early adulthood.

* The transition to young adulthood brings potential turning points.
* An age-graded theory was developed to emphasize informal social controls that are transformative as individuals age.
  * Delinquency and other antisocial conduct are strongly related to troublesome adult behavior across a variety of experiences.
  * One mechanism is called "cumulative disadvantage" whereby serious delinquency undermined things such as employability and enhanced chances of continued offending.
* A fundamental thesis of the age-graded theory of informal social control is that whereas individual traits and childhood experiences are important to understand behavior, experiences in young adulthood and beyond can redirect criminal trajectories in a more positive or negative way.
* There is a need to further understand age and crime and to delve deeper into a person-based exploration of the life course.

Following the Glueck Men

The authors followed up the men from the Gluecks' original study, *Unraveling Juvenile Delinquency*, to investigate the following areas:
* Age and crime—they concluded that a middle-ground position was necessary in that there is enormous variability in individual age-crime curves and yet age has a direct effect on offending. This has implications for developmental criminology and the conceptual meaning of the age-crime relationship.
* Mechanisms of persistence and desistance—they wanted to better understand patterns of stability and change in offending over the life course. Turning points such as marriage and military service are implicated in the process of desistance from crime.
* The long-term follow-up data are quite relevant to examining trajectories of crime and thus the existence of life-course-persistent offender groups.

NOTE: The findings show that antisocial behavior in children is a good predictor of antisocial behavior in adults, yet most antisocial children do not become antisocial adults—we cannot distinguish well who will persist or desist as adults.

Predictability

Is there a small group of offenders who maintain a distinctly high rate of offending over the full life course? Areas looked at are
* predictability of life-course-persistent offending,
* childhood risk and family adversity,
* latent class models of desistance, and
* age at desistance.

Turning Points

A major issue is the role of turning points in development and growth.
* The authors have modified their views in light of the fact that many important life events are repeating in nature.
* Marriage is a good example of a process that leads to desistance from crime by cutting off the person's past, providing new relationships, new levels of supervision, structured routines focused on family life, and situations that allow for the emergence of a new script about the self.

Human Agency

A vital feature that emerged was the role of human agency (the purposeful execution of choice and will) in the process of desisting from crime and persistent offending.

- Former delinquents often develop a new sense of self and an identity as a desister from crime as they become family men and hard workers.
- Some men persist in crime simply because of the rewards they perceive from crime or as a willful resistance to authority.
  - They perceive injustice resulting from experiences with the criminal justice system and express alienation from elite society.

NOTE: Human beings make choices to participate in crime or not, and human social action cannot be left out of the theoretical picture.

Conclusions The authors view this article as offering a dual critique of social science theory and current policy about crime over the life course.

- Some believe that childhood and adolescent risk characteristics are all that really matter. This article pleads that we also look at turning points in later life, in the purposeful actions of men and women, and in the workings of chance.
- The authors' work is also critical of "structuralist" approaches wherein it is argued that location in the social structure (such as poverty and social class) are what really matter in explanations of crime.
- Evidence was exhibited that certain institutions, such as marriage, predicted crime even when each man served as his own control.

NOTE: Long-term outcomes cannot be easily predicted—by emphasizing time-varying events, the authors learned that stability and change do not neatly fit a simple linear "growth" model of development.

Offender Classifications and Treatment Effects in Developmental Criminology: A Propensity/Event Consideration

Michael R. Gottfredson,
University of California, Irvine

Background Interest in classification of the offender population is frequently associated with efforts to discover differential treatment choices, under the assumption that not all offenders are alike.

- Empirical classification requires important methodological issues, including
  - the selection and measurement of classification elements,
  - the rules used to assess similarity and difference, and
  - the reliability of empirically derived classes.
- These issues cannot be adequately resolved independent of theories about the causes of the behavior in question.
- What distinguishes current typological research is the promise from developmental criminology that by adding age (or time) offender typologies might yield enhanced prediction or a more complete explanation for offending.
- Some scholars are skeptical about the prospects for criminology of the typological approach because of

◦ versatility in offending,
◦ general propensities for crime and deviance,
◦ a preference for parsimony,
◦ uncertainty about differential treatment effectiveness,
◦ concerns with how types of offenders are identified, and
◦ advances in explanatory models for crime and delinquency.

Q
R
S

Time and Age   The typologist's problem is to identify those ways in which some offenders are alike and different from others in nontrivial ways.
- The problem is to do so in a way that makes time or age essential.
- Two sets of findings in the recent work of Laub and Sampson should be considered in an interrelated way.
  ◦ Their analyses of the likelihood of enhanced predictions of offending over the life course focused on the time of offending at different ages.
  ◦ Analyses suggesting that some events during the adult life course have major effects on the probability of future offending.
NOTE: These findings have major implications for long-standing discussions about the meaning of age effects, the notion of "careers," and the validity of general theories.

Individual   Individuals differ in their tendency to engage in delinquency and crime; these
Differences   differences are robust over time and place.
- The author's theory emphasizes how individuals come to differ in their susceptibility to (mostly) informal controls on behavior.
- These differences influence the tendency to commit crimes and the environments and life circumstances that make crime more or less likely.
- Propensities and events are not independent of each other—school completion affects employment prospects and certain life circumstances affect opportunities for criminal involvement.
- The event-propensity distinction is useful for conceptualizing and measuring the dependent variable in delinquency research.
  ◦ The event quality of acts creates a cloud over the clear meaning for an interpretation of measures of delinquency.
  ◦ It is possible that all children, as they age from six to thirteen, reduce their delinquency in highly structured settings such as a classroom—toleration of bad behavior is less tolerated even if a child generally increases delinquency elsewhere.
NOTE: The author's propensity-event theory of crime emphasizes socialization experiences in the early years in life and on the lifelong influences that childhood experiences seem to have. Control theory could account for different onsets and different trajectories over a portion of the life course.

The Age Effect   The predictions derived from a ubiquitous decline in offending with age are as follows:
- Incapacitation will be ineffective in reducing the crime rate.
- Absent control group comparisons, all treatments permitting selection by the offender postadolescence will appear effective as long as the follow-up is long enough.
- Programs that seek to change the propensity for crime at a young age have the best chance of substantial individual crime reductions.

Conclusion   A general theory can account for differences in propensity that have a high degree of stability.
- A theory that allows for change in offending at different times in life.

• A theory that recognizes the general decline in crime with age.
• A theory that dispenses with offender classifications that have little added predictive or explanatory value.

NOTE: Criminology will be greatly advantaged by attending to these implications.

Explaining When Arrests End for Serious Juvenile Offenders: Comments on the Sampson and Laub Study

Lee N. Robins, Washington University
(St. Louis) School of Medicine

Background

This article points out achievements and problems observed by Lee Robins in the article by Sampson and Laub, "A Life-Course View of the Development of Crime." Achievements include locating a high proportion of the men at seventy who were initially studied about age thirteen, collecting arrest and death records for them, and getting very interesting interviews with fifty-two of them. Problems identified were the following:

• *Lack of information about incarceration and ill health*. This meant that the authors could not exclude periods when these men were not at risk of committing crimes.
• *Crimes committed that did not appear in the arrest records obtained*. These include the following:
  ◦ Crimes committed while in prison.
  ◦ Crimes committed while in military service.
  ◦ Arrests in other states that were not reported to the FBI
  ◦ Crimes committed which were attributed to someone else.
  ◦ Crimes against persons who chose not to press charges
  ◦ Undetected crimes.

Missing crimes may cause an underestimate of the length of the active criminal career.

• *Possible missing deaths*—The National Death Index was not initiated until several years after the Gluecks' effort to locate these men for interview. Even after its initiation, it would unavoidably misidentify deaths of men who changed their names and would admit any whose bodies were not identified.
• *Age as a marker of vitality*—Street crimes taper off with aging because it diminishes agility and energy, but the speed with which they diminish varies greatly across individuals. This study had no way to assess physical fitness per se and used age as an imperfect indicator of it.
• *The interviews*—Only a small proportion of the men for whom addresses were known were interviewed.
• *Limited record sources*—Current privacy rules make it virtually impossible to get records without written permission. Because subjects who were not located cannot be asked for permission and some of those located would be

unwilling to give it, no attempt was made to get records other than arrests and deaths.
- *Reliance on men's own explanations for their desistance*—Among the fifty-two men interviewed, those who had desisted were asked to explain it. They gave interesting answers, but many of them may not themselves have understood why it happened.
- *No early predictors of desistance found*—While childhood factors predicted the level of offending, taken together, they were not found to significantly predict the age at last arrest. Looking at these factors individually might have found some that did predict age at desistance.
- *Sample homogeneity may have prevented finding childhood predictors of the time of desistance*—Perhaps the subjects of this study had such uniformly bad early behavior and poor family conditions that their childhoods were too much alike to allow finding predictors of future desistance there.

Conclusion

Comparison of the Sampson and Laub study with any other study of antisocial children is hampered by the fact that no other has dealt with such severely antisocial children and no other has had so long a follow-up period.
- Nonetheless, this study agrees with other studies on certain important results:
    - Childhood and adolescent antisocial behavior are powerfully associated with adult criminality.
    - Despite their troubled childhoods, some of these youngsters with serious antisocial behavior do not become highly antisocial adults. Those without adult arrests had better employment records.

NOTE: Because the article by Sampson and Laub shows that all serious delinquents eventually desist, one can argue for changing the focus of research on the longitudinal view of street crime from explanations of desistance to explanations for persistence. We still do not know what keeps a minority of street criminals active beyond their thirties.

The Future

This study concentrates on only a portion of the world of crime—that committed by adults who already had serious delinquency as children or adolescents. To broaden the range of childhoods found to be criminogenic would seem to require a very large sample to include the relatively rare white-collar criminal and those with adult onset. To reduce the number of cases needed, a first study might interview subsamples representing each type of adult criminality about their childhoods. This could provide a more diverse set of backgrounds likely to be criminogenic, which could be oversampled to reduce the final sample size of a prospective study. For the second, prospective study, subjects could be selected in childhood from the general population, oversampling each of the childhood patterns thought to be criminogenic. Such a study, with last follow-up at about age fifty, when almost all will have desisted but fewer will have died, should provide a more complete picture of patterns of desistance over the whole range of adult criminality, with ample numbers available for interview.

Response—When Prediction Fails: From Crime-Prone Boys to Heterogeneity in Adulthood

Robert J. Sampson, Harvard University;
and John H. Laub, University of Maryland

Background

This article is a response to formal commentaries by Michael Gottfredson and Lee Robins on the article by Robert Sampson and John Laub in this volume titled "A Life-Course View of the Development of Crime."

The Problem

Referring to changes in offending over the life course due to events such as marriage, Gottfredson says, "In propensity-event theories, such changes in offending can come about either because the propensity for involvement in crime and related behaviors changes or because the opportunities to engage in crime change." The authors, Sampson and Laub, respond,

- We believe marriage has an effect on *both* criminal propensity and criminal events, especially in shaping opportunities to offend.
- In earlier work, we conceived of marriage as a single turning point, largely affecting propensity, whereas in our current work we conceive of marriage in more dynamic (time-varying) terms.
- Additional evidence on marriage can be found in our life-history narrative data (Laub and Sampson 2003).

Causal Homogeneity

Robins says that we underestimated the effect of causal "homogeneity" in the Gluecks' delinquent sample in *Unraveling Juvenile Delinquency (UJD)*.

- Robins specifically contends the sample is homogeneous on crucial childhood and adolescent variables of causal interest—for her this is not an adequate data set to test developmental theories of offending.
- We acknowledge certain limitations in the *UJD* design as well as our own follow-up study of the delinquent men, such as the restricted scope of official records and possible retrospective bias in our follow-up interviews.
- We also concur that our data cannot be used to definitively assess the validity of the adolescent-limited hypothesis of Moffitt (1993).
- However, there are other important predictions in developmental theory that our data speak directly to, in particular by providing the opportunity to examine long-term trajectories of crime and the purported existence of life-course-persistent offender groups.

The Authors' Response

We are not saying that adult crime cannot be predicted in general or that there are no adult offenders who persist longer than others—rather, our argument is twofold in nature.

- All offenders eventually desist from crime as they age—in this fundamental sense the age effect is "invariant."
- Conditioned on childhood risk or juvenile delinquency, we cannot predict the wide variability in long-term trajectories of offending.

NOTE: Robins claims this lack of prediction is because of causal homogeneity—the boys were all delinquent and thus similar on causal variables. From this perspective, the boys were selected to become adult offenders and any test of childhood prediction is therefore unfair.

Further
Analysis

Logically, if heterogeneous adult outcomes exist when childhood factors are "homogeneous," then by definition the childhood paradigm cannot provide the answer and we must look to explanatory factors in the adult life course.

- Moreover, we can directly test the causal homogeneity critique. In new analysis presented in our *Annals* response that is contrary to Robins's expectations, most of the measures of child risk in the Glueck delinquent-group data do in fact predict individual differences in adult crime before controlling for delinquency—supporting our strategy.
- Childhood risk factors predict a fractal set of age-crime curves (varying in level) rather than qualitatively distinct trajectory groups.

Sample Selec-
tion for Life-
History
Interviews

Critics have questioned the nature of our sample selection criteria and the notion that our fifty-two men are similar to or representative of the rest of the five hundred delinquents in potentially causal variables. Our strategy was as follows:

- Using criminal history records, our goal was to yield maximum variability in trajectories of adult crime.
- We classified eligible men into strata that reflected persistence in crime, desistance, and "zigzag" offending patterns.
- Our interview completion rate (66 percent) was beyond what we expected and compares favorably with other long-term follow-up studies with high-risk samples.
- Finally, in new analysis presented in the *Annals* response, the results clearly show that our targeted sample of interviewed men is indistinct from the larger pool from which they were drawn.

Conclusion

We offer a life-course conception of crime as a temporally emergent, socially interactive, and hence relational process as one of the core ideas to organize future theory and research on the development of crime.

What Has Been Learned from Group-Based Trajectory Modeling? Examples from Physical Aggression and Other Problem Behaviors

Daniel S. Nagin, Carnegie Mellon University; and Richard E. Tremblay, University of Montreal

Background

The purpose of this article is threefold:

- to summarize some key findings from the application of group-based trajectory models.
- to clarify the proper statistical interpretation of a trajectory group.
- to lay out some guidelines on the types of problems for which use of group-based trajectory modeling may be particularly productive.

Model
Comparisons

There is a key distinction between standard growth curve modeling and group-based modeling.

- In conventional growth curve modeling, the unknown distribution of parameters describing individual-level trajectories by assumption is approximated with a specific continuous distribution function.
- In the semiparametric group-based trajectory model, the distribution of parameters is approximated by a finite number of trajectory groups.

Useful Findings   A summary of findings based on group-based trajectory modeling that showcase its strengths include the following:

- Late onset physical aggression is the exception, not the rule—A large body of evidence based on group-based trajectory modeling shows that the peak frequency of physical aggression occurs during early childhood and that trajectories of physical aggression generally decline thereafter. Examples of groups following a trajectory that can be characterized as late onset physical aggression are unusual.
- Clarifying developmental taxonomies—There is a long tradition in developmental psychology of taxonomic analysis and theorizing about both normal and pathological development. Group-based trajectory modeling is very useful in clarifying and testing such analyses/theories. For example, consider an analysis of the predictors of desistance. A desisting trajectory of offending is characterized by a period in which the offending rate is substantial followed by a decline to a negligible rate. This approach identifies a far more interesting and distinctive group of individuals than the conventional static definition of desistance that typically includes large numbers of individuals who have committed only a few minor delinquent acts in adolescence and none thereafter.
- Clarifying predictors and consequences of developmental trajectories—Trajectory groups can be thought of as latent strata in longitudinal data that distinguish clusters of individuals following distinctive developmental paths. An illustration of the utility of this form of data stratification is a study that shows that the most powerful predictors of membership in high-aggression trajectory groups compared to lower-aggression trajectories were high levels of hyperactivity and opposition assessed in kindergarten. However, only maternal characteristics distinguished between a trajectory of chronic physical aggression and that which started high in childhood but declined during adolescence.

Guidelines   Guidelines for the use of group-based trajectory modeling: for what types of problems is the methodology particularly appropriate?

- One guideline relates to the adjective "growth" that modifies "curve modeling." The prototypical application of standard growth curve modeling involves a process in which population's members follow a common developmental pattern of either increase or decline. However, for "multinomial" developmental phenomena for which the conception of a common growth process does not naturally fit, a group-based approach is particularly appropriate.
- A second guideline concerns the motivation for the analysis. One common aim of analyses of longitudinal data is to uncover distinctive developmental trends in the outcome variable of interest. For example, do sizable numbers of youths follow a trajectory of adolescent onset conduct disorder? The group-based approach is ideally suited for testing whether such distinctive patterns are present in the data.
- A third guideline concerns the possibility of path dependencies in the response to turning point events such as marriage or to treatments such as hospitalization for a psychiatric disorder. Path dependencies occur when

the response to a turning point event or treatment is contingent upon the individual's developmental history. The group-based trajectory model is well suited for identifying and testing whether the response to a turning point event or treatment is contingent upon the individual's developmental trajectory.

Q R S

Conclusion The rapid growth of group-based trajectory modeling stems in part from its usefulness in summarizing complexity.
- A hallmark of modern longitudinal studies is the variety and richness of study subjects and their circumstances.
- Researchers should not be so bogged down in complexity that lessons learned from data are lost on them and their audience.
- Group-based trajectory modeling improves a researcher's ability to identify, summarize, and communicate complex patterns in longitudinal data.

Developmental Trajectory Modeling: A View from Developmental Psychopathology

Barbara Maughan, Institute of Psychiatry, King's College London

Categorical and Dimensional Models of Behavior The distinctive feature of the group-based approach to trajectory modeling derives from its assumption that there may be clusters or groupings of individuals whose development on any given behavior of interest follows differing age-related patterns in its developmental course.
- Specified categories can enhance communication and may provide a useful framework in which to examine interactions among hypothesized risks.
- Researchers widely recognize that many of the behaviors that we study are dimensionally distributed and do not show clear-cut points differentiating "normality" and "pathology."
- Latent groupings may differ in degree rather than kind; the heuristic value of group-based approaches derives in part from their capacity to allow for direct tests of a range of hypothesized patterns of association.
- There is a need to entertain categorical and dimensional conceptions and to explore and contrast models and findings from each.

Heterogeneity in Antisocial Behavior Although variations in course may be key pointers to heterogeneity in antisocial behavior, other features may also be important.
- In general, criminal career studies have identified only limited evidence of specialization in offending in adulthood.
- The developmental literature, by contrast, has highlighted a variety of distinctions that seem likely to carry important implications for the understanding of early developmental processes:
  - some on different manifestations of antisocial tendencies,
  - some on age at onset, and
  - some on associated features such as hyperactivity.
- Nagin and Tremblay focus predominantly on physical aggression, and have amassed extensive evidence to show

Q
R
S

* that the peak age for physical aggression is not, as had been assumed, in the teens, but in early childhood; and
* that this pattern also holds for subgroups of children following quite different aggression trajectories—peak levels for the great majority are already evident in the preschool years.

Implications   The conclusions have wide-ranging implications.
* Much aggression is likely to reflect an innate tendency that most children unlearn or learn to control early in childhood.
* If the origins of aggression lie early in development, environmentally oriented risk research also needs to focus there.
* In terms of process, if the typical pattern is one in which most young children are helped to control aggressive tendencies over the toddler period, more may be learned at this stage from exploring failures in proactive parenting than focusing on the coercive processes that have proven so productive in understanding exacerbations in troublesome behavior later in childhood.

NOTE: The findings provide beginning pointers to sources of heterogeneity in childhood antisocial behavior. Nagin and Tremblay's work on aggression provides a model for the type of detailed, systematic focus on well-characterized phenotypes that will form the building blocks for such efforts.

Developmental   Developmental criminology involves two main areas of study:
Perspectives   • The development and dynamics of offending over age.
* The identification of explanatory or causal factors that predate or co-occur with behavioral development and affect its course.

NOTE: Nagin and Tremblay provide numerous examples of the contribution of the group-based trajectory approach to each of these domains of inquiry. As their work also illustrates, tracking the dynamics of behavior raises the issue of why some behavioral trajectories vary so strikingly with age.

Developmental   To address the above concern, we need to turn to a different type of
Processes   covariate, reflecting not preconditions for offending but other aspects of individual development or social context that co-occur with observed changes in behavior and may help understand variations over age. Chronological age may index a variety of processes:
* Changes in social experience: leaving school, starting work are examples that hold implications for antisocial behavior.
* Duration of exposure to risks or to the cumulating consequences of prior behavioral difficulties.
* Changes in cognitive level.
* Variations in biological maturity.

NOTE: Substituting one or more of these metrics for chronological age may cast further light on developmental processes associated with age-related change in antisocial behavior and crime.

Exploring the   The author's recent work has been exploring how far some of the known
Effect of   changes of the adolescent years might illuminate the sharp rise in overall lev-
Changes in   els of offending reflected in the age-crime curve, in age-trends in conduct
Adolescent   disorder (CD) and in a more nuanced way, in some of the specific trajectory
Years   groupings identified by Nagin and Tremblay.

Conclusion   A developmental perspective offers major advantages but, along with them, raises key challenges such as the need to match conceptualizations with appropriate methodological tools. Nagin and Tremblay have done much to advance those ends.

How Do We Study
"What Happens Next"?

Stephen W. Raudenbush, University of Chicago

Background

A key purpose of longitudinal research is to generate knowledge that can support effective social interventions.
- Longitudinal records of behavior are artifacts of a flow of social action unfolding in continuous time: a person's actions generate social reactions, and social interventions trigger varied individual responses.
- We want to know "what happens next?" Given a person's past behavior, what interventions does a person experience and how does that person respond?
- How does "trajectory group modeling" contribute to such knowledge?

Do Trajectory Groups Exist?

- In applied work, Nagin and Tremblay assert that real structural differences exist between members of "trajectory groups" and that formal statistical modeling provides a firm basis for making inferences about such groups. This way of thinking is attractive to clinicians, who seek to classify persons for the purpose of diagnosis and treatment.
- Yet in a recent methodological paper, Nagin and Tremblay warn that trajectory groups should not be regarded as real, that group-based modeling provides an approximation to a more complex reality, and that users of the approach have erred in "reifying" the existence of groups.
- If groups do not exist, a key question arises: What is gained by this kind of approximation? Does the concept of trajectory groups improve predictions of future behavior? If not, it may be advisable to avoid tempting researchers into believing that such groups exist. We would then not need to warn them against reification of the model assumptions.

Conflicting Views of Human Development

- Researchers have found that statistical inferences about the number of groups and their composition change over time. Nagin and Tremblay offer one explanation; the current article offers an alternative explanation.
- Nagin and Tremblay have adopted a view of development as revealed essence. At any time, inferences about developmental trajectories are imperfect because underlying differences between people have not yet fully unfolded. Additional waves of data collection reveal these differences ever more clearly. As more data are collected, shifts in inferences about the number and composition of groups represent improved approximations to true underlying differences.
- An alternative view is that each participant possesses a large number of potential trajectories, depending upon the time-varying interventions that each participant will experience. The interplay between individual differences at any time and later time-varying interventions ensures ever-increasing developmental complexity over time.

Implications for Statistical Modeling

- Rather than conceiving of trajectory groups to approximate developmental complexity, the author recommends an approach that combines a model for individual differences with a model for time-varying interventions. Such models, while seemingly quite simple, can generate developmental complexity consistent with what social scientists actually observe when they look closely at behavior over time.

- This approach is illustrated in two examples. The first concerns children's cognitive growth during elementary school: children differ in their expected growth curves given "typical" teachers, but teacher differences generate deflections from expected growth. The interplay between individual differences and time-varying deflections generates developmental complexity. The second example concerns violent offending during adolescence. Expected trajectories of offending, given a common history, follow a family of age-crime curves. However, data on multiple cohorts reveal the interplay between individual differences and differences in historical experience. The interplay between individual differences and historical experiences generates developmental complexity.

Response—Further Reflections on Modeling and Analyzing Developmental Trajectories: A Response to Maughan and Raudenbush

Daniel S. Nagin, Carnegie Mellon University;
and Richard E. Tremblay, University of Montreal

Raudenbush Commentary

The Raudenbush commentary argues that hierarchical linear modeling (HLM) is a better statistical approach to modeling change than group-based trajectory modeling. The logic of his argument seems to be as follows:

- The group-based trajectory model requires every member of a group to have exactly the same trajectory.
- Trajectory groups are empirically unstable.
- A model based on a finite number of groups "waiting to be revealed as we collect data" cannot possibly explain the diversity of developmental paths present in the data.

Response to Raudenbush

The response to Raudenbush is as follows:

- All statistical models including HLM involve approximation; the issue of approximation error should be framed in comparative, not absolute, terms—"How do the costs and benefits of alternative modeling approximations stack up against one another?"
- As to the first criticism, the argument that the group-based model requires every member of a trajectory group to follow exactly the same trajectory is no more true than the statement that in the HLM framework all individuals follow their trajectories in lock step.
- As to the second criticism, Raudenbush is referring to changes in the shapes and sizes of trajectory groups that attend adding successively more time periods of longitudinal data. Had HLM been applied to these same data measured over successively longer periods of time, equivalent instabilities would have been observed. Trajectory models, whether estimated in a

group-based format or as an HLM, are models of data that have been collected, not of data that have yet to be collected.
- As to the third criticism:
  - The group-based trajectories are no more paths waiting to be revealed or, as Raudenbush also asserts, "immanent in persons at the outset of the study" than are the individual-level trajectories based on random effects that underlay HLM.
  - Contrary to Raudenbush's seeming suggestion, covariates such as marital status or participation in therapeutic interventions can readily be embedded in group-based trajectory models (see Nagin et al. [2003] and Nagin [2005]). Furthermore, Haviland and Nagin (forthcoming) describe an approach based on group-based trajectory modeling for making more confident inferences about causal effects of such events. A firmer statistical basis for making valid causal inference is surely central to modeling "what happens next."
  - The Raudenbush commentary simply asserts that HLM will predict better than the group-based model. This conclusion does not follow from the structure of the models, and the commentary provides no empirical evidence in support of this assertion.

Judging a Model

A model should be faithful to the observed data, and should aid understanding. It must be judged by both an empirical and a cognitive standard.
- Organizing data according to trajectory groups has several important transparency virtues: the abundance of data in modern longitudinal studies is accompanied by complexity; trajectory groups are powerful devices for organizing complexity.
- Trajectory groups describe the trajectory of behavior that has occurred; that behavior is not reified but real.
- Nothing in the structure of a group-based trajectory asserts that a trajectory is permanent, that no intervention can change it, or that it will continue beyond the period of the observed data.

Closing Observation on Raudenbush Commentary

Nagin and Tremblay do not advocate the primacy of group-based statistical modeling compared to HLM. They also caution readers against accepting arguments for the primacy of any other statistical method including HLM. The complexity of studying developmental trajectories is too great to be left to any one statistical method.

Response to Maughan

Nagin and Tremblay agree with most of Maughan's comments and use them as an opportunity to reflect further on research questions and strategies that will help in better understanding human development. These include the following:
- To understand the development of antisocial behaviors, we need to rethink what we mean by oppositional, antisocial, delinquent, and criminal behaviors. It will be helpful to have descriptive data on the development of each of the behaviors presumed to be antisocial. Behaviors should be aggregated only if they have the same developmental trajectories. Once we know the development of antisocial behaviors, then we can start looking at the development of other correlates such as hyperactivity and callousness toward others to create subcategories of antisocial development.
- One important task of longitudinal research is to trace the development of each type of antisocial and criminal behavior. This is not an easy task because there are numerous forms of antisocial behavior, developmental precursors

of criminal behavior often start early in life, and these behaviors can continue until old age. By piecing together results from different longitudinal studies, we can get an idea of the general trends from womb to tomb.

- To understand variation over age in antisocial behavior, we need to study other aspects of individual development and social context that co-occur with observed changes in antisocial behavior. These variables should not displace age as the main covariate. The four covariates proposed by Maughan need to be studied with reference to age, not instead of age—they all vary with age because they depend on age.

Explaining Multiple Patterns of Offending across the Life Course and across Generations

Terence P. Thornberry,
University of Colorado at Boulder

Patterns

The most central aspects that developmental theories of delinquency should explain involve the following:

- *Onset of offending*—There is a challenge to account for the age of onset of offending:
  - They need to offer a conceptualization of age of onset, how variable it is, and if its variability is discrete or continuous.
  - They need to offer an explanation for why people begin to offend when they do.
- *Course*—A developmental model should include a conceptualization of the course of offending with respect to whether there is a tight or loose association between age of onset and the length of criminal careers and whether that association is discrete or continuous.
  - It must account for persistence and give a causal explanation of the association between age of onset and persistence.
- *Desistance*—Developmental theories should include an explanation of the social and psychological processes that lead to desistance.
  - There should be an explicit consideration of whether desistance occurs suddenly or whether it is gradual.
  - Theories should address whether the causes are simply the reverse of those associated with onset.
  - Models should explain the link between age of onset and both the likelihood and timing of desistance.

Manifestations of Behavior

The manifestations of antisocial behavior vary over the life course, and during childhood and adolescence they center on delinquency and substance use.

- Interactional theory offers these expectations about onset:
  - Offending is relatively commonplace—a majority will be involved in antisocial behavior.
  - Relatively few offenders will have extensive criminal careers.
  - Onset is continuously distributed across the age distribution.
  - There can be late bloomers or late onset.

- Interactional theory is a sociogenetic model of the course of human development in which the human organism always remains open and responsive to changing social environments.
- The theory views desistance as composed of two processes:
  - The first reflects the downward movement from the peak of involvement to the start of noninvolvement.
  - The second reflects the maintenance of behavior at zero or near-zero level of offending.

NOTE: Interactional theory does not anticipate sharp turning points that quickly deflect offending trajectories from high levels to zero.

- There is some association between the timing of onset and the timing of desistance.
- Desistance is likely a product of changing life circumstances.

Trajectory Approach

Nagin and Land's (1993) trajectory approach summarizes developmental patterns of behavior, including criminal behavior, and the relationship between level of offending and age.

- It models onset, varying levels of offending without severe restrictions on the shape or number of inflection points.
  - It does not constrain the pattern of offending to be the same for all individuals.
- One of the limitations is whether the trajectory groups (individuals sharing a similar offense history) represent discrete groups with different etiologies or reflect more dense areas from a single underlying distribution.
- The method is a convenient way of describing a complex phenomenon by dividing it into smaller descriptive units.

Desistance

The process of desistance occurs at numerous ages, not just at the transition from adolescence to adulthood as implied by the age-crime curve.

- The movement toward desistance occurs before one is likely to see the impact of marriage, work, and family—the typical explanations.
- Three factors are hypothesized to lead to desistance:
  - As the age of onset increases, the strength of the causal factors associated with antisocial behavior diminishes.
  - The causal factors for this behavior are not strongly coupled.
  - These youth are less likely to experience strong negative consequences from feedback effects from delinquent behavior.

Offending Theory

If the onset of offending is continuously distributed, then the theoretical task is twofold:

- Theories need to account for why some offend and some do not.
- They need to account for why some start earlier and others later.

NOTE: The author indicates that earlier-onset offenders are more likely to continue offending because of the stability in the strength of the causal forces that led to early onset and the negative consequences of that behavior. He also says that continuing economic and relationship problems, combined with the use of alcohol and drugs, is likely to lead to offending well into the adult years for late bloomers.

Prosocial Careers

A small portion of the population manages to avoid involvement in delinquency entirely.

- A pattern of prosocial behavior requires conditions that either prevent the development of predispositions or are able to compensate for these conditions so they do not lead to antisocial behavior.

● Economic means to provide for one's family reduces the risk.
● Strong bond to family helps foster prosocial behavior.

Inter-
generational
Relationships

● An intergenerational perspective leads to two questions:
  ○ Does a parent's own involvement in antisocial behavior generate risk for his or her children?
  ○ If it does, what are the mediating processes that link the generations?
● The author presents a life-course model of the mediators associated with intergenerational continuity in antisocial behavior.
NOTE: The model identifies at least some of the mediating processes.
● Other mediating pathways are likely to incorporate into a fuller explanation.
● The focus on continuity addresses the dominant part of intergenerational linkages—there are clear patterns of discontinuity also.

Discussion

These intergenerational results have a number of interesting implications for understanding the origins of delinquency.
● There is some intergenerational transfer of risk.
● Parent characteristics and behaviors are important in understanding delinquency.
● Results also indicate that parenting behaviors are systematically related to earlier aspects of the parent's own development.
● The impact of parenting is not confined solely to the impact of parents. Grandparents also appear to have a role.

Making Sense of Crime and the Life Course

D. Wayne Osgood, Pennsylvania State University

Interactional
Theory and the
Life Course

Interactional theory treats criminal career features such as onset, frequency, and duration as phenomena worthy of attention but not as deriving from separate causal processes.
● The theory unites them through a unified explanation, thereby using a parsimonious and general framework to give serious attention to the phenomena highlighted by the criminal career paradigm.
● Thornberry and Krohn build this unifying position around the simple idea that offending at all ages is the result of the total magnitude of all relevant forces.
● Thornberry follows and extends Sampson and Laub's (1993) life-span development orientation through attention to the age-graded relevance of the key causal factors.
  ○ In interactional theory, this varying relevance is due to the age differences in the levels of the causal variables.
  ○ The age difference in causal contribution is because the levels rather than causal impacts of these factors vary with age.
● This framework would also predict that heavy exposure to delinquent peers at a young age could engender early-onset offending and a shift from good to bad parenting could produce late-onset offending.
NOTE: Thornberry wisely reserves the possibility that a variable's causal impact would change with age for exceptional cases when that is justified by a

strong life-course argument. Strong parental guidance cannot compensate for these weaknesses after youth leave home to face challenges in life.

Duration of
Offending

Interactional theory takes a unified approach to explaining the stability of offending and its association with age of onset.
- Thornberry, making good use of the idea that offending is a product of the total causal force, accounts for stability of offending through the combination of stable causes and the correlation of earlier causes with later ones.
- Thornberry differs from Moffitt in that he views the age of onset as a continuous variable of modest predictive power, rather than a key marker for a typology of persistent versus short-term offending.

Osgood's
Suggestions

Osgood has a few suggestions for modest alterations in the current presentation of interactional theory that may tighten its consistency around the features of its general explanatory approach.
- Avoid the "risk factor" approach of dichotomizing continuous variables, such as converting an extensive measure of parenting skills to poor versus adequate parenting.
- Thornberry should rethink the position that extreme levels of causal factors are inherently stable—a simpler position would be that, when risk is extreme, even a moderate improvement is likely to leave sufficient causal force to produce continued offending.
- We should follow Thornberry's lead in seeking unifying explanations that make sense of the differences in results produced by alternative offense criteria.

Typological
Theory versus
Empirical
Findings

Tensions remain between typological theory and the empirical findings.
- On one hand, many trajectory typology studies have found evidence of the groups hypothesized by Moffitt (1993): long-term, high-rate trajectories that match life-course-persistent offenders and late-onset, short-term trajectories that match adolescent-limited offenders.
- On the other hand, virtually all of these studies identify additional groups not hypothesized, such as low-rate chronic offenders and late-onset, but long-term offenders.
- The use of categorical research approaches does not require accepting that offenders actually fall into discrete and homogeneous groups.
NOTE: Thornberry's article not only demonstrates a pragmatic stance about the categorical research approach but also shows the continuing relevance of the debate about categorical versus continuous conceptions of individual differences in offending over time.
- He views age onset as a continuous basis for differentiating pathways in offending, in contrast to Moffitt's view of age of onset as the key marker differentiating her two types of offenders.
- Osgood says in this article that there are many shades of gray between the white and black of saints and serial killers.
- It is important that developmental and life course criminologists give greater prominence to continuous conceptions of offending rather than unreservedly adopting a categorical approach.

Growth Curve
Models

Although growth curve models are very useful, they provide a view of individual change that is restricted in a way that has important conceptual ramifications.

- Growth curves reflect only a portion of within-individual change because a polynomial function is constrained to be smooth.
- It is highly unlikely that the typical growth curve model will capture all meaningful change.

NOTE: This limitation is not really a shortcoming of these useful methods, but understanding it is critically important for properly interpreting results and seeing the need for additional conceptual approaches and analytical tools.

Beyond Growth Curves

There is more to explaining change than accounting for individual differences in growth curves.

- If much of the variation around those curves represents genuine change, then it is worthy of attention.
- The short-term variations cannot be explained by the type of theory often offered for growth curves.
- Because growth curves summarize the entire pattern of change over an extended period, many find it appealing to explain them in terms of early experiences or unchanging characteristics.
- Statistical models of growth curves are well suited to this approach because they permit unchanging individual characteristics to serve as explanatory variables for the parameters of the growth curves.

Other Methods

Available theory gives good reason to study the effects of changing experience on offending.

- If growth curve models are not adequate for studying effects of life experience, what methods are needed?
  - Multilevel regression methods used for growth curve analysis are well suited to the task.
  - There is only the need to loosen the growth curve conceptual framework by adding time-varying explanatory variables.
  - The statistical model used provides a means to study what accounts for the age-crime curve.

Conclusions

Osgood offers a few summary comments of his views about how to best enhance the ability to make sense of crime and the life course.

- We must strive for cohesive and unifying theory that integrates various aspects of offending over time.
- We must keep in mind the possibility that there are not just a few types of criminal careers but rather that differences in offense patterns over time vary continuously—we must appreciate the shades of gray.
- We will make better sense of crime and the life course if we recognize that growth curve models of all types present a simplified and incomplete picture of individual change over time.
- The discrepancies between growth curves and short-term change point to the need for research on the effects of changing life experience.
- Models with time-varying covariates enable us to address one of the interesting and important challenges—explaining the age-crime curve.

Explaining Patterns of Offending across the Life Course: Comments on Interactional Theory and Recent Tests Based on the RYDS-RIS Data

Janet L. Lauritsen, University of Missouri–St. Louis

Interactional Theory

According to Thornberry and Krohn (2005), three fundamental aspects of interactional theory are as follows:

- The theory takes a life-course perspective—the belief that delinquency involvement "unfolds over time."
- Delinquency and many of its causes often become involved in mutually reinforcing casual loops as delinquent careers unfold—ineffective parenting may be causal and parents' responses to delinquent behavior may further increase that behavior.
- Multiple causes of delinquency vary in magnitude across persons due to the presence of offsetting assets or protective factors.

Other Theory Assertions

Interactional theory includes other assertions and hypotheses.

- Early involvement in antisocial behavior is the result of the intense coupling of structural, individual, and parental influences at a time when the causal force associated with childhood antisocial behavior is near a maximum.
- Childhood delinquency is strongly associated with families and neighborhoods in poverty and disorganization.
- Onset of offending appears to be a reflection of increased peer influence, decreased parental supervision, and rebelliousness.
- Late starters are hypothesized to have lower intelligence and academic competence but to have had a supportive family and school environment keeping them from delinquent behavior in their early years.

NOTE: In many ways, interactional theory is very ambitious in that it attempts to provide a comprehensive understanding of crime across the life course and to organize knowledge about delinquency and its consequences.

Is It Really a Theory?

The author of this article believes that in its current formulation, interactional theory is not a theory per se but rather a broader orientation to studying crime across the life course.

- The theory needs greater formalization—without attention to structure, it is very difficult to use the theory to organize data collection, test specific hypotheses, or examine logical coherence and assumptions.
- It is not clear how a researcher should determine what behaviors do or do not need to be included.
- Greater clarification is needed for determining how some hypotheses might be falsified.
- Greater clarification is needed to determine what kinds of evidence would falsify key hypotheses involving the relationships between various factors and offending.

Q
R
S

Rochester Study

Interactional theory is most closely associated with the Rochester Youth Development Study (RYDS) that began in 1988. (It continued as the Rochester Intergenerational Study [RIS].)
- The generalizability of the study's findings to other families and children must be made very carefully because
  - the study involves high-risk youth from one city,
  - the sample cannot assess potentially important period effects, and
  - the third-generation sample is not random (the cases on which these analyses are based are selected according to the correlates of teen childbearing).
- the authors of the Rochester study agree that more work needs to be done and that understanding the causal mechanisms underlying intergenerational continuity is a complex task.

Conclusion

The author of this article finds it difficult to use the theory and findings to develop a subsequent research agenda because of the following:
- It is very difficult to know what kinds of models the RYDS and RIS data can assess because the data are not accessible to many researchers.
- The theory is a broad attempt to integrate a variety of theories under one life-course framework.
- There is a lack of formalization of the theory.
- There is a broader concern about how researchers decide when enough data have been gathered.

NOTE: It is important to understand the limitations of longitudinal data. This would permit more sound interpretations of our findings and theories and help determine how much data we should ask subjects to provide in the name of further research.

Response—Notes on Theory Construction and Theory Testing: A Response to Osgood and Lauritsen

Terence P. Thornberry,
University of Colorado at Boulder

Response to Osgood

Thornberry's response to Osgood includes four issues.
- He agrees with Osgood to avoid a risk factor approach.
- He agrees that he did argue that extreme levels of causal factors are more stable than moderate levels. That is, for extreme deficits, even if change occurs, it is unlikely to move the person out of the portion of the distribution that causes delinquency.
- The most challenging issue Osgood raises concerns the definition of offending. Thornberry responds, "We extended interactional theory to account for behavior at younger ages and this led to a stronger focus on general antisocial behavior in childhood, followed by delinquency in adolescence."
- He concurs with Osgood that focusing on shades of gray and on continuous conceptions of offending are good things for developmental criminology.

Response to
Lauritsen

Thornberry responds to three issues that Lauritsen raises.

- Theoretical issues:
  - Lauritsen claims that interactional theory is a broad attempt at theoretical integration and then critiques it for not satisfying some of the conditions of theoretical integration. Thornberry argues that interactional theory is not an integrated theory and that integration diverts attention from the fundamental purpose of theory construction. In its place he argues for theoretical elaboration.
  - She says interactional theory shares common premises, propositions, and hypotheses with other theories and is therefore not unique.
    - Thornberry states that theories are distinguished by how their theoretical propositions are bundled, not by the inclusion of any particular proposition.
    - Second, he says the concern over uniqueness is logically flawed as a criterion for judging the adequacy of any theory.
  - Lauritsen claims interactional theory is not falsifiable, whereas Thornberry says it is presented as a probabilistic theory of behavior and does not differ from any of the other criminological theories presented by Lauritsen. Furthermore, Thornberry points out the examples she presents are misleading.
  - She comments on the definition and measurement of delinquency, crime, and antisocial behavior over the life course. He agrees it is a difficult issue and needs to be considered more fully.
- Empirical issues:
  - Lauritsen contends that the empirical tests are not complete because they do not control for all possible predictors of the outcome. Thornberry agrees that these investigations test only part of the overall model and lists two fundamental problems with her approach:
    - It is entirely atheoretical.
    - To include all the variables in one analysis would be statistically impossible.
  - She criticizes the use of the child's other caregiver and teacher as the measurement source for antisocial behavior. He says the literature shows she misses the mark.
  - She says it is difficult to assess the effect size of the coefficients since means and standard deviations for the original measures are not provided. He says he did not include them due to space limitations, but they are available in his article from 2003 (Thornberry, Freeman-Gallant, et al. 2003, 178).
- Data sharing and data collection:
  - Lauritsen says that the instruments have never been published. Thornberry responds that the volume is enormous but that he has always shared his instruments and continues to do so.
  - Lauritsen argues for the release of the data. Thornberry responds that release of collected data is limited due to how much of it is deemed sensitive data that can easily be linked to participants, which violates the pledge of confidentiality.
  - Another concern is about deciding when too much data have been collected. He feels her concern is misplaced given that the Rochester project is no different from a host of other longitudinal projects in scope and duration.

Q
R
S

° She is also concerned that probing interviews and observations might contaminate the studies and affect the subjects in positive but also negative ways. Thornberry disagrees.

Q
R
S

Final Thoughts—
An Overview of the Symposium
and Some Next Steps

Alfred Blumstein, Carnegie Mellon University

Nagin and
Tremblay

The Nagin and Tremblay article focuses primarily on the group-based trajectory method that has provided insights into trajectories of offending patterns by being applied to richly developed longitudinal data collected on multiple cohorts by Tremblay.

- The strength of the method is that it approaches a set of individual trajectories in a statistically rigorous way, finding groups that resemble each other closely and then assigning each of the others to the group that it most closely resembles.
- This identifies a handful of aggregate groups that are easier to deal with analytically than hundreds of individual trajectories—then one can seek to identify what characteristics distinguish the individuals comprising each of the groups, with a focus on the most troublesome.

Thornberry

The Thornberry article reports on his research as part of one of the most innovative government ventures in supporting longitudinal research.

- Three projects were set up that proceeded in different ways to draw their samples, investigate origins of delinquency, and study the delinquency and criminal careers of their subjects.
- His work has emphasized his "interactional theory" and the insights it brings to understanding phenomena by looking across the offending patterns of his subjects.
  ° He explores the intergenerational transmission of delinquency.

Longitudinal
Strength

The strength of the longitudinal approach is the continuity of the same individuals tracked over time.

- This permits analysis of the developmental processes within particular individuals—each serving as his own control.
- The longitudinal study allows one to examine in detail the connections among onset, course, and desistance.
- In terms of shaping policy, it allows one to examine the duration of a criminal career, especially the residual duration after an individual is arrested, convicted, and awaiting sentencing.

Meaningful
Theories

Phenomena associated with crime and antisocial behavior are so diverse that theories that explain one aspect may be found wanting when applied to others.

- The different sequence of phases of a criminal career from early childhood into adulthood can have very different antecedents, which are difficult to bring under one umbrella.
- If one tries to put a grand framework over all of the associations between individual characteristics, their parents' characteristics and their peer's

characteristics, and how each of these affects propensity to engage in different kinds of crime, one is left with lots of correlations, but nothing as concise as one would like in a theory.
- Any theory must be structured differently if it is to help describe the initiation of offending, reflecting the draw of offenders from a general population, compared to termination of offending, which reflects the distinction among offenders of those who stop from those who go on.
  - The factors that contribute to initiation may be quite different from those that contribute to termination.

Empirical Observation

A theory must comport with empirical observation.
- In this case, the theory must help explain the classic age-crime curve.
- That relationship usually shows a rapid rise from an early age to a peak, usually in the late teens, and then a relatively slower decline.
- There are many age-crime curves, one for each crime type, and those relationships could change dramatically over time.
  - Some argue all of these curves are invariant—whether they are seen as the same or different depends on whether one is trying to put many phenomena into a single box or is interested in identifying which factors contribute to the differences.
  - The Sampson and Laub article is in the former category, and Thornberry is in the latter—we need to find an optimum mixture.

Falsifiability

Lauritsen raises the entirely reasonable use of falsifiability in the context of Thornberry's formulation of his interactional theory.
- It is hard to find any theory in criminology or criminological development that could survive this test.
- The various theories must be seen as conjectures or descriptions that are often or mostly correct, but one could always find counterexamples where they do not hold.

Labeling versus Homogeneity

One important theme that pervades much theory development is the iterative effects that result from various experiences.
- Thornberry highlights such effects in the self-reinforcing effects of early onset of delinquency and of prosocial activities.
- This opens the question of whether the intervention by the criminal justice system labels an individual as "criminal," causing him to act that way, or whether his criminality is a manifestation of heterogeneity (he had a greater proclivity toward criminal behavior).
- The above issue warrants pursuit in any longitudinal data analysis.

Career Length

The data that Sampson and Laub collected on the Glueck men into their seventies is an opportunity to study the duration of their careers.
- An important feature of this perspective on career length is the desirability of distinguishing the factors contributing to the decline of the age-crime curve following its peak.
  - How much of the decline is due to termination of the career and how much to slowing down of offending frequency?
  - Different factors may affect the termination rate than those that affect the slowing down.
- There is a need for much more detailed analysis of career patterns not yet available in the data.

Offender Groups

One of the continued debates is the value of grouping.

- We can find an inherent value in grouping if we can identify which groups are amenable to one or more interventions and others that are not. This would be helpful in making group assignments.
- Grouping could be done on theoretical grounds if there is some distinction between groups beyond the quantitative distinction of some small number of observable factors.
- Grouping could be done on empirical grounds as in the trajectory analysis developed by Nagin in Nagin and Land (1993).
- The ultimate test of grouping should be based on whether we find benefit in aggregating individuals into groups, and that will depend on the context of the analysis to be done.
- Identifying useful groupings could lead to theoretical insights that would be more precisely formulated for each group.
- Finding such groupings provides the means for analyzing interactions with various predictor variables or intervention approaches that may be high for one group and low for another.
- The value will inevitably lie in the degree of homogeneity within the group in terms of some conceptual or operational similarity that does not prevail with other groups.

Improvements

The introduction of richer multivariate regression models is an important methodological improvement.

- There is an appeal to being able to introduce an additional variable into the model that enables the claim that that factor is "controlled for."
- But this ignores the possibility of a nonlinear effect of that variable and the interaction effects with other included variables—there is important benefit in being able to identify subgroups of a population because the appropriate model could be different with each group.
- The introduction of theoretically different groups or empirically based groups offers an even richer possibility because one such group may differ from others in terms of multiple observables and interactions with other covariates.
- There is a reasonable possibility that insights would be revealed that are not evident in the normal course of analysis by applying a single model to all members of a sample.

NOTE: There is a continuing need for new and diverse methodological approaches to address the rich array of the already collected longitudinal data.

Access to Data

An issue raised by Lauritsen is the need to provide access to the rich array of longitudinal data to a wider community of researchers.

- This will help with the replication needed to validate observations.
- It would be a more efficient use of resources.
- The challenge is finding ways that resolve competing concerns among researchers.

NOTE: It would be very reasonable to seek means of requiring the original researchers to provide greater access to the longitudinal data they collected, at least after some reasonable time period.

Working Together

These important streams of research should join up in some ways so that the results would be stronger than those resulting from each of the authors alone.

- We see some joining in Thornberry's use of trajectory methods, but it would be even better to see some greater mixture of integration across the various investigators.

The Future

- It would be desirable to see some culmination by building on each other's and other investigators' work.
- We must seek means to build an interacting research community that will share ideas and data and critique each other's work.

One approach would be to organize under government sponsorship a "developmental criminology forum" to propose new approaches to addressing some agreed upon key questions that will resolve controversies in the field. Some proposed issues are as follows:

- The Moffitt proposal for an adolescent limited and life-course persistent grouping.
- The disaggregation of the effects of slowing down compared to career termination after the peak age of offending as shown in the age-crime curve.
- A focus on the nature of crime-type choice over the course of a criminal career.
- The issue of marriage serving to change the propensity or reduce the opportunity for offending.

Q
R
S

STATEMENT OF OWNERSHIP, MANAGEMENT, AND CIRCULATION
P.S. Form 3526 Facsimile

1. TITLE: THE ANNALS OF THE AMERICAN ACADEMY OF POLITICAL AND SOCIAL SCIENCE
2. USPS PUB. #: 026-060

3. DATE OF FILING: October 1, 2005

4. FREQUENCY OF ISSUE: Bi-Monthly
5. NO. OF ISSUES ANNUALLY: 6
6. ANNUAL SUBSCRIPTION PRICE: Paper-Bound Institution $ 522.24 Cloth-Bound Institution $ 590.40

7. PUBLISHER ADDRESS: 2455 Teller Road, Thousand Oaks, CA 91320
   CONTACT PERSON: Michael Rafter, Director of Circulation
   TELEPHONE: (805) 499-0721

8. HEADQUARTERS ADDRESS: 2455 Teller Road, Thousand Oaks, CA 91320

9. PUBLISHER: Sage Publications Inc., 2455 Teller Road, Thousand Oaks, CA 91320
   EDITORS: Dr. Robert W. Pearson, Univ., of Pennsylvania,
   3814 Walnut St., Philadelphia, PA 19104
   MANAGING EDITOR: Julie Odland

10. OWNER: The American Academy of Political and Social Science, 3814 Walnut St. Philadelphia, PA 19104-6197

11. KNOWN BONDHOLDERS, ETC.
    None

12. NONPROFIT PURPOSE, FUNCTION, STATUS:
    Has Not Changed During Preceding 12 Months

13. PUBLICATION NAME: THE ANNALS OF THE AMERICAN ACADEMY OF POLITICAL & SOCIAL SCIENCE

14. ISSUE FOR CIRCULATION DATA BELOW: JULY 2005

15. EXTENT & NATURE OF CIRCULATION:

		AVG. NO. COPIES EACH ISSUE DURING PRECEDING 12 MONTHS	ACT. NO. COPIES OF SINGLE ISSUE PUB. NEAREST TO FILING DATE
A.	TOTAL NO. COPIES	3430	3842
B.	PAID CIRCULATION		
	1. PAID/REQUESTED OUTSIDE-CO, ETC	1855	1722
	2. PAID IN-COUNTY SUBSCRIPTIONS	0	0
	3. SALES THROUGH DEALERS, ETC.	63	0
	4. OTHER CLASSES MAILED USPS	0	0
C.	TOTAL PAID CIRCULATION	1918	1722
D.	FREE DISTRIBUTION BY MAIL		
	1. OUTSIDE-COUNTY AS ON 3541	105	118
	2. IN-COUNTY AS STATED ON 3541	0	0
	3. OTHER CLASSES MAILED USPS	0	0
E.	FREE DISTRIBUTION OTHER	0	0
F.	TOTAL FREE DISTRIBUTION	105	118
G.	TOTAL DISTRIBUTION	2023	1840
H.	COPIES NOT DISTRIBUTED		
	1. OFFICE USE, ETC.	1407	2002
	2. RETURN FROM NEWS AGENTS	0	0
I.	TOTAL	3430	3842
	PERCENT PAID CIRCULATION	95%	94%

16. NOT REQUIRED TO PUBLISH.

17. I CERTIFY THAT ALL INFORMATION FURNISHED ON THIS FORM IS TRUE AND COMPLETE. I UNDERSTAND THAT ANYONE WHO FURNISHES FALSE OR MISLEADING INFORMATION ON THIS FORM OR WHO OMITS MATERIAL OR INFORMATION REQUESTED ON THE FORM MAY BE SUBJECT TO CRIMINAL SANCTIONS (INCLUDING FINES AND IMPRISONMENT) AND/OR CIVIL SANCTIONS (INCLUDING MULTIPLE DAMAGES AND CIVIL PENALTIES).

8/30/2005
Date

Michael Rafter
Director of Circulation
Sage Publications, Inc.